Active Reading Skills

Second Edition

Kathleen T. McWhorter
Niagara County Community College

Brette McWhorter Sember

PEARSON
Longman

New York   San Francisco   Boston
London   Toronto   Sydney   Tokyo   Singapore   Madrid
Mexico City   Munich   Paris   Cape Town   Hong Kong   Montreal

Acquisitions Editor: Melanie Craig
Development Editor: Gillian Cook
Senior Supplements Editor: Donna Campion
Marketing Manager: Thomas DeMarco
Production Manager: Bob Ginsberg
Project Coordination, Text Design, and Electronic Page Makeup:
    Pre-PressPMG
Cover Design Manager and Cover Designer: John Callahan
Cover Images: *(top)* © Age Fotostock; *(bottom left)* courtesy of iStockphoto; *(bottom right)*
    courtesy of Gettty Images
Photo Researcher: Jody Potter
Senior Manufacturing Buyer: Alfred C. Dorsey
Printer and Binder: Quebecor World, Taunton
Cover Printer: Coral Graphic Services, Inc.

For permission to use copyrighted material, grateful acknowledgment is made to the copyright holders on pp. 539–542, which are hereby made part of this copyright page.

Visit us at www.ablongman.com

Student Edition ISBN-13: 978-0-205-53249-0
Student Edition ISBN-10:   0-205-53249-7
Annotated Instructor's Edition ISBN-13: 978-0-205-53262-9
Annotated Instructor's Edition ISBN-10:   0-205-53262-4

3 4 5 6 7 8 9 10—QWT—10 09

Detailed Contents

Directions for Accessing Online
Chapter:
1. Type in URL http://www.
   ablongman.com/mcwhorter
2. Click on cover of text
3. Click on link to Online
   Chapter

Preface

Active Reading Skills is the second book in a two-book reading series that is designed to improve students' reading and thinking skills through concise skill instruction, extensive guided practice, assessment, and feedback. It was written to provide students at both two- and four-year colleges with a foundation of reading and thinking skills that will enable them to handle their college courses. The text offers brief strategies and extensive skill application for the reading skills essential to college success: active reading and thinking, vocabulary development, literal and critical comprehension, and organizing information. The first book in the series, *Essential Reading Skills,* is intended for use in first-level reading courses; *Active Reading Skills* is intended for second- or upper-level courses.

Chapter Format

Each chapter follows a regular format and sequence, giving students the benefit of a predictable, consistent structure.

Think About It! Each chapter opener consists of an eye-catching visual (a photograph, cartoon, or drawing) and thought-provoking text to elicit student response. This section immediately engages the students, sparks their interest, demonstrates the relevance of chapter content, and motivates them to progress through the chapter.

Concise Skill Instruction. Chapter skills are presented briefly and concisely, using frequent examples. This section tells students what they need to know in the simplest terms possible.

Practice Exercises. Interspersed within the concise skill instruction section are numerous exercises that provide students with ample opportunity to develop and apply skills. The exercises usually involve small steps, leading students through skills gradually and sequentially.

What Have You Learned? This quiz reviews factual chapter content and enables students to determine whether they have understood and learned chapter concepts and ideas. Students may use this feature for review or as a self-test.

What Vocabulary Have You Learned? This exercise provides students with practice with vocabulary words used in the chapter's examples and exercises. These exercises reinforce the importance of ongoing vocabulary development.

Practice Tests.   Three review tests at the end of every chapter encourage students to synthesize the skills they have learned. Often, these tests are based on slightly longer material.

Mastery Tests.   Three mastery tests conclude each chapter. They may be used by students as additional practice or by the instructor as evaluative instruments. The first two tests require students to apply and integrate chapter-specific reading skills to paragraphs and short passages. The third mastery test, based on a full-length reading selection, includes general comprehension questions as well as questions on the specific skills taught within the chapter.

Special Features

The following features enhance the text's effectiveness and directly contribute to student success:

- **Emphasis on essential reading comprehension skills.** A chapter on main ideas, a chapter on supporting details, a chapter on implied main ideas, and two chapters on patterns of organization offer the student reader the basic building blocks for reading success.

- **Emphasis on critical reading skills.** Students need extensive instruction and practice to develop critical reading skills. Three chapters are devoted to critical reading skills and another to reading and evaluating arguments. Topics include inference, author's purpose, fact and opinion, tone, and bias.

- **Full chapter on argument.** Unlike many other texts, this book offers complete coverage of reading arguments. It includes recognizing the parts of an argument, evaluating arguments, and recognizing errors in logical reasoning.

- **Visual elements.** Increasingly, college students have become visual learners as visual literacy has become critical to success in today's world. This four-color book uses visual material to teach key concepts. Photographs, diagrams, and charts are used to clarify relationships, depict sequences, and demonstrate paragraph organization.

- **Extensive practice.** Numerous exercises enable students to successfully apply their learning. The chapter tests provide students with observable, measurable evidence that they are learning and improving their skills. Students may use these exercises as practice tests—as the "test before the test."

- **Full-length reading selections.** Students are given ample opportunity to apply their skills to full-length reading selections. Each chapter concludes with a full-length reading as part of Mastery Test 3. Topics include environmental racism, drug doping, volunteer hotlines, personal safety online, and animals at play. Another three full-length selections appear in the Current Issues Reader.

- **Writing component after each Mastery Test 3 and Additional Practice Readings.** Following the objective apparatus in each Mastery Test 3 and in the Additional Practice Readings, Writing Activities allow students to address issues suggested in the reading and develop their expressive skills.

Changes to the Second Edition

The second edition of *Active Reading Skills* contains numerous changes and additions that recognize and accommodate the needs and skills levels of students using the book.

- **NEW Textbook Challenge Exercise** at the end of every chapter. This exercise provides students with practice using vocabulary words that appear in the chapter's examples and exercises. These exercises reinforce the importance of ongoing vocabulary development.

- **NEW Current Issues Reader.** Replacing the Additional Readings in the previous edition, this collection of six readings addresses six contemporary issues: equity in education, poverty in America, the right to privacy, voting rights and responsibilities, the environment at risk, and species loss. Three of the readings are taken from textbooks; the other three were first published in periodicals. The apparatus that follows each reading uses the same format as Mastery Test 3 Readings at the end of each chapter, allowing instructors to substitute readings as desired.

- **NEW Chapter Opening Photographs** have been chosen to appeal to our diverse student audience.

- **Integration of Expanding Your Horizons.** The Internet activity from the first edition that appears at the end of each full length reading in Mastery Test 3 has been integrated into the Writing Activities, providing students with Internet-based writing activities.

- **NEW Exercise on Implied Main Ideas.** A new exercise has been added that provides students with additional practice in expressing main ideas in their own words.

Text-Specific Supplements

Annotated Instructor's Edition.   This is an exact replica of the student text, with answers provided on the write-on lines in the text. (ISBN 0205532624)

Instructor's Manual.   This manual includes an answer key and describes in detail the basic features of the text. This manual also offers suggestions for structuring the course, teaching non-traditional students, and approaching each chapter of the text. (ISBN 0205532632)

Test Bank.   The Test Bank offers a series of skill and reading quizzes for each chapter, formatted for ease of copying and distribution. (ISBN 0205532640)

MyReadingLab (www.myreadinglab.com). The MyReadingLab Web site provides unparalleled reading practice and assessment for college reading courses. A combination of the best-selling Reading Road Trip skill tutorial and the Lexile Framework® for Reading by MetaMetrics, MyReadingLab gives the unprecedented ability to diagnose, assess, practice, test, and report both reading skills and reading levels, tracking student progress during the course.

MyReadingLab complements textbook learning and improves reading ability with these features:

- **Thoroughly revised and redesigned Reading Road Trip.** New questions have been written for each location, including open ended questions, and a new bank of combined skills tests.
- **Accurate assessment of students' reading levels.** Students are offered a unique set of exercises designed to help them improve their reading level through mastery-based practice.
- **Personalized student study plans.** Generated based on results of the diagonostic tests, individualized study plans direct students to the skills they need to work through to improve reading ability.
- **Progress-tracking grade book.** Available for students and instructors, the gradebook shows individual student's progress or the performance of an entire class.
- **Access to Study Skills, Vocabulary, and Research Navigator Web sites.** Subscriptions to these popular sites are included with MyReadingLab.

Companion Website.   For additional quizzes, readings, and internet-based activities, be sure to visit *Active Reading Skills* online at www.ablongman.com/mcwhorter.

Vocabulary Supplement.   Instructors may choose to shrink-wrap *Active Reading Skills* with a copy of *Vocabulary Simplified*. Written by Kathleen T. McWhorter, this book works well as a supplemental text, providing additional instruction and practice in vocabulary. Students can work through the text independently, or units may be incorporated into weekly lesson plans. Topics covered include methods of vocabulary learning, contextual aids, word parts, connotative meanings, idioms, euphemisms, and many more interesting and fun topics. The book concludes with vocabulary lists and exercises representative of 11 academic disciplines. To preview this book, contact your Longman representative for an exam copy.

The Longman Developmental Reading Package

Longman is pleased to offer a variety of support materials to help make teaching developmental reading easier for teachers and to help students excel in their course work. Visit www.ablongman.com or contact your local Longman sales representative for a detailed listing of our supplements package or for more information on pricing and how to create a package.

Acknowledgements

I wish to express my gratitude to reviewers of this text for their excellent ideas, suggestions, and advice on the preparation and revision of this text:

Idell Adams, Baton Rouge Community College; Estella Albert, Albany State University; Daryl Ann Bettcher, Illinois Valley Community College; Cheyenne Bonnell, Copper Mountain College; Guinee, Portland Community College; Rita Higgins, Essex Community College; Sue Hightower, Tallahassee Community College; Miriam Kinard, Trident Technical College; Kristen Lewis, Fresno City College; Ann Perez, Miami-Dade Community College; Candace Ready, Piedmont Technical College; Adalia M. Reyna, South Texas Community College; Lynn Roberts, Grand Rapids Community College; John Sandin, Tacoma Community College; and Deborah Spradlin, Tyler Junior College.

I am particularly indebted to Gillian Cook, development editor, for overseeing this project and attending to the many details to ready the book for production, and to Melanie Craig, acquisitions editor, for her support and assistance in planning the revision of this book.

Finally, I would like to introduce my new contributing author who has been working on my books throughout much of her life. At age twelve, long before computers, she helped me number manuscript pages. While in high school, being a top-notch student newspaper editor, she proofread my final drafts. As a college student and English major, she was an excellent surce of topics for new readings and a serious critic, as well. While in law school, she began drafting apparatus to accompany new readings. As author of more than 15 law-related books, she has significant writing experience as well as expertise in all the technical details of publishing, including design, page layout, and indexing. Please welcome my daughter—Brette McWhorter Sember. You may visit her Web site at http://BretteSember.com.

KATHLEEN T. MCWHORTER

Part I

Improving Your Skills

THINK ABOUT IT!

The two photographs show two couples. How do they differ?

The first photograph shows a couple actively responding and interacting with each other. The second photograph shows a couple who seem disinterested and uninvolved. The two photographs demonstrate the difference between active participation and passivity. The couple in the first photograph is involved—they are involved in animated conversation. In a similar way, active readers get involved with the material they are reading. They think, question, challenge, and criticize the author's ideas. They try to make the material *their* material. This chapter gives you some tips on how to become an active, successful reader.

CHAPTER 1

Reading Actively

Keys to Academic Success

What does it take to do well in psychology? In history? In your writing class? In business? Many students will answer by saying such things as

- "Hard work!"
- "Knowledge about the subject."
- "A good instructor!"
- "You have to like the course."

Students seldom mention reading as a key to academic success. When you think of college, you think of attending classes and labs, completing assignments, studying for and taking exams, and writing papers. A closer look at these activities, however, reveals that reading is an important part of each one. Reading is not an obvious key to success because it is not evaluated directly. Grades are based on how well you express your ideas in papers and how well you do on exams. Yet reading is the primary means by which you acquire your ideas and gather information. Here are a few tips to get you started using reading to build academic success.

- **Approach an assignment positively and confidently.** Send yourself positive messages. Tell yourself that the assignment is manageable and that you can learn from it. Avoid negative thoughts such as, "This looks boring" or "I don't know if I'll ever get through this." A negative mind-set almost guarantees poor comprehension and concentration. To overcome this, find some way to become interested in the subject. Question or challenge the authors as you read, or try to develop questions about the material.

- **Plan on spending time.** Assignments are not something you can rush through. The time you invest will pay off later in reduced study time and higher grades.
- **Define the task.** Before you begin, decide what you need to learn, how much detail is needed, and what is the best way to approach the task. Will you highlight as you read, take notes, outline, or write a summary, for example? (These techniques are discussed in Chapter 6.)
- **Set goals for yourself.** Don't just start an assignment and plan to work on it as long as you can. Instead, decide how much is reasonable to cover in one session and set a time by which you expect to finish.
- **Search for ideas.** Think of reading as a way of sifting and sorting out what you need to learn from less important information.
- **Stick with an assignment.** If an assignment is troublesome, experiment with different methods of completing it. Try reading difficult sections aloud, for example, or express what you are reading in your own words.

Control External Distractions

A phone ringing, a dog barking, friends arguing, or parents reminding you about errands can break your concentration and cost you valuable time. Each time you are interrupted, you have to find where you left off and refocus your attention.

Although you cannot eliminate all distractions, you can control many of them by choosing wisely when and where you study. For a week or so, analyze the times and places you study. Try to notice situations in which you accomplished a great deal as well as those in which you accomplished very little. At the end of the week, look for a pattern. Where and when did you find it was easy to concentrate? Where and when was it most difficult? Use the information from your analysis along with the following suggestions to choose a regular time and place for study.

- **Choose a place to study that is relatively free of interruptions and distractions.** Consider studying at the campus or neighborhood library. Do not study where you are too comfortable.
- **Choose a time of day when you are mentally alert.** Establish a fixed time for reading or studying. Studying at the same time and place each day

will help you get into the habit of studying more easily. For example, if you establish, as part of a schedule, that you will study in the library right after dinner, soon it will become almost automatic.

Increase Your Attention Span

Most people can keep their minds focused on one task for only a limited period of time. This period of time represents their *attention span*. You can increase your attention span by using the following techniques:

- **Read with a purpose.** If you are looking for specific information as you read, it will be easier to keep your attention focused on the material.
- **Keep a distractions list.** As you are reading, often you will think of something you should remember to do. Keep a piece of paper nearby, and whenever something distracts you or you are reminded of something, jot it down on the paper.
- **Vary your reading.** Work on several assignments in an evening rather than finishing one assignment completely. The variety in subject matter will provide a needed change and maintain your interest.
- **Combine physical and mental activities.** Activities such as highlighting, underlining, making marginal notes, or writing summary outlines provide an outlet for physical energy and supply useful study aids (see Chapter 6).
- **Take frequent breaks.** They will refresh your mind.
- **Establish goals and time limits for each assignment.** Deadlines will keep you motivated and create a sense of urgency that will make you less likely to daydream or become distracted.

| Exercise 1-1 | **Directions:** *Rate each of the following items as either helpful (H) or not helpful (NH) in building academic success. Then discuss how each of the statements marked NH could be changed to be more helpful.* |

_____ 1. Checking with a classmate when you find an assignment difficult or confusing

_____ 2. Studying late at night after going out with friends

_____ 3. Blaming your instructor when you get a low grade on an exam

　　　_____   4. Thinking you've never been very good with numbers, and
　　　　　　　　　 expecting not to do well in a math course

　　　_____   5. Deciding what kinds of information you need to learn before
　　　　　　　　　 beginning to study for a biology test

Read and Learn Actively

　　　Have you ever gone to a ball game and watched the fans? Most do not
sit and watch passively. Instead, they direct the plays, criticize the calls, encourage the players, and reprimand the coach. They care enough to become
actively engaged with the game. Just like interested fans, active readers get
involved. They question, challenge, and criticize, as well as understand.
Table 1-1 contrasts the active strategies of successful readers with the passive ones of less successful readers.

　　　Throughout the remainder of this chapter, you will discover specific
strategies for becoming a more active learner. Not all strategies will work
for everyone. Experiment to discover those that work for you.

TABLE 1-1 Active versus Passive Reading	
Active Readers . . .	**Passive Readers . . .**
Tailor their reading to suit each assignment.	Read all assignments the same way.
Analyze the purpose of an assignment.	Read an assignment *because* it was assigned.
Adjust their speed to suit their purpose.	Read everything at the same speed.
Question ideas in the assignment.	Accept whatever is in print as true.
Compare and connect textbook material with lecture content.	Study lecture notes and textbook separately.
Skim headings to find out what an assignment is about before beginning to read.	Check the length of an assignment and then begin reading.
Make sure they understand what they are reading as they go along.	Read until the assignment is completed.
Read with pencil in hand, highlighting, jotting down notes, and marking key vocabulary.	Simply read.
Develop personalized strategies that are particularly effective.	Follow routine, standard methods.

| Exercise 1–2 | **Directions:** *Choose one of the courses that you are taking this semester. List at least four strategies you will use to become a more active reader.* |

Course: _____

Strategies:

1. _____

2. _____

3. _____

4. _____

_____

Preview Before Reading

You probably would not jump into a pool without checking its depth. You would not buy clothes without trying them on. You would not purchase a CD if you knew nothing about the artist.

Similarly, you should not begin reading a textbook chapter without knowing what it is about and how it is organized. **Previewing** is a way of quickly familiarizing yourself with the organization and content of a chapter or article *before* beginning to read it. Once you try previewing, you will discover that it makes a dramatic difference in how effectively you read and how much you can remember.

How to Preview

Think of previewing as getting a sneak peek at what a chapter will be about. Use the following steps:

1. **Read the title and subtitle.** The title provides the overall topic of the chapter. The subtitle suggests the specific focus, aspect, or approach toward the overall topic.

2. **Read the introduction or the first paragraph.** The introduction or first paragraph serves as a lead-in to the chapter, establishing the overall subject and suggesting how it will be developed.

3. **Read each boldface (dark print) heading.** Headings label the contents of each section, announcing the major topic of the section.

4. **Read the first sentence under each heading.** The first sentence often states the central thought of the section. If the first sentence seems introductory,

read the last sentence; often this sentence states or restates the central thought.

5. **Note any typographical aids.** Italics emphasize important terminology and definitions by using slanted *(italic)* type to distinguish them from the rest of the passage. Notice any material that is numbered 1, 2, 3; lettered a, b, c; or presented in list form.

6. **Note any graphic aids.** Graphs, charts, photographs, and tables often suggest what is important in the chapter. Be sure to read the captions for photographs and the legends on graphs, charts, or tables.

7. **Read the last paragraph or summary.** This provides a condensed view of the chapter, often outlining the chapter's key points.

8. **Read quickly any end-of-chapter material.** This might include references, study questions, discussion questions, chapter outlines, or vocabulary lists. If there are study questions, read them through quickly since they will indicate what is important to remember in the chapter. If a vocabulary list is included, skim through it to identify terms that you will need to learn as you read.

Demonstration of Previewing

The following selection is a section from a textbook. The parts of the text that should be read during previewing are highlighted.

THE CONSUMER BUYING PROCESS

Students of consumer behavior have constructed various models to help marketers understand how consumers come to purchase products. At the core of this and similar models is an awareness of the psychosocial influences that lead to consumption. Ultimately, marketers use this information to develop marketing plans.

Problems/Need Recognition   The buying process begins when the consumer recognizes a problem or need. After strenuous exercise, for example, you may realize that you are thirsty. After the birth of twins, you may find your one-bedroom apartment too small for comfort.

Need recognition also occurs when you have a chance to change your purchasing habits. For example, when you obtain your first job after graduation, your new income may let you purchase items that were once too expensive for you. You may also discover a need for professional clothing, apartment furnishings, and a car. American Express and Sears recognize this shift in typical needs when they market credit cards to college seniors.

Information Seeking   Once they have recognized a need, consumers often seek information. This search is not always extensive. If you are thirsty, for instance, you may simply ask someone to point you to a soft-drink machine. At other times, you may simply rely on your memory for information.

Before making major purchases, however, most people seek information from personal sources, marketing sources, public sources, and experience. For example, if you move to a new town, you will want to identify the best dentist, physician, hair stylist, butcher, or pizza maker in your area. To get this information, you may check with personal sources, such as acquaintances, coworkers, and relatives. Before buying an exercise bike, you may go to the library and read about bikes in *Consumer Reports*.

Evaluation of Alternatives   If you are in the market for a set of skis, you probably have some idea of who makes skis and how they differ. You may have accumulated some of this knowledge during the information-seeking stage and combined it with what you knew previously. By analyzing the attributes that apply to a given product (color, taste, price, prestige, quality, service record) you will consider your choices and compare products before deciding which product best meets your needs.

Purchase Decision   Ultimately, consumers must make purchase decisions. They may decide to defer a purchase until a later time or they may decide to buy now. "Buy" decisions are based on rational motives, emotional motives, or both. Rational motives involve the logical evaluation of product attributes: cost, quality, and usefulness. Although not all irrational decisions are sudden, many spur-of-the-moment decisions are emotionally driven. Emotional motives include sociability, imitation of others, and aesthetics—motives that are common. For example, you might buy the same brand of jeans as your friends to feel comfortable among that group, not because your friends happen to have the good sense to prefer durable, comfortably priced jeans.

Postpurchase Evaluation   Marketing does not stop with the sale of a product. It includes the process of consumption. What happens *after* the sale is important. Marketers want consumers to be happy after the consumption of products so that they are more likely to buy them again. Because consumers do not want to go through a complex decision process for every purchase, they often repurchase products they have used and liked.

Not all consumers are satisfied with their purchases, of course. Dissatisfied consumers may complain to sellers, criticize products publicly, or even file lawsuits. Dissatisfied consumers are not likely to purchase the same products again. Moreover, dissatisfied customers are much more likely to broadcast their experiences than are satisfied customers.

—Ebert and Griffin, *Business Essentials,* pp. 262–263

| Exercise 1–3 | **Directions:** *Indicate whether each of the following statements is true (T) or false (F) based on what you learned by previewing the selection above.* |

_____   1. Marketing plans are based on psychosocial influences that lead to consumption.

_____   2. The buying process begins when a customer enters a store.

_____   3. Customers seek information after forming questions.

_____   4. Marketing does not stop when a product is sold.

_____   5. Dissatisfied customers tend to keep this information to themselves.

This exercise tested your recall of some of the important ideas in the article. Check your answers by referring back to the article. Did you get most or all of the items correct? This exercise demonstrates, then, that previewing helps you learn the key ideas in a selection before actually reading it.

Exercise 1–4

Directions: *For each item, choose the correct answer from the box and write it in the blank space.*

last paragraph	study questions	typographical aids
subtitle	headings	

1. _____ emphasize terminology and definitions.

2. Key points in a chapter are usually condensed in the

   _____.

3. _____ indicate what is important to remember in a chapter.

4. _____ label the content of each section of the chapter.

5. The _____ suggests the specific focus or approach the chapter will take to the topic.

Making Predictions

While previewing a reading assignment, you can make predictions about its content and organization. Specifically, you can anticipate what topics will be covered and how they will be presented. Ask the following questions to sharpen your previewing skills and strengthen your recall of what you read:

- How difficult is the material?
- How is it organized?
- What is the overall subject and how is it approached?
- What type of material is it (for example, practical, theoretical, historical background, or a case study)?
- Where are the logical breaking points where you might divide the assignment into portions, perhaps reserving a portion for a later study session?
- At what points should you stop and review?
- Why was this material assigned?

Exercise 1–5

Directions: *LaTicia is taking a course in anthropology and has been assigned to read an article titled "Recent Skeletal Discoveries in Africa: Rewriting History." She plans to preview the article before reading it. Select the choice that best completes each of the following statements about her situation.*

_____ 1. The main reason LaTicia should preview the assignment is to
   a. determine how long it will take her to read it.
   b. identify the most important ideas in the material.
   c. find out if it contains information she already knows.
   d. evaluate the author's qualifications.

_____ 2. LaTicia can expect the subtitle, "Rewriting History," to
   a. explain how the author is going to organize ideas in the article.
   b. show the perspective the author will give on the topic.
   c. list important points about the article.
   d. reveal a personal story about the author.

_____ 3. The article contains several photographs. When previewing, LaTicia should
   a. read the captions.
   b. draw sketches of them in her notes.
   c. skip them.
   d. compare and contrast them.

_____ 4. The article contains five headings. LaTicia can expect each heading to

a. be the title of a list.

b. start on a separate page.

c. be in italics.

d. introduce a new idea.

_____ 5. LaTicia can expect the first sentence after each heading to

a. be in boldfaced type.

b. summarize the entire reading.

c. state the central thought of that section.

d. ask questions about the reading.

Exercise 1–6	**Directions:** *Match each previewing step listed in column A with the type of information it provides in column B. Use each item only once.*

Column A

_____ 1. first paragraph

_____ 2. typographical aids

_____ 3. section headings

_____ 4. last paragraph

_____ 5. title

Column B

a. identifies the subject

b. provides an overview

c. summarizes the article

d. identify and separate main topics

e. indicate important information

Use Guide Questions

Did you ever read an entire page or more and not remember anything you read? Have you found yourself going from paragraph to paragraph without really thinking about what the writer is saying? Guide questions can help you overcome these problems. **Guide questions** are questions you expect to be able to answer while or after you read. Most students form them mentally, but you can jot them in the margin if you prefer.

The following tips can help you form questions to guide your reading. It is best to develop guide questions *after* you preview but *before* you read.

- **Turn each major heading into a series of questions.** The questions should ask something that you feel is important to know.

- **As you read a section, look for the answers to your questions.** Highlight the answers as you find them.

- **When you finish reading a section, stop and check to see whether you can recall the answers.** Place check marks by those you cannot recall. Then reread.

- **Avoid asking questions that have one-word answers, like** *yes* **or** *no.* Questions that begin with *what, why,* or *how* are more useful.

Here are a few textbook headings and some examples of questions you might ask:

Heading	Questions
Reducing Prejudice	How can prejudice be reduced?
	What type of prejudice is discussed?
The Deepening Recession	What is a recession? Why is it deepening?
Newton's First Law of Motion	Who was Newton? What is his First Law of Motion?

The Textbook Challenge

Part A: Current Issues Reader

Preview the textbook excerpt titled "The Biodiversity Crisis," (p. 530). Then write five guide questions that will help you focus on chapter content. Read the excerpt and write answers to your guide questions.

Part B: A College Textbook

Choose a chapter from one of your own textbooks for another course. Preview the chapter, and then write a list of guide questions that will help you focus on chapter content as you read. Read the chapter and write answers to your guide questions.

What Have You Learned?

Directions: *To check your understanding of the chapter, select the word or phrase from the box below that best completes each of the following statements. Not all of the words in the box will be used.*

| previewing | define | active | passive | predictions |
| attention span | guide | critical | lead | questioning |

1. Before you begin reading an assignment, you should _____ the task, deciding what the assignment is about and how to read it.

2. _____ is a way of finding what an assignment is about before you begin reading it.

3. The period of time that you can concentrate on a task is called your _____.

4. _____ readers read all assignments the same way.

5. Before beginning to read, it is helpful to make _____ about an assignment's difficulty and organization.

6. _____ readers often compare and connect textbook material and lecture content.

7. Questions that you expect to be able to answer after you read are called _____ questions.

What Vocabulary Have You Learned?

Directions: *The words in column A appear in this chapter. Test your mastery of these words by matching each word in column A with its meaning in column B.*

	Column A		Column B
_____	1. aesthetics	a.	qualities or characteristics
_____	2. defer	b.	collected or acquired
_____	3. attributes	c.	logical, reasonable, and sensible
_____	4. accumulated	d.	to put off or postpone
_____	5. rational	e.	consideration of how something looks

ACTIVE READING

Directions: *Use what you have learned in the chapter to select the choice that best completes each of the following statements.*

_____ 1. Typographical aids include all of the following *except*

    a. introductions.   c. colored ink.

    b. numbered lists.   d. italics.

_____ 2. Guide questions should be asked

    a. before previewing.

    b. after previewing but before reading.

    c. after reading.

    d. during review.

_____ 3. The best guide question for an article titled "Using Humor to Improve Your Life" would be

    a. What is humor?

    b. What makes a situation humorous?

    c. Why do some people have a better sense of humor than others?

    d. How can humor improve your life?

_____ 4. Which of the following guide questions would be the best to ask for a section in your history text on the Persian Gulf War?

    a. When did it start?   c. Why did it start?

    b. Where did it start?   d. Did it last very long?

_____ 5. The main purpose of a distractions list is to

    a. keep your study area neat.

    b. organize your time after a study session.

    c. maintain your interest in a reading assignment.

    d. reduce the reminders that come to mind as you study.

_____ 6. The first sentence under a section heading usually

    a. gives the author's qualifications.

    b. further explains the heading.

    c. provides personal examples.

    d. offers an opinion.

_____ 7. A useful guide question would probably begin with the word
    a. *who.*   c. *where.*
    b. *when.*   d. *why.*

_____ 8. Building your concentration includes all of the following *except*
    a. eliminating distractions.
    b. increasing your reading speed.
    c. paying attention.
    d. rewarding yourself.

_____ 9. When reading and studying, you should
    a. speed up your reading whenever possible.
    b. stick with an assignment even if it is difficult.
    c. take breaks when you encounter difficult material.
    d. reread everything.

_____ 10. Scott has begun to preview an article called "Terrorism and Right to Privacy Issues." He can tell that this article will probably discuss
    a. rights of citizens during threats of terrorism.
    b. treatment of terrorists during national emergencies.
    c. causes of terrorism.
    d. the origin of the Bill of Rights.

NAME _____ SECTION _____

DATE _____ SCORE _____

ACTIVE READING

Directions: *Assume you have read the following headings while previewing a section of a sociology textbook chapter on substance abuse. Select the choice that best completes each of the statements that follow.*

Section Title: THE SCOPE OF THE DRUG PROBLEM

Headings:

(1) What Are Drugs?

(2) Americans' Pro-Drug Attitude

(3) The Social Function of Drugs

(4) Social Acceptability of Alcohol

(5) Nicotine: The Deadly Drug

(6) What Is Addiction?

(7) Craving and Withdrawal

(8) Illegal Drugs

(9) Are There Special Cases for Drug Use?

_____ 1. A preview of these headings suggests that the section will focus on

    a. ways to combat drug misuse.

    b. alcohol withdrawal.

    c. types of addictive substances and how they impact society.

    d. addictive substances and legalization.

_____ 2. The best guide question for the heading "Americans' Pro-Drug Attitude" would be

    a. How are Americans pro-drug?

    b. What drugs do Americans use?

    c. Are Americans pro-drug?

    d. Why are Americans using drugs?

3. The first sentence of the section "Social Acceptability of Alcohol" might be
    a. Alcohol is created by fermenting a type of grain.
    b. Alcohol is the most socially accepted drug in America.
    c. Teen drinking is one of the biggest problems facing society.
    d. When something is socially accepted, it is not questioned by the majority of people in a society.

4. The best guide question for the heading "Nicotine: The Deadly Drug" is
    a. When was nicotine first used by humans?
    b. How do people become addicted to nicotine?
    c. Why is nicotine a deadly drug?
    d. Is nicotine a deadly drug?

5. Under which of the following headings would you expect cocaine to be discussed?
    a. What Are Drugs?
    b. Illegal Drugs
    c. The Social Function of Drugs
    d. What Is Addiction?

6. Under which of the following headings would you expect the topic of alcoholism to be addressed?
    a. Are There Special Cases for Drug Use?
    b. Illegal Drugs
    c. Nicotine: The Deadly Drug
    d. Craving and Withdrawal

7. This textbook selection will probably *not* discuss
    a. criminal penalties for drinking and driving.
    b. drug addiction.
    c. chewing tobacco.
    d. rehabilitation programs.

8. Under which heading would you expect to find definitions?
   a. The Social Function of Drugs
   b. Americans' Pro-Drug Attitude
   c. What Are Drugs?
   d. Social Acceptability of Alcohol

9. Under which heading are you likely to find mention of the use of marijuana to treat medical conditions?
   a. Craving and Withdrawal
   b. Are There Special Cases for Drug Use?
   c. What Is Addiction?
   d. Illegal Drugs

10. Under which heading are you likely to find a discussion of the use of alcohol at functions such as weddings, parties, and sporting events?
   a. Are There Special Cases for Drug Use?
   b. Social Acceptability of Alcohol
   c. What Are Drugs?
   d. Illegal Drugs

ACTIVE READING

Directions: *The following excerpt is from a health textbook. Preview by reading* **only** *the highlighted sections of the reading, and then select the choice that best completes each of the statements that follow. Do* **not** *read the section completely.*

PSYCHOSOCIAL SOURCES OF STRESS

Psychosocial stress refers to the factors in our daily lives that cause stress. Interactions with others, the subtle and not-so-subtle expectations we and others have of ourselves, and the social conditions we live in force us to readjust continually. Sources of psychosocial stress include change, hassles, pressure, inconsistent goals and behaviors, and conflict.

Change

Any time change occurs in your normal daily routine, whether good or bad, you will experience stress. The more changes you experience and the more adjustments you must make, the greater the stress effects may be.

Hassles

Psychologists such as Richard Lazarus have focused on petty annoyances and frustrations, collectively referred to as hassles. Minor hassles—losing your keys, slipping and falling in front of everyone as you walk to your seat in a new class, finding that you went through a whole afternoon with a big chunk of spinach stuck in your front teeth—seem unimportant, but their cumulative effects may be harmful in the long run.

Pressure

Pressure occurs when we feel forced to speed up, intensify, or shift the direction of our behavior to meet a higher standard of performance. Pressures can be based on our personal goals and expectations, on concern about what others think, or on outside influences. Among the most significant outside influences are society's demands that we compete and be all that we can be.

Inconsistency between Goals and Behaviors

For many of us, the negative effects of stress are magnified when there is a disparity between our goals (what we value or hope to obtain in life) and our behaviors (actions that may or may not lead to these goals). For instance, you may want good grades, and your family may expect them. But if you party and procrastinate throughout the term, your behaviors are inconsistent with your goals, and significant stress in the form of guilt, last-minute frenzy before exams, and disappointing grades may result. By contrast, if you dig in and work and remain committed to getting good grades, this may eliminate much of your negative stress. Thwarted goals can lead to frustration, and frustration has been shown to be a significant disrupter of homeostasis. Determining whether behaviors are consistent with goals is an essential component of maintaining balance in life.

Conflict

Conflict occurs when we are forced to make difficult decisions concerning two or more competing motives, behaviors, or impulses or when we are forced to face incompatible demands, opportunities, needs or goals. What if your best friends all choose to smoke marijuana and you don't want to smoke but fear rejection? Conflict often occurs as our values are tested. College students who are away from home for the first time often face conflict between parental values and their own set of developing beliefs.

—Donatelle, *Health: The Basics,* pp. 58–61

_____ 1. The title suggests that the reading's general topic will be
   a. health problems caused by stress.
   b. the negative and positive effects of stress.
   c. social and psychological factors that cause stress.
   d. how the environment affects our health.

_____ 2. All of the following previewing aids are found in this selection *except*
   a. a title.
   b. a subtitle.
   c. an introductory paragraph.
   d. section headings.

_____ 3. Having read the introductory paragraph as part of your preview, you would expect the reading to focus on
   a. how people react physically to stress.
   b. what types of people experience the most stress.
   c. how stress is measured.
   d. what causes stress in our daily lives.

4. Change leads to stress when the change
   a. is positive only.
   b. is negative only.
   c. is unexpected.
   d. disrupts your normal daily routine.

5. The "hassles" discussed in this selection refer to
   a. major disagreements with family members.
   b. petty annoyances and frustrations.
   c. harassment and discrimination in the workplace.
   d. financial problems.

6. The most helpful guide question to ask for the heading "Pressure" is
   a. Is pressure related to stress?
   b. Are most people under pressure?
   c. How is pressure related to stress?
   d. Does pressure cause an increase or a decrease in stress?

7. The sentence that follows the heading "Pressure" describes when pressure occurs. In this section you would also expect to read about
   a. factors that create pressure.
   b. health problems related to stress.
   c. being prepared for change.
   d. learning to cope with minor hassles.

8. The most helpful guide question to ask for the heading "Inconsistency between Goals and Behaviors" is
   a. What is inconsistency?
   b. Are goals the same as behaviors?
   c. Is it possible to have inconsistencies between goals and behaviors?
   d. How does inconsistency between our goals and our behaviors lead to stress?

_____ 9. Because the last heading is titled "Conflict," you know that
   a. conflict is another psychosocial source of stress.
   b. conflict is a physical source of stress.
   c. stress is considered a source of conflict.
   d. there are conflicting theories about stress.

_____ 10. Conflict occurs when we must
   a. make hard decisions about competing motives, behaviors, or impulses.
   b. confront incompatible demands, opportunities, needs, or goals.
   c. both a and b
   d. neither a nor b

PRACTICING ACTIVE READING

Directions: *Preview the following selection, which is from a sociology text. So that your instructor can see the parts you read, highlight each part you looked at. (Normally, it is too time-consuming to highlight while previewing.)*

WHO LIVES IN THE CITY?

1   Whether you find alienation or community in the city depends on many factors, but consider the five types of urban dwellers that Gans (1962, 1968, 1991a) identified. Which type are you? How does this affect your chances of finding alienation or community?

      The first three types live in the city by choice; they find a sense of community.

2   **The Cosmopolites.**   The cosmopolites are the city's students, intellectuals, professionals, musicians, artists, and entertainers. They have been drawn to the city because of its conveniences and cultural benefits.

3   **The Singles.**   Young, unmarried people come to the city seeking jobs and entertainment. Business and services such as singles bars, singles apartment complexes, and computer dating companies cater to their needs. Their stay in the city is often temporary, for most move to the suburbs after they marry and have children.

4   **The Ethnic Villagers.**   United by race-ethnicity and social class, these people live in tightly knit neighborhoods that resemble villages and small towns. Moving within a close circle of family and friends, the ethnic villagers try to isolate themselves from what they view as the harmful effects of city life.

5   The next two groups, the deprived and the trapped, have little choice about where they live. As alienated outcasts of industrial society, they are always skirting the edge of disaster.

6   **The Deprived.**   The deprived live in blighted neighborhoods that are more like urban jungles than urban villages. Consisting of the very poor and the emotionally disturbed, the deprived represent the bottom of society in terms of income, education, social status, and work skills. Some of them stalk their jungle in search of prey, their victims usually deprived people like themselves. Their future holds little chance for anything better in life.

7   **The Trapped.**   The trapped can find no escape either. Some could not afford to move when their neighborhood was "invaded" by another ethnic group. Others in this group are the elderly who are not wanted elsewhere, alcoholics and other drug addicts, and the downwardly mobile. Like the deprived, the trapped also suffer high rates of assault, mugging, robbery, and rape.

—Henslin, *Sociology*, pp. 623–624

Directions: *Match each type of urban dweller listed in column A with the correct description in column B.*

	Column A		Column B
_____	1. the cosmopolites	a.	people united by race-ethnicity and social class
_____	2. the singles	b.	people who can find no escape
_____	3. the ethnic villagers	c.	students, intellectuals, professionals, musicians, artists, and entertainers
_____	4. the deprived	d.	young, unmarried people seeking jobs and entertainment
_____	5. the trapped	e.	people who live in blighted neighborhoods that are like urban jungles

PRACTICING ACTIVE READING

A. Directions: *Preview the following selection, which is from a sociology text. So that your instructor can see the parts you read, highlight each part you looked at. (Normally, it is too time-consuming to highlight while previewing.)*

THE MASS MEDIA

The mass media help to shape gender roles. The media give messages to children—and to the rest of us—that certain behaviors are considered "right" for boys and other behaviors "right" for girls. They also give messages about the "proper" relationships between men and women. To get some insight into how this occurs, we will look first at children's books, then at television, music, video games, and advertising.

Children's Books

Children's picture books have been a major focus of sociologists. It is easy to see that illustrated books for children are more than just entertainment; little children learn about the world from the pictures they see and the stories read to them. What the pictures show girls and boys doing becomes part of their view of what is "right."

When sociologists first examined children's picture books in the 1970s, they found that it was unusual for a girl to be the main character. Almost all the books featured boys, men, and even male animals. The girls, when pictured at all, were passive and doll-like, whereas the boys were active and adventuresome. While the boys did things that required independence and self-confidence, most girls were shown trying to help their brothers and fathers (Weitzman et al. 1972). Feminists protested these stereotypes and even formed their own companies to publish books that showed girls as leaders, as active and independent.

The result of these efforts, as well as that of the changed role of women in society, is that children's books now have about an equal number of boy and girl characters. Girls are also now depicted in a variety of nontraditional activities. Researchers find, however, that males are seldom depicted as caring for the children or doing grocery shopping, and they never are seen doing housework (Gooden and Gooden 2001). As gender roles continue to change, I assume that this, too, will change.

More powerful than picture books is television, both because of its moving images and the number of hours that children watch television. In the cartoons that so fascinate young children, males outnumber females, giving the message that boys are more important than girls. A children's TV show that ran from 1987 to 1996, *Teenage Mutant Ninja Turtles,* captures the situation. The original turtles were Michelangelo, Leonardo, Raphael, and Donatello—named after men artists whose accomplishments have been admired for centuries. A female turtle was added. Her name? Venus de

Milo. The female turtle was named not for a person, but for a statue that is world famous for its curvaceous and ample breasts. She never did anything. And, how could she—she has no head or arms ("Getting the Message" 1997).

Adult television reinforces stereotypes of gender, age, and sexuality. On prime time, male characters outnumber female characters, and men are more likely to be portrayed in higher-status positions (Glascock 2001). Starting at age 30, fewer and fewer women are shown, and about 9 out of 10 women on prime time are below the age of 46. Older women practically disappear from television (Gerbner 1998). Women are depicted as losing their sexual attractiveness earlier than men. Men are portrayed as aging more gracefully, with their sexual attractiveness lasting longer.

Music

There are so many kinds (genres) of music that it is difficult to summarize their content accurately. In many songs for teens and preteens, the listeners learn that boys should dominate male–female relationships. A common message for girls is that they should be sexy, passive, and dependent—and that they can control boys by manipulating the boys' sexual impulses. In music videos, females are most often only background ornaments for the dominant males. Some rap groups glorify male sexual aggression and revel in humiliating women. In Country-Western songs, which have become so popular, the common message is that men are aggressive and dominant, whereas women are passive and dependent. These men do have a tender side, however: They cry into their beers after their cheating women have left them. But, never mind, some honkey-tonk woman is waiting to revel in her dominant man.

Video Games

More than any other medium, video games give the message that women are not important: Male characters outnumber female characters seven to one (Beasley and Standley 2002). Matching the depictions of sex roles in the other media, video women show more skin than do video men.

Advertising

Advertising is an insidious propaganda machine for a male supremacist society. It spews out images of women as sex mates, housekeepers, mothers, and menial workers—images that perhaps reflect the true status of most women in society, but which also make it increasingly difficult for women to break out of the sexist stereotypes that imprison them (Komisar 1971:304).

This observation from the 1970s reminds us that little has changed in advertising. Although fewer women are now depicted as "housekeepers, mothers, and menial workers," television advertising continues to reinforce stereotypical gender roles. Commercials aimed at children are more likely to show girls as cooperative and boys as aggressive. They are also more likely to show girls at home and boys at other locations (Larson 2001). Men are portrayed in higher status positions (Coltrane and Messineo 2000). Women make most purchases, they are underrepresented as primary characters, and they are shown primarily as supportive counterparts to men (Ganahal et al. 2003).

Fighting Back

The use of the female body—especially exposed breasts—to sell products also continues. Feminists have fought back. In one campaign, they spray-painted their own lines to billboards (Rakow 1992). One billboard featured a Fiat with a woman reclining on its roof saying, "It's so practical, Darling." Feminists added the spray-painted line, "When I'm not lying on cars, I'm a brain surgeon."

Such resistance, as you know from the average 1,600 ads that pummel you each day (Draper 1986), has had little impact. The major change with how bodies are depicted in advertising is that the male body has become more prominent. More than ever, parts of the male body are also selected for exposure and for irrelevant associations with products.

In Sum

The essential point is that the mass media—children's books, television, music video games, and advertising—influence us. They shape the images that we hold in the way people "ought" to be, and we tend to see one another as men and women through those images. Mostly subtle and beneath our level of awareness, these images channel our behavior, becoming part of the means by which men maintain their dominance in social life. This includes politics, to which we now turn.

—Henslin, *Social Problems*, 7/e, pp. 293–296

B. Directions: *The following guide questions are based on the headings in the selection. Read the entire selection, and then select the choice that best answers each of the following questions.*

_____   1. How do children's books transmit stereotypes?

    a. They do not; they are simply entertainment.

    b. They present positive images of both males and females.

    c. Females in award-winning books are portrayed as more action-oriented than males.

    d. Male characters greatly outnumber females, and portrayals of both males and females are sexist.

_____   2. What message is sent by television?

a. Females outnumber males.

b. Role models are usually based on famous historical figures.

c. Men are more likely to have higher-status positions than women.

d. Accomplishment is not based on gender.

_____ 3. How are male-female relationships portrayed through music and video games?

a. Males are dominant and females are passive and dependent.

b. Males and females are equal partners in relationships.

c. Females control relationships.

d. Both males and females are capable of "rescuing" others in peril.

_____ 4. How does advertising reinforce stereotypes?

a. by using feminists to create advertising campaigns

b. by using more males than females in advertisements

c. by promoting a positive image of male-female relationships

d. by depicting women (and men) as objects for selling products

_____ 5. The summary of this selection indicates that

a. television and video games are more influential than children's literature.

b. we should not be concerned about the influence of the mass media on our lives.

c. the mass media shape our behavior by influencing our perceptions.

d. most men support the images portrayed by the mass media.

DIVERSITY IN U.S. FAMILIES
James M. Henslin

This reading selection, taken from a sociology textbook, explores the family structure of several racial-ethnic groups. Read the selection to discover the family characteristics of each group. Which one is most similar to your family structure?

Vocabulary Preview

These are some of the difficult words in this essay. The definitions here will help you if you can't figure out the meanings from the sentence context or word parts.

diversity (par. 1) the condition of being made up of different characteristics, qualities, or elements

preservation (par. 2) the act of maintaining or keeping

merger (par. 2) combination or union

cultural (par. 4) relating to the behavior patterns, beliefs, and institutions of a particular population

machismo (par. 7) an emphasis on male strength and dominance

emigrated (par. 9) moved away from one country or place to another

permissive (par. 10) tolerant or lenient

assimilate (par. 11) to become part of

DIVERSITY IN U.S. FAMILIES

1   It is important to note that there is no such thing as *the* American family. Rather, family life varies widely throughout the United States. The significance of social class, noted earlier, will continue to be evident as we examine diversity in U.S. families.

African American Families

2   Note that the heading reads African American *families,* not *the* African American family. There is no such thing as *the* African American family any more than there is *the* white family or *the* Latino family. The primary distinction is not between African Americans and other groups, but between social classes. Because African Americans who are members of the upper class follow the class interests reviewed in Chapter 10—preservation of privilege and family fortune—they are especially concerned about the family background of those whom their children marry. To them, marriage is

viewed as a merger of family lines. Children of this class marry later than children of other classes.

3   Middle-class African American families focus on achievement and respectability. Both husband and wife are likely to work outside the home. A central concern is that their children go to college, get good jobs, and marry well—that is, marry people like themselves, respectable and hardworking, who want to get ahead in school and pursue a successful career.

4   African American families in poverty face all the problems that cluster around poverty. Because the men are likely to have few skills and to be unemployed, it is difficult for them to fulfill the cultural roles of husband and father. Consequently, these families are likely to be headed by a woman and to have a high rate of births to single women. Divorce and desertion are also more common than among other classes. Sharing scarce resources and "stretching kinship" are primary survival mechanisms. That is, people who have helped out in hard times are considered brothers, sisters, or cousins to whom one owes obligations as though they were blood relatives. Sociologists use the term *fictive kin* to refer to this stretching of kinship.

5   From Figure A you can see that, compared with other groups, African American families are the least likely to be headed by married couples and the most likely to be

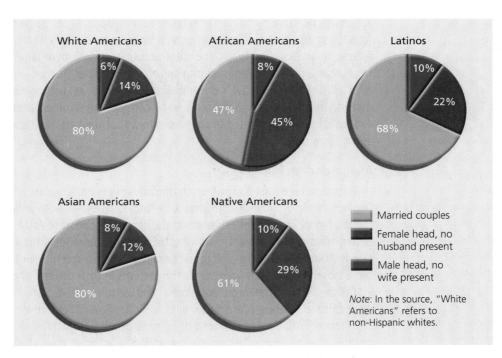

FIGURE A   Family Structure: The Percentage of U.S. Families Headed by Men, Women, and Married Couples

Source: By the author. Based on "American Community . . . "2004; *Statistical Abstract* 2005:Tables 33, 38, 40.

headed by women. Because African American women tend to go farther in school than African American men, they are more likely than women in other racial-ethnic groups to marry men who are less educated than themselves.

Latino Families

6   As Figure A shows, the proportion of Latino families headed by married couples and women falls in between that of whites and African Americans. The effects of social class on families, which I just sketched, also apply to Latinos. In addition, families differ by country of origin. Families from Mexico, for example, are more likely to be headed by a married couple than are families from Puerto Rico. The longer that Latinos have lived in the United States, the more their families resemble those of middle-class Americans (Saenz 2004).

7   With such a wide variety, experts disagree on what distinguishes Latino families. Some point to the Spanish language, the Roman Catholic religion, and a strong family orientation coupled with a disapproval of divorce. Others add that Latinos emphasize loyalty to the extended family, with an obligation to support the extended family in times of need. Descriptions of Latino families used to include **machismo**—an emphasis on male strength, sexual vigor, and dominance—but current studies show that *machismo* now characterizes only a small proportion of Latino husband-fathers. *Machismo* apparently decreases with each generation in the United States. Some researchers have found that the husband-father plays a stronger role than in either white or African American families. Apparently, the wife-mother is usually more family-centered than her husband, displaying more warmth and affection for her children.

8   It is difficult to draw generalizations because, as with other racial-ethnic groups, individual Latino families vary considerably. Some Latino families, for example, have acculturated to such an extent that they are Protestants who do not speak Spanish.

Asian American Families

9   As you can see from Figure A on the previous page, the structure of Asian American families is almost identical to that of white families. As with other racial-ethnic groups, family life also reflects social class. In addition, because Asian Americans emigrated from many different countries, their family life reflects those many cultures (Xie and Garrett 2004). As with Latino families, the more recent their immigration, the more closely their family life reflects the patterns in their country of origin.

10   Despite such differences, sociologist Bob Suzuki (1985), who studied Chinese American and Japanese American families, identified several distinctive characteristics. In child rearing, Asian Americans tend to be more permissive than Anglos. To control their children, they are more likely to use shame and guilt rather than physical punishment. Confucian values provide a distinctive framework for family life: humanism, collectivity,

■ *Although there is no such thing as the* Latino family, *in general, Latinos place high emphasis on extended family relationships.*

self-discipline, hierarchy, respect for the elderly, moderation, and obligation. Obligation means that each member of a family owes respect to other family members and is responsible never to bring shame on the family. Conversely, a child's success brings honor to the family.

Native American Families

11   Perhaps the single most significant issue that Native American families face is whether to follow traditional values or to assimilate into the dominant culture. This primary distinction creates vast differences among families. The traditionals speak

native languages and emphasize distinctive Native American values and beliefs. Those who have assimilated into the broader culture do not.

12   Figure A depicts the structure of Native American families. You can see how close it is to that of Latinos. In general, Native American parents are permissive with their children and avoid physical punishment. Elders play a much more active role in their children's families than they do in most U.S. families: Elders, especially grandparents, not only provide child care but also teach and discipline children. Like others, Native American families differ by social class.

In Sum

13   From this brief review, you can see that race-ethnicity signifies little for understanding family life. Rather, social class and culture hold the keys. The more resources a family has, the more it assumes the characteristics of a middle-class nuclear family. Compared with the poor, middle-class families have fewer children and fewer unmarried mothers. They also place greater emphasis on educational achievement and deferred gratification.

—Henslin, *Sociology*, 8/e, pp. 462–465

━ ∎ ━

Directions: *Select the letter of the choice that best completes each of the following statements.*

CHECKING YOUR COMPREHENSION

_____   1. The purpose of this selection is to
   a. describe the typical American family.
   b. summarize the achievements of successful families in America.
   c. describe the characteristics of families in various racial-ethnic groups in America.
   d. list statistics about marriage and divorce among racial-ethnic groups in America.

_____   2. The selection discusses all of the following racial-ethnic groups *except*
   a. African Americans.   c. Asian Americans.
   b. Arab Americans.   d. Native Americans.

_____ 3. According to the selection, the primary interest of the upper class is

    a. preservation of privilege and family fortune.

    b. acquisition of real estate and material possessions.

    c. strengthening of extended family relationships.

    d. assimilation into the dominant culture.

_____ 4. The group most likely to have families headed by women is

    a. African Americans.

    b. Native Americans.

    c. Asian Americans.

    d. white, non-Hispanic Americans.

_____ 5. According to the reading, "fictive kin" refers to

    a. your spouse's relatives.

    b. people who have helped you that you owe obligations to.

    c. people from your childhood neighborhood.

    d. friends who have sworn a blood vow.

_____ 6. The culture of Latino families is distinguished by all of the following *except*

    a. the Spanish language.

    b. the Roman Catholic religion.

    c. an emphasis on female power.

    d. a strong family orientation.

_____ 7. The structure of white (non-Hispanic) American families is most similar to that of

    a. Asian American families.

    b. African American families.

    c. Native American families.

    d. Latino families.

8. In Asian American families, the term "obligation" specifically means that

   a. Asian Americans must marry other Asian Americans only.

   b. Asian American children are responsible for taking care of their elderly parents.

   c. each family is obliged to maintain the traditions of its country of origin.

   d. each individual owes respect to other family members and must never bring shame on the family.

9. Native American families and Asian American families are similar in that both

   a. are permissive with their children and avoid physical punishment.

   b. downplay the role of elders in the family.

   c. emphasize male strength and dominance.

   d. focus on achievement and respectability.

10. All of the following previewing aids are found in the selection *except*

    a. section headings.

    b. an introduction.

    c. italics.

    d. a subtitle.

11. The most useful guide question for the entire selection would be

    a. Is there a typical American family?

    b. How are families in America diverse?

    c. Which racial-ethnic groups have been studied?

    d. What percentage of U.S. households are part of a racial-ethnic group?

12. According to the selection, the primary distinction between families in the U.S. is determined by

    a. race.

    b. ethnicity.

    c. social class.

    d. geographic location.

REVIEWING DIFFICULT VOCABULARY

Directions: *Complete each of the following sentences by inserting a word from the Vocabulary Preview on page 30 in the space provided. A word should be used only once.*

13. After the _____ was approved by the board of directors, they decided on a name for the newly formed company.

14. The actor's reputation for _____ seemed to conflict with his hobbies of knitting, calligraphy, and yoga.

15. Many immigrants have difficulty trying to _____ into a new country, especially if they do not speak the language.

16. The school was known for its _____; at least twelve different countries were represented among the student body.

17. Many people who live in North America have ancestors who at one time _____ from their native countries.

18. Perhaps because his parents had been so strict with him, Gabriel took a more _____ approach with his own children.

19. The group's mission statement declared that it was dedicated to the _____ of historical buildings and landmarks.

20. Before conducting business in other countries, executives often receive training in local customs and other important _____ differences.

QUESTIONS FOR DISCUSSION

1. Consider your own family and your racial-ethnic group, as well as other groups with which you are familiar. Discuss whether the information in this reading selection accurately reflects your experience.

2. Do you perceive social class as being a more important factor than racial-ethnic identity?

3. Would this reading selection help you to understand someone from a racial-ethnic group different from your own, or has it already?

WRITING ACTIVITIES

1. Write a paragraph describing a person who does or does not fit the characteristics of his or her racial-ethnic profile described in the reading.
2. This reading presents a profile of four racial-ethnic groups. Write a short essay exploring the dangers of such profiling.
3. Visit the Presence of the Past Web site at: http://chnm.gmu.edu/survey/1_4gnrlwat.html. Study the information in this table from a study about the relevance of the past to different racial-ethnic groups. Write a paragraph explaining why you think each group responded the way it did.

Chapter 1:   Reading Actively

RECORDING YOUR PROGRESS

Test	Number Right			Score	
Practice Test 1-1	_____	$\times$ 10	=	_____	%
Practice Test 1-2	_____	$\times$ 10	=	_____	%
Practice Test 1-3	_____	$\times$ 10	=	_____	%
Mastery Test 1-1	_____	$\times$ 20	=	_____	%
Mastery Test 1-2	_____	$\times$ 20	=	_____	%
Mastery Test 1-3	_____	$\times$ 5	=	_____	%

EVALUATING YOUR PROGRESS

Based on your test performance, rate how well you have mastered the skills taught in this chapter by checking one of the boxes below or by writing your own evaluation.

☐ **Need More Improvement**
Tip: Try completing the Active Reading Strategies—New Orleans module in the Reading Skills section on the MyReadingLab Web site at **http://www.ablongman.com/myreadinglab** to fine-tune the skills that you have learned in this chapter.

☐ **Need More Practice**
Tip: Try using the Active Reading Strategies—New Orleans module in the Reading Skills section on the MyReadingLab Web site at **http://www.ablongman.com/myreadinglab** to brush up on the skills taught in this chapter, or visit this textbook's Companion Web site at **http://www.ablongman.com/mcwhorter** for extra practice.

☐ **Good**
Tip: To maintain your skills, quickly review this chapter by using this textbook's Companion Web site at **http://www.ablongman.com/mcwhorter.**

☐ **Excellent**

YOUR EVALUATION: _____

_____

_____

_____

_____

THINK ABOUT IT!

A portion of the photograph below is blocked out. Can you figure out what is missing? Sketch it in the empty box in the photograph now. How did you know what to sketch? You probably used clues from the visible portions of the photograph to figure out what is missing. The image of the athlete suggests he is playing soccer. When reading a sentence or paragraph, if you find a word is missing from your vocabulary, you can figure out its meaning by studying the rest of the sentence or paragraph in which it appears. The words surrounding an unknown word provide clues to its meaning, just as the details in the photograph provide clues about what is missing.

Now read the following brief paragraph. Several words are missing. Try to figure out the missing words and write them in the blanks.

The ideal time to _____ a tree is in the fall. The warm days and cool _____ of autumn allow a tree's root system to develop and become established. The young tree will mature further during the spring season before facing the heat of _____.

CHAPTER 2

Using Context Clues and Word Parts

What Is Context?

Did you insert the word *plant* or *transplant* in the first blank, *nights* in the second blank, and *summer* in the third blank? Most likely, you correctly identified all three missing words. You could tell from the sentence which word to put in. The words around the missing words—the sentence context—gave you clues as to which word would fit and make sense. Such clues are called **context clues.**

While you probably won't find missing words on a printed page, you will often find words that you do not know. Context clues can help you to figure out the meanings of unfamiliar words.

EXAMPLE   During his lecture, the **ornithologist** described his research on western spotted owls as well as many other species of birds.

From the sentence, you can tell that *ornithologist* means "a person who studies birds."

Here's another example:

EXAMPLE   We were so **enervated** by the heat that we decided to go back to our air-conditioned hotel room for a nap before dinner.

You can figure out that *enervated* means "weakened or worn out" by the heat.

Types of Context Clues

There are five types of context clues to look for: (1) definition, (2) synonym, (3) example, (4) contrast, and (5) inference.

Definition Clues

Many times a writer defines a word immediately following its use. The writer may directly define a word by giving a brief definition of the unknown word. Such words and phrases as *means, is, refers to,* and *can be defined as* are often used. Here are some examples:

EXAMPLES

Induction refers to *the process of reasoning from the known to the unknown.*

A **prosthesis** is *an artificial replacement for a missing body part, such as an eye, a limb, or a heart valve.*

Punctuation is often used to signal that a definition clue to a word's meaning is to follow. Punctuation also separates the meaning clue from the rest of the sentence. Three types of punctuation are used in this way. In the examples below, notice that the meaning clue is separated from the rest of the sentence by punctuation.

EXAMPLES

1. Commas

Hypochondria, *excessive worry over one's health,* afflicts many Americans over forty.

Glen was especially interested in **nephology,** *the branch of meteorology that deals with clouds.*

2. Parentheses

Deciduous trees *(trees bearing leaves that are shed annually)* respond differently to heat and cold than **coniferous trees** *(trees bearing cones).*

Middle age *(35 years to 65 years)* is a time for strengthening and maintaining life goals.

3. Dashes

Most societies are **patriarchal**—*males exert dominant power and authority.*

The **rapier**—*a light sword with a narrow, pointed blade*—was traditionally used for thrusting rather than cutting.

Exercise 2–1

Directions: *Using the definition clues in each sentence, select the choice that best defines each boldfaced word.*

_____ 1. There was a **consensus,** or unified opinion, among the students that the exam was difficult.

    a. dispute   c. change

    b. unified opinion   d. question

_____ 2. The continents and ocean basins of the Earth's crust are separated from the Earth's liquid core by the **mantle**—1,800 miles of a solid layer of rock.

    a. crust   c. ocean basins

    b. liquid core   d. solid layer of rock

_____ 3. Jane Goodall has spent many years of her life observing the behavior of animals in their natural settings, a field of study known as **ethology.**

    a. the behavior of animals

    b. the study of animals in their natural environment

    c. the study of the environment

    d. the observation of behavior

_____ 4. The play **satirized** several famous political figures, using wit and sarcasm to expose their folly.

    a. admired   c. defeated

    b. ignored   d. ridiculed

_____ 5. Philippe was upset that he had lost the folder containing his **dossier,** which included his college transcripts, résumé, and letters of recommendation.

    a. wallet   c. license

    b. bank statement   d. collection of papers

_____ 6. In 1898, the Spanish **ceded,** or surrendered possession of, both Guam and Puerto Rico to the United States.

    a. maintained   c. gave up

    b. purchased   d. battled

_____ 7. The professor often used **paradigms,** or models, to illustrate difficult concepts.

    a. typical examples   c. brief reviews

    b. mastery tests   d. illustrated reports

_____ 8. People who practice **totemism**—the worship of plants, animals, or objects as gods—usually select for worship objects that are important to the community.

    a. the worship of community

    b. the worship of gods

    c. the worship of plants, animals, or objects

    d. the worship of no gods

_____ 9. In police investigations, **interrogation** (examination by questioning) is vital, but it can be psychologically and emotionally draining to the person being questioned.

    a. writing answers   c. interfering

    b. asking questions   d. complaining

_____ 10. The **mean**—the mathematical average of a set of numbers—will determine whether grades will be based on a curve.

    a. the highest number in a set

    b. the lowest number in a set

    c. the average of a set of numbers

    d. the total of a set of numbers

Synonym Clues

At other times, rather than formally define the word, a writer may provide a synonym—a word or brief phrase that is close in meaning. The synonym may appear in the same sentence as the unknown word.

EXAMPLE

The author purposely left the ending of his novel **ambiguous,** or _unclear,_ so readers would have to decide for themselves what happened.

Other times, it may appear anywhere in the passage, in an earlier or later sentence.

EXAMPLE

After the soccer match, a **melee** broke out in the parking lot. Three people were injured in the _brawl,_ and several others were arrested.

**Exercise
2-2**

Directions: *Using the synonym clues in each sentence, select the choice that best defines each boldfaced word.*

_____ 1. The mayor's assistant was accused of **malfeasance,** although he denied any wrongdoing.

   a. denial   c. motivation
   b. misconduct   d. authority

_____ 2. The words of the president seemed to **galvanize** the American troops, who cheered enthusiastically throughout the speech.

   a. excite   c. announce
   b. anger   d. discourage

_____ 3. Mia Hamm's superior ability and **prowess** on the soccer field have inspired many girls to become athletes.

   a. meekness   c. exceptional skill
   b. training   d. sound advice

_____ 4. Many gardeners improve the quality of their soil by **amending** it with organic compost.

   a. turning   c. removing
   b. spoiling   d. enriching

_____ 5. Eliminating salt from the diet is a **prudent,** sensible decision for people with high blood pressure.

   a. thoughtless   c. unnecessary
   b. advisable   d. economical

_____ 6. The **cadence,** or rhythm, of the Dixieland band had many people tapping their feet along with the music.

   a. appearance of the band   c. beat of the music
   b. melody   d. noise

_____ 7. Edgar Allan Poe is best known for his **macabre** short stories and poems. His eerie tale, "The Fall of the House of Usher," was made into a horror movie starring Vincent Price.

   a. humorous   c. entertaining
   b. magical   d. frightening

_____   8. While she was out of the country, Greta authorized me to act as her **proxy,** or agent, in matters having to do with her business and her personal bank accounts.

    a. representative   c. partner

    b. adviser   d. accountant

_____   9. The **arsenal** of a baseball pitcher ideally includes several different kinds of pitches. From this supply of pitches, he or she needs to have at least one that can fool the batter.

    a. collection   c. attitude

    b. performance   d. profession

_____   10. A **coalition** of neighborhood representatives formed to fight a proposed highway through the area. The group also had the support of several local businesses.

    a. report or summary   c. alliance or partnership

    b. business or enterprise   d. part or category

Example Clues

Writers often include examples that help to explain or clarify a word. Words and phrases used to introduce examples include _to illustrate, for instance, for example, such as,_ and _including._ Suppose you do not know the meaning of the word _pathogens,_ and you find it used in the following sentence:

EXAMPLE

Microscopic **pathogens,** such as viruses, bacteria, and fungi, constantly threaten our health as we go about our daily lives.

This sentence gives three examples of pathogens. From the examples given, which are known to cause disease or sickness, and from the clue about health, you could conclude that _pathogens_ means "disease-causing agents."

EXAMPLES

Collecting **demographic** data on potential consumers, including age, marital status, and income, is an essential part of market research.

Students in the introductory literature course were required to read several selections in each **genre**—drama, fiction, and poetry.

Orthopterans such as crickets, grasshoppers, and cockroaches thrive in damp conditions.

The symptoms of Erin's **malady** included a high fever, a headache, and an itchy rash.

Exercise 2–3

Directions: *Using the example clues in each sentence, select the choice that best defines each boldfaced word.*

_____   1. Some **debilities** of old age, including loss of hearing, poor eyesight, and diseases such as arthritis, can be treated medically.

   a. deafness   c. weaknesses

   b. medical treatments   d. notices

_____   2. The actor has a wide **repertoire,** including Shakespearean drama, Broadway plays, and classical theater.

   a. budget for artistic performances

   b. stock of material that can be performed

   c. requirements that must be fulfilled

   d. ability to both sing and dance

_____   3. Many people have turned to herbal **remedies,** such as flaxseed, yarrow, and St. John's wort, to treat a variety of health conditions.

   a. foods   c. challenges

   b. payments   d. medicines

_____   4. Children between the ages of three and six occasionally experience some form of **parasomnia**—sleepwalking, night terrors, or bed-wetting.

   a. sleep disorder   c. anger

   b. excitement   d. daydreaming

_____   5. Certain environmental hazards—including asbestos, arsenic, and tar—are considered **carcinogens;** people exposed to these materials are at risk for cancer.

   a. unknown benefits   c. cancer-causing substances

   b. possible pollutants   d. illegal substances

_____   6. The stray dog was **submissive**—crouching, flattening its ears, and avoiding eye contact.

   a. wild and excitable   c. angry and aggressive

   b. yielding and meek   d. active and alert

_____   7. To **substantiate** his theory, Watson offered experimental evidence, case study reports, testimony of patients, and a log of observational notes.

   a. revise   c. withdraw

   b. uncover   d. prove

_____   8. Companies often use **nonmonetary** rewards to motivate their employees. For example, new job titles, compensatory time, privileges, and awards can be effective motivational tools.

   a. private   c. not required

   b. not involving money   d. natural and realistic

_____   9. Many wills include at least one **codicil**, which is appended to the original will, such as an instruction about the disbursement of assets to stepchildren.

   a. additional part   c. fee

   b. error   d. request

_____   10. **Unconditioned responses**, including heartbeat, blinking, and breathing, occur naturally in all humans.

   a. traumas   c. involuntary actions

   b. medical terms   d. learned skills

Contrast Clues

It is sometimes possible to determine the meaning of an unknown word from a word or phrase in the context that has an opposite meaning. Notice, in the following sentence, how a word opposite in meaning to the boldfaced word provides a clue to its meaning:

EXAMPLE

At the wedding reception, the parents of the bride seemed to welcome all the attention, whereas the groom's parents **eschewed** it by staying at their table.

Although you may not know the meaning of *eschewed,* you know that the parents who eschewed the attention were different from the ones who welcomed it. The word *whereas* suggests this. Since one couple enjoyed the attention, you can tell that the other did not; in fact, they avoided it. Thus, *eschew* means the opposite of *welcome;* that is, to avoid.

Words and phrases that suggest a contrasting word or phrase include *on the one hand, on the other hand, however, in contrast, unlike, but, despite, yet, rather,* and *nevertheless.*

| EXAMPLES | Polytheism, the worship of more than one god, is common throughout India; however, **monotheism** is the most familiar religion to Americans. |

Although the cottage appeared **derelict,** we discovered that an elderly man had been living in a portion of it.

My friend is quite **gregarious** at parties, whereas her husband is extremely shy.

The old man lived a **frugal** life, but he left a generous inheritance for his grandchildren.

Exercise 2-4

Directions: *Using the contrast clues in each sentence, select the choice that best defines each boldfaced word.*

_____ 1. Most members of Western society marry only one person at a time, but in other cultures **polygamy** is common and acceptable.
   a. marriage to one person at a time
   b. marriage to more than one person at a time
   c. living together without marriage
   d. divorce

_____ 2. During a drought, plants that are **indigenous** to the area typically do better than non-native plants.
   a. native   c. dry
   b. imported   d. growing

_____ 3. The turkey was overcooked and extremely dry, so we added gravy to make it more **palatable.**
   a. cooked   c. spicy
   b. edible   d. unpleasant

_____ 4. Although every effort was made to ensure that the test was fair, several students complained that the questions were **skewed.**
   a. equal   c. biased
   b. too easy   d. repeated

_____ 5. Everyone on the jury was persuaded of the defendant's innocence except for one juror, who remained **dubious.**
   a. doubtful   c. curious
   b. convinced   d. trusting

_____ 6. Despite the **secular** nature of public schools, many teachers begin each day by leading their students in a short prayer.

   a. spiritual

   b. educational

   c. private

   d. nonreligious

_____ 7. The author seemed **taciturn** during his television interview, but when I met him in person, he was quite sociable.

   a. loud and talkative

   b. anxious and upset

   c. quiet and reserved

   b. unhappy and distraught

_____ 8. While several aspects of the zoo's mission were still open to discussion, its commitment to preserving endangered species was **immutable.**

   a. not decided

   b. not subject to change

   c. too expensive

   d. ideal

_____ 9. Most humans are **omnivores,** in contrast to herbivores such as cattle and deer, which are more selective in their diets and feed mainly on plants.

   a. those who eat plants only

   b. those who eat meat only

   c. those who eat plants and meat

   d. those who are selective about what they eat

_____ 10. One of the school board candidates was **vehement** about the new truancy policy; his opponent, on the other hand, expressed her views calmly and quietly.

   a. forceful

   b. polite

   c. confused

   d. mistaken

Inference Clues

Many times you can figure out the meaning of an unknown word by using logic and reasoning skills. For instance, look at the following sentence:

EXAMPLE

Langston Hughes was a **protean** writer; although he is known mainly for his poetry, he also wrote plays, novels, short stories, children's books, songs, and essays.

You can see that Hughes wrote many different kinds of literature, and you could reason that *protean* means "producing a variety of work."

EXAMPLES   The editor would not allow the paper to go to press until certain passages were **expunged** from an article naming individuals involved in a political scandal.

The differences between the two photo processing centers were **negligible,** so we chose to go to the one closest to our house.

Since the hammering next door had been going on for days, we had become somewhat **inured** to it.

Exercise 2–5

Directions: *Using logic and reasoning skills, select the choice that best defines each boldfaced word.*

_____ 1. Although my grandmother is 82, she is far from **infirm;** she is active, ambitious, and healthy.

   a. weak   c. retired
   b. youthful   d. capable

_____ 2. After leaving Manila, we flew over the Philippine **archipelago,** admiring the islands from our airplane window.

   a. airport   c. group of islands
   b. government   d. population

_____ 3. The senator has served eight **contiguous** six-year terms in office.

   a. intensive   c. unintended
   b. uninterrupted   d. disconnected

_____ 4. One **fallacy** about smokeless tobacco is that it is less harmful than smoking. In fact, smokeless tobacco contains ten times the amount of cancer-producing substances found in cigarettes.

   a. truth   c. advertisement
   b. false belief   d. advantage

_____ 5. The massive **influx** of refugees put such a severe strain on the country's economy that many of the refugees had to be relocated to other countries.

   a. exit   c. money
   b. arrival   d. assistance

_____ 6. After he was caught cheating, the student suffered the **ignominy** of being expelled from the school.

    a. frequency   c. disgrace

    b. agreement   d. attitude

_____ 7. By studying their genealogy, many people hope to **glean** knowledge about their family history and their ancestors.

    a. change   c. authorize

    b. gather   d. hide

_____ 8. Maria was able to **parlay** her computer skills into a successful career as a Web page designer.

    a. use to her advantage

    b. reduce job stress

    c. talk about her talents

    d. question her career choice

_____ 9. In her victory speech, the newly elected state representative thanked her supporters and pledged to be responsive to her **constituency.**

    a. the residents of an electoral district

    b. government officials

    c. state representatives

    d. personal interests

_____ 10. After tasting and eating most of seven different desserts, my appetite was completely **satiated.**

    a. satisfied   c. tempted

    b. unfulfilled   d. created

What Are Word Parts?

Although many people build their vocabulary word by word, studying word parts is a better and faster way to do it. For example, if you learn that _pre-_ means _before,_ then you can begin to figure out hundreds of words that begin with _pre_ (premarital, premix, prepay).

Suppose you came across the following sentence in a child psychology text:

EXAMPLE   The parents thought their child was **unteachable.**

If you did not know the meaning of *unteachable,* how could you figure it out? Since there are no clues in the sentence context, you might decide to look up the word in a dictionary. An easier way, though, is to break the word into parts. Many words in the English language are made up of word parts called *prefixes, roots,* and *suffixes.* A **prefix** comes at the beginning of a word, and a **suffix** comes at the end of a word. The **root**—which contains a word's basic meaning—forms the middle.

Let's look at the word *unteachable* again and divide it into three parts: its prefix, root, and suffix.

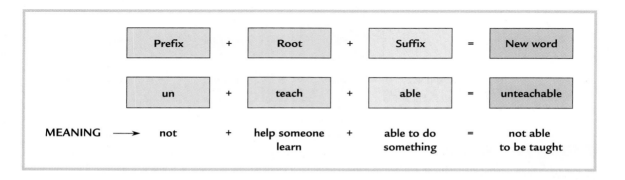

By using word parts, you can see that *unteachable* means "not able to be taught."

EXAMPLE   My friend Josh is a **nonconformist.**
non- = not
conform = go along with others
-ist = one who does something
nonconformist = someone who does not go along with others

To use word parts effectively, you should learn some of the most common ones. The prefixes and roots listed in Tables 2-1 and 2-2 are a good place to start. By knowing just *some* of these prefixes and roots, you can figure out the meanings of thousands of words without looking them up in a dictionary. For instance, more than 10,000 words can begin with the prefix *non-*. Another common prefix, *pseudo-* (which means "false") is used in more than 400 words. As you can see, by learning only a few word parts, you can add many new words to your vocabulary.

Prefixes

Though some English words do not have a prefix, many of them do. Commonly used prefixes are listed in Table 2-1. Prefixes appear at the *beginnings* of words and change the meaning of the root to which they are connected. For example, if you add the prefix *re-* to the word *read*, the word *reread* is formed, meaning "to read again." If *dis-* is added to the word *respect*, the word *disrespect* is formed, meaning "lack of respect."

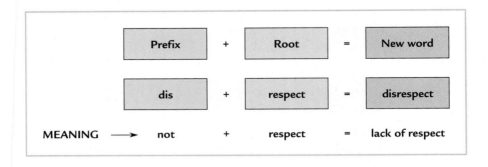

Prefix	+	Root	=	New word
dis	+	respect	=	disrespect

MEANING ⟶ not + respect = lack of respect

Exercise 2-6

Directions: *Using the list of common prefixes in Table 2-1, match each word in column A with its meaning in column B.*

Column A

_____ 1. inedible

_____ 2. bifocal

_____ 3. premeditate

_____ 4. antibacterial

_____ 5. hypertensive

_____ 6. polytonality

_____ 7. postglacial

_____ 8. contravene

_____ 9. transcend

_____ 10. equilateral

Column B

a. using many tonalities in a musical composition

b. plan or arrange ahead of time

c. occurring after a glacial period

d. not fit to be eaten

e. to act against

f. having all sides or faces equal

g. having two focal lengths

h. to cross beyond the limits

i. having high blood pressure

j. destroying or inhibiting the growth of bacteria

TABLE 2-1   Common Prefixes

Prefix	Meaning	Sample Word
Prefixes Referring to Amount or Number		
mono/uni	one	monocle/unicycle
bi/di/du	two	bimonthly/divorce/duet
tri	three	triangle
quad	four	quadrant
quint/pent	five	quintet/pentagon
deci	ten	decimal
centi	hundred	centigrade
milli	thousand	milligram
micro	small	microscope
multi/poly	many	multipurpose/polygon
semi	half	semicircle
equi	equal	equidistant
Prefixes Meaning "Not" (Negative)		
a	not	asymmetrical
anti	against	antiwar
contra	against, opposite	contradict
dis	apart, away, not	disagree
in/il/ir/im	not	incorrect/illogical/irreversible/impossible
mis	wrongly	misunderstand
non	not	nonfiction
un	not	unpopular
pseudo	false	pseudoscientific
Prefixes Giving Direction, Location, or Placement		
ab	away	absent
ad	toward	adhesive
ante/pre	before	antecedent/premarital
circum/peri	around	circumference/perimeter
com/col/con	with, together	compile/collide/convene
de	away, from	depart
dia	through	diameter
en/em	into, within	encase/embargo
ex/extra	from, out of, former	ex-wife/extramarital
hyper	over, excessive	hyperactive
inter	between	interpersonal
intro/intra	within, into, in	introduction
post	after	posttest
re	back, again	review
retro	backward	retrospect
sub	under, below	submarine
super	above, extra	supercharge
tele	far	telescope
thermo	heat	thermometer
trans	across, over	transcontinental

Directions: *Select a prefix from the box below to complete the word indicated in each of the following sentences.*

bi	ir	sub	circum	multi
tele	deca	post	dis	pseudo

1. We _____ vented the problem by calculating in metrics.

2. Because of its _____ standard performance on safety tests, the release of the new model car was delayed.

3. The new _____ purpose building contained conference rooms, a dining area, and a gym.

4. The damaging effects of long-term exposure to the sun are _____ reversible.

5. After surgery, patients should discuss their _____ operative care with their physician.

6. A _____ nary star system contains two stars.

7. In a _____ thlon, each athlete competes in ten track and field events.

8. Samuel Langhorne Clemens is better known by his _____ nym, Mark Twain.

9. Production of the camera was _____ continued because of declining sales.

10. Amateur astronomers use a _____ scope to view the sky.

Roots

Think of roots as being at the core of a word's meaning. You already know many roots—like *bio* in *biology* and *sen* in *insensitive*—because they are used in everyday speech. Thirty-one of the most common and useful roots are listed in Table 2-2. Learning the meanings of these roots will help

TABLE 2-2	Common Roots	
Root	**Meaning**	**Sample Word**
aud/audit	hear	audible/auditory
aster/astro	star	asteroid/astronaut
bene	good, well	benefit
bio	life	biology
cap	take, seize	captive
chron(o)	time	chronology
corp	body	corpse
cred	believe	incredible
dict/dic	tell, say	dictate/predict
duc/duct	lead	introduce/conduct
fact/fac	make, do	factory/factor
graph	write	telegraph
geo	earth	geophysics
log/logo/logy	study, thought	logic/psychology
mit/miss	send	permit/dismiss
mort/mor	die, death	immortal/mortician
path	feeling	sympathy
phono	sound, voice	telephone
photo	light	photosensitive
port	carry	transport
scop	seeing	microscope
scrib/script	write	scribe/inscription
sen/sent	feel	sensitive/sentiment
spec/spic/spect	look, see	retrospect/spectacle
tend/tent/tens	stretch or strain	tendon/tension
terr/terre	land, earth	terrain/territory
theo	god	theology
ven/vent	come	convention/venture
vert/vers	turn	invert/inverse
vis/vid	see	invisible/video
voc	call	vocation

you unlock the meanings of many words. For example, if you knew that the root *dic/dict* means "tell or say," then you would have a clue to the meanings of such words as *dictate* (to speak for someone to write down) or *dictionary* (a book that "tells" what words mean).

When you see a word you don't know and you can't figure it out from the sentence context, follow these tips:

1. **Look for the root first.**
2. **Keep in mind that the spelling of a root may change a bit if it is combined with a suffix.**
   (Table 2-2 includes some examples of spelling changes.)

Exercise 2-8

Directions: *Using the list of common roots in Table 2-2, match each word in column A with its meaning in column B. To help you, the root in each word in column A is in italics.*

Column A	Column B
_____ 1. *spect*ator	a. happening at the same time
_____ 2. *mort*ality	b. a scholarly piece of writing on a single subject
_____ 3. syn*chron*ous	c. a device for looking at objects below the surface of water
_____ 4. *aud*ial	d. the quality of being subject to death
_____ 5. *dict*ion	e. related to the sense of hearing
_____ 6. mono*graph*	f. a person who looks on at an event
_____ 7. sub*terr*anean	g. centering on God
_____ 8. hydro*scope*	h. beneath the earth's surface; underground
_____ 9. *theo*centric	i. to call on for help or support
_____ 10. in*voke*	j. choice and use of words in speech and writing

Exercise 2-9

Directions: *Select the word from the box below that best completes each of the following sentences. Refer to the list of roots in Table 2-2 if you need help.*

asters	benefactor	capacity	chronology	exportation
graphology	pathos	phototropic	sensor	transmit

1. The witness carefully described the _____ of events to the detective.

2. Certain countries forbid the _____ of endangered animals.

3. We planted _____ because we loved their star-shaped flowers.

4. Mosquitoes _____ the West Nile virus from infected birds to humans.

5. Our skin serves as a _____ for heat, cold, pressure, touch, and pain.

6. An anonymous _____ donated $10,000 worth of books to the school library.

7. The final scene of the play was one of _____ and sorrow.

8. The study of handwriting is known as _____.

9. On the night of the debate, the town hall was filled to

   _____.

10. Most plants are _____; that is, they grow in the direction of their light source.

Suffixes

Suffixes are word *endings*. Think of them as add-ons that make a word fit grammatically into a sentence. For example, adding the suffix *y* to the noun *cloud* forms the adjective *cloudy*. The words *cloud* and *cloudy* are used in different ways:

EXAMPLES

The rain **cloud** above me looked threatening.

It was a **cloudy,** rainy weekend.

You can often form several different words from a single root by adding different suffixes.

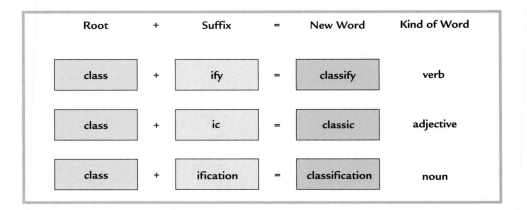

Root	+	Suffix	=	New Word	Kind of Word
class	+	ify	=	classify	verb
class	+	ic	=	classic	adjective
class	+	ification	=	classification	noun

As you know, when you find a word that you do not know, you should look for the root first. Then try to figure out what the word means with the suffix added. A list of common suffixes and their meanings appears in Table 2-3.

Sometimes you may find that the spelling of the root word changes because of the suffix. For instance, a final *e* may be dropped, a final consonant may be doubled, or a final *y* may be changed to *i*. Keep these possibilities in mind when you're trying to identify a root word.

EXAMPLES

David's article was a **compilation** of facts.
Root: compil(e)
Suffix: -ation
New word: compilation (something that has been compiled, or put together, in an orderly way)

We were concerned with the **legality** of our decision about our taxes.
Root: legal
Suffix: -ity
New word: legality (involving legal matters)

Our college is one of the most **prestigious** in the state.
Root: prestig(e)
Suffix: -ious
New word: prestigious (having prestige or distinction)

TABLE 2-3	Common Suffixes		
Suffix	**Sample Word**	**Suffix**	**Sample Word**
Suffixes Referring to a State, Condition, or Quality			
able	touchable	ive	permissive
ance	assistance	like	childlike
ation	confrontation	ment	amazement
ence	reference	ness	kindness
ful	playful	ous	jealous
ible	tangible	ty	loyalty
ion	discussion	y	creamy
ity	superiority		
Suffixes Meaning "One Who"			
an	Italian	ent	resident
ant	participant	er	teacher
ee	referee	ist	activist
eer	engineer	or	advisor
Suffixes Meaning "Pertaining to or Referring to"			
al	autumnal	hood	brotherhood
ship	friendship	ward	homeward

Exercise 2–10

Directions: *From each list of four words, select the choice that best completes the following sentence. Write your answer in the space provided.*

1. *uniforms, uniformity, uniformed, uniforming*

   The _____ of a law requires that it be applied to all relevant groups without bias.

2. *competed, competitor, competition, competitive*

   When food sources are not large enough to support all the organisms in a habitat, environmental _____ occurs.

3. *effective, effected, effectively, effectiveness*

   When evaluating a piece of art, consider its _____ —how well the artist's message has been conveyed to the audience.

4. *instruction, instructor, instructive, instructs*

   The lecture on Islamic traditions was _____.

5. *attendees, attendance, attends, attending*

   All _____ at the conference received a complimentary tote bag.

6. *inherit, inheritable, inherited, inheritance*

   The university was stunned by the size of its _____ from one of its former students.

7. *driven, driver, drivable, drivability*

   After the accident, our car was not _____ so we called a tow truck.

8. *participate, participation, participant, participative*

   Students in the workshop were graded partly on their _____ in class discussions.

9. *identify, identifier, identifiable, identification*

   Taxonomy is the branch of science concerned with the _____ and classification of species.

10. *internship, internist, interned, interning*

    During my senior year in college, I accepted an _____ at the local newspaper.

The Textbook Challenge

Part A: Current Issues Reader

The following words appear in the textbook excerpt, "Air Pollution and Global Warming," (p. 523). For each word, use context to write a definition of the word as it is used in the excerpt.

1. incineration (par. 4) _____

2. biodegradable (par. 4) _____

3. plummet (par. 6) _____

4. receded (par. 8) _____

5. erode (par. 10) _____

6. altitude (par. 11) _____

Part B: A College Textbook

Choose a chapter from one of your textbooks for another course. Identify ten words that you are able to determine the meaning of using context or word parts. Write the words and their meanings.

What Have You Learned?

Directions: *Indicate whether each of the following statements is true (T) or false (F).*

_____   1. The words around an unfamiliar word in a sentence or paragraph are known as its context.

_____   2. A synonym always appears in the same sentence as the word it corresponds to.

_____   3. When you figure out the meaning of a word by using logic and reasoning skills, you are using inference.

_____   4. The part of a word that carries its core meaning is known as the root.

_____   5. All English words have prefixes and suffixes.

_____   6. Prefixes appear at the beginning of words.

_____   7. Suffixes are word endings.

What Vocabulary Have You Learned?

Directions: *The words in column A appear in this chapter. Test your mastery of these words by matching each word in column A with its meaning in column B.*

	Column A		Column B
_____	1. terrain	a.	the payment of money
_____	2. genealogy	b.	opposite or reverse
_____	3. inverse	c.	surface features of the earth
_____	4. disbursement	d.	family history
_____	5. exert	e.	apply, bring to bear

CONTEXT AND WORD PARTS

Directions: *Using context clues and/or word parts, select the choice that best defines the boldfaced word in each sentence.*

_____ 1. It is more efficient to take lecture notes in your own words than to try to record the lecture **verbatim.**

     a. word for word   c. using verbs

     b. using abbreviations   d. using an outline

_____ 2. In some societies, young children are on the **periphery** instead of in the center of family life.

     a. focus   c. edge

     b. inside   d. middle

_____ 3. Amelia enjoys all **equestrian** sports, including jumping, riding, and racing horses.

     a. group   c. organized

     b. indoor   d. horseback

_____ 4. Despite his love of the country, he **renounced** his citizenship when war broke out.

     a. kept   c. gave up

     b. publicized   d. applied for

_____ 5. After we bought a grill on the Internet, we were **inundated** with e-mail offers for related items.

     a. sold   c. convinced

     b. flooded   d. investigated

_____ 6. To treat the inflammation, the patient must receive shots **intramuscularly.**

     a. within the muscle   c. between muscles

     b. next to the muscle   d. away from the muscle

_____ 7. The students reacted to the extra assignment with **incredulity.**

     a. relief   c. excitement

     b. indifference   d. disbelief

_____ 8. The poll was conducted by a **nonpartisan** group based in Maryland.
   a. associated with several political parties
   b. not associated with a political party
   c. locally funded
   d. volunteer

_____ 9. A key part of the experiment involved **photosensitive** cells.
   a. responsive to light   c. responsive to sound
   b. responsive to heat   d. responsive to color

_____ 10. The surface of the moon appears to be **abiotic.**
   a. without heat   c. producing heat
   b. without life   d. producing life

CONTEXT AND WORD PARTS

Directions: *From the box below, select the word that best defines the boldfaced word in each of the following sentences and write it in the space provided. Not all of the words in the box will be used.*

not critical	after the war	examine carefully
complimentary	crowded	roomy
convincing	lose their leaves	overly critical
series	go around	experienced
not changeable	before the war	thrive

1. The prosecutor presented such a **cogent** argument that the jury reached a guilty verdict in twenty minutes. _____

2. The quarterback **sustained** numerous injuries: a fractured wrist, two broken ribs, and a bruised hip. _____

3. To qualify for high-security jobs, applicants must undergo a **battery** of tests designed to measure physical and mental aptitude.

   _____

4. Miriam is **hypercritical** of her daughter's eating habits.

   _____

5. An expedition formed by Ferdinand Magellan was first to **circumnavigate** the Earth. _____

6. I always **scrutinize** my bank statement to make sure there are no mistakes on it. _____

7. Certain house plants may **defoliate** when they are moved from one room to another. _____

8. The annual tour of homes featured several **antebellum** estates.

   _____

9. For a small car, the new Mini Cooper is surprisingly **capacious** inside.

   _____

10. The designation of beneficiary on the life insurance policy was

    irrevocable. _____

CONTEXT AND WORD PARTS

Directions: *Using context clues and/or word parts, select the choice that best defines each boldfaced word from the following paragraphs.*

If you have ever tried to perform heavy manual labor on a hot summer day, you may have become weak and dizzy as a result. If your **exertions** were severe, you may have even collapsed and lost **consciousness** momentarily. If this has happened to you, then you have experienced *heat exhaustion.* Heat exhaustion is a **consequence** of the body's effort to regulate its temperature—in particular, its efforts to get rid of **excess** heat. When the body must get rid of a large quantity of heat, **massive** quantities of sweat can be produced, leading to a significant **reduction** in blood volume. In addition, blood flow to the skin increases markedly, which **diverts** blood from other areas of the body. Together, these changes produce a reduction in blood pressure, which reduces blood flow to the brain and **precipitates** the symptoms just described.

A far more serious condition is *heat stroke,* in which the body's temperature rises out of control due to failure of the **thermoregulatory** system. The skin of individuals experiencing heat stroke has a flushed appearance but will also be dry, in contrast to the **profuse** sweating of heat exhaustion. If someone is experiencing heat stroke, immediate medical attention is of the utmost importance.

—adapted from Germann and Stanfield, *Principles of Human Physiology,* p. 9

_____ 1. exertions
  a. temperature   c. breaks
  b. conditions   d. efforts

_____ 2. consciousness
  a. sense of right and wrong   c. state of awareness
  b. carefulness   d. insensitivity

_____ 3. consequence
  a. cause   c. difference
  b. result   d. complication

_____ 4. excess
  a. quality   c. scarce
  b. normal   d. extra

_____ 5. massive

    a. huge   c. minor

    b. harmless   d. immediate

_____ 6. reduction

    a. increase   c. strengthening

    b. decrease   d. improvement

_____ 7. diverts

    a. redirects   c. continues

    b. forms   d. conceals

_____ 8. precipitates

    a. prevents   c. brings on

    b. follows   d. alters

_____ 9. thermoregulatory

    a. controlling hearing   c. controlling feeling

    b. controlling vision   d. controlling heat

_____ 10. profuse

    a. dry   c. extensive

    b. scarce   d. healthy

CONTEXT AND WORD PARTS

Directions: *Using context clues and/or word parts, select the word from the box below that best defines each of the boldfaced words in the following paragraph. Not all of the words in the box will be used.*

The movies have reinforced the **fallacy** that all Indians constituted a single type with a common lifestyle. The mounted, war-bonneted warrior of the plains has too often been considered the **archetype** of the "Red Man." Yet early European settlers found the North American Indians as **diverse** as the Europeans themselves. Two hundred **distinct** North American languages have been classified, and numerous physical differences in the continent's **inhabitants** have been identified. The **indigenous** societies of North America presented a wide **spectrum** of variation: from small bands of hunter-gatherers and farmers to well-organized states. A similar diversity was found in their arts and crafts; various regions **excelled** in basketry, metalwork, weaving, sculpture, totem-carving, and boatmaking. They survived by hunting and fishing until knowledge of food-raising **migrated** north from Mexico and Central America, resulting in more **stable** settlements in which men cleared the fields and women tended the crops.

—adapted from Brummett et al., *Civilization Past & Present*, pp. 239–40

unmoving	range	residents	foreign	failed
enemy	false belief	native	model	identical
varied	different	moved	performed well	

1. fallacy _____

2. archetype _____

3. diverse _____

4. distinct _____

5. inhabitants _____

6. indigenous _____

7. spectrum _____

8. excelled _____

9. migrated _____

10. stable _____

CONTEXT AND WORD PARTS

Directions: *Using context clues and/or word parts, select the word from the box below that best defines each of the boldfaced words in the following paragraph. Not all of the words in the box will be used.*

Thomas Jefferson had no desire to surround himself with pomp and ceremony; the excessive formality and punctilio of the Washington and Adams administrations had been **distasteful** to him. From the moment of his election, he played down the **ceremonial** aspects of the presidency. In the White House he often wore a **frayed** coat and carpet slippers, even to receive the representatives of foreign powers when they arrived, **resplendent** with silk ribbons and a sense of their own importance, to present their **credentials.** At social affairs he paid little **heed** to the status and **seniority** of his guests. The guests, carefully chosen to make **congenial** groups, were seated at a round table to encourage general conversation, and the food and wine were first-class. These were **ostensibly** social occasions—shop talk was avoided—yet they paid large political **dividends.**

—adapted from Nash, *The American Nation*, pp. 175–6

qualifications	dazzlingly impressive	related to formal occasions
worn out	unpleasant	rank based on length of service
seemingly	agreeable	benefits
attention	drawbacks	up-to-date

1. distasteful _____

2. ceremonial _____

3. frayed _____

4. resplendent _____

5. credentials _____

6. heed _____

7. seniority _____

8. congenial _____

9. ostensibly _____

10. dividends _____

UNFAIR ADVANTAGE
Teresa Audesirk, Gerald Audesirk, and Bruce E. Byers

This essay describes the illegal use of blood doping by some athletes attempting to gain a competitive edge in bicycle racing. Read it to find out what blood doping is, how it works, and the issues surrounding its use.

Vocabulary Preview

These are some of the difficult words in this passage. The definitions here will help you if you can't figure out the meanings from the sentence context or word parts.

arcane (par. 2) known or understood by only a few people; mysterious

molecules (par. 5) the smallest particles of an element or compound that have all the properties of that substance

glucose (par. 6) a monosaccharide sugar occurring in most plant and animal tissue; an important source of cellular energy

fiasco (par. 8) a complete failure

metabolism (par. 8) the total of all chemical reactions that occur in the body

1   On a sunny July morning in 1998, the members of the Festina bicycle racing team, the top-rated team in the world, sat in a French café. Nearby, dozens of other professional bicyclists made their final preparations for the impending start of the day's segment of the grueling Tour de France race. The Festina riders, however, would not be joining the race. Hours earlier, the entire team had been expelled from the Tour de France for the offense of blood doping.

2   The dramatic expulsion of top athletes from the world's premier bicycle race focused attention on the arcane practice of blood doping. By using blood-doping techniques, some athletes try to gain a competitive edge. But what is blood doping, and how does it enhance athletic performance?

3   Blood doping increases a person's physical endurance by increasing the capacity of the blood to carry oxygen. One crude method for accomplishing this goal is to simply inject extra red blood cells into the bloodstream. Red blood cells transport oxygen to the body's tissues, so simply adding more of them is a straightforward way of increasing the amount of oxygen that reaches the tissues. In recent years, however, blood-doping athletes have increasingly turned to injections of erythropoietin (Epo) as a more effective approach to increasing blood oxygen.

4   Epo is a protein molecule that is present in a normal human body, where it functions as a chemical messenger that stimulates bone marrow to produce more red blood cells. Under normal circumstances, the body produces just enough Epo to ensure that red blood cells are replaced as they age and die. An injection of extra Epo, however, can stimulate the production of a huge number of extra red blood cells. The extra cells greatly increase the oxygen-carrying capacity of the blood. Unfortunately, the excess blood cells also thicken the blood and make it harder to move through blood vessels, so those who inject Epo suffer increased risk of heart failure.

5   Why would professional athletes take such a risk to get more oxygen molecules into their bloodstreams? How does extra oxygen increase endurance? The answers to those questions lie in the role of oxygen in supplying energy to muscle cells.

6   Human cells most efficiently extract energy from glucose when an ample supply of oxygen is available to them. The aim of blood-doping cyclists, then, is to extend as long as possible the period in which their muscle cells have access to oxygen. During a difficult hill-climb, a cyclist who has doped his blood with erythropoietin may be able to pedal efficiently, his muscle cells using the Krebs cycle to turn out abundant ATP. At the same time, his "clean" competitor may labor painfully, leg muscles laden with lactate from fermentation.

7   The extra endurance that Epo supplies can tempt elite athletes to risk their health for an extra edge, despite the penalties that await those who are caught using a banned substance. The temptation may be especially large in the case of Epo. Because this substance forms naturally in the human body, its abuse is hard to detect; standard drug-screening procedures cannot distinguish between natural Epo and that injected in blood doping. In fact, the Festina team that was banned from the 1998 Tour de France was caught not by any blood or urine test, but only because a large supply of Epo was found in the team's car at a border crossing.

8   Since the Festina fiasco, however, researchers have worked hard at developing better tests for blood doping with Epo. A new urine test for Epo was introduced at the 2000 summer Olympics. This test detects a subtle chemical difference between the breakdown products of natural Epo and those of the manufactured version that is used in doping injections. Olympic officials, however, are not totally confident in the accuracy of the new urine test, and they use it only in conjunction with blood tests that screen for unusually high density of blood cells. Only athletes who fail both tests are disqualified. Meanwhile, researchers continue to explore the chemistry of Epo metabolism in hope of discovering a definitive test for blood doping.

━━ ▪ ━━

Directions: *Select the letter of the choice that best completes each of the following statements.*

CHECKING YOUR COMPREHENSION

_____ 1. The main point of the reading is that
- a. bicyclists in the Tour de France have been caught using illegal drugs.
- b. the drug Epo is a naturally occurring substance that should not be banned in athletic competitions.
- c. researchers are attempting to create a safe and legal form of Epo.
- d. athletes risk penalties and their health by using Epo to enhance their performance in races.

_____ 2. The main idea of paragraph 3 is that
- a. red blood cells transport oxygen to the body's tissues.
- b. blood doping enhances physical endurance by increasing blood oxygen.
- c. blood-doping techniques are complicated and ineffective.
- d. the drug Epo stimulates the production of red blood cells.

_____ 3. The Festina bicycling team was banned from the 1998 Tour de France because
- a. a blood test revealed that members of the team had used steroids.
- b. a urine test revealed that members of the team had used Epo.
- c. a member of the team was caught injecting Epo.
- d. the team's car was found to contain Epo.

_____ 4. Athletes use Epo (or blood doping) in order to
- a. extend the period in which their muscle cells have access to oxygen.
- b. decrease the amount of oxygen that reaches their tissues.
- c. reduce their risk of heart failure during a strenuous race.
- d. decrease the period in which their muscle cells require oxygen.

_____ 5. Before a race, athletes introduce Epo into their bodies typically by

    a. injecting a manufactured version of Epo.

    b. swallowing a protein supplement that contains Epo.

    c. rubbing an ointment containing Epo on their legs.

    d. working out to increase the quantities of naturally occurring Epo in their bodies.

USING CONTEXT CLUES AND WORD PARTS

_____ 6. In paragraph 1, **impending** means

    a. historic.　　　　　c. dangerous.

    b. about to happen.　　d. unofficial.

_____ 7. In paragraph 1, **grueling** means

    a. shocking.　　　　　c. exhausting.

    b. pleasant.　　　　　d. training.

_____ 8. In paragraph 2 **expulsion** means

    a. elimination.　　　　c. participation.

    b. attendance.　　　　d. reception.

_____ 9. In paragraph 3, **capacity** means

    a. decrease.　　　　　c. changeable.

    b. production.　　　　d. ability.

_____ 10. In paragraph 6, **laden** means

    a. heavy or filled.　　　c. strong and forceful.

    b. necessary.　　　　　d. missing.

_____ 11. In paragraph 7, **elite** means

    a. amateur.　　　　　c. top quality.

    b. educated.　　　　　d. worst.

_____ 12. In paragraph 7, **banned** means

    a. unnatural.　　　　　c. forbidden.

    b. large quantity.　　　d. inefficient.

_____ 13. In paragraph 8, **subtle** means
    a. strange.   c. physical.
    b. hardly noticeable.   d. obvious.

_____ 14. In paragraph 8, **density** means
    a. concentration.   c. variation.
    b. quality.   d. similarity.

_____ 15. In paragraph 8, **disqualified** means
    a. allowed.   c. competed.
    b. examined.   d. denied participation.

REVIEWING DIFFICULT VOCABULARY

Directions: *Complete each of the following sentences by inserting a word from the Vocabulary Preview on page 73 in the space provided. Each word should be used only once.*

16. The most common monosaccharides, or simple sugars, include

    _____, fructose, and galactose.

17. The dinner party was a _____: the guests were

    late, the food was overcooked, and the ceiling began to leak halfway

    through dinner.

18. After describing several _____ economic

    theories, the professor moved on to the more familiar and well-known

    Keynesian theories.

19. When an animal hibernates, its _____ slows

    down and its temperature drops.

20. In the process of diffusion, _____ of a

    substance spread evenly through a gas, liquid, or solid.

QUESTIONS FOR DISCUSSION

1. In what other sports is the use of drugs to enhance performance an issue?

2. Do you think all athletes should be screened for drug use before each performance? Discuss the advantages and disadvantages of such a policy.

3. Why do athletes resort to the use of drugs to enhance their performance? Discuss whether athletics have become too competitive.

WRITING ACTIVITIES

1. Brainstorm a list of characteristics of professional athletes. Consider whether these characteristics are appropriate for national heroes or for role models of aspiring athletes. Write a paragraph summarizing your findings.

2. In a letter to the captain of the Festina bicycle racing team, explain your reactions to his team's use of blood doping.

3. Each sport, special interest, or hobby has its own special language. Visit the White House's Web page on drugs and sports http://www.whitehousedrugpolicy.gov/prevent/sports/doping.html. Write a paragraph that summarizes the information, including a definition of doping and examples of illegal substances and their effects.

Chapter 2:   Using Context and Word Parts

RECORDING YOUR PROGRESS

Test	Number Right		Score
Practice Test 2-1	_____ × 10 =		_____ %
Practice Test 2-2	_____ × 10 =		_____ %
Practice Test 2-3	_____ × 10 =		_____ %
Mastery Test 2-1	_____ × 10 =		_____ %
Mastery Test 2-2	_____ × 10 =		_____ %
Mastery Test 2-3	_____ × 5 =		_____ %

EVALUATING YOUR PROGRESS

Based on your test performance, rate how well you have mastered the skills taught in this chapter by checking one of the boxes below or by writing your own evaluation.

☐ **Need More Improvement**
Tip: Try completing the Vocabulary—The Library of Congress, Washington, D.C. module in the Reading Skills section on the MyReadingLab Web site at **http://www.ablongman.com/myreadinglab** to fine-tune the skills that you have learned in this chapter.

☐ **Need More Practice**
Tip: Try using the Vocabulary—The Library of Congress, Washington, D.C. module in the Reading Skills section on the MyReadingLab Web site at **http://www.ablongman.com/myreadinglab** to brush up on the skills taught in this chapter, or visit this textbook's Companion Web site at **http://www.ablongman.com/mcwhorter** for extra practice.

☐ **Good**
Tip: To maintain your skills, quickly review this chapter by using this textbook's Companion Web site at **http://www.ablongman.com/mcwhorter**.

☐ **Excellent**

YOUR EVALUATION: _____

_____

_____

_____

THINK ABOUT IT!

Look at the photograph below. Write a sentence describing what is happening in the photograph.

_____

_____

   The sentence you have written states the main idea—or main point—the photo conveys. However, unless you interviewed the person in the photograph, you would not know the details of the situation: what sport event the man won or where the competition took place, for example. When you study a paragraph, you also start with its general idea and then try to figure out its main point. Then you move on to examine its details. This chapter focuses on identifying main ideas. Then, in Chapter 4 you will learn more about details that explain and support the main idea.

CHAPTER 3

Locating Main Ideas

What Is a Main Idea?

When a friend asks you to go to a movie you haven't heard of, you probably ask "What's it about?" As you watch the movie, you come to understand the characters and the story. Eventually, you grasp the point the film is making—you realize what all the conversations and action, taken together, mean.

Understanding a paragraph involves a similar process. You first need to know what the paragraph is about, then you have to understand each of the sentences and how they relate to one another. Finally, to understand the paragraph's main point, you need to grasp what all the sentences, taken together, mean.

The one general subject a whole paragraph is about is called the **topic.** The most important point a whole paragraph makes is called the **main idea.** For example, read the following paragraph:

Today, super-sized meals are the norm at many restaurants. Biscuits and gravy, huge steaks, and plate-filling meals are popular fare. Consider the 25-ounce prime rib dinner served at a local steak chain. At nearly 3,000 calories and 150 grams of fat for the meat alone, this meal both slams shut arteries and adds on pounds. Add a baked potato with sour cream and/or butter, a salad loaded with creamy salad dressing, and fresh bread with real butter, and the meal may surpass the 5,000-calorie mark and ring in at close to 300 grams of fat. In other words, it exceeds what most adults should eat in two days!

—Donatelle, *Health the Basics*, p. 283

In this paragraph, the topic is "super-sized meals," and the main idea is that "super-sized meals have become common in many restaurants." Here the main point of the paragraph is stated in the first sentence. The rest of the sentences then support or back up the main idea. As you will see later, however, the main idea doesn't always come first.

Understanding General Versus Specific Ideas

To identify topics and main ideas in paragraphs, it helps to understand the difference between general and specific. A *general* idea applies to a large number of individual items. The term *television programs* is general because it refers to a large collection of shows—soap operas, sports specials, sit-coms, and so on. A *specific* idea or term is more detailed or particular. It refers to an individual item. The word *reality TV,* for example, is more specific than the word *program*. The title "Survivor" is even more specific.

EXAMPLES

General:	Cakes	*General:*	Vegetables
Specific:	chocolate	*Specific:*	carrots
	spice		corn
	angel food		peas

General:	Continents	*General:*	Parts of Speech
Specific:	Asia	*Specific:*	noun
	Africa		verb
	Australia		adjective

Exercise 3–1

Directions: *Choose the letter that represents the most general term in each group of words.*

_____ 1. (a) American literature   (b) college courses   (c) anthropology   (d) biochemistry

_____ 2. (a) horror films   (b) westerns   (c) movies   (d) comedies

_____ 3. (a) computers   (b) laptops   (c) notebooks   (d) mainframes

_____ 4. (a) parkas   (b) windbreakers   (c) coats   (d) raincoats

_____ 5. (a) station wagons   (b) vehicles   (c) SUVs   (d) minivans

_____   6. (a) volleyball   (b) soccer   (c) football   (d) sports

_____   7. (a) hardbacks   (b) e-books   (c) books   (d) paperbacks

_____   8. (a) brothers   (b) grandmothers   (c) relatives   (d) cousins

_____   9. (a) math   (b) geometry   (c) algebra   (d) calculus

_____ 10. (a) pines   (b) trees   (c) maples   (d) oaks

Exercise 3-2

Directions: *For each list of items, select the choice that best describes that grouping.*

_____   1. dodo bird, tyrannosaurus rex, woolly mammoth, stegosaurus
   a. extinct animals   c. endangered animals
   b. animals   d. zoo animals

_____   2. single-parent, divorced, two-career, married
   a. children   c. familes
   b. incomes   d. societies

_____   3. for money, for experience, to meet people
   a. reasons to attend a party
   b. reasons to get a part-time job
   c. reasons to apply for loans
   d. reasons to date

_____   4. U.S. Constitution, Bill of Rights, Federalist Papers, Twenty-fifth Amendment
   a. policies   c. historical documents
   b. historical events   d. party politics

_____   5. Mars, Saturn, Jupiter, Mercury
   a. asteroids   c. galaxies
   b. solar systems   d. planets

Now that you are familiar with the difference between general and specific, you will be able to use these concepts in the rest of the chapter.

Identifying the Topic

You already know that the topic is the general subject of an entire paragraph. Every sentence in a paragraph in some way discusses or explains this topic. To find the topic of a paragraph, ask yourself: What is the one idea the author is discussing throughout the paragraph? Read the following paragraph with that question in mind:

> The major motive for excuse making seems to be to maintain our self-esteem, to project a positive image to ourselves and to others. Excuses are also offered to reduce stress that may be created by a bad performance. We feel that if we can offer an excuse—especially a good one that is accepted by those around us—it will lessen the negative reaction and the subsequent stress that accompanies poor performance.
>
> —DeVito, *Human Communication: The Basic Course*, p. 178

In this example, the author is discussing one topic—making excuses—throughout the paragraph. Notice that the word *excuse* is used several times. As you can see, the repeated use of a word often serves as a clue to the topic.

Exercise 3-3

Directions: *After reading each of the following paragraphs, choose the letter of the choice that best represents the topic of the paragraph.*

_____ 1. Magazines are a channel of communication halfway between newspapers and books. Unlike newspapers or books, however, many of the most influential magazines are difficult or impossible to purchase at newsstands. With their color printing and slick paper (in most cases), magazines have become a showplace for exciting graphics. Until the 1940s most consumer (general) magazines offered a diverse menu of both fiction and nonfiction articles and miscellany such as poetry and short humor selections. With television providing a heavy quotient of entertainment for the American home, many magazines discovered a strong demand for nonfiction articles, their almost exclusive content today.

—Agee, Ault, and Emery, *Introduction to Mass Communication*, p. 153

a. magazine graphics c. entertainment
b. magazines d. communication

_____ 2. Businesses do not operate in a vacuum, but rather exist within a business environment that includes economic, legal, cultural, and competitive factors. Economic factors affect businesses by influencing what and how many goods and services consumers buy. Laws and regulations have an impact on many activities in a business. Cultural and social factors influence the characteristics of the goods and services sold by businesses. Competition affects what products and services a business offers, and the price it charges.

—Nickerson, *Business and Information Systems*, p. 30

a. business environment

b. economic factors in business

c. business activities

d. competition in business

_____ 3. The process of becoming hypnotized begins when the people who will be hypnotized find a comfortable body position and become thoroughly relaxed. Without letting their minds wander to other matters, they focus their attention on a specific object or sound, such as a metronome or the hypnotist's voice. Then, based on both what the hypnotherapist expects to occur and actually sees occurring, she or he tells the clients how they will feel as the hypnotic process continues. For instance, the hypnotist may say, "You are feeling completely relaxed" or "Your eyelids are becoming heavy." When people being hypnotized recognize that their feelings match the hypnotist's comments, they are likely to believe that some change is taking place. That belief seems to increase their openness to other statements made by the hypnotist.

—Uba and Huang, *Psychology*, p. 148

a. hypnosis results

b. relaxation

c. hypnosis process

d. suggestion during hypnosis

_____ 4. Although there were unions in the United States before the American Revolution, they have become major power blocks only in the last 60 years or so. Directly or indirectly, managerial decisions in almost all organizations are now influenced by the effect of unions. Managers in unionized organizations must operate through the union in dealing with their employees instead of acting alone. Decisions affecting employees are made collectively at the bargaining tables and through arbitration, instead of individually by the supervisor when and where the need arises. Wages, hours, and other terms and conditions of employment are largely decided outside of management's sphere of discretion.

—Mosley, Pietri, and Magginson, *Management: Leadership in Action*, p. 317

a. union membership   c. power of unions

b. history of unions   d. establishment of unions

_____ 5. Automated radio has made large gains, as station managers try to reduce expenses by eliminating some of their on-the-air personnel. These stations broadcast packaged taped programs obtained from syndicates, hour after hour, or material delivered by satellite from a central program source. The closely timed tapes contain music and commercials, along with the necessary voice introductions and bridges. They have spaces into which a staff engineer can slip local recorded commercials. By eliminating disc jockeys in this manner, a station keeps its costs down but loses the personal touch and becomes a broadcasting automaton. For example, one leading syndicator, Satellite Music Network, provides more than 625 stations with their choice of seven different 24-hour music formats that include news and live disc jockeys playing records.

—Agee, Ault, and Emery, *Introduction to Mass Communication*, p. 225

a. satellite radio   c. local radio commercials

b. radio costs   d. automated radio

Finding the Main Idea

You learned earlier that the **main idea** of a paragraph is its most important point. The main idea is also the most *general* statement the writer makes about the topic. Pick out the most general statement among the following sentences.

1. Animals differ according to when they sleep.
2. Some animals sleep during daylight while others sleep during darkness.
3. Animals' sleeping habits differ in a number of ways.
4. Hibernation is another kind of sleep for some animals.

Did you choose item 3 as the most general statement? Now we will change this list into a paragraph by rearranging the sentences and adding a few facts.

> Animals' sleeping habits differ in a number of ways. They differ according to what time of day they sleep. Some animals sleep during daylight hours while others sleep during darkness. They also differ in the length of time they sleep. Other animals sleep for weeks or months at a time when they hibernate.

In this brief paragraph, the main idea is expressed in the first sentence. This sentence, known as the **topic sentence,** is the most general statement in the paragraph. All the other sentences are specific details that explain this main idea.

Tips for Finding the Main Idea

Here are some tips that will help you find the main idea.

1. **Identify the topic.** As you did earlier, figure out the general subject of the entire paragraph. In the preceding sample paragraph, "animals' sleeping habits" is the topic.

2. **Locate the most general sentence (the topic sentence).** This sentence must be broad enough to include all of the other ideas in the paragraph. The topic sentence in the sample paragraph ("Animals' sleeping habits differ in a number of ways") covers all of the other details in that paragraph. The tips in the next section will help you locate topic sentences.

3. **Study the rest of the paragraph.** The main idea must make the rest of the paragraph meaningful. It is the one idea that ties all of the other details together. In the sample paragraph, sentences 2, 3, 4, and 5 all give specific details about how animals' sleeping habits differ.

Tips for Locating the Topic Sentence

Although a topic sentence can be located anywhere in a paragraph, it is usually *first* or *last*.

Topic Sentence First   In most paragraphs, the topic sentence comes first. The author states his or her main point and then explains it.

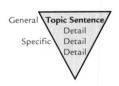

> There is some evidence that colors affect you physiologically. For example, when subjects are exposed to red light, respiratory movements increase; exposure to blue decreases respiratory movements. Similarly, eye blinks increase in frequency when eyes are exposed to red light and decrease when exposed to blue. This seems consistent with intuitive feelings about blue being more soothing and red being more arousing. After changing a school's walls from orange and white to blue, the blood pressure of the students decreased while their academic performance improved.
>
> —DeVito, *Human Communication*, p. 182

Here, the writer first states that there is evidence of the physiological effects of colors. The rest of the paragraph presents that evidence.

Topic Sentence Last   The second most likely place for a topic sentence to appear is last in a paragraph. When using this arrangement, a writer leads up to the main point and then states it at the end.

> Is there a relationship between aspects of one's personality and that person's state of physical health? Can psychological evaluations of an individual be used to predict physical as well as psychological disorders? Is there such a thing as a disease-prone personality? Our response is very tentative, and the data are not all supportive, but for the moment we can say yes, there does seem to be a positive correlation between some personality variables and physical health.
>
> —Gerow, *Psychology: An Introduction*, p. 700

In this paragraph, the author ponders the relationship between personality and health and concludes with the paragraph's main point: they are related.

Topic Sentence in the Middle   If a topic sentence is placed neither first nor last, then it may appear somewhere in the middle of a paragraph. In this arrangement, the sentences before the topic sentence lead up to or introduce the main idea. Those that follow the main idea explain or describe it.

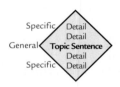

> There are 1,500 species of bacteria and approximately 8,500 species of birds. The carrot family alone has about 3,500 species, and there are 15,000 known species of wild orchids. Clearly, the task of separating various living things into their proper groups is not an easy task. Within the insect family, the problem becomes even more complex. For example, there are about 300,000 species of beetles. In fact, certain species are disappearing from the earth before we can even identify and classify them.
>
> —Wallace, *Biology: The World of Life*, p. 283

In this paragraph, the author first gives several examples of living things for which there are numerous species. Then he states his main point: Separating living things into species is not an easy task. The remainder of the paragraph offers an additional example and provides further information.

Topic Sentence First and Last   Occasionally writers put the main idea at the beginning of a paragraph and again at the end. Writers may do this to emphasize the main point or to clarify it.

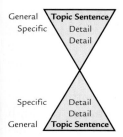

General
Specific

Specific
General

Topic Sentence
Detail
Detail

Detail
Detail
Topic Sentence

Many elderly people have trouble getting the care and treatment they need for their ailments. Most hospitals, designed to handle injuries and acute illnesses that are common to the young, do not have the facilities or personnel to treat the chronic degenerative diseases of the elderly. Many doctors are also ill-prepared to deal with such problems. As Fred Cottrell points out, "There is a widespread feeling among the aged that most doctors are not interested in them and are reluctant to treat people who are as little likely to contribute to the future as the aged are reputed to." Even with the help of Medicare, the elderly in the United States often have a difficult time getting the health care that they need.

—Coleman and Cressey, *Social Problems*, p. 277

The first and last sentences together explain that many elderly people in the United States have difficulty obtaining needed health care.

Exercise 3–4

Directions: *Underline the topic sentence in each of the following paragraphs.*

1. Early biologists who studied reflexes, kineses, and fixed action patterns assumed that these responses are inherited, unlearned, and common to all members of a species. They clearly depend on internal and external factors, but until recently, instinct and learning were considered distinct aspects of behavior. However, in some very clever experiments, Jack Kailman of the University of Wisconsin showed that certain stereotyped behavior patterns require subtle forms of experience for their development. In other words, at least some of the behavior normally called instinct is partially learned.

   —Mix, *Biology, The Network of Life*, p. 532

2. Color, a component of light, affects us directly by modifying our thoughts, moods, actions, and even our health. Psychologists, as well as designers of schools, offices, hospitals, and prisons, have acknowledged that colors can affect work habits and mental conditions. People surrounded by expanses of solid orange or red for long periods often

experience nervousness and increased blood pressure. In contrast, some blues have a calming effect, causing blood pressure, pulse, and activity rates to drop to below normal levels.

—Preble, Preble, and Frank, *Artforms*, p. 64

3. The pawnshop industry has been in decline in most parts of the world. In Great Britain in 1900 there were 3,000 pawnshops; in the 1990s there are fewer than 150. In the United States, however, the pawnshop business actually grew during the same time period, from under 2,000 to more than 7,000 today. Pawnshops in this country currently make about 40 million loans a year with an aggregate dollar amount over $1 billion. Most of these pawnshops are in the Southeast and Rocky Mountain areas. One of the reasons for the growth of pawnshops is that many states have relaxed their restrictions (called *usury laws*) on the maximum interest rates that can be charged. Pawnshops in these states can now legally charge the high rates needed to stay in business. Further, the percentage of U.S. citizens classified as low-income has risen in recent decades. These individuals cannot get loans from mainstream financial institutions, such as banks and savings and loan associations, and so must turn to alternatives, one of which is the pawnshop.

—Miller, *Economics Today*, p. 213

4. Dirty words are often used by teenagers in telling off-color stories and this can be considered part of their sex education. As their bodies grow and change, both boys and girls wonder and worry. To keep from being overwhelmed by these fears, they turn them into jokes or dirty-word stories. By telling and retelling off-color stories, they learn that they aren't the only ones in the group disturbed about their future roles in courtship and marriage. Using dirty words and stories to laugh at sexual doubts and fears may make them less frightening.

—Brothers, "What Dirty Words Really Mean" in *Good Housekeeping*

5. Bone is one of the hardest materials in the body and, although relatively light in weight, it has a remarkable ability to resist tension and other forces acting on it. Nature has given us an extremely strong and exceptionally simple (almost crude), supporting system without giving up mobility. The calcium salts deposited in the matrix give bone its hardness, whereas the organic parts (especially the collagen fibers) provide for bone's flexibility and great tensile strength.

Marieb, *Essentials of Human Anatomy and Physiology*, p. 119

6. Many people assume that the law is based on the consent of citizens, that it treats citizens equally, and that it serves the best interest of society. If we simply read the U.S. Constitution and statutes, this assumption may indeed be justified. But focusing on the *law on the books,* as William Chambliss (1969) pointed out, may be misleading. The law on the books does indeed say that the authorities ought to be fair and just. But are they? To understand crime, Chambliss argued, we need to look at the *law in action,* at how legal authorities actually discharge their duty. After studying the law in action, Chambliss concluded that legal authorities are actually unfair and unjust, favoring the rich and powerful over the poor and weak.

—Thio, *Sociology,* p. 180

7. The functions of desktop publishing software are similar to those of word processing programs, except that some capabilities are more sophisticated. A user can enter text using the desktop publishing program in the same way that he or she can enter text with a word processing program. In addition, the user can retrieve text from a file created by another program. For example, the user may enter, edit, and save text using a word processing program and then retrieve the saved text using the desktop publishing program.

—Nickerson, *Business and Information Systems,* p. 249

8. Body mass is made up of protoplasm, extracellular fluid, bone, and adipose tissue (body fat). One way to determine the amount of adipose tissue is to measure the whole-body density. After the on-land mass of the body is determined, the underwater body mass is obtained by submerging the person in water. Since water helps support the body by giving it buoyancy, the apparent body mass is less in water. A higher percentage of body fat will make a person more buoyant, causing the underwater mass to be even lower. This occurs because fat has a lower density than the rest of the body.

—Timberlake, *Chemistry: An Introduction to General, Organic, and Biological Chemistry,* p. 30

9. Faces are so visible and so sensitive. Because one pays more attention to people's faces than to any other nonverbal feature, the face has become an efficient and high-speed means of conveying meaning. Gestures, posture, and larger body movements require some time to change in response to a changing stimulus, whereas facial expressions can change instantly, sometimes even at a rate imperceptible to the human

eye. As an instantaneous response mechanism, it is *the* most effective way to provide feedback to an ongoing message. This is the process of using the face as a regulator.

—adapted from Weaver, *Understanding Interpersonal Communication*, p. 220

10. At some time or another, many close relationships go through a conflict phase. "We're always fighting," complains a newlywed. But if she were to analyze these fights, she would discover important differences among them. According to communication researchers Miller and Steinberg, most conflicts fit into three different categories. There is (1) pseudoconflict—triggered by a lack of understanding. There is (2) simple conflict—stemming from different ideas, definitions, perceptions, or goals. Finally there is (3) ego conflict—which occurs when conflict gets personal.

—adapted from Beebe, Beebe, and Redmond, *Interpersonal Communication*, pp. 243, 248

Finding the Central Thought

Just as a paragraph has a main idea, so articles, essays, and sections of textbook chapters have a main point. The main point of a group of paragraphs appearing together as a unit is called the **central thought.** You may also hear it called a thesis statement, especially in your writing classes. A central thought states what the entire piece of writing is about. It is often stated in a single sentence. The central thought often appears in the first or second paragraph of a piece of writing, although it may appear anywhere in the selection.

To find the central thought, ask yourself, "What big, general idea is discussed throughout the selection?" Now, use this question to find the central thought of the following brief article.

CLONING ENDANGERED SPECIES

Environmentalists tend to be skeptical of claims that biotechnology can help solve environmental problems, but one group of scientists is determined to apply bioengineering to conservation problems. Researchers at the biotech company Advanced Cell Technologies (ACT) have embarked on an ambitious plan to clone species that are in danger of extinction. In early 2001, they had their first success with the birth of a guar, a wild ox native to India and southeast Asia. Guars are very rare and in danger of extinction, as their habitat is disappearing rapidly.

The guar was cloned using a preserved skin cell from an individual that had died 8 years earlier. The genetic material from this cell was inserted into a cow egg from which the nucleus had been removed. The resulting cloned embryo was implanted in the uterus of a surrogate mother cow. The embryo developed properly and the cow gave birth to the guar calf. Unfortunately, the calf died 2 days later of dysentery, an infection that the researchers say was unrelated to the cloning procedure.

Buoyed by their first success, the cloning team plans to move its project forward. They recently received permission from the Spanish government to clone the bucardo, a mountain goat species of Europe that is already extinct. The scientists from ACT have spoken of being especially inspired by the idea of resurrecting an extinct species (they will use preserved bucardo tissues that are in storage in Spain). The researchers have also focused on the endangered and charismatic giant panda, as well as endangered big cats such as tigers, cheetahs, and leopards. The techniques for cloning such species, however, have not yet been developed. Unlike guars and bucardos, these species are not closely related to the few types of domestic animals that have already been cloned.

—adapted from Audesirk, *Life on Earth*, p. 201

In this selection from a biology book, the central thought is that the biotech company ACT is attempting to use bioengineering to solve conservation problems. The central thought is stated in the first sentence of the selection. The remainder of the selection provides details about the company's success in cloning a guar and its plans to clone other species.

Exercise 3–5

Directions: *In each of the following groups of sentences, three of the sentences are topic sentences in an article. The fourth is the central thought of the entire article. Select the central thought in each group of sentences.*

_____   1. a. Monotheism is a belief in one supreme being.

b. Polytheism is a belief in more than one supreme being.

c. Theisms are religions that worship a god or gods.

d. Monotheistic religions include Christianity, Judaism, and Islam.

_____ 2. a. Vincent Van Gogh is an internationally known and respected artist.

   b. Van Gogh's art displays an approach to color that was revolutionary.

   c. Van Gogh created seventy paintings in the last two months of his life.

   d. Van Gogh's art is respected for its attention to detail.

_____ 3. a. The Individuals with Disability Education Act offers guidelines for inclusive education.

   b. The inclusive theory of education says that children with special needs should be placed in regular classrooms and have services brought to them.

   c. The first movement toward inclusion was mainstreaming—a plan in which children with special needs were placed in regular classrooms for a portion of the day and sent to other classrooms for special services.

   d. Families play an important role in making inclusive education policies work.

_____ 4. a. Stress can have a negative effect on friendships and marital relationships.

   b. Stress can affect job performance.

   c. Stress is a pervasive problem in our culture.

   d. Some health problems appear to be stress related.

Learning More About Paragraphs

When you read a paragraph now, you should be pretty good at figuring out its topic and finding its topic sentence. Obviously, though, there is more to a paragraph than these two items. What about all of the other sentences? These are the **details**—the sentences that explain the main idea. To connect sentences, writers use **transitions,** words like *first, however,* and *finally.* You will learn more about details and transitions in the next chapter.

The Textbook Challenge

Part A: Current Issues Reader

Using the textbook excerpt "Whether to Vote: A Citizen's First Choice," (p. 514) highlight the topic sentence in each paragraph.

Part B: A College Textbook

Choose a chapter that you have been assigned to read in a textbook for one of your other courses. Underline the topic sentence of each paragraph in the first five pages.

What Have You Learned?

Directions: *To check your understanding of the chapter, select the choice that best completes each of the following statements.*

_____ 1. The main idea of a paragraph is the
   a. most important point made in the paragraph.
   b. topic of a paragraph.
   c. noun that is the subject of a sentence.
   d. object of the predicate.

_____ 2. The topic of a paragraph is the
   a. first sentence.
   b. important detail in a paragraph.
   c. general subject of the paragraph.
   d. conclusion of the paragraph.

_____ 3. The sentence that expresses the main idea of a paragraph is known as the
   a. opening sentence.   c. topic sentence.
   b. general sentence.   d. main sentence.

_____ 4. Where can a topic sentence most likely be found in a paragraph?
   a. first sentence   c. last sentence
   b. second sentence   d. in the middle

_____   5. The topic sentence is the sentence that is the most
                a. technical.   c. detailed.
                b. general.   d. noticeable.

_____   6. The main point of an article or essay is called its
                a. organizational pattern.   c. main idea.
                b. major heading.   d. central thought.

What Vocabulary Have You Learned?

Directions: *The words in column A appear in this chapter. Test your mastery of these words by matching each word in column A with its meaning in column B.*

	Column A		Column B
_____	1. motive	a.	slowly worsening
_____	2. intuitive	b.	reason
_____	3. correlation	c.	ability to move
_____	4. degenerative	d.	relationship
_____	5. mobility	e.	known automatically

GENERAL VS. SPECIFIC

A. Directions: *Select the choice that best describes each grouping.*

_____ 1. cleats, bat, shin guards, shoulder pads
  a. types of sports uniforms
  b. types of clothing
  c. types of sports equipment
  d. types of safety gear

_____ 2. *Sports Illustrated, Glamour, Good Housekeeping, Mad*
  a. women's magazines
  b. magazines
  c. fashion magazines
  d. news magazines

_____ 3. to get in shape, to feel good, to lose weight
  a. reasons to exercise
  b. reasons to diet
  c. reasons to see a doctor
  d. reasons to take a vacation

_____ 4. Italian, Southern, Chinese, Cajun
  a. types of cuisine
  b. nationalities
  c. types of languages
  d. states

_____ 5. Amazon, Nile, St. Lawrence, Missouri
  a. rivers
  b. bookstores
  c. states
  d. U.S. landmarks

B. Directions: *For each general idea, write four specific ideas that "fit" within it. An example is provided for each entry.*

6. <u>General idea</u>: types of candy   <u>jelly beans</u>

   _____   _____   _____   _____

7. <u>General idea</u>: music   <u>jazz</u>

   _____   _____   _____   _____

8. <u>General idea</u>: pets   <u>guinea pig</u>

   _____   _____   _____   _____

9. <u>General idea</u>: political office   <u>mayor</u>

   _____   _____   _____   _____

10. <u>General idea</u>: career   <u>nurse</u>

   _____   _____   _____   _____

FINDING MAIN IDEAS

Directions: *For each of the following paragraphs, (1) select the choice that best represents the topic of the paragraph, and (2) underline the topic sentence.*

_____ 1. Contrary to popular assumption, slavery was not usually based on racism, but on one of three other factors. The first was debt. In some cultures, an individual who could not pay a debt could be enslaved by the creditor. The second was crime. Instead of being killed, a murderer or thief might be enslaved by the family of the victim as compensation for their loss. The third was war and conquest. When one group of people conquered another, they often enslaved some of the vanquished (Starna and Watkins 1991). Historian Gerda Lerner (1986) notes that the first people enslaved through warfare were women. When premodern men raided a village or camp, they killed the men, raped the women, and then brought the women back as slaves. The women were valued for sexual purposes, for reproduction, and for their labor.

—Henslin, *Sociology: A Down-to-Earth Approach*, p. 246

a. war and conquest   c. causes of slavery

b. debt and slavery   d. warfare among women

_____ 2. At Steelcase Inc., the country's largest maker of office furnishings, two very talented women in the marketing division both wanted to work only part-time. The solution: They now share a single full-time job. With each working 2.5 days a week, both got their wish and the job gets done—and done well. In another situation, one person might work mornings and the other afternoons. The practice, known as work sharing (or job sharing) has "brought sanity back to our lives," according to at least one Steelcase employee.

—Ebert and Griffin, *Business Essentials*, p. 208

a. creative solutions   c. women in the workforce

b. dissatisfied employees   d. job sharing

_____ 3. Suppose a friend holds up her hand, palm flattened to signal "stop" to someone standing across the room from you. A basketball coach may motion "time out" with his hands to communicate to a player on the court that the player should signal the referee to stop play so that the team can discuss a new strategy. Both of these situations demonstrate the use of emblems—body motions that take the place of words. In order for emblems to be an effective form of nonverbal communication, both parties must readily understand the motions being used. A spectator unfamiliar with sports might not understand the "time out" motion used by those involved in the game and therefore might question why the referee officially signaled time out. Emblems can also be used effectively when there are obstacles to verbal communication. The example of the basketball game applies here as well; the coach may signal to a player to call for time out because the crowd is generating too much noise for the coach to be heard by the player.

—adapted from Dunn and Goodnight, *Communication: Embracing the Difference*, p. 92

    a. speech

    b. nonverbal communication

    c. hand signals

    d. emblems

_____ 4. Homelessness has arisen from at least three social forces. One is the increased shortage of inexpensive housing for poor families and poor unattached persons because of diminishing government subsidy of such housing. Another social force is the decreasing demand for unskilled labor that has occurred since the 1980s, which has resulted in extremely high unemployment among young men in general and African Americans in particular. A third social force is the erosion of public welfare benefits that has occurred over the last two decades. These three social forces have not directly caused homelessness. But they have enlarged the ranks of the extremely poor, thereby increasing the chances of these people becoming homeless.

—Thio, *Sociology: A Brief Introduction*, p. 187

    a. social forces impacting homelessness

    b. public welfare

    c. shortage of inexpensive housing

    d. decreasing demand for unskilled labor

_____ 5. Homelessness is not new. There have always been homeless people in the United States. But homeless today differ in some ways from their counterparts of the 1950s and 1960s. More than 40 years ago, most of the homeless were old men, only a handful were women, and virtually no families were homeless. Today, the homeless are younger and include more women and families with young children. Today's homeless people also are more visible to the general public because they are much more likely to sleep on the streets or in other public places. In recent years, however, most cities have cracked down on the homeless, removing them from the streets.

—Thio, *Sociology: A Brief Introduction*, p. 187

a. how homelessness has changed over time
b. the types of people that are homeless
c. where the homeless sleep
d. how homelessness will change in the future

TOPICS, MAIN IDEAS, AND CENTRAL THOUGHTS

Directions: *After reading the following passage, select the choice that best completes each of the statements that follow.*

HARMLESS DIETARY SUPPLEMENTS OR DANGEROUS DRUGS?

1   When serious athletes hear of natural substances that build muscles and provide energy, they are bound to wonder whether supplementing their diets with these substances could improve their athletic performance. Mark McGwire's incredible 70 home runs in the 1998 baseball season drew attention to two substances that he was taking at the time: the steroid androstenedione ("andro") and creatine, a compound found in the muscle tissue of vertebrates.

2   Should these substances be classified as dietary supplements or as drugs? This is a legal distinction with wide-ranging repercussions. Because both andro and creatine are classified as dietary supplements under the Dietary Supplement and Health Act of 1994, they can be sold over the counter to anyone, without first being subjected to the extensive scientific testing necessary for substances classified as drugs. Before you start seasoning your steaks with andro and creatine, however, several important questions should be answered.

Are They Safe?

3   Although small amounts of androstenedione and testosterone in the body are essential to good health, introducing larger than normal amounts into one's system has potentially serious side effects, including gland cancer, hair loss, impotence, and acne. Increased testosterone levels in women can lead to a deeper voice and facial hair.

Are They Effective?

4   It has been found that when a typical 100-mg dose of androstenedione is consumed, all but a small percentage is destroyed in the liver, and what is left boosts testosterone levels only temporarily. It is not clear whether this has a significant effect on muscle building. According to the National Strength and Conditioning Association (a professional society for athletic trainers, sports medicine physicians and researchers, professional coaches, and physical therapists), there is no reliable evidence that andro improves athletic performance.

5   Research suggests that taking creatine does lead to a small improvement in some physical tasks, but there is still doubt whether supplemental amounts have any significant value. Meat contains creatine. Assuming that adequate amounts of meat are eaten, one's liver will normally produce about 2 g of the substance per day. The creatine is stored in the muscles, but any excess is promptly removed by the kidneys.

Are They Legal?

6   As of this writing, andro is banned in the NFL, the Olympics, and the NCAA, but it is still permitted in baseball and basketball, which ban only illegal drugs. For this reason, Mark McGwire could take it, but shot putter Randy Barnes, the 1996 Olympic gold medallist and world record holder, was banned from Olympic competition for life for doing so. (Barnes claims that he was not told about the ban and is appealing the decision.)

7   Did andro and creatine make a significant difference in Mark McGwire's ability to hit home runs? Edward R. Laskowski, M.D., co-director of the Sports Medicine Center at the Mayo Clinic in Rochester, Minnesota, says, "Mark McGwire has all the tools within himself to do what he did. If you ask elite athletes in any sport what they did to get to the top, they often break it down to the basics—training, conditioning and practice."

—Bishop, *Introduction to Chemistry,* p. 750

_____   1. The central thought of the passage is
     a. research is inconclusive about the value of creatine.
     b. there is a debate as to whether andro and creatine should be classified as drugs or supplements.
     c. creatine and andro are dangerous drugs.
     d. creatine and andro should be illegal.

_____   2. At the time the article was written, andro and creatine were classified as
     a. dietary supplements.
     b. drugs.
     c. legal only for athletes.
     d. hormones.

_____   3. The topic of paragraph 1 is
     a. athletes' use of natural substances.
     b. Mark McGwire.
     c. the steroid androstenedione.
     d. building muscles and providing energy.

_____   4. Paragraph 2 primarily concerns
     a. consumption of substances.
     b. effects of substances.
     c. distribution of substances.
     d. classification of substances.

5. The topic of paragraph 3 is
   a. regulation.   c. safety.
   b. testosterone levels.   d. side effects.

6. The main idea of paragraph 3 is
   a. small doses of andro should be used with caution.
   b. large doses of andro have serious side effects.
   c. women should not use andro.
   d. testosterone levels vary between men and women.

7. The main idea of paragraph 4 is
   a. andro can destroy the liver.
   b. sports medicine physicians do not approve of andro.
   c. the effectiveness of andro is unclear.
   d. testosterone levels must be closely monitored in users of andro.

8. The main idea of paragraph 5 is
   a. one's body produces enough creatine.
   b. meat, especially liver, contains creatine.
   c. the body requires 2 grams of creatine.
   d. creatine provides a small improvement in physical performance, but supplemental amounts are questionable.

9. The topic sentence of paragraph 6 appears in
   a. the first sentence.   c. the third sentence.
   b. the second sentence.   d. the first and third sentences.

10. The main idea of paragraph 7 is
   a. Mark McGwire should not have used andro.
   b. Laskowski is an expert on andro use.
   c. elite athletes rely on training, condition, and practice.
   d. athletes must decide for themselves whether to use andro.

FINDING MAIN IDEAS

Directions: *After reading the following passage, select the choice that best completes each of the statements that follow.*

CHRONEMICS

Chronemics, the study of how we use our time, reveals several important uses of time. In our culture, time is viewed as a commodity or thing we can trade or buy. Think about the words we use to describe time: We *save* time by taking a short cut; we *budget* our time by working longer hours on Thursday so we can leave early on Friday; our group *invested* so much time in this project in order to get our grade up; and we *waste* time by watching television. As Anderson (1999) says, "Psychologically and rhetorically, most Americans treat time like their most prized possession or like money itself: something to be earned, saved, spent, and treasured."

We send messages by our use of time. What does being prompt or on time mean? What about being late? If you are consistently late for class, how might the instructor think about you and your attitude toward the course? Probably not very positively. We value promptness because it communicates professionalism, caring and respect. Spending a lot of time with someone is also considered a sign of caring and respect. In one study, the amount of time spent with someone was the leading predictor of relational satisfaction and understanding.

Time can communicate status. Think about the people who can keep you waiting. We often wait thirty minutes to an hour to see a physician. We accept that our supervisor, instructor, or other authority figure can and will make us wait because their time is perceived as more valuable.

—adapted from Dunn and Goodnight, *Communication: Embracing Difference,* p. 103

_____ 1. The central thought of the selection is
   a. time is important to everyone.
   b. time reveals attitudes and feelings.
   c. chronemics has limited usefulness.
   d. chronemics demonstrates several uses of time.

_____ 2. The topic of the first paragraph is
   a. trading time.   c. the value of time.
   b. loss of time.   d. wasting time.

3. In paragraph 1, the word **chronemics** means

   a. the study of the use of time.

   b. the study of time.

   c. cultural views about time.

   d. time is prized.

4. In paragraph 1, the word **commodity** means

   a. something fleeting.

   b. something saved.

   c. something bought or traded.

   d. an item measured by time.

5. In paragraph 2, the word **predictor** means

   a. effect.   c. distress.

   b. indicator.   d. device.

6. The topic of the second paragraph is the

   a. importance of being on time.

   b. messages people send by their use of time.

   c. importance of measuring the amount of time you spend with people.

   d. importance of spending time on relationships.

7. In the second paragraph, the topic sentence begins with the words

   a. "Spending a lot of time."

   b. "We value promptness."

   c. "What does being."

   d. "We send messages."

8. According to the selection, which of the following is *not* correct?

   a. Time is not highly valued in our society.

   b. Spending a lot of time with someone is a sign of caring.

   c. Time is often viewed as a commodity.

   d. Time is often treated like a prized possession.

_____ 9. According to the selection, one way that we demonstrate the value of time is
a. by hurrying.
b. through the use of language.
c. by checking our watches often.
d. through setting alarms.

_____ 10. The paragraphs in this reading support the idea that a topic sentence often comes
a. in the middle.
b. first.
c. last.
d. first and last.

FINDING MAIN IDEAS

Directions: *After reading the following passage, select the choice that best completes each of the statements that follow.*

PICKING PARTNERS

Just as males and females may find different ways to express emotions themselves, the process of partner selection also shows distinctly different patterns. For both males and females, more than just chemical and psychological processes influence the choice of partners. One of these factors is *proximity,* or being in the same place at the same time. The more you see a person in your hometown, at social gatherings, or at work, the more likely that an interaction will occur. Thus, if you live in New York, you'll probably end up with another New Yorker. If you live in northern Wisconsin, you'll probably end up with another Wisconsinite.

The old adage that "opposites attract" usually isn't true. You also pick a partner based on *similarities* (attitudes, values, intellect, interests). If your potential partner expresses interest or liking, you may react with mutual regard known as *reciprocity.* The more you express interest, the safer it is for someone else to return the regard, and the cycle spirals onward.

Another factor that apparently plays a significant role in selecting a partner is *physical attraction.* Whether such attraction is caused by a chemical reaction or a socially learned behavior, males and females appear to have different attraction criteria. Men tend to select their mates primarily on the basis of youth and physical attractiveness. Although physical attractiveness is an important criterion for women in mate selection, they tend to place higher emphasis on partners who are somewhat older, have good financial prospects, and are dependable and industrious.

—Donatelle, *Health: The Basics,* p. 105

_____ 1. The central thought of the entire selection is
   a. several factors influence choice of partners.
   b. physical attraction is more important to men than to women.
   c. proximity is the key to mate selection.
   d. opposites attract.

_____ 2. The topic sentence of the first paragraph begins with the words
   a. "For both."   c. "The more."
   b. "One of these."   d. "Just as."

3. In paragraph 1, the word **proximity** means
   a. interaction based on attraction.
   b. being in the same place at the same time.
   c. state-by-state attraction.
   d. partner selection.

4. The easiest way to figure out the meaning of the word **reciprocity** in the second paragraph is to
   a. use word parts.
   b. use a dictionary.
   c. use sentence context.
   d. reread the entire paragraph.

5. The topic of the second paragraph is
   a. physical attraction.   c. the old adage.
   b. interaction.   d. similarities.

6. In the second paragraph, the topic sentence begins with the words
   a. "You also pick."
   b. "The more you express."
   c. "If your potential."
   d. "The old adage."

7. In paragraph 2, the word **adage** means
   a. saying.   c. fact.
   b. information.   d. joke.

8. The topic of the third paragraph is
   a. differences between men and women.
   b. physical attraction.
   c. chemical reactions.
   d. behavioral characteristics.

9. In paragraph 3, the word **criteria** means
   a. standards.   c. criticisms.
   b. faults.   d. charms.

_____ 10. According to the selection,
  a. men are never attracted to women who are not physically attractive.
  b. physical location is the most important partner selection criterion.
  c. women are more attracted to men they are different from.
  d. men and women have different attraction criteria.

ENVIRONMENTAL RACISM
Rebecca J. Donatelle

This reading selection, taken from a textbook titled *Health: The Basics,* published in 2003, explores the topic of environmental racism, the practice of treating minority racial groups unfairly in the protection of their environment. Read it to find out where environmental racism has occurred and what is being done about it.

Vocabulary Preview

These are some of the difficult words in this essay. The definitions here will help you if you can't figure out the meanings from the sentence context or word parts.

indigenous (par. 2) native, belonging to a place

malnourishment (par. 2) poor diet and nutrition that lead to physical harm

decimation (par. 2) complete destruction

hydrocarbons (par. 4) a group of flammable chemicals

creosote (par. 5) a wood preservative derived from coal tar

arsenic (par. 5) poisonous metallic element

mortality (par. 5) death

1   Environmental racism has meant, among other things, that toxic waste dumps, landfills, and industrial plants are much more likely to be placed in communities of color and in the developing world than in predominantly white communities. The interconnectedness of race and poverty has contributed to the disparities in risks faced by ethnic minority communities. In the United States, minorities bear a disproportionate risk of living in an unhealthy environment because race of the local population has been a significant determining factor in the location of hazardous waste facilities nationwide.

2   The adverse health effects of environmental racism have been devastating for people of color in the United States and throughout the world. A clear example comes from the Amazon rain forest of Ecuador. Over a 21-year period, an American oil company systematically dumped more than 16 million gallons of oil and toxic wastewater into the Ecuadorian Amazon. Three indigenous groups lived in the area where the oil company operated—the Cofan, the Secoya, and the Siona. The Cofan, who numbered approximately 15,000 when the oil company built its first well in 1971, now number only a few hundred. The Secoya and Siona have likewise experienced reductions in their populations. Each of

these three groups was a fishing culture when the oil company first came to the Amazon. Now, because of oil contamination, they can no longer fish in the rivers and so face malnourishment. Often young people migrate to the cities and take low-wage jobs. The result of the contamination of the environment has been the practical decimation of these three indigenous cultures.

3   In the mid-1990s, the remaining indigenous people filed suit against the oil company, claiming that they had violated the people's right to a healthy environment. They said that the company's decision to dump millions of gallons of toxins in the rain forest led to the cultural genocide of the three tribes; this, they claimed, amounts to racial and ethnic discrimination. One of the tribes' attorneys commented, "The fact is when [the oil company] drills for oil where white people live, they do so safely and according to the industry standards. When they drilled in the headwaters of the Amazon river, however, they blatantly ignored these standards while knowingly wreaking havoc on the local people, almost all of whom are people of color." As late as September 1999, the oil company was continuing to fight the lawsuit and refusing to clean up the Amazon. Indigenous leaders launched a national media campaign in the United States, charging the oil company with racism. The company denied that race played any role in its actions.

4   Scientific literature clearly demonstrates that crude oil and toxic wastewater produced by oil drilling are highly carcinogenic. A September 1999 public health study of San Carlos, an Ecuadorian town containing more than 30 oil wells, found cancer rates 30 times greater than normal, despite the fact that local inhabitants do not smoke, have a healthy diet, and are not exposed to urban contamination. Additionally, no other industries in the area release cancer-causing toxins. The water in San Carlos had nearly 150 times the amount of hydrocarbons considered safe by internationally recognized limits.

5   Examples of environmental racism can also be found throughout the United States. Consider these examples:

- In Los Angeles, recycling plants were located in low-income, primarily Latino neighborhoods. Residents consistently complained of dustlike glass particles in the air throughout the community.
- In Augusta, Georgia, a wood preservant factory leaked creosote into the ground, and a scrap metal company leaked arsenic. This ethnic minority community now evidences high rates of cancer and skin disease. The plants are also located near an elementary school, and students there experience high rates of learning disabilities, allergies, and asthma.
- In the predominantly African American area of Chester, Pennsylvania, four hazardous and municipal waste facilities are located. That area has the highest percentage of low-weight births in the state as well as mortality and lung cancer rates 60 percent higher than in the rest of the country.

6   Many health, civil rights, and environmental activists have become proponents of environmental justice. Proponents of environmental justice argue that people of color have the right to be protected from hazardous substances and that public policy be developed based on mutual respect and justice for all people.

— ∎ —

Directions: *Select the letter of the choice that best completes each of the following statements.*

CHECKING YOUR COMPREHENSION

_____   1. The central thought of the passage is
      a. indigenous people are unaware of environmental racism.
      b. environmental racism occurs only in South America.
      c. environmental decisions are often made in a racist manner.
      d. oil drilling causes environmental racism.

_____   2. In paragraph 3, the environmental racism occurred because
      a. the oil company used different drilling procedures where white people live.
      b. the indigenous people belonged to a fishing culture.
      c. the oil company denied that race played any role.
      d. the indigenous people ignored industry standards.

_____   3. According to paragraph 4,
      a. scientific literature does not show a link between oil drilling and cancer.
      b. urban contamination is a key cause of cancer.
      c. indigenous people are unconcerned about carcinogenic risks.
      d. a study in Ecuador linked oil drilling with high cancer rates.

_____   4. According to the article, environment racism occurs often when race is interconnected with
      a. poverty.   c. rain forests.
      b. fear.   d. knowledge.

_____ 5. Other examples of environmental racism mentioned in the article included
  a. Augusta, Georgia; Miami; and Los Angeles.
  b. Chester, Pennsylvania; Los Angeles; and Augusta, Georgia.
  c. Los Angeles; Uniontown, Michigan; and Augusta, Georgia.
  d. Chester, Pennsylvania; New York City; and Chicago.

USING WHAT YOU KNOW ABOUT MAIN IDEAS

_____ 6. The topic of paragraph 2 is
  a. the effect of indigenous wastewater.
  b. the effect of drilling on three Ecuadorian tribes.
  c. tribal justice.
  d. drilling processes in the Amazon.

_____ 7. The topic sentence of paragraph 3 begins with the words
  a. "They said that."   c. "One of the tribes'."
  b. "In the mid-1990s."   d. "As late as."

_____ 8. The topic sentence of paragraph 4 begins with the words
  a. "Scientific literature."   c. "A September."
  b. "The water."   d. "Additionally, no."

_____ 9. The topic of paragraph 5 is
  a. low-weight births and toxins.
  b. cancer in Georgia.
  c. community response to toxins.
  d. other examples of environmental racism.

_____ 10. The topic of paragraph 6 is
  a. environmental justice.   c. people of color.
  b. civil rights activists. d. hazardous substances.

USING CONTEXT CLUES AND WORD PARTS

_____ 11. In paragraph 1, the word **predominantly** means
  a. definitely.   c. likely.
  b. primarily.   d. carefully.

_____ 12. In paragraph 1, the word **disparities** means
  a. differences.   c. similarities.
  b. degrees.   d. toxins.

_____ 13. In paragraph 1, the word **disproportionate** means
  a. primary.   c. likely.
  b. essential.   d. unequal.

_____ 14. In paragraph 4, the word **carcinogenic** means
  a. cancer-causing.   c. full of asbestos.
  b. healthy.   d. dirty.

_____ 15. In paragraph 6, the word **proponents** means
  a. developers.   c. supporters.
  b. scientists.   d. opponents.

REVIEWING DIFFICULT VOCABULARY

Directions: *Complete each of the following sentences by inserting a word from the Vocabulary Preview on page 111 in the space provided. A word should be used only once.*

16. When the lumber mill processed wood, it emptied

    _____ into the creek.

17. Children who live in drought-stricken areas of the world often face

    _____.

18. The citrus crop in Florida suffered complete _____
    from the frost.

19. The _____ rate for women with ovarian cancer is
    quite high.

20. _____ has been used to poison someone.

QUESTIONS FOR DISCUSSION

1. Discuss what steps could be taken to reduce environmental racism in the United States.
2. Discuss examples of environmental racism in your community that you have observed or read about.
3. In what ways should victims of environmental racism be compensated?

WRITING ACTIVITIES

1. Write a paragraph describing an environmental problem or issue in your community, or describe how an important environmental problem was resolved.
2. Brainstorm about the meaning of the term *environmental justice,* considering such questions as these: What problems and issues does it encompass? What rights should it preserve? Should it apply only to humans? Then write a brief essay expressing your ideas on the topic.
3. In this chapter, we focus on locating main ideas in textbook passages. Not all printed sources follow the same conventions that textbooks do. Read this article about the relationship between race and the damage caused by Hurricane Katrina: http://www.kersplebedeb.com/mystuff/katrina/wright_21_09_2005.html. Write a paragraph in response to the claims made here.

Chapter 3: Locating Main Ideas

RECORDING YOUR PROGRESS

Test	Number Right			Score
Practice Test 3-1	_____	× 10	=	_____ %
Practice Test 3-2	_____	× 20	=	_____ %
Practice Test 3-3	_____	× 10	=	_____ %
Mastery Test 3-1	_____	× 10	=	_____ %
Mastery Test 3-2	_____	× 10	=	_____ %
Mastery Test 3-3	_____	× 5	=	_____ %

EVALUATING YOUR PROGRESS

Based on your test performance, rate how well you have mastered the skills taught in this chapter by checking one of the boxes below or by writing your own evaluation.

☐ **Need More Improvement**
Tip: Try completing the Main Idea–Maine Woods module in the Reading Skills section on the MyReadingLab Web site at **http://www.ablongman.com/myreadinglab** to fine-tune the skills that you have learned in this chapter.

☐ **Need More Practice**
Tip: Try using the Main Idea–Maine Woods module in the Reading Skills section on the MyReadingLab Web site at **http://www.ablongman.com/myreadinglab** to brush up on the skills taught in this chapter, or visit this textbook's Companion Web site at **http://www.ablongman.com/mcwhorter** for extra practice.

☐ **Good**
Tip: To maintain your skills, quickly review this chapter by using this textbook's Companion Web site at **http://www.ablongman.com/mcwhorter**.

☐ **Excellent**

YOUR EVALUATION: _____

_____

_____

_____

THINK ABOUT IT!

Look at the photograph below, which shows students attending a study group. Did this study group just "happen," or did someone have an idea and then follow it up with work and planning? Suppose you decide to organize a study group for your biology course. Your *main idea* is that you want to get a small group of classmates together to study for an upcoming exam. In order for the study group be successful, though, you also need to pay attention to the *details*—selecting classmates to include, selecting a time and place, deciding how to organize the review session, and so forth.

Studying a paragraph can be a little bit like planning a study group. First you find the paragraph's main idea, and then you look for the details that support it.

CHAPTER 4

Identifying Supporting Details

What Are Supporting Details?

Just as selecting participants and choosing a time and place are details that help you organize a study group, the details writers use in a paragraph help them back up the point they want to make. **Supporting details** are those facts and ideas that prove or explain the main idea of a paragraph. As you read, you will notice that some details are more important than others. Pay particular attention to the **major details**—the most important details that directly explain the main idea. You should also note **minor details**—details that may provide additional information, offer an example, or further explain one of the major details.

Figure 4-1 on page 120 shows how details relate to the main idea. As you recall from Chapter 3, the main idea is usually stated in a topic sentence.

Read the following paragraph and then study the diagram in Figure 4-2 (p. 120).

The Abkhasians (an agricultural people who live in a mountainous region of Georgia, a republic of the former Soviet Union) may be the longest-lived people on earth. Many claim to live past 100—some beyond 120 and even 130. Although it is difficult to document the accuracy of these claims, government records indicate that an extraordinary number of Abkhasians do live to a very old age. Three main factors appear to account for their long lives. The first is their diet, which consists of little meat, much fresh fruit, vegetables, garlic, goat cheese, cornmeal, buttermilk and wine. The second is their lifelong physical activity. They do slow down after age 80, but even after the age of 100 they still work about four hours a day. The third factor—a highly developed sense of community—goes to the very heart of the Abkhasian culture. From child-hood, each individual is integrated into a primary group, and remains so throughout life. There is no such thing as a nursing home, nor do the elderly live alone.

—adapted from Henslin, *Sociology*, pp. 380–381

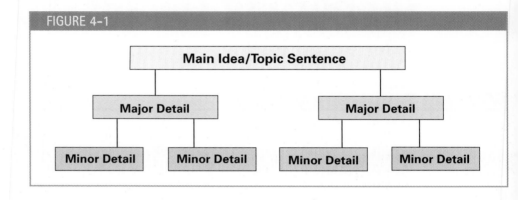

FIGURE 4-1

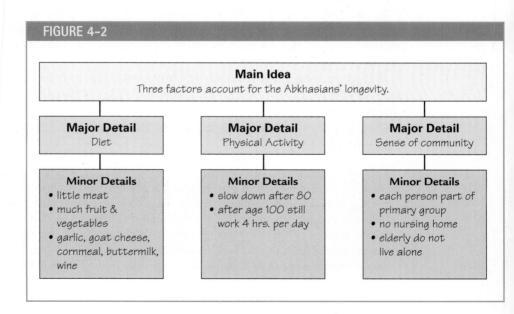

FIGURE 4-2

From Figure 4-2 you can see the three main reasons why Abkhasians live long lives. These are the **major details.** The minor details are less important than the major details. **Minor details** may provide additional information, offer an example, or further explain one of the major details. In the paragraph above, the example about Abkhasians' primary group structure provides further information and is a minor detail. The minor details are the sentences that explain other, more important details.

Look at the paragraph again, and notice how the author has used **transitions**—words that lead you from one major detail to the next. The words *first, second,* and *third* are a few of the transitions that can help you find the major details in a paragraph. Be on the lookout for transitions as you read; they are discussed more fully later in this chapter.

Exercise 4–1

A. Directions: *Read the following paragraph and then complete the diagram that follows. Some of the items have been filled in for you.*

Small group discussions progress through four phases. The first is orientation, when the members become comfortable with each other. Second is the conflict phase. Disagreements and tensions become evident. The amount of conflict varies with each group. The third phase is known as emergence. The members begin to try to reach a decision. The members who created conflict begin to move toward a middle road. The final phase is the reinforcement phase when the decision is reached. The members of the group offer positive reinforcement toward each other and the decision.

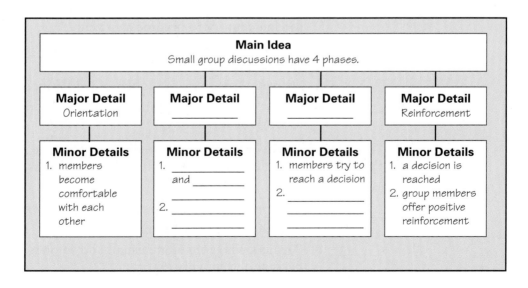

B. Directions: *Read the paragraph again and list the four transitions the writer uses to help you find the four major details.*

1. _____   2. _____   3. _____   4. _____

The diagram you completed in the exercise above is a **map**—a visual way of organizing information. By filling in—or drawing—maps you can "see" how ideas in a paragraph or essay are related. Chapter 6 gives you more information about mapping (see page 190) and about other ways of organizing information.

Exercise 4–2

Directions: *Each of the following topic sentences states the main idea of a paragraph. After each topic sentence are sentences containing details that may or may not support the topic sentence. Read each sentence and write an "M" beside those that contain major details that support the topic sentence.*

1. *Topic sentence:* Most Mexican Americans are in the United States as a result of immigration that has taken place since 1900.

   Details:

   _____ a. Puerto Rico was added as a territory of the United States in 1898.

   _____ b. Emigration is the process of permanently leaving one's country, while immigration is the process of entering a foreign country to become a citizen.

   _____ c. Mexico's economic problems prompted many people to emigrate.

   _____ d. Hispanic Americans are often called Latinos.

   _____ e. Many Mexican immigrants came to California in order to work in agriculture.

2. *Topic sentence:* Divorce and out of wedlock births have led to a rise in the number of single-parent families in the United States.

   Details:

   _____ a. In 1970 there were 3 million single-parent families, while in 2000 there were 12 million.

   _____ b. Partners who cohabitate usually do so on a temporary basis and eventually marry.

_____ c. Most single-parent families are headed by females.

_____ d. Blended families make up one-third of all U.S. families.

_____ e. There has been an increase in the number of couples attending marriage counseling since 1980.

3. *Topic sentence:* The Internet has allowed people to become more socially connected and engage in more communication with greater numbers of people.

   Details:

   _____ a. Technology has made contact with others easier and less expensive than it used to be.

   _____ b. The Internet allows people to choose friends based on interest rather than geography.

   _____ c. The Internet allows people to work from home and decreases their one-on-one exposure to other people.

   _____ d. The Internet allows people to make contact with others while still maintaining anonymity, making it easier to take personal risks in relationships.

   _____ e. E-mail and chat rooms allow for communication at any time of the day, making interpersonal communication more accessible.

Exercise 4-3

Directions: *Read the following paragraph and answer the questions that follow.*

A person's personality type can determine how he or she creates and reacts to self-imposed stress. The first kind of personality type is known as Type A. Type A personalities work hard, are anxious, competitive, and driven and often create high expectations for themselves. Type As are more likely than others to have heart attacks. Type B is the second personality type. Type Bs tend to be relaxed, laid-back, and noncompetitive. A third personality type is Type C. Type Cs are Type A's who thrive under stress, achieve things, and experience little or no stress-related health problems. Most people can't be categorized as one personality type and display characteristics of different types at different times.

1. Does the topic sentence occur first, last, or in the middle of the paragraph? _____

2. List the paragraph's three major details:

   _____

   _____

   _____

3. What transition words does the writer use to take the reader from one major detail to the next? _____

4. In the third sentence, what does the word *expectations* mean?

   _____

   _____

5. Is the last sentence the main idea of the paragraph, a major detail, or a minor detail? _____

Recognizing Transitions

As you know, **transitions** are linking words or phrases that lead the reader from one idea to another. If you get into the habit of recognizing transitions, you will see that they often help you read a paragraph more easily.

In the following paragraph, notice how the underlined transitions lead you from one detail to the next.

When Marcita takes an exam, she follows a certain procedure. <u>First of all</u>, she tries to find a seat in the room away from others. She might sit at the back of the room, <u>for example</u>, or sit in the front row so no one is in front of her. <u>Next</u>, she gets her supplies ready, <u>such as</u> pencils, pens, and paper. Sometimes, <u>however</u>, she brings things like a calculator or textbook if the instructor permits them. <u>Finally</u>, she sits quietly for a moment before the test begins. She does this because it usually helps her relax and clear her mind.

Not all paragraphs contain such obvious transitions, and not all transitions serve as such clear markers of details. As you can see, transitions may be used for a variety of reasons. They may alert you to what will come next in the paragraph, they may tell you that an example will follow, or they may predict that a different, opposing idea is coming. Table 4-1 lists some of the most common transitions and indicates what they tell you.

TABLE 4-1	Common Transitions	
Type of Transition	**Example**	**What They Tell the Reader**
Time sequence	first, later, next, finally	The author is arranging ideas in the order in which they happened.
Example	for example, for instance, to illustrate, such as	An example will follow.
Enumeration	first, second, third, last, another, next	The author is marking or identifying each major point. (Sometimes these may be used to suggest order of importance.)
Continuation	also, in addition, and, further, another	The author is continuing with the same idea and is going to provide additional information.
Contrast	on the other hand, in contrast, however	The author is switching to a different, opposite, or contrasting idea than previously discussed.
Comparison	like, likewise, similarly	The writer will show how the preceding idea is similar to what follows.
Cause/effect	because, thus, therefore	The writer will show a connection between two or more things, how one thing caused another, or how something happened as a result of something else.

Exercise 4-4

Directions: *Select the transitional word or phrase from the box below that best completes each of the following sentences. Some of the transitions in the box may be used more than once.*

on the other hand	for example	because
in addition	similarly	after
next	however	also

1. Typically, those suffering from post-traumatic stress disorder are soldiers after combat. Likewise, civilians who have experienced events such as the World Trade Center destruction can _____ experience this syndrome.

2. Columbus was determined to find an oceanic passage to China _____ finding a direct route would mean increased trading and huge profits.

3. In the event of a heart attack, it is important to first identify the symptoms. _____, call 911 or drive the victim to the nearest hospital.

4. In the 1920s, courtship between men and women changed dramatically. _____, instead of paying calls at the woman's home with her parents there, men now invited women out on dates.

5. Direct exposure to sunlight is dangerous because the ultraviolet rays can lead to skin cancer. _____, tanning booths also emit ultra violet rays and are as dangerous as, if not more dangerous than, exposure to sunlight.

6. Lie detector tests are often used by law enforcement to help determine guilt or innocence. _____, since these tests often have an accuracy rate of only between 60 and 80 percent, the results are not admissible in court.

7. The temporal lobes of the brain process sound and comprehend language. _____, this area of the brain is responsible for storing visual memories.

8. The theory of multiple intelligences holds that there are many different kinds of intelligence, or abilities. _____, musical ability, control of bodily movements (athletics), spatial understanding, and observational abilities are all classified as different types of intelligence.

9. During World War II, Japanese Americans were held in relocation camps. _____ the war was over, the United States paid reparations and issued an apology to those who were wrongfully detained.

10. Support continues to grow for the legalization of marijuana.

_____, legalization has not yet been passed in any state and it is unlikely this will happen anytime soon.

Exercise 4-5

Directions: *Many transitions have similar meanings and can sometimes be used interchangeably. Match each transition in column A with a similar transition in column B.*

Column A	Column B
_____ 1. because	a. therefore
_____ 2. in contrast	b. also
_____ 3. for instance	c. likewise
_____ 4. thus	d. after that
_____ 5. first	e. since
_____ 6. one way	f. finally
_____ 7. similarly	g. on the other hand
_____ 8. next	h. one approach
_____ 9. in addition	i. in the beginning
_____ 10. to sum up	j. for example

Putting It All Together

In Chapters 3 and 4 you have learned the four essential ingredients of a paragraph and how to find them. You know how to locate the general *topic* of a paragraph and its *main idea* in a topic sentence. You also know how to identify *details* and how to use *transitions* to help you. In short, you can recognize and put together all of the important parts of a paragraph. Sometimes, though, as you have probably noticed in your reading, the main idea of a paragraph is not stated directly. Instead of being in a topic sentence—like the paragraphs you've been working with—a main idea may be **implied.** Paragraphs with implied main ideas will be covered in Chapter 5.

The Textbook Challenge

Part A: Current Issues Reader

Using the textbook excerpt "Air Pollution and Global Warming," (p. 523) highlight the major supporting details of each paragraph. Circle the transitions.

Part B: A College Textbook

Choose a chapter that you have been assigned to read in a textbook for one of your other courses. For the first five pages, underline the major supporting details of each paragraph. Circle the transitions.

What Have You Learned?

Directions: *To check your understanding of the chapter, select the word or phrase from the box below that best completes each of the following sentences. Not all of the words in the box will be used.*

finally	minor details	because	first	for example
transitions	main idea	major details	next	on the other hand

1. The details in a paragraph are intended to prove or explain the

   _____.

2. The most important details in a paragraph are its

   _____.

3. _____ are words or phrases that lead the reader from one idea to another.

4. Words such as *first*, _____, and *finally* tell you that the writer is putting ideas in the order in which they happened.

5. The word _____ tells you that the writer is going to explain the reason for a concept or fact.

What Vocabulary Have You Learned?

Directions: *To check your mastery of the vocabulary used in this chapter, select the word or phrase from the box below that best completes each of the following sentences. Not all of the words in the box will be used.*

integrated	emergence	reinforcement	emigration
cohabitate	anonymity	noncompetitive	reparations

1. After a few weeks, first-year students are completely
   _____ into college life.

2. Because of the personal nature of the subject, the reporter maintained
   the _____ of her sources.

3. During the war in Afghanistan, there was a dramatic increase in
   _____ from Afghanistan to Pakistan.

4. Because he is _____, Rich refuses to participate
   in sports.

5. The couple was reluctant to marry, so they decided to
   _____.

IDENTIFYING DETAILS

Directions: *Read the following paragraph and then complete the diagram below. Some of the items have been filled in for you.*

What can you do if you have trouble sleeping? Four techniques may help. *Restrict your sleeping hours to the same nightly pattern.* Keep regular sleeping hours. Avoid sleeping late in the morning, napping longer than an hour, or going to bed earlier than usual, all of which will throw you off schedule, creating even more sleep difficulties. And try to get up at the same time every day, even on weekends or days off. *Control bedtime stimuli* so that things normally associated with sleep are associated only with sleep. Use your bed only for sleep (don't read or watch tv in bed). *Avoid ingesting substances with stimulant properties.* Don't smoke cigarettes or drink beverages with alcohol or caffeine in the evening. Alcohol may cause initial drowsiness, but it has a "rebound effect" that leaves many people wide awake in the middle of the night. Don't drink water close to bedtime; getting up to use the bathroom can lead to poor sleep. *Consider meditation or progressive muscle relaxation.* Either technique can be helpful, if used regularly.

—adapted from Kosslyn and Rosenberg, *Fundamentals of Psychology,* pp. 368–369

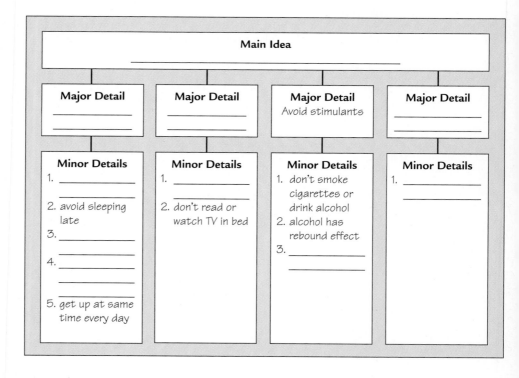

USING TRANSITIONAL WORDS

Directions: *Select the transitional word or phrase from the box below that best completes each of the following sentences. Use each transition only once.*

next	because	second	finally	on the other hand
first	another	to illustrate	likewise	such as

When you paint a room, _____ you must prepare the walls by wiping them clean. _____, you need to tape off woodwork _____ baseboards, molding, and windows _____ paint can be difficult to remove from these areas. _____, be sure to put down drop cloths to protect the floor or floor covering in the room. _____, begin preparing your paint by mixing it well. _____ the importance of mixing the paint, open up a paint can and take a look at how the paint separates. Putting it on your walls in this condition will create streaks. _____ important step is to prepare your brushes or rollers. Make sure they are clean and dry. _____, if you are using a sponge or rag for a painting technique, make sure the sponge or rag is damp. _____, pour your paint and begin rolling or brushing it on the walls.

UNDERSTANDING PARAGRAPH STRUCTURE

Directions: *After reading each paragraph below, select the choice that best completes each of the statements that follow.*

Paragraph A

Two general types of meaning are essential to identify: denotation and connotation. The term denotation refers to the meaning you'd find in a dictionary; it's the meaning that members of the culture assign to a word. Connotation is the emotional meaning that specific listeners give to a word. Take as an example the word *death*. To a doctor this word might mean (denote) the time when the heart stops. This is an objective description of a particular event. On the other hand, to a mother who is informed of her son's death, the word means (connotes) much more. It recalls her son's youth, ambitions, family, illness, and so on. To her, *death* is a highly emotional, subjective, and personal word. These emotional, subjective, or personal associations are the word's connotative meaning. The denotation of a word is its objective definition. The connotation of a word is its subjective or emotional meaning.

—DeVito, *Messages: Building Interpersonal Communication Skills,* p. 121

_____   1. The main idea of the paragraph is that
   a. the word *death* has several meanings.
   b. denotation refers to dictionary meanings.
   c. words have emotional meanings.
   d. there are two types of meaning for many words.

_____   2. The phrase *on the other hand* suggests that
   a. a reason is to follow.
   b. a contrasting idea will follow.
   c. a list will follow.
   d. more detailed information will follow.

_____   3. The fifth sentence, which begins with "To a doctor," is
   a. a transition.
   b. a major detail.
   c. the topic sentence.
   d. a minor detail.

_____ 4. The second sentence of the paragraph, which begins with "The term denotation," is

    a. the topic sentence.

    b. a major detail.

    c. a transitional statement.

    d. a minor detail.

_____ 5. According to the paragraph,

    a. doctors do not use emotional language.

    b. connotative meanings are the same for everyone in a culture.

    c. connotative meanings vary from person to person.

    d. descriptions can never be truly objective.

Paragraph B

Communicating your emotions and responding appropriately can be difficult, but it is helpful to view the process as involving a number of specific tasks. Your first task is to understand the emotions you're feeling. For example, consider how you would feel if your best friend just got the promotion you wanted or if your brother, a police officer, was shot while breaking up a street riot. Try to answer the question, "Why am I feeling this way?" or "What happened to lead me to feel as I do?" Your second task is to decide, if, in fact, you want to express your emotions. In circumstances in which you have time to think before you react, ask yourself whether you wish to communicate your emotions. Remember, it is not always wise to give vent to every feeling you have. If you do decide to express your emotions, the third task is to evaluate your communication options in terms of both effectiveness and ethics (what is right or morally justified). When thinking in terms of effectiveness, consider, for example, the time and setting, the persons you want to reveal these feelings to, and the available methods of communication. When thinking in terms of ethics, consider the legitimacy of appeals based on emotions.

—adapted from DeVito, *Messages: Building Interpersonal Communication Skills,* pp. 197–198

_____ 1. The main idea of the paragraph is expressed in

    a. the first sentence.   c. the fifth sentence.

    b. the second sentence.   d. the last sentence.

_____ 2. The second sentence, which begins with "Your first task," is

    a. the main idea.   c. a minor detail.

    b. a transitional sentence.   d. a major detail.

3. Which of the following is a transitional word or phrase?
   a. Remember
   c. Try to answer
   b. Your second task
   d. When thinking in

4. The third sentence, which begins with "For example, consider," is
   a. the topic sentence.
   c. a minor detail.
   b. a transitional sentence.
   d. a major detail.

5. According to the passage,
   a. emotions do not always need to be expressed.
   b. it is never morally justified to withhold your feelings.
   c. you never have time to think before you react emotionally.
   d. you can never express emotions effectively; they just happen.

RECOGNIZING DETAILS

Directions: *After reading the following passage, select the choice that best completes each of the statements that follow.*

PHYSICAL APPEARANCE AND CLOTHING

In our Western culture, appearance matters. People's perceptions of our outward appearance make a big difference in our opportunities to establish relationships, find jobs, and succeed in school. Studies have shown that we care about appearance, and attractive people, overall, find it easier to make friends, gain employment, and earn good grades. What messages are you sending by wearing several earrings or piercing your nose or belly button? In some social groups, this is a sign of being cool or stylish. How might a future employer at a bank, for example, perceive the body piercings? Our physical appearance matters, and we need to be aware that others may view us differently because of it.

The way we dress becomes part of the message we send to others, whether we intend it to or not. Our clothes and style of dress contribute to the way we see ourselves and the way others perceive us. Our style of clothing also reflects our ability or willingness to adjust to a variety of social situations. In other words, what we choose to wear can reflect our desire to gain acceptance within a given social situation. For instance, if we wanted to "fit in" among the other guests at a formal dinner party, we would wear a tuxedo or an appropriate evening dress. Moreover, our choice of dress reveals information about ourselves and affects our impact in both interpersonal and public communication settings.

What specifically does our clothing communicate? One thing it can indicate is our age or an age we wish to project. If, for example, we want to appear youthful, we would dress according to the latest styles or trends. Beware, however, that we can inadvertently give away our age by wearing clothes considered to be out of date.

Certain types of dress identify individuals as members of particular groups or professions. When we see someone dressed in a blue uniform, we presume (usually correctly) that he or she is a member of a police department. Other examples include black collars worn by priests, military uniforms worn by men and women in the armed forces, uniforms representing different sports, leather jackets worn by members of motorcycle gangs, and native dress representing foreign nations (sarongs worn by Indian women, for example).

—Dunn and Goodnight, *Communication: Embracing Difference,* pp. 100–101

_____ 1. The central thought of the entire selection is
  a. body piercings may send the wrong message.
  b. the way we dress identifies us as a group member.
  c. clothing helps you to fit into social situations.
  d. physical appearance, as evidenced by what we wear, matters.

_____ 2. The topic of paragraph 1 is
  a. dressing for careers.
  c. styles of clothing.
  b. group membership.
  d. physical appearance.

_____ 3. In paragraph 1, which of the following is a minor detail?
  a. Appearance affects the establishment of relationships.
  b. People may view us differently because of our physical appearance.
  c. Attractive people find it easier to build friendships, find jobs, and get good grades.
  d. Body piercing may be a sign of being cool.

_____ 4. The topic sentence of paragraph 2 begins with the words
  a. "For instance, if."
  b. "The way we dress."
  c. "Moreover, our choice."
  d. "In other words."

_____ 5. In paragraph 2, all the following are major supporting details _except_
  a. Clothing and style of dressing contribute to our self-image.
  b. Our style of clothing reflects our willingness to fit into a social situation.
  c. A tuxedo or evening dress is appropriate formal attire.
  d. Choice of clothing affects both interpersonal and public communication.

_____ 6. In paragraph 2, the transitional word _moreover_ signals
  a. the topic.
  c. a major detail.
  b. another example.
  d. a minor detail.

7. The second sentence of paragraph 3, which begins with the words "One thing," is
   a. a minor detail.   c. a transition.
   b. a major detail.   d. the paragraph's main idea.

8. The transitional phrase "other examples" in paragraph 4 indicates that the writers will
   a. put ideas in order.
   b. offer examples.
   c. switch to an opposite idea.
   d. show how one thing caused another.

9. In paragraph 4, which of the following is *not* a minor detail?
   a. Priests wear collars.
   b. Motorcycle gang members wear leather jackets.
   c. Dress can identify people as members of groups.
   d. Members of the armed forces wear uniforms.

10. According to the selection,
   a. people are judged only by appearance.
   b. appearance has an important impact on how we are perceived.
   c. clothing only sends messages when we intend it to.
   d. we should change how we dress to gain acceptance.

RECOGNIZING DETAILS

Directions: *After reading the following passage, select the choice that best completes each of the statements that follow.*

ADVANTAGES AND DISADVANTAGES OF MODIFIED SCHEDULES AND ALTERNATIVE WORKPLACES

Flextime [a system that allows employees to set their own daily work schedules] gives employees more freedom in their professional and personal lives. It allows workers to plan around the work schedules of spouses and the school schedules of young children. Studies show that the increased sense of freedom and control reduces stress and thus improves individual productivity.

Companies also benefit in other ways. In urban areas, for example, such programs can reduce traffic congestion and similar problems that contribute to stress and lost work time. Furthermore, employers benefit from higher levels of commitment and job satisfaction. John Hancock Insurance **http://www.jhancock.com,** Atlantic Richfield **http://www.arco.com,** and Metropolitan Life **http://www.metlife.com** are among the major American corporations that have successfully adopted some form of flextime.

Conversely, flextime sometimes complicates coordination because people are working different schedules. For example, Sue may need some important information from Joe at 4:30 PM, but because Joe is working an earlier schedule, he leaves for the day at 3:00. In addition, if workers are paid by the hour, flextime may make it difficult for employers to keep accurate records of when employees are actually working.

As for telecommuting and virtual offices, although they may be the wave of the future, they may not be for everyone. For example, consultant Gil Gordon points out that telecommuters are attracted to the ideas of "not having to shave and put on makeup or go through traffic, and sitting in their blue jeans all day." However, he suggests that would-be telecommuters ask themselves several other questions: "Can I manage deadlines? What will it be like to be away from the social context of the office five days a week? Can I renegotiate the rules of the family, so my spouse doesn't come home every night expecting me to have a four-course meal on the table?" One study has shown that even though telecommuters may be producing results, those with strong advancement ambitions may miss networking and rubbing elbows with management on a day-to-day basis.

—Griffin and Ebert, *Business Essentials,* pp. 210–211

_____ 1. The central thought of the entire selection is that
   a. there are both advantages and disadvantages to flextime and to working at home.
   b. telecommuting creates problems for workers who are not self-directed.
   c. flextime benefits employers as well as employees.
   d. flextime increases workers' sense of freedom and reduces stress.

_____ 2. In paragraph 1, the word **productivity** means
   a. ability to get work done.
   b. expenses created by a worker.
   c. quality of work done.
   d. training needed by a worker.

_____ 3. In paragraph 1, the major details explain
   a. the advantages and disadvantages of flextime.
   b. how flextime creates stress.
   c. that flextime has a negative impact on productivity.
   d. how flextime benefits employees.

_____ 4. In paragraph 2, the sentence that begins with the words "Furthermore, employees benefit," is
   a. the paragraph's main idea.
   b. a minor detail.
   c. a major detail.
   d. an example.

_____ 5. The last sentence of paragraph 2 is
   a. a minor detail.   c. a major detail.
   b. a transition.   d. the main idea.

_____ 6. In paragraph 2, the topic sentence is expressed in the
   a. first sentence.   c. third sentence.
   b. second sentence.   d. last sentence.

7. When the writers move from discussing the benefits of flextime to the discussion in paragraph 3 of its problems, they use the transition
   a. *for example.*
   b. *conversely.*
   c. *in contrast.*
   d. *on the other hand.*

8. In paragraph 3, the word **coordination** means
   a. simplifying complex things.
   b. flexibility.
   c. scheduling.
   d. working together.

9. The major supporting details of paragraph 4 explain
   a. the advantages and disadvantages of telecommuting.
   b. why virtual offices and telecommuting are not for everyone.
   c. how to renegotiate family rules.
   d. why telecommuters like to wear blue jeans.

10. According to the selection,
    a. flextime is the best option for workers.
    b. companies as well as employees benefit from flextime.
    c. flextime costs companies a lot of money.
    d. telecommuting usually has a negative impact on home life.

TALKING A STRANGER THROUGH THE NIGHT
Sherry Amatenstein

This reading first appeared in *Newsweek*. Read it to find out how one woman connected with another person in an impersonal city and saved a life.

Vocabulary Preview

These are some of the difficult words in this essay. The definitions here will help you if you can't figure out the meanings from the sentence context or word parts.

Holocaust (par. 1) extermination of Jewish people during World War II

empathetic (par. 2) understanding others' emotions and feelings

idealism (par. 3) naïve belief in the good aspects of something

succession (par. 3) series occurring one after another, in an orderly line

untethered (par. 4) alone and not connected to anyone

rationale (par. 4) line of reasoning

imminent (par. 5) immediate, happening soon

dictum (par. 7) pronouncement, rule

---

1   The call came 60 minutes into my third shift as a volunteer at the crisis hot line. As the child of Holocaust survivors, I grew up wanting to ease other people's pain. But it wasn't until after September 11 that I contacted Help Line, the nonprofit telephone service headquartered in New York. The instructor of the nine-week training course taught us how to handle a variety of callers, from depressed seniors to "repeats" (those who checked in numerous times a day).

2   We spent two sessions on suicide calls but I prayed I wouldn't get one until I felt comfortable on the line. Drummed over and over into the 30 trainees' heads was that our role wasn't to give advice. Rather, we were to act as empathetic sounding boards and encourage callers to figure out how to take action.

3   My idealism about the hot line's value faded that first night, as in quick succession I heard from men who wanted to masturbate while I listened, repeats who told me again and again about their horrific childhoods, know-nothing shrinks and luckless lives, and three separate callers who railed about the low intellect of everyone living in Queens (my borough!). Sprinkled into the mix were people who turned abusive when I refused to tell them how to solve their problems.

4   I tried to remain sympathetic. If I, who had it together (an exciting career, great friends and family) found New York isolating, I could imagine how frightening it was for people

so untethered they needed a hot line for company. That rationale didn't help. After only 10 hours, I no longer cringed each time the phone rang, terrified it signified a problem I wasn't equipped to handle. Instead I wondered what fresh torture this caller had up his unstable sleeve.

5   Then Sandy's (not her real name) quavering voice nipped into my ear: "I want to kill myself." I snapped to attention, remembering my training. Did she have an imminent plan to do herself in? Luckily, no. Sandy knew a man who'd attempted suicide via pills, threw them up and lived. She was afraid of botching a similar attempt. Since she was handicapped, she couldn't even walk to her window to jump out.

6   Sandy's life was certainly Help Line material. Her parents had disowned her 40 years before. She'd worked as a secretary until a bone-crushing fall put her out of commission. Years later she was working again and had a boyfriend who stuck with her even after a cab struck Sandy and put her back on the disabled list. They became engaged, and then, soap-opera like, tragedy struck again. Sandy's boyfriend was diagnosed with cancer and passed away last year. Now she was in constant pain, confined to a dark apartment, her only companion a nurse's aide. "There's nothing left," she cried. "Give me a reason to live."

7   Her plea drove home the wisdom of the "no advice" dictum. How could I summon the words to give someone else's life meaning? The best I could do was to help Sandy fan the spark that had led her to reach out. I tossed life-affirming statements at her like paint on a canvas; hoping some would stick. I ended with "Sandy, I won't whitewash your problems. You've had more than your share of sorrow. But surely there are some things that have given you pleasure."

8   She thought hard and remembered an interest in books on spirituality. The downside followed immediately. Sandy's limited eyesight made it difficult for her to read. She rasped, "My throat hurts from crying, but I'm afraid if I get off the phone I'll want to kill myself again."

9   I said, "I'm here as long as you need me."

10   We spoke another two hours. She recalled long-ago incidents—most depressing, a few semi-joyful. There were some things she still enjoyed: peanuts, "Oprah," the smell of autumn. I again broached the topic of spirituality. My supervisor, whom I'd long ago motioned to listen in on another phone, handed me a prayer book. I read, and Sandy listened. After "amen," she said, "I think I'll be all right for the night."

11   Naturally, she couldn't promise to feel better tomorrow. For all of us, life is one day, sometimes even one minute, at a time. She asked, "When are you on again?"

12   I said, "My schedule is irregular, but we're all here for you, anytime you want. Thanks so much for calling."

13   As I hung up, I realized the call had meant as much to me as to Sandy, if not more. Despite having people in my life, lately I'd felt achingly lonely. I hadn't called a hot line, but I'd manned one, and this night had been my best in a long time. Instead of having dinner at an overpriced restaurant or watching HBO, I'd connected with another troubled soul in New York City.

▬ ▪ ▬

Directions: *Select the letter of the choice that best completes each of the following statements.*

CHECKING YOUR COMPREHENSION

_____ 1. The main point of the selection can be stated as follows:

    a. A woman helped herself by reaching out to others.

    b. Hot lines receive a variety of calls, and not all are what you would expect.

    c. Hot line operators are not permitted to offer advice to callers.

    d. New York City is a lonely place where many people contemplate suicide.

_____ 2. Which statement best summarizes Sandy's state of mind at the end of the hotline call?

    a. Sandy was comforted and hoped to talk to the author again.

    b. Sandy will not consider suicide again.

    c. Sandy is more depressed than before the hotline call.

    d. Sandy lost her idealistic view of a hotline.

_____ 3. After a few hours of calls, the author

    a. believed there were more calls for help than could be handled.

    b. felt afraid that each call might be a person threatening suicide.

    c. wanted to go home.

    d. believed that most of the calls were not really people seeking help.

_____ 4. According to paragraph 2, a hot line operator should

    a. pray with callers.

    b. listen and help the callers decide what to do.

    c. give advice to callers.

    d. suggest callers see a therapist.

_____ 5. How did Sandy's call change the author's attitude about the hot line?

    a. The call made her realize she needed a supervisor's help with the challenging calls.

    b. The call depressed her because she realized she couldn't really solve the callers' problems.

    c. The call showed her that dealing with serious emotional problems is something you need training for.

    d. The call helped her to realize that she could connect with people in need and make a difference in their lives.

USING WHAT YOU KNOW ABOUT SUPPORTING DETAILS

_____ 6. In paragraph 2, the transition _but_ tells the reader that

    a. an example will follow.

    b. the author will show how one thing caused another.

    c. the author will switch to a contrasting idea.

    d. the author will identify each major point.

_____ 7. In paragraph 6, the sentence that begins with the words "Sandy's life" is a

    a. minor detail.   c. major detail.

    b. transition.   d. main idea.

_____ 8. The details in paragraph 6

    a. suggest that Sandy is a hypochondriac.

    b. provide background about Sandy's predicament.

    c. offer reasons why Sandy should not commit suicide.

    d. point to Sandy's spirituality.

_____ 9. In paragraph 7, where does the topic sentence occur?

    a. first sentence

    b. second sentence

    c. fourth sentence

    d. last sentence

_____ 10. In paragraph 10, which of the following is a minor detail?
   a. The author read from a prayer book.
   b. Sandy recalled events from the past.
   c. The supervisor handed the author a prayer book.
   d. Sandy still enjoys peanuts.

USING CONTEXT CLUES AND WORD PARTS

_____ 11. In paragraph 3, the word **horrific** means
   a. terrible.   c. poor.
   b. exciting.   d. short-lasting.

_____ 12. In paragraph 3, the word **abusive** means
   a. gentle and calm.
   b. bored and indifferent.
   c. slow and careful.
   d. insulting and harmful.

_____ 13. In paragraph 4, the word **signified** means
   a. wrote.
   b. meant.
   c. acted out.
   d. demanded.

_____ 14. In paragraph 7, the word **dictum** means
   a. hurdle.
   b. crisis.
   c. department.
   d. rule.

_____ 15. In paragraph 7, the word **summon** means
   a. pronounce.
   b. enjoy.
   c. strengthen and intensify.
   d. gather together.

REVIEWING DIFFICULT VOCABULARY

Directions: *Complete each of the following sentences by inserting a word from the Vocabulary Preview on page 141 in the space provided. A word should be used only once.*

16. The British history class studied the _____ of English monarchs.

17. I explained my _____ for selling my car to my father.

18. Sara looked up at the dark sky and knew that rain was

    _____.

19. The _____ in Professor Stark's class is that cell phones must be turned off.

20. As Alfredo explained his problem, I tried to be _____ and understand what was bothering him.

QUESTIONS FOR DISCUSSION

1. Discuss why it is the hotline's policy not to offer advice.
2. If you worked at a hotline, what would be your reaction to frequent callers who take advantage of the service? How would you react?
3. Evaluate the level of training and supervision this hotline offered its volunteers.

WRITING ACTIVITIES

1. Brainstorm a list of volunteer options available in your community. Write a paragraph explaining where you could make the best possible contribution and why. Explain the tasks involved and the talents you bring to the task.
2. Have you ever found it necessary to be a good listener to a friend with a problem? Write a paragraph describing your feelings. Was it difficult not to offer advice? What did your friend expect or not expect of you?
3. Many Americans spend time each year volunteering. Look over the report from the U.S. Bureau of Labor Statistics at http://www.bls.gov/news.release/volun.nr0.htm. Write a paragraph that analyzes a part of the report that interests or surprises you.

Chapter 4:   Identifying Supporting Details

RECORDING YOUR PROGRESS

Test	Number Right		Score
Practice Test 4-1	_____	× 10 =	_____ %
Practice Test 4-2	_____	× 10 =	_____ %
Practice Test 4-3	_____	× 10 =	_____ %
Mastery Test 4-1	_____	× 10 =	_____ %
Mastery Test 4-2	_____	× 10 =	_____ %
Mastery Test 4-3	_____	× 5 =	_____ %

EVALUATING YOUR PROGRESS

Based on your test performance, rate how well you have mastered the skills taught in this chapter by checking one of the boxes below or by writing your own evaluation.

☐ **Need More Improvement**
Tip: Try completing the Supporting Details—St. Louis Arch, Missouri module in the Reading Skills section on the MyReadingLab Web site at **http://www.ablongman.com/myreadinglab** to fine-tune the skills that you have learned in this chapter.

☐ **Need More Practice**
Tip: Try using the Supporting Details—St. Louis Arch, Missouri module in the Reading Skills section on the MyReadingLab Web site at **http://www.ablongman.com/myreadinglab** to brush up on the skills taught in this chapter, or visit this textbook's Companion Web site at **http://www.ablongman.com/mcwhorter** for extra practice.

☐ **Good**
Tip: To maintain your skills, quickly review this chapter by using this textbook's Companion Web site at **http://www.ablongman.com/mcwhorter**.

☐ **Excellent**

YOUR EVALUATION: _____

_____

_____

_____

_____

THINK ABOUT IT!

Study the cartoon below. The point the cartoonist is making is clear—videos are a threat to the book market. Notice, however, that this point is not stated directly; instead, it is implied. To get the cartoonist's point, you have to study the details in the cartoon and then figure out what the cartoonist is trying to communicate.

When you read a paragraph that lacks a topic sentence, you need to use the same reasoning process. You have to study all of the details and figure out the writer's main point. This chapter will show you how to figure out implied main ideas.

CHAPTER 5

Understanding Implied Main Ideas

What Does Implied Mean?

Just as you figured out the cartoonist's main point, you often have to figure out the implied main ideas of speakers and writers. When an idea is **implied,** it is suggested but not stated outright. Suppose you discover that the gas gauge in your car is on empty and you remember that your sister recently borrowed your car. Thus you say to her, "If I run out of gas on the way to the station, I'll be sure to call you." This statement does not directly accuse your sister of failing to refill the tank, but your message is clear— Don't leave the gas tank empty!

Speakers and writers often imply ideas rather than state them directly. Here is another statement. What is the writer implying?

EXAMPLE
You couldn't pay me to eat in that restaurant.

You can figure out that the writer does not want to eat in the restaurant under any circumstances, even though this is not stated directly.

Directions: *For each of the following statements, select the choice that best explains what the writer is implying or suggesting.*

_____ 1. The lead singer in Henry's band sounded like an injured moose.

   a. The singer was hurt.

   b. The singer had a terrible voice.

   c. The singer was imitating an animal.

   d. Henry's band needed practice.

_____ 2. We were on the edge of our seats during the entire movie.

   a. Our seats were uncomfortable.

   b. We wanted to leave.

   c. We were deeply engrossed in the movie.

   d. Our seats were broken.

_____ 3. The airplane was crowded and hot, the flight was bumpy, we missed our connecting flight, and the airline lost our luggage. We'll be driving next time.

   a. We enjoyed our travel experience.

   b. We had an exciting trip.

   c. The airline handled our difficulties well.

   d. We had an unpleasant travel experience.

_____ 4. During the lecture, Alex could barely keep his eyes open.

   a. The lecture was scary.

   b. The lecture was boring.

   c. The room was too bright.

   d. Alex's eyes were dry.

_____ 5. The paint on the house was faded and peeling; the shutters dangled to one side and the front windows were boarded shut; the yard was full of weeds and pieces of rusted metal.

   a. There had just been a storm.

   b. The house was for sale.

   c. The house was abandoned.

   d. The homeowners were on vacation.

Remembering General Versus Specific Ideas

When trying to figure out the implied main idea of a paragraph, it is important to remember the distinction between general and specific. In Chapter 3 you learned that a *general* idea applies to many items or ideas, whereas a *specific* idea refers to a particular item. The word *color,* for instance, is general because it refers to many other specific colors—purple, yellow, red, and so forth. The word *jewelry* is general because it can apply to many types of body adornment, such as rings, bracelets, earrings, and necklaces. (For more information on general and specific ideas, see Chapter 3, p. 82.)

Exercise 5–2

Directions: *For each set of specific items or ideas, select the choice that best applies to them. When choosing a general idea, be careful that it is not too general or too narrow.*

_____ 1. Martha Washington, Jacqueline Kennedy, Rosalynn Carter, Laura Bush

    a. famous twentieth-century women

    b. famous American parents

    c. wives of American presidents

    d. famous women

_____ 2. mosquito, wasp, gnat, butterfly

    a. garden pests   c. living creatures

    b. harmful insects   d. insects

_____ 3. watching videos, reading travel magazines, vacationing in new cities, talking with international students

    a. ways to spend your vacation

    b. ways to spend an evening

    c. ways to meet new people

    d. ways to learn about other places

_____ 4. landscaping your yard, painting your house, adding a deck, remodeling the kitchen

    a. inexpensive activities   c. home improvements

    b. outdoor activities   d. daily chores

_____ 5. to support your community, to help others in need, to feel good about yourself, to meet people

    a. reasons to give money to charity

    b. reasons to become a volunteer

    c. reasons to go to a movie

    d. reasons to start a business

You also know from Chapter 3 that the main idea of a paragraph is not only its most important point but also its most *general* idea. *Specific* details back up or support the main idea. In the paragraphs you studied in Chapters 3 and 4, the main idea was always stated in a topic sentence. In this chapter, however, because main ideas are implied, you have to look at the specific details to figure out the main idea. Like main ideas that are stated directly, implied main ideas are usually larger, more important, and more general than the details.

What larger, more general idea do the following specific details and the accompanying photograph point to?

The wind began to howl at over 90 mph.

A dark gray funnel cloud was visible in the sky.

Severe storms had been predicted by the weather service.

Together these three details and the photograph suggest that a tornado had devastated the area.

What general idea do the following specific sentences suggest?

The doctor kept patients waiting hours for an appointment.

The doctor was hasty and abrupt when talking with patients.

The doctor took days to return phone calls from patients.

You probably determined that the doctor was inconsiderate and managed her practice poorly.

Exercise 5-3

Directions: *Read the specific details in each item, and then select the word or phrase from the box below that best completes the general idea in the sentence that follows. Make sure that each general idea fits all of its specific details. Not all words or phrases in the box will be used.*

different factors	genetic	contributes	nonverbal messages
store's image	advertisers	characteristics	
process	problems	dangerous effects	

1. a. Major life catastrophes, such as natural disasters, can cause stress.
   b. Significant life changes, such as the death of a loved one, elevate one's level of stress.
   c. Daily hassles, such as long lines at the drugstore, take their toll on a person's well-being.

   General idea: A number of _____ contribute to stress.

2. a. Humorous commercials catch consumers' attention.
   b. Fear emphasizes negative consequences unless a particular product or service is purchased.
   c. "Sex sells" is a common motto among those who write commercials.

   General idea: _____ use a variety of appeals to sell products.

3. a. Acid rain may aggravate respiratory problems.
   b. Each year millions of trees are destroyed by acid rain.
   c. Acid rain may be hazardous to a pregnant woman's unborn child.

   General idea: Acid rain has _____.

4. a. Facial expressions reveal emotions.

   b. Hand gestures have meanings.

   c. Posture can reveal how a person feels.

   General idea: The body communicates _____.

5. a. The smell of a store can be appealing to shoppers.

   b. Colors can create tension or help shoppers relax.

   c. The type of background music playing in a store creates a distinct impression.

   General idea: Retailers create a _____ to appeal to consumers.

6. a. Creative people are risk takers.

   b. Creative people recognize patterns and make connections easily.

   c. Creative people are self-motivated.

   General idea: A number of different _____ contribute to creativity.

Exercise 5–4

Directions: *Study the photo shown here and then answer each of the following questions.*

1. What do you think is happening in the photograph?

   _____

   _____

   _____

   _____

2. What general idea is the photographer trying to express through the photograph?

   _____

   _____

   _____

   _____

How to Find Implied Main Ideas in Paragraphs

As you know, when a writer leaves his or her main idea unstated, it is up to you, the reader, to look at the details in the paragraph and figure out the writer's main point.

The details, when taken together, will all point to a general and more important idea. You might want to think of such a paragraph as the pieces of a puzzle. You must put together the pieces or details to determine the meaning of the paragraph as a whole. Use the following steps as a guide to find implied main ideas.

1. **Find the topic.** As you know from earlier chapters, the *topic* is the general subject of the entire paragraph. Ask yourself: "What is the one thing the author is discussing throughout the paragraph?"

2. **Figure out what is the most important idea the writer wants you to know about that topic.** Look at each detail and decide what larger idea is being explained.

3. **Express this main idea in your own words.** Make sure that the main idea is a reasonable one. Ask yourself: "Does it apply to all of the details in the paragraph?"

EXAMPLE

Men's friendships are often built around shared activities—attending a ball game, playing cards, working on a project at the office. Women's friendships, on the other hand, are built more around a sharing of feelings, support, and "personalism." One study found that similarity in status, in willingness to protect one's friend in uncomfortable situations, in academic major, and even in proficiency in playing Password were significantly related to the relationship closeness of male-male friends but not of female-female or female-male friends.

—DeVito, *Messages: Building Interpersonal Communication Skills*, p. 290

The general topic of this paragraph is friendships. More specifically, the paragraph is about the differences between male and female friendships. Three details are given: (1) men's friendships are based on shared activities, (2) women's friendships are based on shared feelings, and (3) similarity is important in men's friendships but not in women's. Each of the three details is a difference between male and female friendships. The main point the writer is trying to make, then, is that men and women have different criteria for building friendships. You can figure out this writer's main idea even though no single sentence states this directly. You might visualize this paragraph as follows:

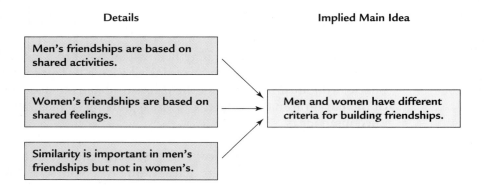

Here is another paragraph. Read it and then fill in the diagram that follows:

By now most people know that the herb echinacea may help conquer the common cold. Herbal remedies that are less well known include flaxseed, for treating constipation, and fennel, for soothing an upset stomach. In addition, the herb chamomile may be brewed into a hot cup of tea for a good night's sleep.

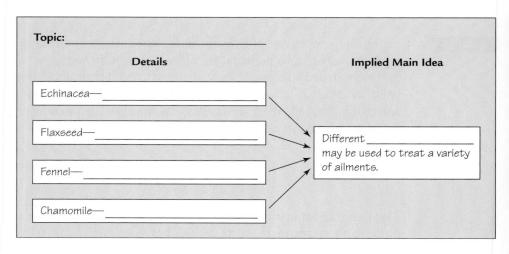

After you come up with a main idea, make sure it is broad enough. Every sentence in the paragraph should support the idea you have chosen. Work through the paragraph sentence by sentence. Check to see if each sentence explains or gives more information about the main idea. If some sentences do not explain your chosen idea, it probably is not broad enough. You may need to expand your idea and make it more general.

Exercise 5-5

Directions: *After reading each of the following paragraphs, complete the diagram that follows.*

1. The average American consumer eats 21 pounds of snack foods in a year, but people in the West Central part of the country consume the most (24 pounds per person) whereas those in the Pacific and Southeast regions eat "only" 19 pounds per person. Pretzels are the most popular snack in the mid-Atlantic area, pork rinds are most likely to be eaten in the South, and multigrain chips turn up as a favorite in the West. Not surprisingly, the Hispanic influence in the Southwest has influenced snacking preferences—consumers in that part of the United States eat about 50 percent more tortilla chips than do people elsewhere.

—adapted from Solomon, *Consumer Behavior,* p. 184

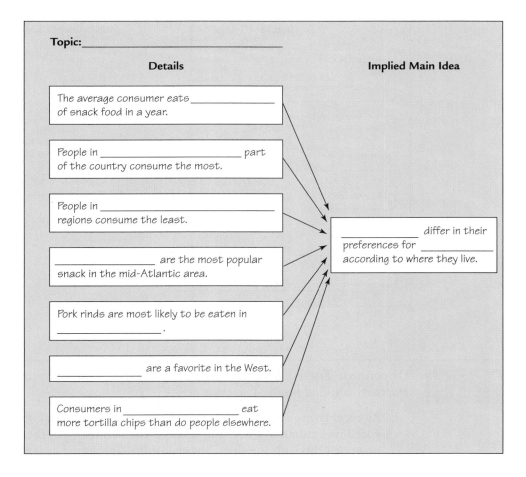

Topic:_____

Details

The average consumer eats _____ of snack food in a year.

People in _____ part of the country consume the most.

People in _____ regions consume the least.

_____ are the most popular snack in the mid-Atlantic area.

Pork rinds are most likely to be eaten in _____.

_____ are a favorite in the West.

Consumers in _____ eat more tortilla chips than do people elsewhere.

Implied Main Idea

_____ differ in their preferences for _____ according to where they live.

2. The process of becoming hypnotized begins when the people who will be hypnotized find a comfortable body position and become thoroughly relaxed. Without letting their minds wander to other matters, they focus their attention on a specific object or sound, such as a metronome or the hypnotist's voice. Then, based on both what the hypnotist expects to occur and actually sees occurring, she or he tells the clients how they will feel as the hypnotic process continues. For instance, the hypnotist may say, "Your eyelids are becoming heavy." When people being hypnotized recognize that their feelings match the hypnotist's comments, they are likely to believe that some change is taking place. That belief seems to increase their openness to other statements made by the hypnotist.

—Uba and Huang, *Psychology,* p. 148

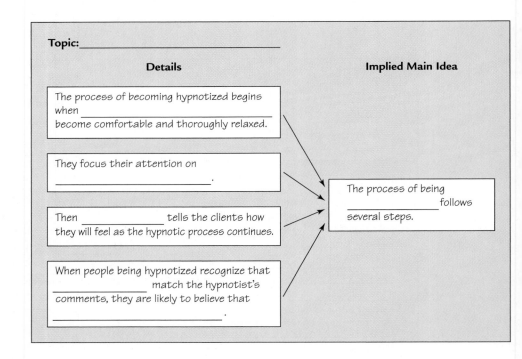

Topic:_____

Details   **Implied Main Idea**

The process of becoming hypnotized begins when _____ become comfortable and thoroughly relaxed.

They focus their attention on _____.

Then _____ tells the clients how they will feel as the hypnotic process continues.

When people being hypnotized recognize that _____ match the hypnotist's comments, they are likely to believe that _____.

The process of being _____ follows several steps.

Exercise 5–6

Directions: *For each of the following paragraphs, write a sentence that states its implied main idea.*

1. As recently as 20 years ago, textbooks on child psychology seldom devoted more than a few paragraphs to the behaviors of the neonate—the newborn through the first 2 weeks of life. It seemed as if the neonate did not do much worth writing about. Today, most child psychology texts

devote substantially more space to discussing the abilities of newborns. It is unlikely that over the past 20 years neonates have gotten smarter or more able. Rather, psychologists have. They have devised new and clever ways of measuring the abilities and capacities of neonates.

—Gerow, *Psychology: An Introduction*, p. 319

Implied main idea: _____

_____

2. Severe punishment may generate such anxiety in children that they do not learn the lesson the punishment was designed to teach. Moreover, as a reaction to punishment that they regard as unfair, children may avoid punitive parents, who therefore will have fewer opportunities to teach and guide the child. In addition, parents who use physical punishment provide aggressive models. A child who is regularly slapped, spanked, shaken, or shouted at may learn to use these forms of aggression in interactions with peers.

—Newcombe, *Child Development*, p. 354

Implied main idea: _____

_____

3. Chat groups such as you'll find on the commercial Internet Service Providers and the increasingly popular Internet Relay Chat groups enable you to communicate with others in real time (called *synchronous conversation* as opposed to *asynchronous conversation* in which there's a delay between the message-sending and the message-receiving). Real time communication obviously has its advantages; you can ask questions, respond to feedback, and otherwise adjust your message to the specific receivers. One great disadvantage, however, is that you may not find anyone you want to talk with when you log on. Unlike e-mail, you can't leave a message. Chat groups, like listservs and newsgroups, are subject specific and, because there are so many of them (they number in the thousands), you're likely to find some dealing with the topics you're researching. Another advantage of chat rooms and IRC channels is that you can establish one yourself. With other members of your class, you can then discuss the topics you're interested in. The problem with chat groups is that everyone has to be online at the same time.

—DeVito, *The Elements of Public Speaking*, pp. 132–133

Implied main idea: _____

_____

Working with Paragraphs

Now that you have read Chapters 3 through 5, you know a lot about paragraphs. You know, for instance, that they always have a *topic* and a *main idea*. In some paragraphs, the main idea is stated directly in a *topic sentence*. In other paragraphs, like the ones you worked with in this chapter, the main idea is *implied* or suggested. In all paragraphs, the main idea is backed up by *details*. As you move on to Chapter 6, you will learn some ways to keep track of the kinds of information you've been learning. The methods in that chapter will help you with all kinds of reading—for this course, for other college courses, and for reading you do on the job or just for fun.

The Textbook Challenge

Part A: Current Issues Reader

Using the reading "His Name Is Michael," (p. 494) write a sentence that states the implied main idea of paragraph 3.

_____

_____

Part B: A College Textbook

Choose a chapter that you have been assigned to read in a textbook for one of your other courses. For the first five pages, underline the topic sentence of each paragraph. If any main ideas are implied, write a sentence for each that states the implied main idea.

What Have You Learned?

Directions: *To check your understanding of the chapter, select the word or phrase from the box below that best completes each of the following sentences. Not all words or phrases in the box will be used.*

main ideas	in the writer's words	general
missing	specific	topic
in your own words	implied	identity

1. When an idea is _____, it is suggested but not stated directly.

2. To figure out the main idea of a paragraph, it is important to understand the distinction between _____ and _____.

3. _____ are larger, more general, and more important than details.

4. The first step in finding an implied main idea is to find the _____ of the entire paragraph.

5. Once you figure out the main idea of a paragraph, you should be able to express this idea _____.

What Vocabulary Have You Learned?

Directions: *The words in column A appear in this chapter. Test your mastery of these words by matching each word in column A with its meaning in column B.*

	Column A	Column B
_____	1. status	a. level of skill
_____	2. proficiency	b. from a culinary or medicinal plant
_____	3. significantly	c. position or standing
_____	4. herbal	d. device that uses a pendulum to create rhythm
_____	5. metronome	e. not accidentally or randomly

IMPLIED MAIN IDEAS

Directions: *Read the specific details in each item, and then select the word or phrase from the box below that best completes the general idea in the sentence that follows. Make sure that each general idea fits all of its specific details. Not all words or phrases in the box will be used.*

valuable	indoor air pollution	interaction
importance	placement of goods	emotions
communicate	differentiate	valuable experiences
specific fears	gender	specific purposes
benefits		

1. a. Achievement tests measure what you have already learned.
   b. Aptitude tests predict your ability to learn a new skill.
   c. Mastery tests measure your ability to perform a particular task.

   General idea: Tests differ in what they measure and are designed for

   _____.

2. a. Preschool teaches children to get along with other children.
   b. Children learn to separate from their parents by attending preschool.
   c. Children learn the routine of a classroom in preschool.

   General idea: Preschool provides _____ for young children and readies them for school.

3. a. Many people are afraid of snakes.
   b. Some people suffer agoraphobia, the fear of public places.
   c. Social phobia is the fear of being scrutinized by others.

   General idea: There are a variety of phobias, or _____, of an object, activity, or situation.

4. a. Women are more likely to attempt suicide than men.
   b. Men are more likely to succeed in a suicide attempt.
   c. Men are more likely to choose a foolproof method.

   General idea: There are _____ differences among those who attempt suicide.

5. a. Work makes people feel productive.

   b. Work gives people a chance to prove their competency.

   c. Work gives people a sense of accomplishment.

   General idea: Work is _____ and contributes to well-being.

6. a. Formaldehyde is a dangerous gas that is present in some carpeting, furniture, and adhesives.

   b. Asbestos, present in some pre-1970 building materials, can cause lung damage.

   c. Furnace emissions can contain deadly carbon monoxide.

   General idea: There are numerous sources of _____.

7. a. One drug can reduce or eliminate the effects of another.

   b. Drugs used in combination can produce dangerous physical reactions.

   c. Taking two or more drugs may cause the effects of each individual drug to be multiplied beyond what is expected for taking each alone.

   General idea: Drug _____ can have serious consequences.

8. a. Exercise reduces the risk of heart disease.

   b. Regular physical activity can reduce blood pressure.

   c. The circulatory and respiratory systems are improved by physical acitivity.

   General idea: There are many _____ of regular exercise.

9. a. Women tend to interrupt less than men do during a conversation.

   b. Men are more concerned than women with obtaining information during a conversation.

   c. Men tend to reveal fewer emotions than women during a conversation.

   General idea: Men and women _____ differently.

10. a. Low markup items are placed high in narrow aisles in a store.

    b. The highest-profit items are placed in wide aisles in prominent view.

    c. Impulse buying items, such as candy and gum, are placed near the checkout.

    General idea: Retailers control the _____ in a store to enhance sales.

IMPLIED MAIN IDEAS

Directions: *After reading each of the following paragraphs, complete the diagram that follows by filling in each blank line.*

1. The constellation [group of stars] that the Greeks named Orion, the hunter, was seen by the ancient Chinese as a supreme warrior called *Shen*. Hindus in ancient India also saw a warrior, called *Skanda*, who rode a peacock. The three stars of Orion's belt were seen as three fishermen in a canoe by Aborigines of northern Australia. As seen from southern California, these three stars climb almost straight up into the sky as they rise in the east, which may explain why the Chemehuevi Indians of the California desert saw them as a line of three sure-footed mountain sheep.

—adapted from Bennett et al., *The Cosmic Perspective*, p. 40

Topic:_____

Details

The constellation that the Greeks called _____ was called _____ by the Chinese.

Hindus called the constellation _____ and saw it as a warrior who rode _____ .

The _____ of northern Australia saw the stars of Orion's belt as fishermen in a canoe.

The Chemehuevi Indians of the _____ _____ saw the stars as a line of sure footed mountain _____ .

Implied Main Idea

People of many cultures gave different _____ to the Orion constellation and saw different shapes.

2. Initially, many computers entered homes as children's games. But the trend spread fast, from simple games to more sophisticated ones. Soon they became a favorite pastime both for children and young adults. This group of people showed an almost natural ability to adapt to computers; software developers saw the opportunity for the market and developed increasingly challenging games as well as educational programs. Many parents were then tempted to buy computers for home use and this, in turn, led to a situation where people of all ages and backgrounds saw the benefit of computers not only for young people but also for adults who used them for personal and business purposes.

—Bandyo-padhyay, *Computing for Non-specialists*, p. 4

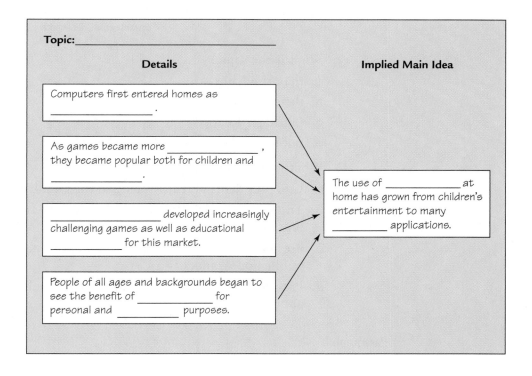

Topic:_____

Details

Computers first entered homes as _____.

As games became more _____, they became popular both for children and _____.

_____ developed increasingly challenging games as well as educational _____ for this market.

People of all ages and backgrounds began to see the benefit of _____ for personal and _____ purposes.

Implied Main Idea

The use of _____ at home has grown from children's entertainment to many _____ applications.

IMPLIED MAIN IDEAS

Directions: After reading each of the following paragraphs, select the choice that best answers the questions that follow.

Paragraph A

John Kennedy, the first "television president," held considerably more public appearances than did his predecessors. Kennedy's successors, with the notable exception of Richard Nixon, have been even more active in making public appearances. Indeed, they have averaged more than one appearance every weekday of the year. Bill Clinton invested enormous time and energy in attempting to sell his programs to the public. George W. Bush has followed the same pattern.

—Edwards et al., *Government in America,* p. 422

_____ 1. What is the topic?

    a. the presidency

    b. the effects of television

    c. President Kennedy

    d. public appearances of the president

_____ 2. What main idea is the writer implying?

    a. U.S. presidents all enjoy being in the public eye.

    b. The successors of President Kennedy have tried to imitate him.

    c. Presidents have placed increasing importance on making public appearances.

    d. Presidents spend too much time making public appearances.

Paragraph B

When speaking on the telephone be sure to speak clearly, enunciating carefully. It is also a good practice to speak just a bit slower than if you were talking with someone face-to-face. When responding to an answering machine or voice mail, be brief but to the point. Give your name, telephone number, and a brief explanation of why you called. State what time would be best to return your call. It is also helpful to give your phone number a second time as a conclusion to your message.

—adapted from Cook, Yale, and Marqua, *Tourism: The Business of Travel,* p. 370

_____ 3. What is the topic?
   a. telephone manners   c. telemarketing
   b. public speaking   d. customer service

_____ 4. What is the writer saying about the topic?
   a. People today have terrible phone manners.
   b. Telephone manners are not as important as those used in face-to-face conversations.
   c. Speaking on the telephone requires clarity, brevity, and conciseness.
   d. Telephone messages should be kept to a minimum.

Paragraph C

All the nutrients in the world are useless to humans unless oxygen is also available. Because the chemical reactions that release energy from foods require oxygen, human cells can survive for only a few minutes without oxygen. Approximately 20% of the air we breathe is oxygen. It is made available to the blood and body cells by the cooperative efforts of the respiratory and cardiovascular systems.

—adapted from Marieb, *Anatomy and Physiology*, p. 9

_____ 5. What is the topic?
   a. humans   c. oxygen
   b. nutrients   d. the respiratory system

_____ 6. What main idea is the writer implying?
   a. All chemical reactions require oxygen.
   b. Oxygen is vital to human life.
   c. Less than a fourth of the air we breathe is oxygen.
   d. The respiratory system and the cardiovascular system work together.

_____ 7. Which one of the following details does *not* support the paragraph's implied main idea?
   a. All the nutrients in the world are useless to humans.
   b. The chemical reactions that release energy from foods use oxygen.
   c. Plants release oxygen into the air through the process of photosynthesis.
   d. The respiratory and cardiovascular systems supply oxygen to the blood and body cells.

Paragraph D

People's acceptance of a product may be largely determined by its packaging. In one study the very same coffee taken from a yellow can was described as weak, from a dark brown can as too strong, from a red can as rich, and from a blue can as mild. Even your acceptance of a person may depend on the colors worn. Consider, for example, the comments of one color expert: "If you have to pick the wardrobe for your defense lawyer heading into court and choose anything but blue, you deserve to lose the case. . . . " Black is so powerful it could work against the lawyer with the jury. Brown lacks sufficient authority. Green would probably elicit a negative response.

—adapted from DeVito, *Messages: Building Interpersonal Communication Skills,* p. 161

8. What is the topic?
   a. packaging
   b. marketing
   c. colors
   d. dressing for success

9. What is the writer saying about the topic?
   a. Colors influence how we think and act.
   b. A product's packaging determines whether or not we accept it.
   c. A lawyer's success depends on the color of his or her wardrobe.
   d. Color experts consider blue to be the most influential color.

10. Which one of the following details does *not* support the paragraph's implied main idea?
    a. The same coffee is judged differently depending on the color of the coffee can.
    b. The colors a person is wearing may influence your opinion of that person.
    c. Lawyers who wear blue in court deserve to be defeated.
    d. Green is not considered a good color to wear in the courtroom.

IMPLIED MAIN IDEAS

Directions: After reading each of the following paragraphs, select the choice that best completes each of the statements that follow.

Paragraph A

Anybody anywhere can communicate via the Internet with people who speak his or her own language, but the Internet was born in the United States, so about 80 percent of home pages (Web sites) are in English. The second greatest number of sites are in Japanese (only 2.5 percent), followed by German, French, and Spanish. English accounts for about 97 percent of all pages linked to secure servers, however—that is, pages used in electronic business transactions. The English-language advantage in access will probably decrease as more international users log on and as computer translation improves. A unicode devised in 1995 allows computers to represent the letters and characters of virtually all the world's languages, and commercial services now offer translations on the Web. Ministers from French-speaking countries met in Montreal in 1997 to promote French-language use of the Web. They proposed government subsidies to French-language Web sites. The number of Chinese Internet users and Web pages is increasing rapidly.

—Bergman and Renwick, *Introduction to Geography*, p. 263

_____ 1. The implied main idea of the paragraph is that

    a. every language is represented on the Internet.

    b. English is the primary language on the Internet.

    c. computer translation should be improved to increase access for non-English speakers.

    d. French-language use of the Web is being promoted by representatives from French-speaking countries.

_____ 2. The statement that can reasonably be inferred from the details given in the paragraph is that

    a. most people prefer to speak English.

    b. most countries offer government subsidies to Web sites that use their language.

    c. most international companies use English in their business transactions.

    d. the Internet was first developed in Japan.

3. The second most common language on the Web is
   a. German.   c. Japanese.
   b. English.   d. French.

4. As more international users log on to the Internet, the "English-language advantage" will probably
   a. increase.
   b. remain the same.
   c. disappear completely.
   d. decrease.

5. One detail that does *not* support the main idea of this paragraph is
   a. The unicode developed in 1995 does not include English as one of its languages.
   b. The Internet originated in the United States.
   c. English accounts for almost all pages used in electronic business transactions.
   d. Commercial services offer translations on the Web from English to other languages.

Paragraph B

Who controls the market—companies or consumers? This question is even more complicated as new ways of buying, having, and being are invented every day. It seems that the "good old days" of *marketerspace,* a time when companies called the shots and decided what they wanted their customers to know and do, are dead and gone. Many people now feel empowered to choose how, when, or if they will interact with corporations as they construct their own *consumerspace.* In turn, companies need to develop and leverage brand equity in bold new ways to attract the loyalty of these consumer "nomads." People still "need" companies—but in new ways and on their own terms.

—adapted from Solomon, *Consumer Behavior,* p. 19

6. the implied main idea of this paragraph is that
   a. the marketplace should return to the "good old days."
   b. companies should work on increasing consumer loyalty.
   c. companies still control the marketplace.
   d. consumers have gained power in the marketplace.

_____ 7. According to the paragraph, the power in the marketplace has shifted from
   a. consumers to corporations.
   b. corporations to consumers.
   c. buyers to sellers.
   d. traditional brick-and-mortar stores to Internet businesses.

_____ 8. The term "marketerspace" is defined as a time when
   a. people developed new ways of buying, having, and being.
   b. people felt empowered about their interactions with corporations.
   c. companies decided what they wanted their customers to know and do.
   d. companies developed and leveraged brand equity in bold new ways.

_____ 9. When the author states that "People still 'need' companies," he means that
   a. companies offer products that people want.
   b. people need companies as employers.
   c. people need companies to show them what they want.
   d. companies convince people to buy unnecessary products.

_____ 10. As used in the paragraph, the term *nomads* refers to someone who
   a. travels a lot.
   b. is a native of a desert region.
   c. has immigrated from another country.
   d. moves from one product brand to another.

IMPLIED MAIN IDEAS

Directions: *Read the following excerpt from an essay titled "The Family Farm," by David Mas Masumoto. Then read each statement and decide whether it is an implied idea that can reasonably be drawn from the information presented in the passage. If the statement is reasonable, write R in the space provided; if it is not reasonable, write NR.*

THE FAMILY FARM

1   I grew up knowing my father's work. He was a peach and grape farmer, and I saw him at work daily, sometimes working alongside him. As a young child I knew some of the crises he faced. I cringed at the sight of worms attacking ripe fruit. I too could feel the searing heat of the summer sun as it blistered exposed fruit.

2   Now I farm the California land that my father and mother farmed, the land where my grandparents labored as farm workers. My children will know the work of their father, too. But where my father rarely showed emotion, I show it all. My daughter has seen me yell at the sky as September rain clouds approach my raisins or curse about lousy fruit prices when no one wants my peaches. It is a family farm—my parents, wife, and children spend time in the fields—and our family is bound to the land. Our farm survives as both a home and a workplace.

3   When I was in college, I asked friends about their parents' work. I thought my questions would be a safe way of getting to know someone. But most of my friends never ventured beyond one-line answers: "My dad is an engineer" or "He works for a bank" or "He handles sheet metal for an air-conditioning company."

4   I would respond, "What kind of engineer?" or "Why'd he choose banking?" or "How's the sheet-metal business?" Such questions alienated some of my friends: family seemed to be a painful subject. After I told them my dad was a farmer, rarely did they ask a second question. I stopped interpreting their initial response, "Oh, really?" as one of positive surprise.

5   Returning home after college, I felt uncomfortable telling others, "I farm." I translated blank looks as disdain mixed with condescension. I could see images flashing through their minds of Old MacDonald and hayseeds who spend weekends watching corn grow. As my peers were securing their corporate jobs and advancing as professionals in law or medicine, I spent long hours talking with my dad, getting to know fifty acres of vines and twenty acres of peach trees, preparing to take over the farm.

6   I'd listened for hours before I noticed that Dad's stories of growing up on the farm seemed to revolve around the pronoun *they*. "They" meant my grandparents and the entire family of four sons and two daughters. I had to adjust my thinking. My image of work was singular in nature, one man in one job, not a family's combined effort to make a living. I learned the significance of work that is inseparable from home, when work is also the place you live and play and sleep.

—adapted from Masumoto, "The Family Farm," *Epitaph for a Peach*

NR   1. The author is a worker on someone else's farm.

NR   2. Most of the author's college friends also grew up on farms.

NR   3. The author's college friends did not want to talk about their families.

R   4. After he came home from college, the author thought people looked down on him for being a farmer.

?   5. The author wishes he had pursued a career in law or medicine.

?R   6. The author's attitude toward farming has changed as he has grown older.

R   7. The family farm is very important to the author.

NR   8. The author's father wants him to sell the farm.

R   9. The author is proud of his family's way of life.

NR   10. The author is teaching his children to care about the family farm.

SEX AND SYMMETRY

Teresa Audesirk, Gerald Audesirk, and Bruce E. Byers

This excerpt from a biology textbook describes unexpected similarities between humans and the insect world. Read it to find out what you and scorpionflies may have in common.

Vocabulary Preview

These are some of the difficult words in this essay. The definitions here will help you if you can't figure out the meanings from the sentence context or word parts.

symmetrical (par. 2) having exact correspondence in size, shape, and position of parts on opposite sides of a dividing line; beautiful as a result of such balance

copulate (par. 2) to engage in sexual intercourse; to mate

correlated (par. 4) having a cause–effect relationship

embryological (par. 6) having to do with the early stages of development of an organism

genotype (par. 6) the genetic makeup of an organism or group of organisms

1   For a male Japanese scorpionfly, finding a mate can be a real struggle. Female scorpionflies will mate only with males that can offer a tasty meal (usually a dead insect). Competition for dead insects is fierce and, typically, once a male finds an insect, he must defend it from other males. The competition for insects often erupts in bitter combat, characterized by repeated head-butting and grappling with sharp-pointed genital claspers.

2   In the competition to gain access to mates, not all male Japanese scorpionflies can be equally successful. The most successful males have qualities that help them defeat other males in combat and that are especially attractive to females. Biologist Randy Thornhill has found that one quality in particular accurately predicts the mating success of male scorpionflies. In Thornhill's experiments and observations, the most successful males were those whose left and right wings were equal or nearly equal in length, in other words—symmetrical. Males with one wing longer than the other were less likely to win fights or to copulate; the greater the difference between the two wings, the lower the likelihood of success.

3   Thornhill's work with scorpionflies led him to wonder if the advantages of symmetry also extend to humans. Working with psychologist Steven Gangestad, he devised some

■ *Both this male scorpionfly and this male human are exceptionally attractive to females of their species. The secret to their sex appeal may be that both have highly symmetrical bodies.*

fascinating studies to investigate the role of symmetry in human sexual relationships. He found that women find symmetrical men more attractive, and highly symmetrical human males do indeed appear to gain some of the advantages that accrue to symmetrical scorpionflies. The preferences of human females resemble, as least in this one respect, those of female scorpionflies. One could almost say that insects and humans share a standard of beauty.

4   To assess whether male body symmetry is correlated with male "mating success" in humans, Randy Thornhill, Steven Gangestad, and their colleagues began by measuring symmetry in some young adult males. Each man's degree of symmetry was assessed by measurements of his ear length and the width of his foot, ankle, hand, wrist, elbow, and ear. From these measurements, the researchers derived an index that summarized the degree to which the size of these features differed between the right and left sides of the body.

5   The researchers found that, among the males in their sample, the most symmetrical men were judged (by a panel of female observers who were unaware of the nature of the study) to be more attractive than other men. A survey of the study subjects revealed that the more symmetrical men also tended to begin having sex earlier in life and to

have had a larger number of different sexual partners. Apparently, symmetry is a powerful characteristic.

6   Why would male body symmetry affect mating success? The most likely explanation is that symmetry is an indicator of good physical condition. As developmental biologists have long known, disruptions of normal embryological development can cause bodies to be asymmetrical, so a highly symmetrical body indicates healthy, normal development. It also may indicate a high-quality genotype that was able to overcome any disturbances (such as diseases or exposure to toxic substances) during development. Females that mate with individuals whose health and vitality are announced by their symmetrical bodies might have offspring that are similarly healthy and vital. Natural selection would thus favor females who chose to mate with symmetrical males, and that kind of mating behavior would come to predominate.

— · —

Directions: Select the letter of the choice that best completes each of the following statements.

CHECKING YOUR COMPREHENSION

_____ 1. The main point of this selection is that

a. the Japanese scorpionfly has difficulty finding potential mates.

b. certain species of insects are attracted only to symmetrical mates.

c. physical symmetry is an important factor in sexual relationships.

d. humans and insects are alike in many ways.

_____ 2. The topic of paragraph 1 is

a. insects.

b. Japanese scorpionflies.

c. competition.

d. combat among insects.

_____ 3. The degree of symmetry in the human male subjects was assessed by

a. taking their physical measurements.

b. asking female observers.

       c. monitoring their physical performance during a workout.

       d. consulting their personal physicians.

_____ 4. The main finding of Thornhill and Gangestad's study was that

       a. symmetrical men are in better physical shape than other men.

       b. women do not care whether men are symmetrical.

       c. symmetry is the result of genetic factors.

       d. symmetrical men are considered more attractive than other men.

_____ 5. According to the selection, one likely reason that male body symmetry affects mating success is that

       a. a symmetrical body indicates good physical condition.

       b. symmetrical males have fewer sexual partners.

       c. symmetrical females have a larger number of offspring.

       d. males are more attracted to symmetrical females.

USING WHAT YOU KNOW ABOUT IMPLIED MAIN IDEAS

_____ 6. The main idea of paragraph 2 is that

       a. the most important predictor of mating success for male scorpionflies is symmetry.

       b. male Japanese scorpionflies are highly competitive.

       c. not all male scorpionflies find mates.

       d. male scorpionflies with unequal wing lengths are less likely to win fights.

_____ 7. The main idea of paragraph 3 is that

       a. the study of insect symmetry led to the study of human symmetry.

       b. a biologist and a psychologist designed the human symmetry study.

       c. human females have the same preferences as female scorpionflies.

       d. male symmetry is important in human sexual relationships.

8. The last sentence of paragraph 3 means that
   a. humans and insects both base their relationships on physical beauty.
   b. symmetry is one characteristic of beauty that appeals to both humans and insects.
   c. insects and humans are both beautiful in their own ways.
   d. insects and humans are equally symmetrical.

9. The main idea of paragraph 5 is that
   a. the most symmetrical men in the study were also the most attractive.
   b. the female observers were unaware of the purpose of the study.
   c. the most symmetrical men in the study had sex at an earlier age.
   d. a man's sexual activity and attractiveness appear to be directly related to his symmetry.

10. The main idea of paragraph 6 is that
   a. symmetrical male bodies suggest physical health and ability to produce healthy offspring.
   b. exposure to toxic substances has no effect on embryological development.
   c. symmetrical bodies are a result of healthy, normal development in the embryo.
   d. symmetry may indicate superior intellectual capacity.

USING CONTEXT AND WORD PARTS

C 11. In paragraph 2, the word **access** means
   a. attack mode.   c. complete and full attention.
   b. possibility of approaching.   d. defensive action.

C 12. In paragraph 3, the word **accrue** means
   a. ignore.   c. accumulate.
   b. avoid.   d. compete.

_____D_____ 13. In paragraph 4, the word **derived** means
          a. allowed.   c. removed.
          b. required.   d. obtained.

_____B_____ 14. In paragraph 6, the word **asymmetrical** means
          a. joined.   c. perfectly shaped.
          b. not balanced.   d. oversized.

_____a_____ 15. In paragraph 6, the word **predominate** means
          a. be most common.   c. seem unavailable.
          b. appear weakened.   d. have no effect.

REVIEWING DIFFICULT VOCABULARY

Directions: Complete each of the following sentences by inserting a word from the Vocabulary Preview on page 174 in the space provided.

16. The number of traffic accidents on a given day often is directly correlated to the weather.

17. Female Japanese scorpionflies are more likely to copulate with symmetrical males.

18. A person's genotype reveals his or her genetic composition.

19. Denise admired the perfectly symmetrical handmade ceramic bowl.

20. Researchers studied the embryological development of the starfish.

QUESTIONS FOR DISCUSSION

1. Discuss the idea of symmetry in another context, such as photography, sculpture, painting, art, or literature. Do you think symmetrical shapes, arrangements, and themes are more "attractive" than asymmetrical ones?

2. Other than symmetry, what other factors contribute to beauty or physical attractiveness?

3. Discuss the importance of Thornhill's research. Why is it important to understand the mating habits of scorpionflies?

WRITING ACTIVITIES

1. Write a paragraph evaluating the importance of physical attractiveness in mate selection.

2. Brainstorm a list of factors other than physical attractiveness that are important in mate selection. Choose three factors that are most important to you and write a short essay explaining your choices.

3. Visit the site for FacePrints research at http://web.mac.com/vicjohn/iWeb/FacePrints/Welcome.html. Be sure to participate in the male face experiment. Write a paragraph about your experience with the site.

Chapter 5: Understanding Implied Main Ideas

RECORDING YOUR PROGRESS

Test	Number Right		Score
Practice Test 5-1	_____	× 10 =	_____ %
Practice Test 5-2	_____	× 5 =	_____ %
Practice Test 5-3	_____	× 10 =	_____ %
Mastery Test 5-1	_____	× 10 =	_____ %
Mastery Test 5-2	_____	× 10 =	_____ %
Mastery Test 5-3	_____	× 5 =	_____ %

EVALUATING YOUR PROGRESS

Based on your test performance, rate how well you have mastered the skills taught in this chapter by checking one of the boxes below or by writing your own evaluation.

☐ **Need More Improvement**
Tip: Try completing the Main Idea–Maine Woods module in the Reading Skills section on the MyReadingLab Web site at **http://www.ablongman.com/myreadinglab** to fine-tune the skills that you have learned in this chapter.

☐ **Need More Practice**
Tip: Try using the Main Idea–Maine Woods module in the Reading Skills section on the MyReadingLab Web site at **http://www.ablongman.com/myreadinglab** to brush up on the skills taught in this chapter, or visit this textbook's Companion Web site at **http://www.ablongman.com/mcwhorter** for extra practice.

☐ **Good**
Tip: To maintain your skills, quickly review this chapter by using this textbook's Companion Web site at **http://www.ablongman.com/mcwhorter**.

☐ **Excellent**

YOUR EVALUATION: _____

_____

_____

_____

THINK ABOUT IT!

Study the items shown below. What do they all have in common? Each is a method of organizing information and making it accessible and easy to understand.

Just as there are several ways to keep track of information in everyday life, there are several ways to keep track of information when you read academic assignments.

File   Edit   View   Insert   Format   Tools   Data   Window   Help   Adobe PDF

D7   fx

	A	B	C	D
	Dept. of English COURSE NO.	COURSE TITLE	DAYS/TIMES	CREDITS
1	ENG 001	Written Expression	MWF 0900a–1000a	3
2	ENG 004	Engl for Internatl Stdnts	MWF 0300p–0400p	3
3	ENG 005	First Year Seminar	TTh 1030a–1200p	3
4	ENG 011	Types of Literature	MWF 0100p–0300p	3
5	ENG 012	Introduction to Drama	TTh 0530p–0700p	3
6	ENG 013	Introduction to Fiction	TTh 0530p–0700p	3
7	ENG 014	Introduction to Poetry	MWF 1100a–1200p	3
8	ENG 024	American Literature	MWF 0200p–0300p	3

Sheet1 / Sheet2 / Sheet3 /

MAY 2007

Sunday	Monday	Tu
April 29	30	
6	7	8
13	14	15
20	21	22
27	28	29

16   17   18   19

23
8:00 a.m. Study for biology test
12:00 p.m. Lunch
2:00 p.m. Read Chpt 3 psychology
7.15 p.m. Dinner
8:15 p.m. Movie w/Juan

24
8:00 a.m. Biology test
10:15 a.m. Take a break!
12:00 p.m. Lunch
1:00 p.m. Language lab
3:00 p.m. Group meeting for Eng. Comp.
5:15 p.m. Library — don't forget Africa books!

25   26

30   31   June 1   2

File   Edit   View   Favorites   Tools   Help

Back ▾

Add to Favorites...
Organize Favorites...

Search ⭐ Favorites 🌐 Med

Address http://w

old
camping
Nature publishing
gateway

RS ▾ ▾ ▾ ▾

law   SOSIG Law Gate
science
music

CHAPTER 6

Keeping Track of Information

Why Keep Track of Information?

As you plan a vacation, you often begin to collect all sorts of information—newspaper articles on various cities, brochures, restaurant suggestions from friends, and so forth. If you don't keep track of the various pieces of information, you soon discover that they are hard to find and thus not very useful. For a trip to Texas, for instance, you might decide to sort what you've collected by city, putting everything for San Antonio in one large envelope, everything for Dallas in another envelope, and so forth.

When you read, the ideas and details you are learning about also become more useful if you can organize them in some way. In the preceding chapters, you discovered how to find main ideas and the details that support them. This chapter will show you five ways to keep track of this kind of information: (1) highlighting, (2) marking, (3) outlining, (4) mapping, and (5) summarizing. You may decide to use only a few of these methods, or you may decide to use different ones for different kinds of reading assignments. Whatever approach you take, keep in mind that all of these methods can help you remember what you have read—an important skill for studying and taking tests in college.

Highlighting and Marking

Highlighting and marking important facts and ideas as you read are effective ways to keep track of information. They are also big time-savers for college students. Suppose it took you four hours to read an assigned chapter in sociology. One month later you might need to review that chapter to prepare for an exam. If you did not highlight or mark the chapter the first time, then you would have to spend another four hours rereading it. However, if you had highlighted and marked as you read, you could review the chapter fairly quickly.

Highlighting Effectively   Here are a few basic suggestions for highlighting effectively:

1. **Read a paragraph or section first.** Then go back and highlight what is important.
2. **Highlight important portions of any topic sentence.** Also highlight any supporting details you want to remember (see Chapter 4).
3. **Be accurate.** Make sure your highlighting reflects the content of the passage.
4. **Highlight the right amount.** If you highlight too little, you may miss valuable information. On the other hand, if you highlight too much, you are not zeroing in on the most important ideas, and you will wind up rereading too much material when you study. As a general rule of thumb, highlight no more than 20 to 30 percent of the material.

Read the following paragraph. Notice that you can understand its meaning from the highlighted parts alone.

> The results of resistance training in men and women are quite different. Women don't normally develop muscle to the same extent that men do. The main reason for the difference between the sexes is that men and women have different levels of the hormone testosterone in their blood. Before puberty, testosterone levels in blood are similar for both boys and girls. During adolescence, testosterone levels in boys increase dramatically, about ten-fold, but testosterone levels in girls are unchanged. Women's muscles will become larger as a result of resistance training exercise but typically not to the same degree as in adult males.
>
> —Donatelle, *Health: The Basics*, p. 286

Exercise 6–1

Directions: *Read the following paragraph, which has been highlighted two different ways. Look at each highlighted version, then answer the questions that follow.*

Example 1

Chemistry begins defining **matter** by dividing it into two broad types, *pure substances* and *mixtures*. In **pure substances**, only a single type of matter is present. **Mixtures** occur when two or more pure substances are intermingled with each other. For example, table salt is a pure substance. So is water. And so is table sugar. If you put salt and sugar in a jar together and shake, however, you have a mixture. Dissolve sugar in water and you have another mixture. Some things that you might not think of as mixtures actually do fit the definition—a rock, for example. In most rocks, you'll see a mixture of different minerals, each a different pure substance.

—Russo and Silver, *Introductory Chemistry Essentials*, pp. 3–4

Example 2

Chemistry begins defining **matter** by dividing it into two broad types, *pure substances* and *mixtures*. In **pure substances**, only a single type of matter is present. **Mixtures** occur when two or more pure substances are intermingled with each other. For example, table salt is a pure substance. So is water. And so is table sugar. If you put salt and sugar in a jar together and shake, however, you have a mixture. Dissolve sugar in water and you have another mixture. Some things that you might not think of as mixtures actually do fit the definition—a rock, for example. In most rocks, you'll see a mixture of different minerals, each a different pure substance.

1. The topic sentence begins with the word _____.

2. Is Example 1 or Example 2 the better example of effective highlighting? _____

3. Why isn't the highlighting in the other example effective?

   _____

4. According to the writer, what two broad types of matter are there in chemistry?

   a. _____   b. _____

Marking to Record Ideas   Although highlighting can be very helpful, sometimes you may want to circle a word, ask a question, or write some other kind of note to yourself as you read. In these instances, try making notes in the margin in addition to highlighting.

Here are just a few ways to use marking:

1. **Circle words you do not know.**
2. **Mark definitions with "def."**
3. **Make notes to yourself**—such as "good example," "test question," "reread," or "ask instructor."
4. **Put question marks next to confusing words/passages.**

In the following passage a student taking a marketing course has used marking as well as highlighting.

With so many stores competing for customers, how do consumers pick one over another? As with products, stores may be thought of as having "personalities." Some stores have very clearly defined images (either good or bad). Others tend to blend into the crowd. They may not have anything distinctive about them and may be overlooked for this reason. This personality, or **store image**, is composed of many different factors. Store features, coupled with such consumer characteristics as shopping orientation, help to predict which shopping outlets people will prefer. Some of the important dimensions of a store's profile are location, merchandise suitability, and the knowledge and congeniality of the sales staff.

What does this mean?

Test question?

Because a store's image is now recognized as a very important aspect of the retailing mix, store designers pay a lot of attention to **atmospherics,** or the conscious designing of space and its various dimensions to evoke certain effects in buyers. These dimensions include colors, scents, and sounds. A store's atmosphere in turn affects purchasing behavior—one recent study reported that the extent of pleasure reported by shoppers five minutes after entering a store was predictive of the amount of time spent in the store as well as the level of spending there.

def.

—adapted from Solomon, *Consumer Behavior,* p. 301

Notice how the student has used marking to circle a word and a phrase she's not sure of, to point out a definition, and to call attention to a possible test question.

Exercise 6-2

Directions: *Read the following paragraphs, which are a continuation of the preceding passage. Highlight and mark the paragraphs in a way that would help you remember the material and study it later.*

Many elements of store design can be cleverly controlled to attract customers and produce desired effects on consumers. Light colors impart a feeling of spaciousness and serenity, and signs in bright colors create excitement. In one subtle but effective application, fashion designer Norma Kamali replaced fluorescent lights with pink ones in department store dressing rooms. The light had the effect of flattering the face and banishing wrinkles, making female customers more willing to try on (and buy) the company's bathing suits. Wal-Mart found that sales were higher in areas of a store lit in natural daylight compared to the more typical artificial light. One study found that brighter in-store lighting influenced people to examine and handle more merchandise.

In addition to visual stimuli, all sorts of cues can influence behaviors. For example, patrons of country-and-western bars drink more when the jukebox music is slower. Similarly, music can affect eating habits. Another study found that diners who listened to loud, fast music ate more food. In contrast, those who listened to Mozart or Brahms ate less and more slowly.

—Solomon, *Consumer Behavior,* p. 316

Outlining

Making an outline is another good way to keep track of what you have read. **Outlining** involves listing major and minor ideas and showing how they are related. When you make an outline, follow the writer's organization. An outline usually follows a format like the one below:

I. Major topic
   A. First major idea
      1. First key supporting detail
      2. Second key supporting detail
   B. Second major idea
      1. First key supporting detail
         a. Minor detail or example
         b. Minor detail or example
      2. Second key supporting detail
II. Second major topic
   A. First major idea

Suppose you had just read a brief essay about your friend's vacation in San Francisco. An outline of the essay might begin like this:

I. Favorite places
   A. Chinatown
      1. Restaurants and markets
         a. Fortune cookie factory
         b. Dim sum restaurants
      2. Museums
         a. Chinese Culture Center
         b. Pacific Heritage Museum
   B. Fisherman's Wharf
      1. Pier 39
         a. Street performers
         b. Sea lions sunning themselves on the docks
      2. Ghiradelli Square

Notice that the most important ideas are closer to the left margin. The rule of thumb to follow is this: The less important the idea, the more it should be indented.

Here are a few suggestions for using the outline format:

1. **Don't worry about following the outline format exactly.** As long as your outline shows an organization of ideas, it will work for you.
2. **Use words and phrases or complete sentences,** whichever is easier for you.
3. **Use your own words, and don't write too much.**
4. **Pay attention to headings.** Be sure that all the information you place underneath a heading explains or supports that heading. In the outline above, for instance, the entries "Chinatown" and "Fisherman's Wharf" are correctly placed under the major topic "Favorite Places." Likewise, "Pier 39" and "Ghiradelli Square" are under "Fisherman's Wharf," since they are located in the Wharf area.

Read the following paragraph on how children learn to manage their emotions, and then study its outline.

Children learn how to manage their emotions in at least three ways. First, they learn how they *should* feel. For example, they should love their parents and they should feel guilty for displeasing their parents. Second, children learn how to *display* or *conceal* emotions. They should look happy at a wedding, seem sad at a funeral, and appear reverent at a religious service. Sometimes children learn to display an emotion that they do not have in them or to conceal a feeling that they do have. If a grandparent gives them a present they do not like, they are taught to show how much they like it. Finally, while they learn to display or conceal certain emotions, children also learn how to *change* some feelings in themselves. When children are feeling sad, they may learn to manipulate that feeling by, for example, telephoning or visiting a friend.

—Thio, *Sociology*, pp. 70–71

In this outline, the major topic of the paragraph, "How children learn to manage their emotions," is listed first. The writer's three main ideas are listed as A, B, and C. Supporting details are then listed under the ideas. When you look at this outline, you can easily see the writer's most important points.

I. How children learn to manage their emotions
   A. They learn how they are supposed to feel
      1. Love parents
      2. Feel guilty for displeasing parents

> B. They learn to show or hide what they feel
>   1. Show happiness, sadness, reverence in different situations
>   2. Display positive feelings and hide negative feelings
> C. They learn how to change what they feel
>   1. Change sadness by contacting a friend

Exercise 6-3

Directions: *After reading the following passage and the incomplete outline that follows, fill in the missing information in the outline.*

HOW AMERICANS PARTICIPATE IN POLITICS

Political participation encompasses the many activities in which citizens engage to influence the selection of political leaders or the policies they pursue. Although the line is hard to draw, political scientists generally distinguish between two broad types of participation: conventional and unconventional. Conventional participation includes many widely accepted modes of influencing government—voting, trying to persuade others, ringing doorbells for a petition, running for office, and so on. In contrast, unconventional participation includes activities that are often dramatic, such as protesting, civil disobedience, and even violence.

For a few, politics is their lifeblood; they run for office, work regularly in politics, and live for the next election. The number of Americans for whom political activity is an important part of their everyday life is minuscule; they number at most in the tens of thousands. To these people, policy questions are as familiar as slogans on TV commercials are to the average citizen. They are the political elites—activists, party leaders, interest group leaders, judges, members of Congress, and other public officials.

Millions take part in political activities beyond simply voting. In two comprehensive studies of American political participation, samples of Americans were asked twice at 20 year intervals about their role in various kinds of political activities. Included were voting, working in campaigns, contacting government officials, and working on local community issues. Voting was the only aspect of political participation that a majority of the population reported engaging in, but also the only political activity for which there is evidence of a decline in participation in recent years. Substantial increases in participation were found on the dimensions of giving money to candidates and contacting public officials, and small increases are evident for all the other activities. Thus, although the decline of voter turnout is a development Americans should rightly be concerned about, a broader look at political participation reveals some positive developments for participatory democracy.

—adapted from Edwards, Wattenberg, and Lineberry,
Government in America, pp. 196–197

  I. Two types of participation
     A. Conventional methods
        1. Voting
        2. Persuading others
        3. _____
        4. _____
     B. _____
        1. Protesting
        2. _____
        3. _____
 II. Political activity as part of everyday life
     A. Small percentage of population
     B. Political elite
        1. Activists
        2. _____
        3. Interest group leaders
        4. _____
        5. Members of Congress
        6. _____
III. Studies of political participation
     A. Voting
        1. Majority of the population voted
        2. _____
     B. Giving money to candidates increased substantially
     C. _____
     D. Small increases for all other activities
     E. Overall positive developments for participatory democracy

Mapping

In Chapter 4 you learned a little bit about **mapping** (p. 122), which is a visual method of organizing information. It involves drawing diagrams to show how ideas in a paragraph or chapter are related. Some students prefer mapping to outlining because they feel it is freer and less tightly structured.

Maps can take many forms. You can draw them in any way that shows the relationships between ideas. Figures 6-1 and 6-2 (p. 192) show two sample maps of the paragraph about children's emotions. Look at the maps and then look again at the outline of the emotions paragraph. Notice how the important information is included by each method—it's just presented differently.

As you draw a map, think of it as a picture or diagram that shows how ideas are connected. You can hand draw maps or use a word processor. Use the following steps, which can be seen in Figures 6-1 and 6-2:

1. **Identify the overall topic or subject.** Write it in the center or at the top of the page.

2. **Identify major ideas that relate to the topic.** Using a line, connect each major idea to the central topic.

3. **As you discover supporting details that further explain an idea already mapped, connect those details with new lines.**

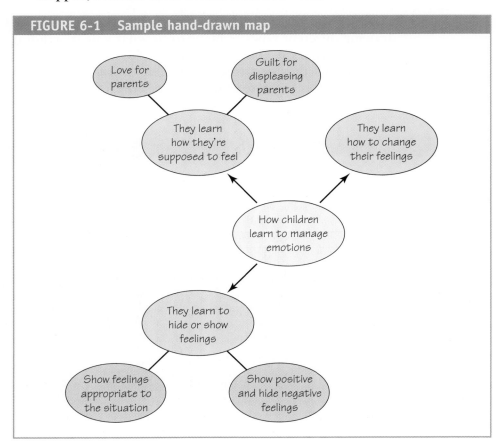

FIGURE 6-1   Sample hand-drawn map

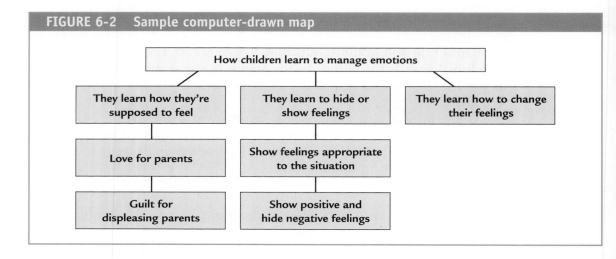

FIGURE 6-2   Sample computer-drawn map

How children learn to manage emotions

| They learn how they're supposed to feel | They learn to hide or show feelings | They learn how to change their feelings |

Love for parents

Show feelings appropriate to the situation

Guilt for displeasing parents

Show positive and hide negative feelings

Once you are skilled at drawing maps, you can become more creative, drawing different types of maps to fit what you are reading. For example, you can draw a *time line* (see Figure 6-3) to show historical events in the order in which they occurred. A time line starts with the earliest event and ends with the most recent. Another type of map is one that shows a

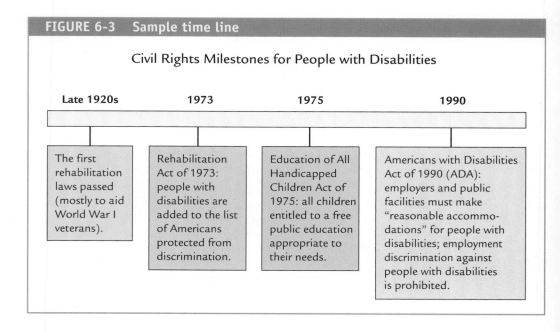

FIGURE 6-3   Sample time line

Civil Rights Milestones for People with Disabilities

| Late 1920s | 1973 | 1975 | 1990 |

| The first rehabilitation laws passed (mostly to aid World War I veterans). | Rehabilitation Act of 1973: people with disabilities are added to the list of Americans protected from discrimination. | Education of All Handicapped Children Act of 1975: all children entitled to a free public education appropriate to their needs. | Americans with Disabilities Act of 1990 (ADA): employers and public facilities must make "reasonable accommodations" for people with disabilities; employment discrimination against people with disabilities is prohibited. |

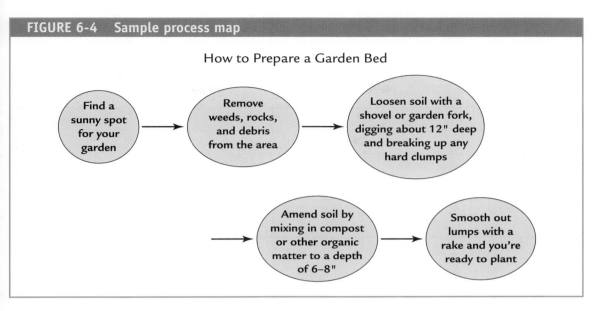

FIGURE 6-4   Sample process map

How to Prepare a Garden Bed

process—the steps involved in doing something (see Figure 6-4). When you study chronological order and process in Chapter 7 (p. 230), you will discover more uses for these kinds of maps.

Exercise 6-4

Directions: *Read the following paragraph and complete the map below, filling in the writer's main points in the spaces provided. Then answer the question that follows the map.*

Because complaints are often preludes to conflict in the workplace, they need to be listened to and responded to appropriately. Here are some suggestions for dealing with complaints. First, let the person know that you're open to complaints; you view them as helpful sources of information, and you're listening. (Be careful not to fall into the trap of seeing someone who voices a complaint as someone to avoid.) Second, try to understand both the thoughts and the feelings that go with the complaint. Express not only your concern about the problem but also your understanding of the frustration this person is feeling. Third, respect confidentiality. Let the person know that the complaint will be treated in strict confidence or that it will be revealed only to those he or she wishes. Fourth, ask the person what he or she would like you to do. Sometimes all a person wants is for someone to hear the complaint and appreciate its legitimacy. Other times, the complaint is presented in hopes that you will do something specific. Finally, thank the person for voicing the complaint, and assure him or her of your intention to follow up.

—adapted from DeVito, *Messages*, p. 317

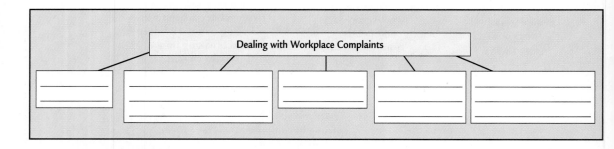

1. What five transition words does the writer use to introduce the main points?

   a. _____   b. _____   c. _____   d. _____   e. _____

Exercise 6–5

Directions: *After reading the following paragraphs, complete the map of the passage. Fill in the writer's main points as well as some supporting details.*

TWO TYPES OF ORGANISMS THAT RELEASE NUTRIENTS

Among the most important strands in a food web are the detritus feeders and decomposers. The detritus feeders are an army of mostly small and often unnoticed animals and protists that live on the refuse of life: molted exoskeletons, fallen leaves, wastes, and dead bodies. (Detritus means "debris.") The network of detritus feeders is complex; in terrestrial ecosystems it includes earthworms, mites, centipedes, some insects, land-dwelling crustaceans, nematode worms, and even a few large vertebrates such as vultures. These organisms consume dead organic matter, extract some of the energy stored in it, and excrete it in a further decomposed state. Their excretory products serve as food for other detritus feeders and for decomposers.

The decomposers are primarily fungi and bacteria (the black coating or gray fuzz you may notice on decaying tomatoes and bread crusts are fungal decomposers). Decomposers digest food outside their bodies by secreting digestive enzymes into the environment. They absorb the nutrients they need, and the remaining nutrients are released to the environment.

—Audesirk, Audesirk, and Byers, *Life on Earth*, pp. 584–585

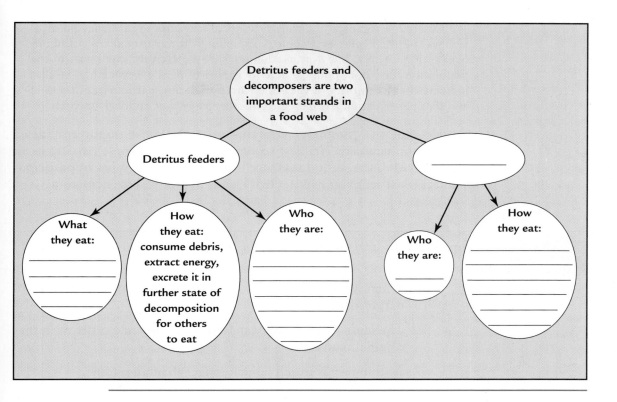

Summarizing

Summarizing is another good way to remember and keep track of information. A **summary** is a brief statement that pulls together the most important ideas in something you have read. It is much shorter than an outline and contains less detailed information. At times, you may want to summarize a paragraph, an essay, or even a chapter.

To write a good summary you need to understand the material and identify the writer's major points. Here are some tips to follow:

1. **Underline each major idea in the material.**
2. **Write one sentence that states the writer's most important idea.** This sentence will be the topic sentence of your summary.
3. **Be sure to use your own words rather than those of the author.**
4. **Focus on the author's major ideas,** not on supporting details.
5. **Keep the ideas in the summary in the same order as they appear in the original material.**

Read the following summary of "How Americans Participate in Politics," which appeared in Exercise 6–3 on page 189.

Citizens participate in different political activities to influence political leaders and their policies. People participate in conventional ways and unconventional ways. The "political elites" are a relatively small part of the population for whom political activity is part of their everyday life. Studies indicate that a majority of the American population participates in voting and that participation has increased in other aspects of political activities.

Notice that this summary contains only the most important ideas. Details are not included. The first sentence shows why people participate in political activities, the second sentence lists the two basic types of participation, and the last sentence lists general trends in political participation.

Exercise 6-6

A. Directions: *Indicate whether each of the following statements is true (T) or false (F).*

_____ 1. When writing a summary, you should focus on the author's major ideas.

_____ 2. The ideas in a summary should be in the same order as in the original material.

_____ 3. A summary is usually much longer than an outline.

_____ 4. A summary should be in your own words rather than those of the author.

B. Directions: *After reading the following paragraphs, circle the letter of the choice that best summarizes each one.*

_____ 5. The tourist potential of any spot depends upon its "three A's": accessibility, accommodations, and attractions. The rich bird life on the islands of Lake Nicaragua, the lions of Kenya, and the tropical vegetation in many countries are important tourist destinations. Overall, the countries best endowed for tourism have both natural and cultural attractions, pleasant climates, good beaches, and reasonably well-educated populations. Political stability is a necessity. Despite Africa's wealth of ecological and cultural attractions, political instability and lack of accommodations have restricted its income to only 2.2 percent of global tourist dollars.

—adapted from Bergman and Renwick,
Introduction to Geography, pp. 495–496

a. The tourist potential of a place depends upon its accessibility, accommodations, and attractions. Important tourist destinations include Lake Nicaragua, Kenya, and tropical countries. However, despite Africa's many attractions, its income is only 2.2 percent of global tourist dollars due to political instability and lack of accommodations.

b. Tourists typically want to visit places that offer the three A's. They also want pleasant weather, nice beaches, and an educated population.

c. A country's ability to attract tourism is determined by how accessible it is and by the accommodations and attractions it provides. Countries that are tourist destinations offer a variety of activities, mild weather, attractive beaches, and a population that is educated and politically stable.

d. Tourists are interested in places that offer political stability, excellent beaches, nice weather, and well-educated people. A tourist spot has to have natural and cultural attractions and a variety of accommodations.

_____ 6. The common cold is responsible for more days lost from work and more uncomfortable days spent at work than any other ailment. Caused by any number of viruses (some experts claim there may be over 200 different viruses responsible for the common cold), colds are always present to some degree among people throughout the world. In the course of a year, Americans suffer over 1 billion colds. Cold viruses are carried in the nose and throat most of the time. These viruses are held in check until the host's resistance is lowered. It is possible to "catch" a cold—from the airborne droplets of another person's sneeze or from skin-to-skin or mucous membrane contact—though recent studies indicate that the hands may be the greatest avenue of colds and transmission of other viruses. Although many people believe that a cold results from exposure to cold weather or from getting chilled or overheated, experts believe that such things have little or no effect on cold development. Stress, allergy disorders that affect the nasal passages, and menstrual cycles do, however, appear to increase susceptibility.

—adapted from Donatelle, *Health: The Basics*, p. 350

a. More workers are affected by the common cold than by any other illness. Colds are caused by viruses and result from exposure to another person's virus through the air or by physical contact. Stress, nasal allergies, and certain stages of the menstrual cycle may make people more susceptible to colds.

b. People who suffer from the common cold often miss work or are uncomfortable at work. Experts say that over 200 different viruses may be responsible for the common cold, which is always present in people all over the world. In America, people suffer over 1 billion colds every year.

c. The common cold is caused by different viruses that are carried in the nose and throat most of the time. These viruses wait until a person's resistance is low; then the person may catch a cold from someone else, through either a sneeze or some other contact.

d. Cold viruses exist all over the world, and Americans suffer more than 1 billion colds each year. More than 200 different viruses may be responsible for causing the common cold.

Good Reasons to Keep Track of Information

As you know, you will do a lot of reading in your college courses, and you will often be tested on what you have read. If you keep track of information as you go along, you will remember more of the material, and studying for tests or exams will be much easier. Instead of rereading everything, you can study from the notes, outlines, or maps you have already made. You now know five ways to keep track of information—highlighting, marking, outlining, mapping, and summarizing. Try out a few of these methods as you read the next chapters.

The Textbook Challenge

Part A: Current Issues Reader

Using the textbook excerpt "Whether to Vote: A Citizen's First Choice," (p. 514) highlight the major supporting details of each paragraph. Circle the transitions.

Part B: A College Textbook

Choose a chapter that you have been assigned to read in a textbook for one of your other courses. For the first five pages, underline the major supporting details of each paragraph. Circle the transitions.

What Have You Learned?

Directions: *To check your understanding of the chapter and to review its major points, indicate whether each of the following statements is true (T) or false (F).*

_____ 1. In general, you should highlight no more than 20 to 30 percent of the material.

_____ 2. Marking should not be used with material that has already been highlighted.

_____ 3. When you outline material, you should follow the writer's organization.

_____ 4. In an outline, the most important ideas are closest to the left margin.

_____ 5. Mapping is more structured than outlining.

_____ 6. Maps should include major ideas as well as supporting details.

_____ 7. A process map shows the steps involved in doing something.

_____ 8. Supporting details are not included in summaries.

What Vocabulary Have You Learned?

Directions: *The words in column A appear in this chapter. Test your mastery of these words by matching each word in column A with its meaning in column B.*

Column A	Column B
_____ 1. congeniality	a. minor events that come before a more important or significant event
_____ 2. minuscule	b. living or growing on land; related to the earth or its inhabitants
_____ 3. preludes	c. friendliness, sociability
_____ 4. terrestrial	d. likelihood of being affected by something
_____ 5. susceptibility	e. very small

SUMMARIZING

Directions: *After reading the following passage, select words and phrases from the box that follows the selection to complete the summary. Use each word or phrase only once. Not all words or phrases in the box will be used.*

ON VISITING AN ART MUSEUM, (OR HOW TO ENJOY LOOKING AT ART WITHOUT BEING OVERWHELMED BY MUSEUM FATIGUE)

Art museums can be mind-expanding or sleep-inducing, depending on how you approach them. It is a mistake to enter a museum with the belief that you should like everything you see—or even that you should see everything that is there. Without selective viewing, the visitor to a large museum is likely to come down with a severe case of museum exhaustion.

It makes sense to approach an art museum the way a seasoned traveler approaches a city for a first visit: Find out what there is to see. In the museum, inquire about the schedule of special shows, then see those exhibitions and outstanding works that interest you. Museums are in the process of rethinking their buildings and collections in order to meet the needs of changing populations and changing values. It is not unusual to find video exhibits, performances of all kinds, and film showings as part of regular museum programming.

If you are visiting without a specific exhibition in mind, follow your interests and instincts. Browsing can be highly rewarding. Zero in on what you feel are the highlights, savoring favorite works and unexpected discoveries.

Don't stay too long in a museum. Take breaks. Perhaps there is a garden or café in which you can pause for a rest. The quality of your experience is not measured by the amount of time you spend in the galleries or how many works you see. The most rewarding experiences can come from finding something that "speaks" to you, then sitting and enjoying it in leisurely contemplation.

—Preble and Preble, *Artforms,* p. 110

mind-expanding	selective viewing	exhaustion	overwhelmed
art museum	sleep-inducing	offer	too long
overload	highlights	instincts	breaks
outstanding works	speaks	special exhibitions	

Summary

When you are visiting an _____, you should practice

_____. Find out what the museum has to _____.

Decide what _____ and _____ appeal to you.

Follow your _____ and focus on the _____.

Don't stay _____ in the museum, and take frequent

_____. Find art that _____ to you and take time

to enjoy it.

HIGHLIGHTING AND MARKING

Directions: *After reading the following passage, select the choice that best completes each of the statements that follow.*

APPETITE: A MOVING TARGET

1   The early phases of eating depend on the taste of food. When you take the first bites of a meal or snack, you probably experience the *appetizer effect;* if those first bites taste good, your appetite is stimulated. This effect is driven in part by opioids in the brain; as you might suspect from their name, **opioids** are chemicals that behave like opium-derived drugs and cause you to experience pleasure. The opioids are released when you first eat food that tastes good.

2   As you continue to eat, your responses to food-related stimuli change. After eating some fresh-baked cookies, the smell of them doesn't seem quite as heavenly as it did before you ate them. If people have had their fill of a certain food, they rate its odor as less pleasant than they did before eating it. However, when the flavor, texture, color, or shape of a food is changed, people will eat more of the same food. After you've eaten a few chocolate chip cookies, you might find yourself not interested in more cookies, but happy to have some fresh-baked bread.

3   Not surprisingly, these changes in your appetite are linked to events in the hypothalamus. Neurons in the lateral hypothalamus initially fire to the sight or taste of a food, and then reduce their firing after an animal has eaten its fill of that food. These neurons are selective: After they stop responding to one food, they can still be stimulated by another.

4   Eating is not simply about events in the brain. The presence of other people influences how much you eat. People report eating a greater amount when more people are present for a meal. Part of this effect may simply reflect the fact that when more people are present, the meal takes longer to complete. But this can't be all there is to it: When people eat in groups, they do not vary the size of their meals to reflect their degree of hunger—for example, by eating less for dinner if they had a late lunch—but they do make such adjustments when eating alone.

5   Anything that reminds you of good food you've eaten on a previous occasion can increase hunger. This effect occurs in part because your body responds not only to perceptions of food but also to thoughts of food by secreting **insulin.** Insulin is a hormone that stimulates the storage of food molecules in the form of fat. Thus, insulin reduces the level of food in the blood, which may increase hunger.

—adapted from Kosslyn and Rosenberg, *Fundamentals of Psychology,* pp. 260–261

1. In paragraph 1, the word group that is *least* important to highlight is
   a. the taste of food.
   b. your appetite is stimulated.
   c. as you might suspect from their name.
   d. opioids are released.

2. In paragraph 1, the best use of marking would be to underline
   a. the first few words of each sentence.
   b. the word *opioids* and write "def" in the margin next to its definition.
   c. all of the words that have also been highlighted.
   d. only words that have not been highlighted.

3. In paragraph 2, the word group that is *most* important to highlight is
   a. responses to food-related stimuli change.
   b. some fresh-baked cookies.
   c. doesn't seem quite as heavenly.
   d. a few chocolate chip cookies.

4. The main idea of paragraph 2 is that
   a. eating too many cookies can make you sick.
   b. the smell of cookies baking is usually better than the taste.
   c. your responses to food-related stimuli change as you eat.
   d. people will eat more of the same food if its flavor is changed.

5. In paragraph 3, the word group that is *least* important to highlight is
   a. not surprisingly.
   b. changes in . . . appetite . . . linked to . . . hypothalamus.
   c. neurons . . . fire to . . . sight or taste of food.
   d. neurons are selective.

6. In paragraph 3, the word **fire** is used to mean
   a. heat.   c. remove.
   b. bake.   d. respond.

_____ 7. The main idea of paragraph 4 is that

  a. the brain controls how much you eat.

  b. meals take longer to complete when more people are present.

  c. people tend to eat less dinner when they've had a late lunch.

  d. the presence of other people influences how much food you eat.

_____ 8. In paragraph 4, the word group that is _least_ important to highlight is

  a. presence of other people influences.

  b. greater amount when more people are present.

  c. for example, by eating less for dinner.

  d. adjustments when eating alone.

_____ 9. In paragraph 5, the best use of marking would be to

  a. cross out any unnecessary information.

  b. write "def" in the margin next to the definition of insulin.

  c. circle the transition words _but_ and _thus_.

  d. underline all four sentences.

_____ 10. Insulin works to increase hunger by

  a. reducing the level of food in the blood.

  b. decreasing the levels of fat stored in the body.

  c. releasing chemicals that behave like opium-derived drugs.

  d. stimulating the release of neurons in the brain.

NAME _____   SECTION _____
DATE _____   SCORE _____

PRACTICE TEST 6-3

OUTLINING

Directions: *After reading the following passage, fill in the missing informa-tion in the outline that follows.*

GANGS AS FORMAL ORGANIZATIONS

Inner-city gangs provide a good example of a formal organization. According to a study of 37 different gangs comprising Chicano, Jamaican, Irish, African American, and other ethnic groups, certain basic elements are common to all gang organizations. First, like all organizations, gangs are organized to achieve specific goals—such as securing money, protecting members, gaining prestige in a neighborhood, and providing alternatives to mainstream low-pay, dead-end jobs.

Second, all gangs have defined organizational structures that take three basic forms. Many of the larger ones subscribe to a *hierarchical model* of organization, with a president or "godfather," a vice-president in charge of administrative tasks, a war-lord whose job it is to maintain order within ranks, and a treasurer who collects and manages the gang's finances. A second type, favored by Chicano gangs, which are often smaller and more cohesive than those hierarchically arranged, is the *horizontal organizational model*. It, too, has four offices but they have roughly equal authority and different individuals may assume duties based on preference and need. The *influential model* has neither formal written duties for leaders nor formal titles, but relies instead on charismatic authority. According to gang members, leaders appear "naturally," perhaps because of superior fighting skills, mediating abilities, or some other unique talent that gang members deem important.

—adapted from Thompson and Hickey, *Society in Focus,* p. 147

I. Gangs are organized to _____

   A. Secure money

   B. _____

   C. _____

   D. Provide alternatives to dead-end jobs

II. Gangs have defined organizational structures

    A. _____

        1. President or "godfather"

        2. Vice-president—administrative tasks

        3. _____

        4. _____

    B. Horizontal model

        1. Four offices

            a. _____

            b. Different members may assume duties based on _____

    C. Influential model

        1. No formal written duties or titles for leaders

        2. Natural, charismatic authority established by:

            a. _____

            b. Mediating abilities

            c. _____

MAPPING

Directions: *After reading the following passage from a marketing textbook, select the choice that best completes each of the statements that follow. Then fill in the missing information in the map on page 209.*

THE PRODUCT LIFE CYCLE

The life of a product may be measured in months or years. The humble zipper is an example of a product that has managed to live an exceptionally long life. Invented in the 1800s for use on high-buttoned shoes, the zipper did not make its way onto a pair of trousers until the 1930s; basically unchanged nearly seventy years later, the zipper continues to be an essential part of our wardrobes. From zippers to zip drives, the life of a product can be divided into four separate stages: introduction, growth, maturity and decline.

The first stage of the product life cycle is **introduction,** when customers get their first chance to purchase the good or service. During this early stage, a single company usually produces the product. If the product is accepted and profitable, competitors will follow with their own versions. The goal during this stage is to get first-time buyers to try the product. Sales increase at a steady but slow pace. The company does not make a profit during this stage for two reasons: research and development costs and heavy spending for advertising and other promotional costs. How long the introduction stage lasts depends on a number of factors, including marketplace acceptance and producer willingness to support the product during its start-up.

Not all products make it past the introduction stage. For a new product to be successful, consumers must first know about it. Then they must believe that the product is something they need. Thus, marketing during this stage often focuses on informing consumers about the product, how to use it, and its benefits. Overall, 38 percent of all new products fail.

The second stage in the product life cycle, the **growth stage,** sees a rapid increase in sales while profits increase and peak. The goal here is to encourage brand loyalty by convincing the market that this brand is superior to others in the category. When competitors appear, marketers must use heavy advertising and other types of promotion. Price competition may develop, driving profits down.

The **maturity stage** of the product life cycle is usually the longest. Sales peak and then begin to level off and even decline while profit margins narrow. Competition grows intense when remaining competitors fight for a piece of a shrinking pie. Because most customers have already accepted the product, sales are often to replace a "worn-out" item or to take advantage of product improvements. To remain competitive and maintain market share during the maturity stage, firms may tinker with the marketing mix by adding "bells and whistles" to their products' features, or they may try to attract new users of the product.

The **decline stage** of the product life cycle is characterized by a decrease in sales. Often this is because new technology has made the product obsolete, as when computers caused the decline of the typewriter. Although a single firm may still be profitable, the market as a whole begins to shrink, profits decline, and suppliers pull out. In this stage, there are usually many competitors with no one having a distinct advantage. A firm's major product decision in the decline stage is whether or not to keep the product. Once the product is no longer profitable, it drains resources from the firm—resources that could help develop new products.

—adapted from Solomon and Stuart, *Marketing: Real People, Real Choices,* pp. 266–269

_____ 1. The topic of this passage is
   a. the zipper.
   b. new products.
   c. competition.
   d. the product life cycle.

_____ 2. The longest stage of the product life cycle usually is the
   a. introduction stage.
   b. growth stage.
   c. maturity stage.
   d. decline stage.

_____ 3. The two stages in which profits typically peak are the
   a. introduction and growth stages.
   b. growth and maturity stages.
   c. introduction and maturity stages.
   d. maturity and decline stages.

_____ 4. The primary goal during the introduction stage of a product is to
   a. get first-time buyers to try the product.
   b. encourage brand loyalty by convincing buyers that a particular brand is better than others in the category.
   c. persuade buyers to replace worn-out items or take advantage of product improvements.
   d. decide whether or not to keep the product.

_____ 5. In the last paragraph, the topic sentence begins with the words
   a. "The decline stage."
   b. "Often this."
   c. "Although a single."
   d. "Once the product."

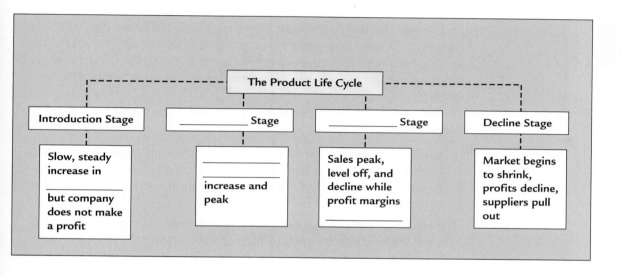

OUTLINING

Directions: *After reading the following passage, fill in the missing informa-tion in the outline that follows.*

CLASSIFYING GOODS AND SERVICES

One way to classify a product is according to expected buyers. Buyers fall into two groups: buyers of consumer products and buyers of industrial products. The consumer and industrial buying processes differ significantly. Not surprisingly, marketing products to consumers is vastly different from marketing them to other companies.

Consumer products are commonly divided into three categories that reflect buyer behavior:

- Convenience goods (such as milk and newspapers) and convenience services (such as those offered by fast-food restaurants) are consumed rapidly and regu-larly. They are inexpensive and are purchased often and with little expenditure of time and effort.

- Shopping goods (such as stereos and tires) and shopping services (such as insur-ance) are more expensive and are purchased less often than convenience prod-ucts. Consumers often compare brands, sometimes in different stores. They may also evaluate alternatives in terms of style, performance, color, price, and other criteria.

- Specialty goods (such as wedding gowns) and specialty services (such as catering for wedding receptions) are extremely important and expensive purchases. Con-sumers usually decide on precisely what they want and will accept no substitutes. They will often go from store to store, sometimes spending a great deal of money and time to get a specific product.

Depending on how much they cost and how they will be used, industrial prod-ucts can be divided into two categories: expense and capital items.

- Expense items are any materials and services that are consumed within a year by firms producing other goods or supplying other services. The most obvious ex-pense items are industrial goods used directly in the production process (for ex-ample, bulkloads of tea processed into tea bags).

- Capital items are permanent (expensive and long-lasting) goods and services. All these items have expected lives of more than a year and typically up to several years. Expensive buildings (offices, factories), fixed equipment (water towers, baking ovens), and accessory equipment (computers, airplanes) are capital goods.

Capital services are those for which long-term commitments are made. These may include purchases for employee food services, building and equipment maintenance, or legal services. Because capital items are expensive and purchased infrequently, they often involve decisions by high-level managers.

—Ebert and Griffin, *Business Essentials,* pp. 266–267

I. Consumer products

    A. Convenience goods and services

        1. Examples: milk, newspapers, fast-food places

        2. Consumed _____

        3. Inexpensive

        4. Purchased _____

        5. Little expenditure of time and effort

    B. Shopping goods and services

        1. Examples: stereos, tires, insurance

        2. More _____

        3. Purchased less often

        4. Brands _____

        5. Alternatives evaluated

            a.   Style

            b.   Performance

            c.   Color

            d.   Price

            e.   Other criteria

    C. _____

        1. Examples: wedding gowns, caterers

        2. Very important and expensive

        3. No substitutes

        4. Large expenditure of _____

II. Industrial products

    A. Expense items

        1. Materials and services consumed within 1 year

        2. Goods used _____

        3. Example: bulk tea packaged into teabags

    B. _____

        1. Permanent goods and services lasting

           _____

        2. Examples of goods

           a.   Expensive buildings

           b.   Fixed equipment

           c.   Accessory equipment

        3. Examples of services

           a.   Employee food services

           b.   Building / equipment maintenance

           c.   Legal services

        4. Decisions involve _____

PERSONAL SAFETY ONLINE
Wendy G. Lehnert

Do you believe that your Internet account is secure? In this selection, you will learn that your computer is not secure on the Internet unless you make it secure.

Vocabulary Preview

These are some of the difficult words in this essay. The definitions here will help you if you can't figure out the meanings from the sentence context or word parts.

access (par. 1) the ability to enter a place (in this case, the Internet)

Netizen (par. 1) a combination of the words *citizen* and *Internet*, meaning someone who is active on the Internet

digital trespasser (par. 3) someone who invades another person's account on the Internet; also known as a hacker

protocol (par. 4) the rules of acceptable conduct or etiquette

ruse (par. 5) a crafty scheme or clever trick designed to fool someone

---

1   The Internet gives you access to a very public space. It might not feel particularly public when you dial in from the privacy of your own home. However, each time that you connect you enter a public space. This means that your conduct will be visible to others, as well as monitored by various network administrators (and others) who may be invisible to you. You have rights as well as responsibilities. To be a good *Netizen* of the Internet, you need to act responsibly. And because of aggressive data collection, intrusive advertisers, underhanded business practices, and malicious miscreants, you need to protect your rights.

2   Being online is not so very different from being offline. When you visit a large city, you plan your trip, tuck your wallet in a safe pocket, obey the law, and use common sense. Going online is much the same. When you log on to the Internet, you need to understand and follow the behavioral codes that are specific to the Net, and you need to minimize your personal risk.

3   Your first line of defense against all kinds of mischief and misery is your password. You probably don't have a password for your personal computer, and that's fine. It's the password on your Internet access account that needs to be handled with care. Someone who breaks into your university account or ISP (Internet Service Provider) account is probably hoping to break into more than only your account. Starting from your account, a digital trespasser might be able to break into other accounts and acquire

access privileges normally reserved for system administrators. You must protect your computer account not only for your own sake but also for that of everyone in your immediate computing environment.

4   In a secure computing environment, passwords are stored by using special techniques so that no one, including the most powerful system administrator, can retrieve a password for a given account. No system administrator will ever need to know your password for the sake of legitimate system maintenance and will never ask for it. Privileged administrators can bypass the usual password protocol if an appropriate circumstance justifies it. Any stranger who asks you for your password is up to no good. No matter what someone tells you, no matter how forceful their argument, don't buy it.

5   Further, if you ever receive an e-mail message from some official-sounding person, with an official-looking return address, that includes a request for your password, realize this is a ruse. Hackers who want to break into computer accounts often use elaborate scenarios in an effort to take advantage of the unwary. This is called **social engineering.** Never give your password to *anyone,* including your own mother. As soon as you share your password with another person, that person also becomes a potential target for social engineering, and you are no longer in control of your own computer account.

6   People can also steal passwords without resorting to social engineering. Computer programs can run through a full dictionary of the English language in an effort to "guess" your password. Dictionaries of common names are also used for the same purpose. You can foil these programs by carefully creating passwords that are not words in a dictionary or proper names. Examples of bad passwords are "television" and "Jessica." An example of a good password is "fiNallY93."

7   Finally, never use the same password at more than one Web site.

8   A safe, secure password always contains the following elements:

- At least six characters (eight is better)
- Both lowercase and uppercase letters
- At least one numeric character

9   Regardless of how carefully you create your passwords, you should still change them every month or two. Passwords can be "sniffed out" by software that is designed to eavesdrop on your Internet communications.

━━ ▪ ━━

Directions: *Select the letter of the choice that best completes each of the following statements.*

CHECKING YOUR COMPREHENSION

_____ 1. The central thought of this selection is that
  a. there are several different methods of computer hacking.
  b. Internet users must protect their passwords.
  c. Internet users should follow rules of behavior on the Internet.
  d. antivirus software is a worthwhile investment.

_____ 2. The main idea of paragraph 1 is that
  a. the Internet is a public place and you need to protect your rights.
  b. network administrators monitor everything you do on the Internet.
  c. data collectors can obtain information about you without your knowledge.
  d. the Internet is private only when you dial in from your home computer.

_____ 3. The topic sentence of paragraph 3 is the
  a. first sentence, which begins "Your first line . . ."
  b. second sentence, which begins "You probably . . ."
  c. fourth sentence, which begins "Someone who . . ."
  d. fifth sentence, which begins "Starting from . . ."

_____ 4. The main idea of paragraph 4 is that your password
  a. is never secure.
  b. is typically required for system maintenance.
  c. can easily be retrieved without your permission.
  d. should not be given to anyone.

_____ 5. In the context of this selection, social engineering occurs when
  a. computer users apply safeguards to protect their privacy while they are online.
  b. software engineers create programs to prevent hackers from breaking into computer accounts.
  c. computer hackers use elaborate scenarios to persuade a person to reveal his or her password.
  d. system administrators bypass the usual security channels to obtain a person's password.

_____ 6. In paragraph 2, the most important group of words to highlight is

  a. "when you visit a large city."

  b. "tuck your wallet in a safe pocket."

  c. "going online is much the same."

  d. "minimize your personal risk."

_____ 7. Of the following choices, the one that best summarizes paragraph 3 is

  a. It doesn't matter if you don't have a password for your personal computer. Most hackers want to break into accounts that give them the privileges of system administrators.

  b. It is important to protect your password to your Internet access account. Hackers may use your account to break into other accounts and gain the access privileges of system administrators. By protecting your own account, you help keep the other accounts in your computing environment safe.

  c. A hacker who breaks into your university account or ISP account can then break into other accounts. Starting from your account, a hacker can cause problems for everyone in your immediate computing environment.

  d. To protect yourself and everyone in your computing environment, you should create a password for your Internet access account. The access privileges that normally are reserved for system administrators are one goal of digital trespassers. You do not need a password for your personal computer.

Questions 8–10 refer to the following map of the selection.

_____ 8. The best word or phrase to fill in the blank labeled A is

  a. only when necessary.   c. every month or two.

  b. once a year.   d. every day.

_____ 9. The best word or phrase to fill in the blank labeled B is

  a. numbers.   c. blank spaces.

  b. your name.   d. different fonts.

_____ 10. The best word or phrase to fill in the blank labeled C is

  a. foreign words.   c. punctuation.

  b. proper names.   d. difficult words.

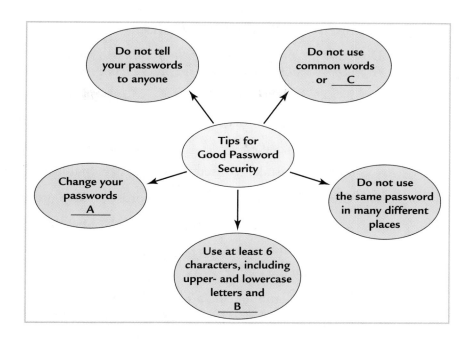

USING CONTEXT AND WORD PARTS

_____ 11. In paragraph 1, **miscreants** means

    a assistants.   c. viewers.

    b. advertisers.   d. wrongdoers.

_____ 12. In paragraph 4, **legitimate** means

    a. useless.   c. valid.

    b. improper.   d. inconsiderate.

_____ 13. In paragraph 5, **elaborate** means

    a. fancy.   c. careless.

    b. complex.   d. sincere.

_____ 14. In paragraph 6, **foil** means

    a. prevent.   c. promote.

    b. allow.   d. follow.

_____ 15. In paragraph 9, **eavesdrop** means

    a. interfere with.   c. discourage.

    b. listen in on.   d. distribute.

REVIEWING DIFFICULT VOCABULARY

Directions: *Complete each of the following sentences by inserting a word from the Vocabulary Preview on page 213 in the space provided.*

16. Lucia's company teaches business executives the _____ for interacting with customers in Latin American countries.

17. Edgar was denied _____ to his bank account when he mistakenly used the wrong personal identification number.

18. Creating the right kinds of passwords can help prevent a _____ from breaking into your ISP account.

19. Being a good _____ means acting responsibly while you are online.

20. The e-mail announcing a new fee for our ISP turned out to be a _____, so we reported it to the system administrator.

QUESTIONS FOR DISCUSSION

1. Have you ever experienced a violation of your computer privacy? Describe what steps you took to avoid repeating the experience.
2. Do you think the freedom offered by the Internet is worth the potential risks to your security? Discuss what limits, if any, you would place on access to the Internet.
3. How will the information in this selection change the way you use the Internet? Describe what you plan to do differently.

WRITING ACTIVITIES

1. Create a list of ways to be a good Netizen. Include "do's and don'ts" of e-mail etiquette (for example, "writing an e-mail message in all capital letters is the same as shouting").
2. Write a paragraph arguing either for or against placing restrictions on Internet users for the sake of security.
3. Explore this government site concerning Internet security: http://onguardonline.gov/index.html. Write a paragraph about one new thing you learned from it.

Chapter 6: Keeping Track of Information

RECORDING YOUR PROGRESS

Test	Number Right		Score
Practice Test 6-1	_____ $\times$ 10	=	_____ %
Practice Test 6-2	_____ $\times$ 10	=	_____ %
Practice Test 6-3	_____ $\times$ 10	=	_____ %
Mastery Test 6-1	_____ $\times$ 10	=	_____ %
Mastery Test 6-2	_____ $\times$ 10	=	_____ %
Mastery Test 6-3	_____ $\times$ 5	=	_____ %

EVALUATING YOUR PROGRESS

Based on your test performance, rate how well you have mastered the skills taught in this chapter by checking one of the boxes below or by writing your own evaluation.

☐ **Need More Improvement**
Tip: Try completing the Outlining and Summarizing—Spring Break in Florida module in the Reading Skills section on the MyReadingLab Web site at **http://www.ablongman.com/myreadinglab** to fine-tune the skills that you have learned in this chapter.

☐ **Need More Practice**
Tip: Try using the Outlining and Summarizing—Spring Break in Florida module in the Reading Skills section on the MyReadingLab Web site at **http://www.ablongman.com/myreadinglab** to brush up on the skills taught in this chapter, or visit this textbook's Companion Web site at **http://www.ablongman.com/mcwhorter** for extra practice.

☐ **Good**
Tip: To maintain your skills, quickly review this chapter by using this textbook's Companion Web site at **http://www.ablongman.com/mcwhorter**.

☐ **Excellent**

YOUR EVALUATION: _____

_____

_____

_____

THINK ABOUT IT!

Study the two photographs below. What do these photographs have in common?

You probably discovered that each photo shows how something is organized. Understanding how a mall, a college campus, or a large discount store is organized makes it easier to get around. You can find what you need easily and avoid wasting time wandering around. Likewise, when reading paragraphs in textbooks, you can find your way around more easily and save time if you know how they are organized.

Good writers try to follow a clear organization, or *pattern*, when they write so that readers can easily find and understand the important points they are making.

CHAPTER 7

Recognizing the Basic Patterns of Organization

What Are Patterns of Organization?

Just as there is no one way to organize a mall or a college campus, there is no one way to organize a paragraph or essay. Writers use a variety of *patterns of organization*, depending on what they want to accomplish. These patterns, then, are the different ways that writers present their ideas.

To help you think a bit about patterns, complete each of the following steps:

1. Study each of the following drawings for a few seconds (count to ten as you look at each one).

2. Cover up the drawings and try to draw each from memory.

3. Check to see how many you had exactly correct.

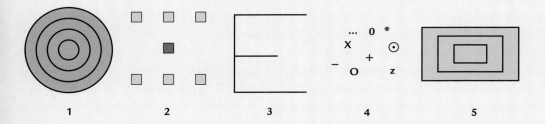

You probably drew all but the fourth correctly. Why do you think you got that one wrong? How does it differ from the others?

Drawings 1, 2, 3, and 5 have patterns. Drawing 4, however, has no pattern; it is just a group of randomly arranged symbols.

From this experiment you can see that it is easier to remember drawings that have a pattern—a clear form of organization. The same is true of written material. If you can see how a paragraph or essay is organized, it is easier to understand and remember. In this chapter you will learn about some of the common patterns writers use and how to recognize them: (1) example, (2) definition, (3) chronological order and process, and (4) listing.

Example

One of the clearest ways to explain something is to give an example. This is especially true when a subject is unfamiliar. Suppose, for instance, you are taking a course in child psychology and your sister asks you to explain what aggressive behavior is in children. You might explain by giving examples of aggressive behavior, such as biting other children, striking playmates, and throwing objects at others. Through examples, your sister would get a fairly good idea of what aggressive behavior is.

When organizing a paragraph, a writer often states the main idea first and then follows it with one or more examples. The preceding paragraph takes this approach. The main idea in the topic sentence is supported by the example about explaining aggressive behavior to a sister. In some paragraphs, of course, a writer might use several examples. And in a longer piece of writing, a separate paragraph may be used for each example.

Here is one way to visualize the example pattern in a paragraph:

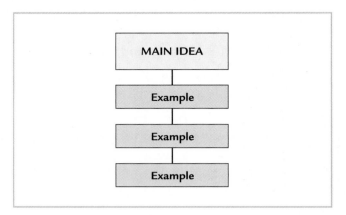

Notice how this example pattern is developed in the following paragraph.

Many animals undergo a metamorphosis as they move from one developmental stage to the next in their growth cycle. A maggot transforms into a fly. A tadpole hatches from an egg and develops into an adult frog. A caterpillar changes from its larval form into a moth or a butterfly.

In the preceding paragraph, the writer explains metamorphosis through a variety of examples. You could visualize the paragraph as follows:

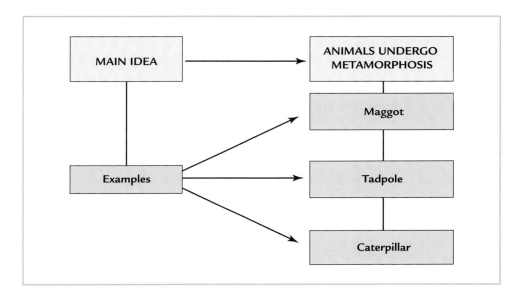

As you recall from Chapter 4, sometimes writers use transitional words—*for example, for instance,* or *such as*—to signal the reader that an example is to follow. The writer of the following paragraph uses transitions in this way:

> New technologies are helping to make alternative sources of energy cost-effective. In Pennsylvania and Connecticut, *for example,* the waste from landfills is loaded into furnaces and burned to generate electricity for thousands of homes. Natural sources of energy, *such as* the sun and the wind, are also becoming more attractive. The electricity produced by 300 wind turbines in northern California, *for instance,* has resulted in a savings of approximately 60,000 barrels of oil per year. Solar energy also has many applications, from pocket calculators to public telephones to entire homes, and is even used in spacecraft, where conventional power is unavailable.
>
> —adapted from Bergman and Renwick, *Introduction to Geography,* p. 343
> and Carnes and Garraty, *The American Nation,* p. 916

By using examples and transitions, the writer describes alternative sources of energy. Although writers don't always use transitions with examples, be on the lookout for them as you read.

Directions: *The following paragraphs, all of which are about dietary fat, use the example pattern. Read each of them and answer the questions that follow.*

A. There are different kinds of dietary fat. **Saturated fats** are found in animal products such as meat, eggs, milk, and dairy products and in palm oil and coconut oil, which come from plants. This is the type of fat that is deposited along the walls of your arteries. The accumulation of this fat is a contributing factor to diseases of the cardiovascular system such as high blood pressure and heart attack. Because of this, the USDA's *Dietary Guidelines for Americans* recommends that saturated fats account for less than 10 percent of your total caloric intake.

—Pruitt and Stein, *HealthStyles*, p. 100

1. What transition does the writer use to introduce the examples of saturated fats?

_____

2. Does the topic sentence occur first, second, or last? _____

3. List the six examples of animal products and plants in which saturated fats are found.

a. _____   d. _____

b. _____   e. _____

c. _____   f. _____

4. List the two examples of diseases of the cardiovascular system.

a. _____   b. _____

B. Unsaturated fats are either polyunsaturated or monounsaturated. Both types of unsaturated fats can lower body cholesterol. Examples of **polyunsaturated fats** are corn oil, soybean oil, and cottonseed oil. Some fish are also sources of polyunsaturated fat. **Monounsaturated fats** are found in peanut oil, olive oil, and canola oil. Although beef fat, lard, and chicken fat have quite a bit of monounsaturated fat, they are also very high in saturated fat. Less than 10 percent of your total daily calories should come from polyunsaturated fat and a little more than 10 percent from monounsaturated fat.

—Pruitt and Stein, *HealthStyles*, p. 100

5. Does the topic sentence occur first, second, or last? _____

6. The writer gives four examples of polyunsaturated fat. List them in the diagram below.

> SOURCES OF POLYUNSATURATED FAT
>
> a. _____
>
> b. _____
>
> c. _____
>
> d. _____

7. The writer also gives six examples of monounsaturated fat. List only the three that are also high in saturated fat

   a. _____   b. _____   c. _____

C. Cholesterol is a fat-like substance that is manufactured by the liver and is necessary for certain bodily processes; for instance, cholesterol is essential to the production of bile. Cholesterol is also taken into the body when you eat animal products such as meat, milk, eggs, and dairy foods. Plant foods do not contain cholesterol.

   —Pruitt and Stein, *HealthStyles*, p. 100

8. What transition does the writer use to introduce one of the functions of cholesterol? _____

9. What other transition does the writer use to signal that examples will follow? _____

10. What type of foods does *not* contain cholesterol?

    _____

Definition

Another pattern writers follow is definition. Let's say that you see a game of lacrosse being played in your neighborhood and you mention this to a friend. Since your friend does not know what lacrosse is, you have to define it. Your definition should describe the sport's characteristics or features, explaining how it is different from other sports. Thus, you might define lacrosse as follows:

> Lacrosse was first played by Native Americans, making it the oldest sport in North America. Modern lacrosse is a fast-paced game played on a field by two teams of ten players each. During the game, players use the crosse—a long-handled stick with a webbed pouch—to maneuver a ball into the opposing team's goal. There are youth lacrosse teams for boys and girls, college and amateur teams for men and women, and professional teams for men.

This definition can be shown as follows:

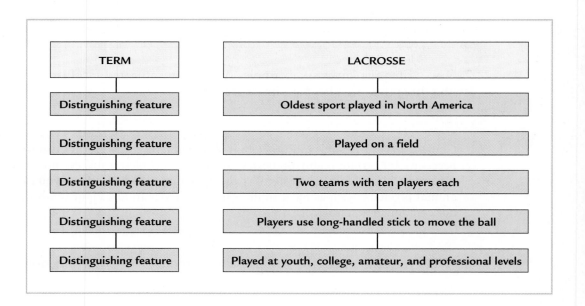

As you read passages that use the definition pattern, keep these questions in mind:

1. What is being defined?
2. What makes it different from other items or ideas?

Apply these questions to the following paragraph:

> **Humid subtropical climates** have several defining characteristics. They occur in latitudes between about 25 and 40 degrees on the eastern sides of continents and between about 35 and 50 degrees on the western sides. These climates are relatively warm most of the year but have at least occasional freezing temperatures during the winter. Most humid subtropical climates have deciduous species of vegetation that lose their leaves in autumn and become dormant in winter. Eastern China, the southeastern U.S., and parts of Brazil and Argentina are the largest areas of humid subtropical climates.
>
> —adapted from Bergman and Renwick, *Introduction to Geography*, p. 80

When you ask yourself the preceding questions, you can see, first of all, that *humid subtropical climates* are being defined. In addition, the definition lists four ways that humid subtropical climates are different from other climates: (1) they occur in latitudes between 25 and 40 degrees on the eastern sides of continents and between 35 and 50 degrees on the western sides, (2) they are warm most of the year but have some freezing temperatures during the winter, (3) they have deciduous species of vegetation that lose their leaves in autumn and become dormant in winter, and (4) the largest areas of humid subtropical climates are in eastern China, the southeastern U.S., Brazil, and Argentina.

Combining Definition and Example

It is important to note that definitions are often combined with examples. For instance, if someone asks you to define the term *fiction writer,* you might begin by saying that a fiction writer is someone who creates novels and stories that describe imaginary people or events. You might also give some examples of well-known fiction writers, such as Ernest Hemingway or Stephen King. When definition and example are used together in this way, you can visualize the pattern as follows:

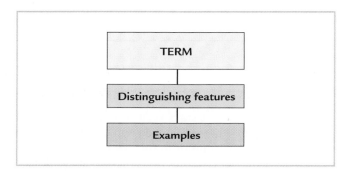

You will often encounter the definition and example pattern in your textbooks. An author will define a term and then use examples to explain it further, as shown in this passage from a health text:

> Generally, positive stress, or stress that presents the opportunity for personal growth and satisfaction, is called **eustress**. Getting married, starting school, beginning a career, developing new friendships, and learning a new physical skill all give rise to eustress.
>
> —Donatelle and Davis, *Access to Health,* p. 65

First the authors define *eustress,* and then they provide several examples to make the definition more understandable. You have probably already noticed that textbook authors often put an important term in **boldface** type when they define it. This makes it easier for students to find definitions as they read or study for tests.

Exercise 7–2

Directions: *Read each of the following paragraphs and answer the questions that follow.*

A. The **integumentary system** is the external covering of the body, or the skin. It waterproofs the body and cushions and protects the deeper tissues from injury. It also excretes salts and urea in perspiration and helps regulate body temperature. Temperature, pressure, and pain receptors located in the skin alert us to what is happening at the body surface.

—Mareib, *Essentials of Human Anatomy and Physiology,* p. 3

1. What term is being defined?

   _____

2. The writer mentions several distinguishing features of this term. List three of them.

   a. _____

   b. _____

   c. _____

B. The patterns of stars seen in the sky are usually called constellations. In astronomy, however, the term constellation refers to a region of the sky. Any place you point in the sky belongs to some constellation; familiar patterns of stars merely help locate particular constellations. For example, the constellation Orion includes all the stars in the familiar pattern of the hunter, along with the region of the sky in which these stars are found.

—Bennett, *The Cosmic Perspective, Brief Edition*, p. 28

3. What term is being defined?

   _____

4. What example is given to illustrate the term being defined?

   _____

5. What transitional phrase does the writer use? _____

C. The name "tale" is sometimes applied to any story, whether short or long, true or fictitious. But defined in a more limited sense, a **tale** is a story, usually short, that sets forth strange and wonderful events in more or less bare summary, without detailed character-drawing. "Tale" implies a story in which the goal is to reveal something marvelous rather than to reveal the character of someone. In the English folk tale "Jack and the Beanstalk," for instance, we take away a more vivid impression of the miraculous beanstalk and the giant who dwells at its top than of Jack's mind or personality.

—adapted from Kennedy and Gioia, *Literature*, p. 7

6. What term is being defined?

   _____

7. What example is given to illustrate the term being defined?

   _____

8. What transitional phrase do the writers use? _____

D. The **nervous system,** the master controlling and communicating system of the body, has three overlapping functions: (1) It uses millions of sensory receptors to monitor changes occurring both inside and outside the body. These changes are called stimuli and the gathered information is called *sensory input.* (2) It processes and interprets the sensory input and decides what should be done at each moment—a process called *integration.* (3) It causes a response by activating our muscles or glands; the response is called *motor output.* An example will illustrate how these functions work together. When you are driving and see a red light ahead (sensory input), your nervous system integrates this information (red light means "stop"), and your foot goes for the brake (motor output).

—Marieb, *Anatomy and Physiology,* p. 387

9. What term is being defined? Enter it in the diagram on the next page.

10. In defining this term, the writer mentions three distinguishing features. List them in the diagram on the next page.

```
TERM: _____

          Distinguishing features:

a. _____
   _____

b. _____
   _____

c. _____
   _____
```

Chronological Order and Process

The terms **chronological order** and **process** both refer to the order in which something occurs or is done. When writers tell a story, they usually present events in chronological order. In other words, they start with the first event, continue with the second, and so on. For example, if you were telling a friend about finding a new part-time job, you would probably start by explaining how you found out about the job, continue by describing your interview, and end with the result—the manager was impressed with you and hired you on the spot. You would put events in order according to the *time* they occurred, beginning with the first event.

Common Transitions in Chronological Order and Process					
first	before	following	second	after	last
later	then	during	next	in addition	when
another	also	until	as soon as	finally	meanwhile

When you read stories for an English class or material in a history or political science text, you will often encounter chronological order. When writers use this pattern, they often include time transitions, such as *first, next,* and *finally* (see box). They may also use actual dates to help readers keep track of the sequence of events.

EXAMPLE

Organized baseball teams first emerged in the 1840s, but the game only became truly popular during the Civil War, when it was a major form of camp recreation for the troops. After the war professional teams began to appear, and in 1876 teams in eight cities formed the National League. The American League followed in 1901. After a brief period of rivalry, the two leagues made peace in 1903, the year of the first World Series.

—adapted from Garraty and Carnes, *The American Nation*, p. 518

As you can see in this paragraph from a history text, the writers use chronological order to discuss the evolution of organized baseball. They use several phrases to show the reader the time sequence—*in the 1840s, during the Civil War, After the war, in 1876, in 1901,* and *in 1903.* As you read, look for such phrases as well as for time transitions.

Writers also follow a time sequence when they use the **process pattern**—when they explain how something is done or made. When writers explain how to put together a bookcase, how to knit a sweater, or how bees make honey, they use steps to show the appropriate order.

EXAMPLE

To make a basic white sauce, follow a few easy steps. First, melt two tablespoons of butter over low heat. Next, add two tablespoons of flour and stir until the flour and butter are combined. Then add one cup of milk and continue stirring over low heat. Finally, when the mixture has thickened, add salt and pepper, or other seasonings, to taste.

This writer uses four time transitions—*first, next, then,* and *finally*—to make the order clear for the reader. Note that she also uses the word *steps* in the topic sentence. In the process pattern and in other patterns as well, the topic sentence often provides a clue as to the kind of pattern that will be used.

You can visualize and draw the chronological order and process patterns as follows:

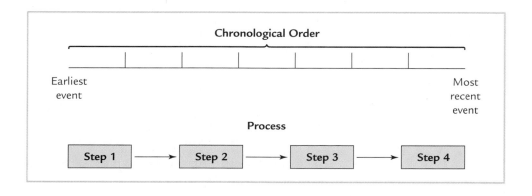

Sample maps showing chronological order and process appear in Chapter 6 (see Figures 6-3 and 6-4, pp. 192–193).

Directions: *Using either chronological order or process, put each of the following groups of sentences in the correct order. For each sentence, write a number from 1 to 4 in the space provided, beginning with the topic sentence.*

1. _____   Rail travel originated in Europe in 1825, and four years later, North America welcomed the advent of passenger rail service.

   _____   Transcontinental service began in the United States in 1869 and in Canada in 1885.

   _____   Passenger rail service has been an important form of domestic transportation for more than 175 years.

   _____   In 1875 Fred Harvey introduced the golden age of passenger railroad service in the U.S., with the addition of dining cars and lodging facilities.

   —adapted from Cook, Yale, and Marqua,
   Tourism: The Business of Travel, p. 102

2. _____   Next, chemicals are released that attract even more platelets to the site.

   _____   Basically, once damage has occurred, blood elements called platelets immediately begin to cling to the injured site.

   _____   This rapidly growing pile-up of platelets initiates the sequence of events that finally forms a clot.

   _____   Blood clotting is a normal response to a break in the lining of a blood vessel.

   —adapted from Marieb, *Anatomy and Physiology*, p. 13

3. _____   A gold rush into Colorado in 1859 sent thousands of greedy prospectors across the Plains to drive the Cheyenne and Arapaho from land guaranteed them in 1851.

   _____   Thus it happened that in 1862, most of the Plains Indians rose up against the whites.

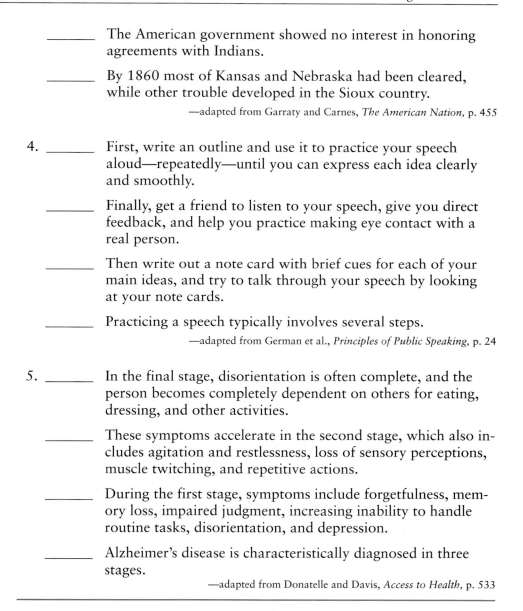

_____ The American government showed no interest in honoring agreements with Indians.

_____ By 1860 most of Kansas and Nebraska had been cleared, while other trouble developed in the Sioux country.

—adapted from Garraty and Carnes, *The American Nation*, p. 455

4. _____ First, write an outline and use it to practice your speech aloud—repeatedly—until you can express each idea clearly and smoothly.

_____ Finally, get a friend to listen to your speech, give you direct feedback, and help you practice making eye contact with a real person.

_____ Then write out a note card with brief cues for each of your main ideas, and try to talk through your speech by looking at your note cards.

_____ Practicing a speech typically involves several steps.

—adapted from German et al., *Principles of Public Speaking*, p. 24

5. _____ In the final stage, disorientation is often complete, and the person becomes completely dependent on others for eating, dressing, and other activities.

_____ These symptoms accelerate in the second stage, which also includes agitation and restlessness, loss of sensory perceptions, muscle twitching, and repetitive actions.

_____ During the first stage, symptoms include forgetfulness, memory loss, impaired judgment, increasing inability to handle routine tasks, disorientation, and depression.

_____ Alzheimer's disease is characteristically diagnosed in three stages.

—adapted from Donatelle and Davis, *Access to Health*, p. 533

Listing

Although writers often want to put events or items in a specific time sequence, sometimes they just want to list them. **Listing**, then, is used when a particular order isn't so important. If you were telling a friend about three places you would like to visit or three stores you like to shop at, you might just list them. It wouldn't matter which place or which store was listed first.

EXAMPLE

The city of San Antonio, Texas, offers many attractions for visitors. One famous site is the Alamo, the eighteenth-century Spanish mission that had a historic role in Texas' revolution against Mexico. Another San Antonio highlight is much more modern: the River Walk, a shopping, dining, and entertainment promenade situated along the San Antonio River. For those interested in wildlife, the San Antonio Zoo and Aquarium houses more than 3,500 animals from 750 species. Visitors may also want to take in the serenity and beauty of the Japanese Tea Gardens next door to the zoo.

In the preceding paragraph, the writer might have put any of San Antonio's attractions first. The order simply depends on how the writer wants to present the material. Specific steps or time sequences are not important. Note, however, that the writer uses the transitions *another* and *also* to link the attractions together.

You can visualize the listing pattern as follows:

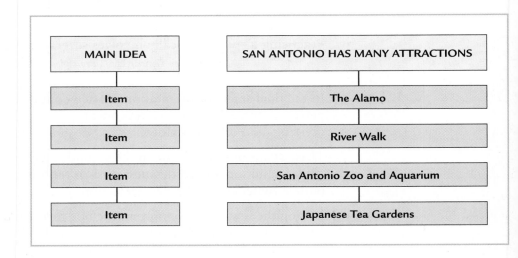

Textbook authors often use listing when they want to present information. The order is the way *they* want to present the material. It is not determined by time or steps.

EXAMPLE

Precisely because the visual system is so complicated, it does not always work perfectly. For example, people with *myopia,* or nearsightedness, have difficulty focusing on distant objects. Myopia is usually caused by an eyeball that is too long to focus the image on the retina properly. Another visual problem is *hypermetropia,* or farsightedness, in which people have difficulty focusing on near objects. Such farsightedness usually results from an eyeball that is too short, or a lens that is too thin, to allow the image on the retina to focus properly. Finally, there is *astigmatism,* a defect in the curvature of the cornea or lens, causing blurriness. Astigmatism, like nearsightedness and farsightedness, can be corrected with eyeglasses (and sometimes with contact lenses).

—adapted from Kosslyn and Rosenberg, *Psychology: The Brain, the Person, the World,* p. 102

The authors of this passage could have listed the visual problems in a different order. They might, for example, have discussed astigmatism first and myopia last. The decision was up to them because they were not talking about something related to time.

As in the paragraph about San Antonio, textbook writers also use transitions to link the items in a list. In the preceding example, the transitions *for example, another,* and *finally* tie together the three types of visual problems. Other transitions—such as *first* and *in addition*—are also used in the listing pattern.

Exercise 7–4

Directions: *After reading the following paragraph, select the choice that best answers each of the questions that follow.*

The federal government has a handful of **government corporations.** These are not exactly like private corporations in which you can buy stock and collect dividends, but they *are* like private corporations—and different from other parts of the government—in two ways. First, they provide a service that *could be* handled by the private sector. Second, they typically charge for their services, though often at rates cheaper than those the consumer would pay to a private-sector producer. Government corporations include the Tennessee Valley Authority (TVA), which provides electricity to millions of Americans in Tennessee and neighboring states, and Comsat, a modern-day government corporation that sells time-sharing on NASA satellites. Of course, the government's largest and most well-known corporation is the U.S. Postal Service.

—adapted from Edwards et al., *Government in America,* pp. 478–479

_____   1. The topic of the paragraph is
          a. the U.S. Postal Service.
          b. government corporations.
          c. private corporations.
          d. government regulations.

_____ 2. In the third and fourth sentences, the writers mention two ways that government corporations resemble private corporations. What pattern of organization do these sentences follow?

    a. chronological order

    b. process

    c. definition

    d. listing

_____ 3. In the last two sentences, the writers mention three government corporations. What pattern of organization do these sentences follow?

    a. process

    b. chronological order

    c. example

    d. definition

4. Complete the following outline of the paragraph. Some items have been filled in for you.

I. Main idea: The federal government has several government corporations.

  A. Government corporations are similar to private corporations.

    1. _____

    2. _____

      _____

  B. There are three examples of government corporations.

    1. _____

      _____

    2. Comsat is a modern-day government corporation that sells time-sharing on NASA satellites.

    3. _____

      _____

Combining Patterns of Organization

As you saw in Exercise 7–4, some pieces of writing may use more than one pattern. In the beginning of this chapter, for instance, you learned how definition and example could be combined, with a writer defining a term and then giving examples to clarify the definition. As you read textbooks, novels, magazine articles, and newspapers, you will see that writers often combine other patterns as well. Within a story that is in chronological order, for instance, a writer might include a list of items. And writers almost always use examples, regardless of the overall pattern they are following. In the next chapter you will learn about two more patterns—comparison/contrast and cause/effect—and how these patterns, too, are often combined with lists, examples, and definitions.

The Textbook Challenge

Part A: Current Issues Reader

Using the textbook excerpt "Whether to Vote: A Citizen's First Choice" (p. 514), identify at least one paragraph for each of the following patterns of organization:

Pattern	Paragraph #
Example	_____
Chronological order	_____
Definition	_____

Part B: A College Textbook

Using a chapter from one of your own textbooks, identify at least one paragraph for each of the following patterns of organization:

Pattern	Page #	Paragraph #
Example	____	____
Listing	____	____
Definition	____	____
Chronological order	____	____
Process	____	____

What Have You Learned?

Directions: *To check your understanding of the chapter, select the word or phrase from the box below that best completes each of the following sentences. Not all of the words in the box will be used.*

listing	first	definitions
patterns of organization	transitional phrases	examples
for instance	chronological order	in contrast
process	boldface type	

1. The different ways that writers present their ideas are known as

   _____.

2. A transitional phrase that signals the reader that an example is to follow is _____.

3. Writers often put important terms in _____ to make it easier for readers to find definitions.

4. When writers tell a story, they usually present events in

   _____.

5. The _____ pattern is used to explain how something is done or made.

6. Common transitions in chronological order and process are

   _____ and *finally*.

7. When a particular order of events or items is not important, writers often use the _____ pattern.

8. Regardless of the overall pattern they are following, writers almost always use _____.

What Vocabulary Have You Learned?

Directions: *The following words appear in the chapter. Test your mastery of these words by selecting the word or phrase from the box that best completes each of the following sentences. Not all of the words in the box will be used.*

disorientation	integrates	accumulation
aggressive	applications	metamorphosis
dormant	fictitious	

1. Many plants remain _____ throughout the winter but rejuvenate in the spring.

2. After the train derailment, many passengers suffered from confusion and _____.

3. The _____ of junk in the attic made it time-consuming to clean.

4. Good health care _____ diagnosis, treatment, and follow-up.

5. The _____ behavior shown in the film made it unsuitable for young children.

IDENTIFYING PATTERNS

Directions: *Use what you have learned in the chapter to select the choice that best answers each of the following questions.*

_____ 1. If you want to explain *slapstick comedy* to someone who is unfamiliar with the term, the best pattern to use is
   a. chronological order.   c. example.
   b. process.   d. listing.

_____ 2. To write a paragraph describing how to assist someone who is choking, the best pattern to use is
   a. listing.   c. definition.
   b. process.   d. example.

_____ 3. Of the following topics, the one that would most likely be developed using the chronological order pattern is
   a. the use of imagery in poetry.
   b. variables affecting group behavior.
   c. the development of conscience in children.
   d. relationships within the extended family.

_____ 4. If you wanted to write a paragraph about your four favorite contemporary authors, the pattern you would most likely use is
   a. listing.   c. process.
   b. chronological order.   d. definition.

_____ 5. Suppose you were explaining the art form of Impressionism to someone. If you talked about the distinctive elements of Impressionism and how it is different from other types of art, the pattern you would be using is
   a. process.   c. definition.
   b. chronological order.   d. listing.

_____ 6. If a paragraph begins with the topic sentence "Marketers typically follow four basic steps in marketing research," the pattern that the paragraph is most likely to follow is
   a. process.   c. definition.
   b. example.   d. listing.

_____ 7. If a paragraph begins with the topic sentence "Adolescents in different parts of the country exhibit what is considered 'cool' in different ways," the pattern that the paragraph is most likely to follow is

a. process.
c. example.
b. chronological order.
d. listing.

_____ 8. If a paragraph begins with the topic sentence "Three of the best-known composers of baroque music are Johann Sebastian Bach, George Frideric Handel, and Georg Philipp Telemann," the pattern that the paragraph is most likely to follow is

a. example.
c. definition.
b. listing.
d. process.

_____ 9. If you were taking an essay exam in a biology course and one question read "Explain the term _homeostasis_," the pattern you would most likely use to organize your answer is

a. definition.
c. chronological order.
b. listing.
d. process.

_____ 10. If you were writing a paper on the important events that led up to the Boer War, the best pattern to use would be

a. process.
c. example.
b. chronological order.
d. definition.

IDENTIFYING PATTERNS

Directions: *For each of the following statements, select the choice that best describes its particular pattern of organization.*

_____   1. In a list of numbers, the **mode** is the number that occurs often. For instance, if the ages of 5 children are 7, 10, 11, 8, and 10, then the mode is 10.

      a. chronological order   c. definition and example

      b. process   d. listing

_____   2. If you want to improve your vocabulary, three reference sources that can help you are a collegiate dictionary, a subject area dictionary, and a thesaurus.

      a. chronological order   c. definition and example

      b. process   d. listing

_____   3. The first step in solving word problems is to identify what is asked for. Then, locate the information that is provided to solve the problem.

      a. chronological order   c. definition and example

      b. process   d. listing

_____   4. When treating a sprained ankle, you should first elevate the ankle to a comfortable position and apply ice to reduce the swelling. Next, wrap the ankle firmly with a cloth bandage. Try to keep it elevated, with ice on it, for 24 hours.

      a. definition   c. example

      b. process   d. listing

_____   5. In late 1778, the British took Savannah. During the next year, most of the other settled areas of Georgia fell, followed by the surrender of Charleston, South Carolina, in 1780.

      a. chronological order   c. definition

      b. process   d. listing

_____   6. Because of the language barrier, many new immigrants are unable to work in their former professions. For instance, Rima taught school in Lithuania, but in America she cleans houses.

      a. chronological order   c. example

      b. process   d. listing

_____ 7. There are four forces of nature: gravity, electromagnetism, strong nuclear force, and weak nuclear force.

    a. chronological order   c. listing

    b. process   d. definition

_____ 8. When a bill is vetoed by the president, he sends it back to the House or Senate and explains why he vetoed it. Congress can then override the veto with a two-thirds vote in both the House and the Senate.

    a. example   c. definition

    b. process   d. listing

_____ 9. An allergen is a substance that causes an allergic reaction. Common allergens include pollen, dust mites, mold spores, and pet dander.

    a. chronological order   c. listing

    b. process   d. definition and example

_____ 10. The explorers began their cross-country journey in early spring. By late fall, they had traveled nearly halfway to their destination.

    a. chronological order   c. example

    b. process   d. listing

IDENTIFYING PATTERNS

Directions: *After reading each of the following passages, complete the exercises that follow.*

A.   Factors that influence our behavior and our decisions to change our behavior can be divided into three general categories. One category is *predisposing factors,* such as our life experiences, knowledge, cultural and ethnic inheritance, and current beliefs and values. Factors that may predispose us to certain conditions include our age, sex, race, income, family background, educational background, and access to health care. For example, if your parents smoked, you are 90 percent more likely to start smoking than someone whose parents didn't.

Another category is *enabling factors.* These include skills or abilities; physical, emotional, and mental capabilities; and resources that make health decisions more convenient or difficult. Positive enablers encourage you to carry through on your intentions, whereas negative enablers work against your intentions to change. For example, if you would like to join a local gym but discover that the closest one is 4 miles away and costs $500 to join, those negative enablers may convince you to stay home.

Finally, *reinforcing factors* may influence you toward positive and/or negative behaviors. These include money, popularity, social support and appreciation from friends, and family interest and enthusiasm for what you are doing. If, for example, you are overweight and you lose a few pounds and your friends tell you how terrific you look, your positive behavior will be reinforced and you will be more likely to continue to diet.

—adapted from Donatelle and Davis, *Access to Health,* p. 25

1. Complete the following map by writing the three types of factors that influence behavior and behavior-change decisions.

MAIN IDEA: FACTORS THAT INFLUENCE BEHAVIOR AND THE DECISION TO CHANGE BEHAVIOR CAN BE DIVIDED INTO THREE CATEGORIES

a. _____

b. _____

c. _____

2. List three transitions used in the passage.

   a. _____

   b. _____

   c. _____

3. The two main patterns of organization used in this passage are listing

   and _____.

B.   The process of digestion begins at the upper end of the gastrointestinal tract. The *mouth* is where food enters and where the processes of mechanical breakdown and digestion begin. In the mouth, food is chewed (a process called **mastication**) and mechanically broken down into smaller particles by the cutting and grinding actions of the teeth. The food is also mixed with **saliva,** which lubricates it and contains an enzyme which begins the digestion of carbohydrates by breaking down starch and glycogen.

   From the mouth, the food-saliva mixture is propelled by the tongue into the **pharynx** (commonly known as the *throat*), a common passageway for food and air. From the pharynx, the passageways for food and air diverge. Whereas air enters the larynx and trachea and proceeds toward the lungs, food enters the esophagus, which runs parallel to the trachea.

   The **esophagus** is a muscular tube whose primary function is to conduct food from the pharynx to the stomach. It can easily stretch to accommodate food as it is swallowed; when food is not present, however, it is normally collapsed.

   —adapted from Germann and Stanfield, *Principles of Human Physiology,* pp. 606–607

4. Complete the following map.

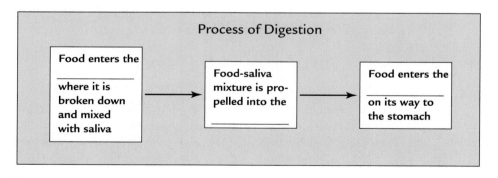

Process of Digestion

Food enters the _____ where it is broken down and mixed with saliva → Food-saliva mixture is propelled into the _____ → Food enters the _____ on its way to the stomach

5. The organizational pattern used in this passage is _____.

IDENTIFYING PATTERNS

Directions: *After reading each of the paragraphs below, select the choice that best answers each of the questions that follow.*

A.　　　Five planets are easy to see with the naked eye: Mercury, Venus, Mars, Jupiter, and Saturn. Mercury can be seen only infrequently, and then only just after sunset or before sunrise because it is so close to the Sun. Venus often shines brightly in the early evening in the west or before dawn in the east; if you see a very bright "star" in the early evening or early morning, it probably is Venus. Jupiter, when it is visible at night, is the brightest object in the sky besides the Moon and Venus. Mars is recognizable by its red color, but be careful not to confuse it with a bright red star. Saturn is easy to see with the naked eye, but because many stars are just as bright as Saturn, it helps to know where to look. (Also, planets tend not to twinkle as much as stars.) Sometimes several planets may appear close together in the sky, offering a particularly beautiful sight.

—Bennett et al., *The Cosmic Perspective,* pp. 58–59

_____　1. The main idea of this paragraph appears in the
　　　　　a. first sentence.　　　　c. fourth sentence.
　　　　　b. third sentence.　　　　d. last sentence.

_____　2. The main pattern of organization used in this paragraph is
　　　　　a. chronological order.　　c. definition.
　　　　　b. listing.　　　　　　　　d. example.

_____　3. The planet that often shines brightly in the early evening or early morning is
　　　　　a. Mercury.　　　　　　c. Venus.
　　　　　b. Jupiter.　　　　　　d. Saturn.

B.　　　**Gender roles** are the culturally determined appropriate behaviors of males versus females. It is one thing to identify yourself as male or female, but something else again to understand what behaviors are appropriate for your gender. Gender roles vary in different cultures, social classes, and time periods; for instance, a proper woman in Victorian England (or, perhaps, 19th-century America) would probably be very surprised to learn that a woman can be a senator or the president of a major corporation today. Conceptions about gender roles develop early. Even preschool boys apparently believe that if they played with cross-gender toys (say, dishes instead of tools), their fathers would think that was "bad." Indeed, by age 2 children have apparently learned about gender role differences.

—adapted from Kosslyn and Rosenberg, Psychology: The Brain, the Person, the World, p. 331

_____ 4. The main idea of this paragraph is that
   a. gender roles have remained the same throughout history.
   b. women can be politicians or presidents of corporations today.
   c. the behaviors considered appropriate for males and females are known as gender roles and are culturally determined.
   d. preschool boys should not play with cross-gender toys.

_____ 5. The main pattern of organization used in this paragraph is
   a. chronological order.   c. process.
   b. listing.   d. definition and example.

_____ 6. The transitional word or phrase that signals an example is to follow is
   a. one.   c. perhaps.
   b. for instance. d. indeed.

C.   The history of maps goes back thousands of years. In Babylonia, in approximately 2300 B.C., the oldest known map was drawn on a clay tablet. The map showed a man's property located in a valley surrounded by tall mountains. Later, around 1300 B.C., the Egyptians drew maps that detailed the location of Ethiopian gold mines and that showed a route from the Nile Valley. The ancient Greeks were early mapmakers as well, although no maps remain for us to examine. It is estimated that in 300 B.C. they drew maps showing the earth to be round. The Romans drew the first road maps, a few of which have been preserved for study today. Claudius Ptolemy, an Egyptian scholar who lived around 150 A.D., drew one of the most famous ancient maps. He drew maps of the world as it was known at that time, including 26 regional maps of Europe, Africa, and Asia.

_____ 7. The main idea of the paragraph appears in the
   a. first sentence.   c. third sentence.
   b. second sentence.   d. last sentence.

_____ 8. The pattern of organization used in this paragraph is

    a. process.   c. chronological order.

    b. definition.   d. example.

_____ 9. Of the following phrases, the only one that is _not_ used as a transition in this paragraph is

    a. thousands of years.   c. in 300 B.C.

    b. Later.   d. around 150 A.D.

_____ 10. According to this passage, the first road maps were drawn by the

    a. Babylonians.   c. Greeks.

    b. Egyptians.   d. Romans.

NAME _____ SECTION _____

DATE _____ SCORE _____

IDENTIFYING PATTERNS

Directions: After reading the excerpt below, taken from a textbook about the Internet, select the choice that best answers each of the questions that follow.

VIRUSES, TROJANS, AND WORMS

1   Computer security experts worry about software that can be used maliciously to put computer users at risk. Over the years, they have found it useful to distinguish different classes of software that are often associated with security problems. Mainstream news outlets tend to call such software a *virus*. However, many fast-spreading troublemakers are actually *worms*, and one of the most insidious forms of software attack is the *Trojan horse*.

2   A **virus** is an executable program that attaches itself to a host program and whose purpose is to replicate itself via files that are transferred from one computer to another. They can propagate through a host program. Some viruses are benign, doing nothing more than leaving the equivalent of their initials on a file somewhere. Others, however, are extremely destructive, capable of destroying files or even entire file systems.

3   A **Trojan horse** is an executable program that slips into a system under the guise of another program. To qualify as a Trojan horse, the program must do something that is undocumented and intended by the programmer that the user would not approve of. Deception is a key characteristic of all Trojan horses. You think that you've installed only a particular program, but you end up getting more than you expected. Some Trojan horses, for instance, are designed to record every key that you hit, such as the credit card account number that you use when online shopping. Your keystrokes might be monitored by the program's author in real time, or they might be saved and sent back to the program's author at a later time.

4   A **worm** is very similar to a virus but differs in its reproductive habits. Whereas viruses propagate via shared floppies or other media and need a host program in order to propagate, a worm depends on active network connections in order to multiply and needs many different hosts that are running the same software. Sophisticated worms can have multiple segments that run on different machines, do different things, and communicate with each other over a network. Some are programmed to act maliciously, whereas others are merely resource hogs that pull down entire networks by tying up too much memory or too many CPU cycles.

5   If you can't remember how these three differ from each other, just remember that everyone who uses computers is vulnerable to attack and must take precautions. There are some steps that you can take to protect your system. Once you know the ropes, good computer security doesn't have to take a lot of your time.

—adapted from Lehnert, *Light on the Web*, pp. 32–33

_____ 1. The general subject of this passage is
  a. problems with antivirus software.
  b. computer software security troublemakers.
  c. evaluation of computer services.
  d. propagation of computer viruses.

_____ 2. The main pattern of organization used throughout this selection is
  a. process.
  b. chronological order.
  c. definition.
  d. listing.

_____ 3. The main idea of paragraph 1 is that
  a. mainstream news outlets tend to call all problems viruses.
  b. three kinds of software are associated with security problems.
  c. *virus* is the general name for software that causes security problems.
  d. the Trojan horse is one of the worst forms of software attack.

_____ 4. The main idea of paragraph 2 appears in the
  a. first sentence.
  b. second sentence.
  c. third sentence.
  d. last sentence.

_____ 5. The best synonym for the word **benign** as used in paragraph 2 is
  a. destructive.
  b. obvious.
  c. humorous.
  d. harmless.

_____ 6. The two patterns of organization used in paragraph 3 are
  a. definition and listing.
  b. listing and process.
  c. definition and example.
  d. example and chronological order.

7. The transitional phrase that signals an example in paragraph 3 is

   a. to qualify.

   b. a key characteristic.

   c. such as.

   d. a later time.

8. According to the selection, one distinguishing characteristic of a *worm* is that it

   a. depends on active network connections in order to multiply.

   b. does nothing more than leave its initials on a file.

   c. monitors keystrokes and sends them back to the program's author.

   d. actually improves the performance of the entire network.

9. The best synonym for the word **propagate** as used in paragraph 4 is

   a. change.

   b. multiply.

   c. damage.

   d. remove.

10. The main idea of paragraph 5 is that

   a. you should be able to identify each type of software threat.

   b. not every computer is vulnerable to attack.

   c. good computer security can be expensive.

   d. everyone who uses a computer should take precautions.

ANIMALS AT PLAY
Teresa Audesirk, Gerald Audesirk, and Bruce E. Byers

Have you ever watched animals playing and wondered about their behavior? This selection from a biology textbook titled *Life on Earth* describes how and why animals play.

Vocabulary Preview

These are some of the difficult words in this essay. The definitions here will help you if you can't figure out the meanings from the sentence context or word parts.

behavioral biologists (par. 1) scientists who study the actions and reactions of human beings and animals through observation and experiments

evolutionarily (par. 1) related to the theory that groups of organisms change over time, mainly as a result of natural selection, so that descendants are different from their ancestors

species (par. 3) biological category or group

natural selection (par. 5) the process in nature that results in the survival of only those organisms that are best adapted to their environment

neural (par. 6) related to nerves or the nervous system

---

1   Pigface, a giant 50-year-old African softshell turtle, spends hours each day batting a ball around his aquatic home in the National Zoo in Washington, D.C., to the delight of thousands of visitors and the puzzlement of behavioral biologists. Play has always been somewhat of a mystery. It has been observed in many birds and in most mammals, but, until zookeepers tossed Pigface a ball a few years ago, it had never been seen in animals as evolutionarily ancient as turtles.

2   Animals at play are fascinating. Pygmy hippopotamuses push one another, shake and toss their heads, splash in the water, and pirouette on their hind legs. Otters delight in elaborate acrobatics. Bottlenose dolphins balance fish on their snouts, throw objects, and carry them in their mouths while swimming. Baby vampire bats chase, wrestle, and slap each other with their wings. Even octopuses have been seen playing a game: pushing objects away from themselves and into a current, then waiting for the objects to drift back, only to push them back into the current to start the cycle over again.

■ *Young animals at play.*

3   Play can be solitary, and this typically consists of a single animal manipulating an object, such as a cat with a ball of yarn, or the dolphin with its fish, or a macaque monkey making and playing with a snowball. Or, play can be social. Often young of the same species play together, but parents may join them. Social play typically includes chasing, fleeing, wrestling, kicking, and gentle biting.

4   What are the features of play? Play seems to lack any clear immediate function and is abandoned in favor of feeding, courtship, and escaping from danger. Young animals play more frequently than do adults. Play typically borrows movements from other behaviors (attacking, fleeing, stalking, and so on) and uses considerable energy. Also, play is potentially dangerous. Many young humans and other animals are injured, and some

are killed, during play. In addition, play can distract an animal from the presence of danger while making it conspicuous to predators. So, why do animals play?

5   The most logical conclusion is that play must have survival value and that natural selection has favored those individuals who engage in playful activities. One of the best explanations for the survival value of play is the "practice theory," first proposed by K. Groos in 1898. He suggested that play allows young animals to gain experience in behaviors that they will use as adults. By performing these acts repeatedly in play, the animal practices skills that will later be important in hunting, fleeing, or social interactions.

6   More-recent research supports and extends Groos's proposal. Play is most intense early in life when the brain is developing and crucial neural connections are forming. John Byers, a zoologist at the University of Idaho, has observed that animals with larger brains tend to be more playful than are animals with smaller brains. Because larger brains are generally linked to increased learning ability, this relationship supports the idea that adult skills are learned during juvenile play. Watch children roughhousing or playing tag, and you will see how strength and coordination are fostered by play and how skills are developed that might have helped our hunting ancestors survive. Quiet play with other children, with dolls, blocks, and other toys helps children prepare to interact socially, nurture their own children, and deal with the physical world.

7   Although Shakespeare tells us "play needs no excuse," there is good evidence that the tendency to play has evolved as an adaptive behavior in animals capable of learning. Play is quite literally "serious fun"!

━━ ∙ ━━

Directions: *Select the letter of the choice that best answers each of the following questions:*

CHECKING COMPREHENSION

_____   1. The main purpose of this selection is to
   a. describe the activities of African softshell turtles.
   b. illustrate how wild animals can be trained.
   c. encourage people to spend more time watching animals play.
   d. explain how and why animals play.

_____ 2. The main idea of paragraph 2 is stated in the
   a. first sentence.   c. third sentence.
   b. second sentence.   d. last sentence.

_____ 3. The main idea of paragraph 3 is that
   a. cats, monkeys, and dolphins are especially playful
      animals.
   b. only animals of the same species play together.
   c. play can take place with just one animal or many animals.
   d. social play is rougher than solitary play.

_____ 4. All of the following are features of play *except*
   a. play borrows movements from other behaviors.
   b. young animals play more frequently than do adults.
   c. play uses considerable energy.
   d. play is always safe.

_____ 5. According to this selection, the most likely purpose of play
   is to
   a. alert animals to the presence of danger.
   b. make animals less conspicuous to predators.
   c. allow young animals to practice important skills and
      behaviors.
   d. improve the bond between young animals and their
      parents.

USING WHAT YOU KNOW ABOUT BASIC PATTERNS

_____ 6. The main pattern of organization followed in paragraph 2 is
   a. example.   c. process.
   b. chronological order.   d. listing.

_____ 7. In paragraph 3, the transitional word or phrase that signals
   an example is to follow is
   a. *typically*.   c. *often*.
   b. *such as*.   d. *includes*.

8. The main pattern of organization followed in paragraph 4 is
   a. example.   c. process.
   b. chronological order.   d. listing.

9. The transitional phrases that signal a list in paragraph 4 are
   a. *more frequently* and *typically*.
   b. *also* and *in addition*.
   c. *many* and *other*.
   d. *while* and *so*.

10. The term that is defined in paragraph 5 is
    a. survival value.
    b. natural selection.
    c. practice theory.
    d. social interactions.

USING CONTEXT AND WORD PARTS

11. In paragraph 2, the word **pirouette** means
    a. whirl about.   c. take control.
    b. speak aloud.   d. show anger.

12. In paragraph 3, the word **solitary** means
    a. unhappy.   c. in a group.
    b. happening alone.   d. frightening.

13. In paragraph 4, the word **predators** means
    a. relatives.   c. companions.
    b. movements.   d. enemies.

14. In paragraph 6, the word **juvenile** means
    a. adult.   c. youthful.
    b. rough.   d. dangerous.

15. In paragraph 6, the word **fostered** means
    a. substituted.   c. forced.
    b. encouraged.   d. not allowed.

REVIEWING DIFFICULT VOCABULARY

Directions: Match each of the following words in column A from the Vocabulary Preview on page 252 with its meaning in column B.

Column A

_____ 16. behavioral biologists

_____ 17. evolutionarily

_____ 18. species

_____ 19. natural selection

_____ 20. neural

Column B

a. biological category or group

b. the process in nature that results in the survival of only those organisms that are best adapted to their environment

c. related to nerves or the nervous system

d. scientists who study the actions and reactions of human beings and animals through observation and experiments

e. related to the theory that groups of organisms change over time so that descendants are different from their ancestors

QUESTIONS FOR DISCUSSION

1. Have you ever watched an animal—perhaps your own pet—at play? Describe what you saw. Do your observations support K. Groos's "practice theory" about why animals play?

2. What similarities have you seen between the play of children and the play of young animals? Do you remember "practicing" behaviors and skills as a child?

3. What do you think adults can gain from play?

WRITING ACTIVITIES

1. Brainstorm a list of activities that you consider to be play. Then write a paragraph describing several that you find most enjoyable.

2. Is sports, either viewing professional sports or participating in sports, a form of play? Write a paragraph that answers this question.

3. Read the information from the American Humane Association at http://www.americanhumane.org/. Write a paragraph about the American Humane Association. Identify its purpose, and summarize the activities it endorses for the care and treatment of animals.

Chapter 7:   Recognizing the Basic Patterns of Organization

RECORDING YOUR PROGRESS

Test	Number Right			Score	
Practice Test 7-1	_____	× 10	=	_____	%
Practice Test 7-2	_____	× 10	=	_____	%
Practice Test 7-3	_____	× 10	=	_____	%
Mastery Test 7-1	_____	× 10	=	_____	%
Mastery Test 7-2	_____	× 10	=	_____	%
Mastery Test 7-3	_____	× 5	=	_____	%

EVALUATING YOUR PROGRESS

Based on your test performance, rate how well you have mastered the skills taught in this chapter by checking one of the boxes below or by writing your own evaluation.

☐ **Need More Improvement**
Tip: Try completing the Patterns of Organization—New York Harbor module in the Reading Skills section on the MyReadingLab Web site at **http://www.ablongman.com/myreadinglab** to fine-tune the skills that you have learned in this chapter.

☐ **Need More Practice**
Tip: Try using the Patterns of Organization—New York Harbor module in the Reading Skills section on the MyReadingLab Web site at **http://www.ablongman.com/myreadinglab** to brush up on the skills taught in this chapter, or visit this textbook's Companion Web site at **http://www.ablongman.com/mcwhorter** for extra practice.

☐ **Good**
Tip: To maintain your skills, quickly review this chapter by using this textbook's Companion Web site at **http://www.ablongman.com/mcwhorter**.

☐ **Excellent**

YOUR EVALUATION: _____

_____

_____

_____

THINK ABOUT IT!

Study the two photographs shown below. Although both photographs show a professor conducting a class, there are dramatic differences between the two classes. Write a list of similarities and differences you observe between the two classes.

Similarities	Differences
1. _____	1. _____
2. _____	2. _____
3. _____	3. _____

When you look at photographs in this way, you are comparing and contrasting them. Writers often use the comparison/contrast pattern in paragraphs and in longer pieces of writing. It helps them explain how items, people, or events are alike and different.

In Chapter 7 you learned four basic patterns of organization: example, definition, chronological order and process, and listing. In this chapter you will learn two other primary patterns—comparison/contrast and cause/effect—as well as several additional patterns.

CHAPTER 8

Recognizing Comparison/Contrast and Cause/Effect Patterns

Comparison/Contrast Patterns

You use comparison and contrast every day—not just when comparing photographs. For example, when you decide which pair of shoes to buy, where to apply for a part-time job, or what topic to choose for a research paper, you are thinking about similarities and differences.

Writers use comparison or contrast to explain how something is similar to or different from something else. **Comparison** treats similarities, whereas **contrast** emphasizes differences. For example, a writer who is *comparing* two U.S. presidents would focus on their shared features: experience in politics, leadership characteristics, and commitment to fulfill the duties of the office. But a writer who is *contrasting* the two presidents would discuss how they differ in foreign policy, education, family background, and so forth.

As you read, you will find passages that only compare, some that only contrast, and some that do both.

Directions: *Choose one of the following subjects: two musical groups, two jobs, two professors, or two cities. Then, using the box below as a guide, make a list of five similarities and five differences.*

Example:

Subject: two restaurants

Items A and B: Blue Mesa and Chico's

Similarities

1. Both specialize in Mexican food.

2. Both serve lunch and dinner.

3. Both are located on the east side of town.

4. Both employ college students.

5. Both have a special menu for children.

Differences

1. Blue Mesa is much more expensive than Chico's.

2. Chico's is a chain, while Blue Mesa is a single restaurant.

3. Only Chico's offers takeout.

4. Blue Mesa is closed on Mondays, while Chico's is open every day.

5. Only Blue Mesa accepts reservations.

Subject: _____

Items A and B: _____

Similarities

1.

2.

3.

4.

5.

Differences

1.

2.

3.

4.

5.

Comparison

A writer who is concerned only with similarities may identify the items to be compared and then list the ways they are alike. The following paragraph describes apparent similarities between two planets, Earth and Mars.

> Early telescopic observations of Mars revealed several uncanny resemblances to Earth. The Martian rotation axis is tilted about the same amount as Earth's, and on both planets a day lasts about 24 hours. In addition, Mars has polar caps, which we now know to be composed primarily of frozen carbon dioxide, with smaller amounts of water ice. Telescopic observations also showed seasonal variations in surface coloration over the course of the Martian year (about 1.9 Earth years). All these discoveries led to the perception that Mars and Earth were at least cousins, if not twins. By the early 1900s, many astronomers—as well as the public—envisioned Mars as nearly Earthlike, possessing water, vegetation that changed with the seasons, and possibly intelligent life.
>
> —adapted from Bennett et al., *The Cosmic Perspective*, p. 249

Such a pattern can be diagrammed as follows:

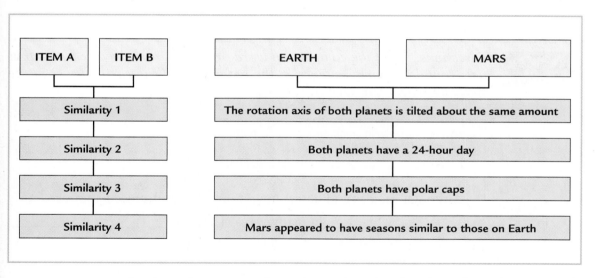

Look at the paragraph again, and notice the clues the writers provide about what kind of pattern they are following. In the first sentence—the topic sentence—the phrase *several uncanny resemblances* tells you that the paragraph will be about the similarities between Earth and Mars. The writers also use the words *same* and *both,* which signal that a comparison is being made. As you read, be on the lookout for words that indicate comparison or contrast.

When writers use comparison or contrast, sometimes they also include transitions to introduce each important point they are making. In the paragraph about Earth and Mars, for example, the writers use the transitions *in addition* and *also* to help the reader follow the main points of the comparison. Although such transitions are not always used in comparison and contrast, you will often find them in longer selections.

Transitions in Comparison and Contrast			
To Show Similarities		**To Show Differences**	
alike	likewise	unlike	in contrast
same	both	different	despite
similar	just as	difference	nevertheless
similarity	each	on the other hand	however
like	in common	instead	but

Exercise 8–2

Directions: *Select the comparison word or phrase from the box below that best completes each sentence in the paragraph. Write each answer in the space provided. Use each choice only once.*

same	in common	both
similarity	alike	

Although beagles and basset hounds are different breeds, they are

_____ in many ways. They are _____

considered part of the hound group, and the physical

_____ between the two breeds is apparent in their

coloring and their typically long, drooping ears. Beagles and bassets have

another, more important characteristic _____: they

share the _____ friendly and sociable disposition,

especially when it comes to children.

Contrast

The following paragraph was written to point out only the differences between two types of tumors:

> Not all tumors are **malignant** (cancerous); in fact, most are **benign** (non-cancerous). Benign and malignant tumors differ in several key ways. Benign tumors are generally composed of ordinary-looking cells enclosed in a fibrous shell or capsule that prevents their spreading to other body areas. Malignant tumors, in contrast, are usually not enclosed in a protective capsule and can therefore spread to other organs. Unlike benign tumors, which merely expand to take over a given space, malignant cells invade surrounding tissue, emitting clawlike protrusions that disrupt chemical processes within healthy cells.
>
> —adapted from Donatelle, *Health: The Basics*, p. 324

Such a pattern can be diagrammed as follows:

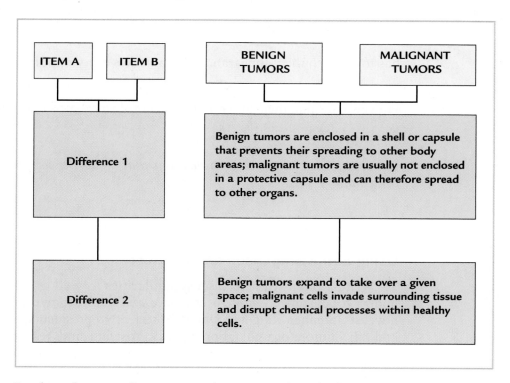

Look at the preceding paragraph again, and circle the contrast clues you can find (use the box on p. 264 to help you). Did you circle the following words and phrases: *differ, in contrast,* and *unlike?*

A. Directions: *Select the contrast word or phrase from the box below that best completes each sentence in the paragraph. Write each answer in the space provided. Use each choice only once.*

contrast	difference	however	on the other hand
different	unlike	but	

Sarah and Rachel may be sisters, but their friends and family agree that the girls couldn't be more _____. To begin with, Sarah has a very active social life; Rachel, _____, is content to curl up at home with a good book. Another _____ between the two sisters is their attitude toward school. Rachel loves school and plans to become a teacher, _____ Sarah is happiest outside of the classroom. One last _____ between Sarah and Rachel has to do with their appearances. Sarah takes every opportunity to dress up, _____ Rachel, who prefers jeans and a sweatshirt. However, despite their differences, each of the two girls considers the other her best friend.

B. Directions: *List the three transitions that the writer uses to introduce her three main points.*

1. _____   2. _____   3. _____

Using Both Comparison and Contrast

Writers often want to discuss similarities as well as differences. They might, for instance, want to compare *and* contrast two popular modern novelists, Stephen King and Danielle Steele; two presidents, George W. Bush and Bill Clinton; or two national parks, Yosemite and Yellowstone.

When writers use comparison and contrast together, they may discuss everything about their first item (say, Stephen King) and then discuss everything about their second item (say, Danielle Steele). Often, though, writers move back and forth from item to item, discussing similarities and differences as they go along. This pattern is shown in the following paragraph, which compares and contrasts the Senate and the House of Representatives.

Congress is bicameral, meaning that it is made up of two houses, the Senate and the House of Representatives. According to the Constitution, all members of Congress must be residents of the states that they have been elected to represent. The Constitution also specifies that representatives must be at least 25 years old and American citizens for 7 years, whereas senators must be at least 30 and American citizens for 9 years. The roles of majority and minority leaders are similar in both houses, and both use committees to review bills and to set their legislative agenda. Despite these similarities, there are many important differences between the two houses. First, the term of office is two years for representatives but six years for senators. Further, each state is guaranteed two senators but its number of representatives is determined by the state's population; thus, the House of Representatives has 435 members and the Senate has 100. Another difference involves procedure: the House places limits on debate, whereas the Senate allows unlimited debate, which sometimes leads to a filibuster.

Exercise 8-4

Directions: After reading the preceding paragraph, select the choice that best answers each of the following questions.

_____ 1. Although the writer is comparing and contrasting the two houses of Congress, what other pattern (from Chapter 7) does she use in the first sentence of the paragraph?

a. example

b. definition

c. process

d. listing

_____ 2. The writer uses many words to indicate similarities and differences. Which of the following is *not* used as a contrast word?

a. whereas

b. but

c. further

d. differences

3. The paragraph includes many similarities and differences between the House of Representatives and the Senate. List some of the similarities and differences on the next page.

The House of Representatives and the Senate

Similarities   *Differences*

1. _____   1. _____

   _____   _____

2. _____   _____

   _____   2. _____

3. _____   _____

   _____   3. _____

                                        _____

                                     4. _____

                                        _____

Cause/Effect Patterns

Writers use the **cause/effect** pattern to explain why an event or action causes another event or action. For example, if you are describing a skiing accident to a friend, you would probably follow a cause/effect pattern. You would tell what caused the accident and what happened as a result.

When a single cause has multiple effects, it can be visualized as follows:

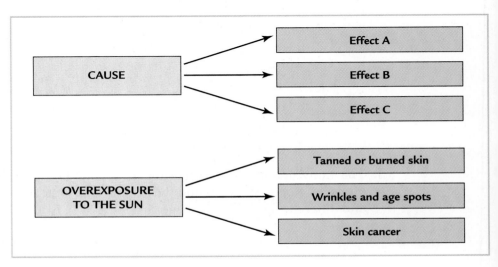

Sometimes, however, multiple causes result in a single effect. This kind of cause/effect pattern can be visualized this way:

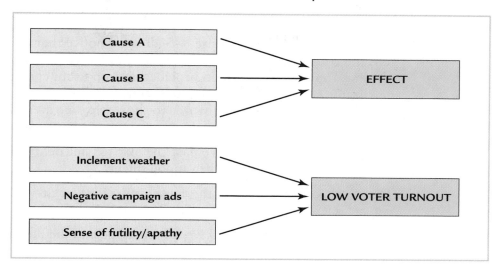

Read the following paragraph, which discusses the multiple causes of a single effect.

Although ulcers are commonly associated with stress, they can be brought on by other risk factors. Chronic use of aspirin and other nonsteroidal anti-inflammatory drugs increases the risk of ulcer because these agents suppress the secretion of both mucus and bicarbonate, which normally protect the lining of the GI tract from the effects of acid and pepsin. The risk of ulcer is also increased by chronic alcohol use or the leakage of bile from the duodenum into the stomach, both of which can disrupt the mucus barrier. Surprisingly, ulcers are usually not associated with abnormally high rates of stomach-acid secretion; more often than not, acid secretion is normal or even below normal in most people with ulcers.

—adapted from Germann and Stanfield, *Principles of Human Physiology*, p. 622

Exercise 8-5

Directions: After reading the preceding paragraph, answer each of the following questions.

1. What effect is the writer discussing? _____

2. List four causes described by the authors.

   a. _____

   b. _____

c. _____

d. _____

As you worked on Exercise 8–5, did you notice that the topic sentence tells the reader that the paragraph will be about causes, referred to as *risk factors?* Topic sentences often provide this important clue in a cause/effect paragraph, so pay close attention to them.

Writers often use specific words to show why one event is caused by another. Look at the following statement:

Shirley accidentally drove past the exit for her dentist's office. Consequently, she was late for her appointment.

The word *consequently* ties the cause—missed the exit—to the effect—being late. Here is another example:

Deion was not in class all week because he had the flu.

In this sentence the word *because* ties the effect—Deion was absent—to the cause—he had the flu. In both of these examples, the cause and effect words help explain the relationship between two events. As you read, watch for words that show cause and effect; some common ones are listed in the box below.

Exercise 8–6

Transitions in Cause and Effect			
cause	since	effect	one result is
because	due to	consequently	therefore
because of	reasons	as a result	thus

A. Directions: *After reading the following paragraph, select the cause/effect word in the box below that best completes each sentence in the paragraph. Write your answer in the space provided. Not all words will be used.*

consequently	effects	reasons
because of	cause	result

Although it was a frightening experience, Bill's heart attack last year has had several positive _____. First, Bill realized that his diet had to change. He has eliminated the high-fat, high-sodium foods that were a major _____ of his health problems, replacing them with healthy, low-fat foods that he can prepare at home. Another aspect of Bill's life that has changed _____ his heart attack is his attitude toward exercise. He used to drive everywhere; now he walks whenever possible. In addition, he has started an exercise program approved by his doctor. As a _____, he looks and feels better than he has in years. Finally, Bill's heart attack served as a powerful reminder of the importance of his family. _____, he has adjusted his work schedule so that he is able to spend more time with the people he loves.

B. Directions: *After reading the preceding paragraph, answer the following questions.*

1. What cause is being discussed? _____

2. What three effects does the writer mention?

    a. _____

    b. _____

    c. _____

3. Does the topic sentence tell you that this will be a cause/effect paragraph? _____

4. Aside from the cause and effect words, list four transitions that the writer uses to lead the reader through the information.

    a. _____   b. _____   c. _____   d. _____

Other Useful Thought Patterns

The patterns presented in Chapter 7 and in this chapter are the most common. However, writers do not limit themselves to these six patterns. Especially in academic writing, you may find one or more of the patterns described in the next pages.

Classification

A common way to explain something is to divide the topic into parts and explain each part. For example, you might explain the kinds of courses taken in college by dividing the courses into such categories as electives, required basic courses, courses required for a specific major, and so on and then describing each category. Textbook writers use the classification pattern to explain a topic that can easily be divided into parts. These parts are selected on the basis of common characteristics. For example, a psychology textbook writer might explain human needs by classifying them into two categories, primary and secondary. Or in a chemistry textbook, various compounds may be grouped or classified according to common characteristics, such as the presence of hydrogen or oxygen. In the following paragraph, the authors describe three types of business strategy.

> Three types of strategy are usually considered by a company. The purpose of **corporate strategy** is to determine the firm's overall attitude toward growth and the way it will manage its businesses or product lines. A company may decide to *grow* by increasing its activities or investment or to *retrench* by reducing them. **Business (or competitive) strategy,** which takes place at the level of the business unit or product line, focuses on improving the company's competitive position. At the level of **functional strategy,** managers in specific areas decide how best to achieve corporate goals by being as productive as possible.
>
> —adapted from Ebert and Griffin, *Business Essentials*, p. 117

Words that signal the classification patterns are shown below.

Transitions for Classification			
another	another kind	classified as	include
is composed of	one	types of	

Statement and Clarification

Many writers make a statement of fact and then proceed to clarify or explain that statement. For instance, a writer may open a paragraph by stating that "The best education for you may not be the best education for someone else." The remainder of the paragraph would then discuss that statement and make its meaning clear by explaining how educational needs are individual and based on one's talents, skills, and goals. In the following paragraph the author makes a statement about computer hackers and then elaborates on the issue.

In recent years, computer hackers have become a serious problem. It is very difficult to catch the culprits because the virus programs they introduce often affect a system afterwards. In fact, very few hacking incidents get reported and even fewer of the hackers get caught. According to the San Francisco–based Computer Security Institute (CSI), only about 17% of companies report hacking incidents because of the fear of adverse publicity, copycat hacking and loss of customer confidence. Out of those reported cases, normally an infinitesimal number of those responsible are caught.

—adapted from Bandyo-Padhyay, *Computing for Non-specialists*, p. 260

Words associated with this pattern are listed below.

Transitions for Statement and Clarification				
in fact	in other words	clearly	evidently	obviously

Summary

A summary is a condensed statement that provides the key points of a larger idea or piece of writing. The summaries at the end of each chapter of many textbooks provide a quick review of the chapter's contents. Often writers summarize what they have already said or what someone else has said. For example, in a psychology textbook you will find many summaries of research. Instead of asking you to read an entire research study, the textbook author will summarize the study's findings. Other times a writer may repeat in condensed form what he or she has already said as a means of emphasis or clarification. In the following paragraph from a sociology text, the author summarizes a general principle of human behavior.

To sum up, the minimax strategy is a general principle of human behavior that suggests that humans try to minimize costs and maximize rewards. The fewer costs and the more rewards we anticipate from something, the more likely we are to do it. If we believe that others will approve an act, the likelihood increases that we will do it. In short, whether people are playing cards with a few friends or are part of a mob, the principles of human behavior remain the same.

—adapted from Henslin, *Sociology*, p. 637

Words associated with this pattern are listed below.

Transitions for Summary			
in summary	in conclusion	in brief	to summarize
to sum up	in short	on the whole	

Addition

Writers often introduce an idea or make a statement and then supply additional information about that idea or statement. For instance, an education textbook may introduce the concept of homeschooling and then provide in-depth information about its benefits. The addition pattern is distinct from the listing pattern discussed in Chapter 7. This pattern is often used to expand, elaborate, or discuss a single idea in greater detail. The listing pattern enumerates items. In the following paragraph, the authors introduce the concept of telecommuting and then describe its advantages.

> Millions of people work at home at computer terminals connected to an office, an arrangement known as **telecommuting.** Telecommuting eases the pressure on transport facilities, saves fuel, and reduces air pollution. Moreover, it has been shown to increase workers' productivity and reduce absenteeism. It also allows employers to accommodate employees who want flexible work arrangements, thus opening employment opportunity to more people, such as women who are still homemakers.
>
> —adapted from Bergman and Renwick, *Introduction to Geography*, p. 404

Words associated with this pattern are shown below.

Transitions for Addition			
furthermore	additionally	also	besides
further	in addition	moreover	again

Spatial Order

Spatial order is concerned with physical location or position in space. Spatial order is used in disciplines in which physical descriptions are important. A photography textbook may use spatial order to describe the parts of a camera. An automotive technology textbook may use spatial order to describe disc brake operation. In the following paragraph from a physiology textbook, the authors use spatial order to describe the human chemoreceptors for taste.

> We can taste food because chemoreceptors in the mouth respond to certain chemicals in food. The chemoreceptors for taste are located in structures called **taste buds,** each of which contains 50–150 receptor cells and numerous support cells. At the top of each bud is a pore that allows receptor cells to be exposed to saliva and dissolved food molecules. Each person has over 10,000 taste buds, located primarily on the tongue and the roof of the mouth, but also located in the pharynx.
>
> —Germann and Stanfield, *Principles of Human Physiology*, pp. 303–304

Words associated with this pattern are listed below.

Transitions for Spatial Order			
above	below	besides	next to
in front of	behind	inside	outside
opposite	within	nearby	

Directions: *After reading each paragraph, select the pattern from the box below that best describes the organization of the paragraph.*

classification	summary	addition
statement and clarification	spatial order	

1. All languages have four key characteristics. First, they have phonology. Phonemes are the basic units of speech, and they are arranged in sequences to form words. Second, languages have grammar. Grammar is a set of rules for combining words that is based on the relationships among parts of speech. Third, languages have semantics, which specify meaning. The semantics of a word arise from its morphemes, small elements of meaning. Fourth, languages have pragmatics, the indirect or implied aspects of meaning. Pragmatics play a key role in understanding whether a question is actually a request, and whether a statement ending with a rising pitch is actually a question.

—adapted from Kosslyn and Rosenberg, *Fundamentals of Psychology:*
The Brain, the Person, the World, p. 197

Organization pattern: _____

2. The **meninges** are three connective tissue membranes that lie just external to the central nervous system organs. The leathery **dura mater,** meaning "tough mother," is the strongest of the meninges. Where it surrounds the brain, it is a two-layered sheet of fibrous connective tissue. Its more superficial layer, the *periosteal layer,* is attached to the inner surface of the skull. The deeper *meningeal layer* forms the true external covering of the brain and continues in the vertebral canal as the dural sheath of the spinal cord. The brain's two dural layers are fused together except in certain areas, where they separate to enclose dural sinuses that collect

venous blood from the brain and direct it into the internal jugular veins of the neck.

—adapted from Marieb, *Anatomy and Physiology,* pp. 402–403

Organization pattern: _____

3. In this chapter, we looked at listening and criticism and offered suggestions for making your listening and your criticism more effective. To sum up, criticism helps to (1) identify a speaker's strengths and weaknesses, (2) identify standards for evaluating different kinds of public speeches, and (3) show that the audience is concerned about the speaker's progress. In short, criticism is crucial to mastering the principles of public speaking.

—adapted from DeVito, *The Essential Elements of Public Speaking,* p. 46

Organization pattern: _____

4. Economic conditions determine spending patterns by consumers, businesses, and governments. Thus, they influence every marketer's plans for product offerings, pricing, and promotional strategies. Among the more significant economic variables, marketers are concerned with inflation, interest rates, recession, and recovery. In other words, they must monitor the general business cycle, which typically features a pattern of transition from periods of prosperity to recession to recovery (return to prosperity).

—Ebert and Griffin, *Business Essentials,* p. 254

Organization pattern: _____

5. Introducing a surprise element in an advertisement can be particularly effective in aiding recall. In addition, mystery ads, in which the brand is not identified until the end of the ad, are more effective at building associations in memory between the product category and that brand—especially in the case of relatively unknown brands

—adapted from Solomon, *Consumer Behavior,* p. 89

Organization pattern: _____

Moving Beyond Patterns

In Chapter 7 and in this chapter you have learned about many of the common patterns writers use—example, definition, chronological order and process, listing, comparison/contrast, and cause/effect. You have seen how these patterns help readers understand what a writer is saying and how writers may use more than one pattern in a piece of writing. In Chapters 9 through 12 you will have a chance to think about other issues involved in reading, including evaluating the author's purpose, making inferences, distinguishing fact from opinion, assessing tone and bias, and analyzing arguments.

The Textbook Challenge

Part A: Current Issues Reader

Using the textbook excerpt "The Biodiversity Crisis" (p. 530), identify three paragraphs that use the cause/effect pattern of organization:

Pattern	Paragraph #
Cause/Effect	_____

Part B: A College Textbook

Using one or more chapters from one of your own textbooks, identify several paragraphs that use the following patterns of organization:

Pattern	Page #	Paragraph #
Comparison/Contrast	_____	_____
Cause/Effect	_____	_____

What Have You Learned?

Directions: To check your understanding of the chapter, select the word or phrase from the following box that best completes each of the following statements. Not all of the choices will be used and others may be used more than once.

spatial order	in fact	process	however
comparison/contrast	cause/effect	summary	in common
addition	classification	topic sentences	comparison

1. The pattern that is most concerned with relationships between events is _____.

2. _____ often provide important clues about the pattern the writer is using.

3. Words such as *consequently* and *because* often suggest the _____ pattern.

4. The pattern that is most concerned with similarities and differences is _____.

5. Writers use the _____ pattern to explain a topic that can easily be divided into parts.

6. A transitional phrase often associated with the statement and clarification pattern is _____.

7. A _____ is a condensed statement that provides the key points of a larger idea or piece of writing.

8. The phrases *next to* and *in front of* often signal the _____ pattern.

9. When a writer introduces an idea or makes a statement and then supplies additional information about that idea or statement, the writer is using the _____ pattern.

10. Words such as *likewise* and *both* signal the _____ pattern.

What Vocabulary Have You Learned?

Directions: The following words appear in this chapter. Test your mastery of these words by selecting the word or phrase from the following box that best completes each of the sentences that follow. Write each answer in the space provided.

protrusions	adverse	suppress
retrench	sheath	

1. The treatment was so mild that there were no _____ effects in most patients.

2. Mineral deposits often create interesting _____ inside caves.

3. We could not _____ our laughter when the dog ran off with my sister's underwear.

4. After recording a loss for the fourth month in a row, the company decided that it must _____.

5. In the central nervous system, special cells form a protective _____ around nerve fibers.

IDENTIFYING PATTERNS

Directions: *Each of the following statements reflects a particular pattern of organization from either Chapter 7 or Chapter 8. Select the choice that indicates the correct pattern for each passage.*

_____ 1. The human brain is divided into two halves, each of which is responsible for separate functions.

      a. example   c. cause/effect

      b. addition   d. comparison/contrast

_____ 2. The battle for women's suffrage was carried out in the late 1800s and early 1900s.

      a. comparison/contrast   c. chronological order

      b. listing   d. cause/effect

_____ 3. A mild stimulant, such as coffee, causes a change in a person's ability to maintain attention and concentration.

      a. addition   c. chronological order

      b. cause/effect   d. spatial order

_____ 4. Geomorphology, the study of landforms and the events and processes that create them, is the topic of the lecture.

      a. chronological order   c. addition

      b. cause/effect   d. definition

_____ 5. When faced with life-threatening illnesses, people move away from denial (rejecting that the illness exists), to anger, to bargaining, and finally to acceptance.

      a. process   c. statement and clarification

      b. comparison/contrast   d. addition

_____ 6. Students who are informed about drugs tend to use them in greater moderation. Furthermore, they tend to help educate others.

      a. comparison/contrast   c. summary

      b. addition   d. classification

_____ 7. A residual check valve that maintains pressure on the hydraulic system is located in the master cylinder at the outlet for the drum brakes.

    a. listing   c. spatial order

    b. example   d. cause/effect

_____ 8. Sociologists study how we are socialized into gender roles, the attitudes expected of males and females. Gender roles, in fact, identify some activities and behaviors as clearly male and others as clearly female.

    a. chronological order   c. summary

    b. listing   d. statement and clarification

_____ 9. In conclusion, it is safe to say that crime by women is likely to increase as greater numbers of women assume roles traditionally held by men.

    a. spatial order   c. classification

    b. summary   d. definition

_____ 10. Patients often consult a lay referral network to discuss their medical problems. Cancer patients, for instance, can access Internet discussion groups that provide both information and support.

    a. comparison/contrast   c. cause/effect

    b. summary   d. example

MAPPING AND OUTLINING PATTERNS

Directions: After reading each paragraph, complete the map or outline that follows.

A. Comedy is often divided into two varieties—"high" and "low." **High comedy** relies more on wit and wordplay than on physical action for its humor. It tries to address the audience's intelligence by pointing out the pretension and hypocrisy of human behavior. High comedy also generally avoids derisive humor. Jokes about physical appearances would, for example, be avoided. **Low comedy** explores the opposite extreme of humor. It places greater emphasis on physical action and visual gags, and its verbal jokes do not require much intellect to appreciate. Low comedy does not avoid derisive humor; rather it revels in making fun of whatever will get a good laugh. Drunkenness, stupidity, lust, senility, trickery, insult, and clumsiness are inexhaustible staples for this kind of comedy.

—adapted from Kennedy and Gioia, *Literature*, pp. 885–886

	Contrasting High and Low Comedy
Difference #1	_____ relies more on wit and wordplay.
Difference #2	_____ tries to speak to the audience's intellect by pointing out certain aspects of human behavior.
Difference #3	_____ usually avoids derisive humor, including jokes about physical appearance.
Difference #4	_____ emphasizes physical action and visual jokes, not intellect.
Difference #5	_____ takes delight in making fun of anything for a good laugh.

B.   The suburbs developed in response to several social forces. The multilane freeways that go around the perimeter of the city (the outerbelts) spurred the development of suburban places along the city's rim. Now, rather than going from the suburb to the central city to work, to shop, to see a doctor, or to enjoy the movies, suburbanites can obtain the same services by driving along the outer belt from one suburban community to another. Another factor has been the decentralization of jobs. Faster transportation and communications have encouraged manufacturing plants and distribution centers to relocate from the central city to the outer rings of the city—that is, to the suburbs. Yet another factor has been the aging of the central city. Facilities in many downtown areas are simply worn out or obsolete. Parking is expensive and inconvenient; buildings are dirty and run-down. In contrast, suburban shopping malls and industrial centers typically have bright new facilities and ample parking.

—Curry et al., *Sociology for the Twenty-First Century,* p. 148

I. Suburbs developed in response to several social forces

A. The development of _____
the city's perimeter

B. The decentralization of _____

   1. Manufacturing plants and distribution centers relocated
   due to _____

C. The aging of _____

   1. Downtown facilities are worn out or obsolete

   2. Parking is expensive and inconvenient

   3. Buildings are dirty and run-down

   4. _____ offer better facilities
   and parking

IDENTIFYING PATTERNS

Directions: *After reading each of the paragraphs below, select the choice that best answers each of the questions that follow.*

A.   The three major types of managerial styles are autocratic, democratic, and free rein. Managers who adopt an **autocratic style** generally issue orders and expect them to be obeyed without question. The military commander prefers and usually needs the autocratic style on the battlefield. Because no one else is consulted, the autocratic style allows for rapid decision making. Another managerial style is the **democratic style.** Managers who adopt this generally ask for input from subordinates before making decisions but retain final decision-making power. For example, the manager of a technical group may ask other group members to interview job applicants, but the manager will ultimately make the hiring decision. Managers who adopt a **free-rein** style typically serve as advisers to subordinates who are allowed to make decisions. The chairperson of a volunteer committee to raise funds for a new library may find a free-rein style most effective.

—adapted from Ebert and Griffin, *Business Essentials,* pp. 212–213

_____ 1. The organizational pattern of this paragraph is

    a. process.   c. spatial order.

    b. cause/effect.   d. classification.

_____ 2. The purpose of the paragraph is to

    a. describe different managerial styles.

    b. summarize the qualities of good managers.

    c. explain the effects of different managerial styles.

    d. show which managerial style is best.

_____ 3. A transitional word or phrase that signals the writers' pattern is

    a. another.   c. for example.

    b. because.   d. however.

_____ 4. A manager who involves subordinates in decision making but retains final decision-making power is using the style known as

    a. autocratic.   c. democratic.

    b. military.   d. free rein.

5. One characteristic of the autocratic style is that it allows for
   a. rapid decision making.
   b. employee creativity.
   c. input from subordinates.
   d. decisions by subordinates.

B.   Most of the asteroids, rocky objects that orbit stars, found outside the asteroid belt [regions in which asteroids are heavily concentrated]—including the Earth-approaching asteroids that pass near Earth's orbit—are probably "impacts waiting to happen." But asteroids can safely congregate in two stable zones outside the main belt. These zones are found along Jupiter's orbit 60 degrees ahead of and behind Jupiter. The asteroids found in these two zones are called the *Trojan asteroids,* and the largest are named for the mythological Greek heroes of the Trojan War. The Trojan asteroids are stable because of a different type of orbital resonance with Jupiter. In this case, any asteroid that wanders away from one of these zones is nudged back into the zone by Jupiter's gravity. The existence of such orbital resonances was first predicted by the French mathematician Joseph Lagrange more than 200 years ago—135 years before the discovery of the first asteroid in such an orbit. It is possible that the population of Trojan asteroids is as large as that of main-belt asteroids, but the greater distance to the Trojan asteroids makes them more difficult to study or even to count from Earth.

—adapted from Bennett et al., *The Cosmic Perspective,* p. 326

6. The topic of this paragraph is
   a. Earth's orbit.   c. the Trojan War.
   b. asteroids.   d. Jupiter.

7. The organizational pattern of this paragraph is
   a. comparison/contrast.   c. spatial order.
   b. classification.   d. cause/effect.

8. All of the following transitional words from the paragraph signal the writers' pattern *except*
   a. outside.   c. behind.
   b. into.   d. but.

_____ 9. One characteristic of asteroids outside the main belt is that they
   a. are totally unstable.
   b. are found only near Earth's orbit.
   c. can congregate safely in two zones along Jupiter's orbit.
   d. immediately crash into each other.

_____ 10. This paragraph is concerned primarily with
   a. differences between Trojan asteroids and main-belt asteroids.
   b. similarities between Trojan asteroids and main-belt asteroids.
   c. general characteristics of all types of asteroids.
   d. the physical position of asteroids outside the main belt.

RECOGNIZING PATTERNS

Directions: *After reading the following passage, select the choice that best answers each of the questions that follow.*

FOLK CULTURE AND POPULAR CULTURE

1   Today's rapid pace of cultural change requires us to distinguish between folk culture and popular culture. The term **folk culture** refers to a culture that preserves traditions. Folk groups are often bound by a distinctive religion, national background, or language, and folk cultures are conservative and resistant to change. Most folk-culture groups are rural, and relative isolation helps these groups maintain their integrity. Folk-culture groups, however, also include urban neighborhoods of immigrants struggling to preserve their native cultures in their new homes.

2   Cultural geographers have identified a surprising number of folk cultures across the United States. Folk geographic studies in the U.S. range from studies of songs, foods, medicine, and folklore to objects of folk material culture as diverse as locally produced pottery, clothing, tombstones, farm fencing, and even knives and guns. In addition, houses, barns, and other structures are built in distinct architectural styles that reveal the origins of their builders.

3   In North America the Amish provide an example of a folk culture. The Amish stand out because they wear plain clothing and shun modern education and technology. They prosper by specializing their farm production and marketing their produce, but they severely curtail the choice of goods that they will accept in return.

4   In contrast to folk culture, **popular culture** is the culture of people who embrace innovation and conform to changing norms. Popular culture may originate anywhere, and it tends to spread rapidly, especially wherever people have time, money, and inclination to indulge in it.

5   Popular material culture usually means mass culture—that is, items such as clothing, processed food, books, CDs, and household goods that are mass produced for mass distribution. Popular culture is largely defined by consumption, so it is usually more closely related to social class, as defined by income and education, than folk cultures are. The consumer items people buy are largely determined by what they can afford.

—adapted from Bergman and Renwick, *Introduction to Geography,* pp. 215–217

_____ 1. The primary purpose of this passage is to
   a. describe the history of folk groups in America.
   b. explain how geographers study different cultural groups.
   c. contrast the characteristics of folk culture and popular culture.
   d. give geographical locations for folk groups in America.

_____ 2. Popular material culture usually refers to items such as
   a. houses and other structures.
   b. locally produced pottery.
   c. farm fencing.
   d. consumer goods that are mass produced.

_____ 3. According to this passage, the Amish stand out because they
   a. wear plain clothing and shun modern education and technology.
   b. will accept anything in exchange for the goods they market.
   c. build in distinct architectural styles.
   d. strive to adapt to changing norms.

_____ 4. One transitional word or phrase in the passage that signals the writers' pattern is
   a. however.   c. in contrast.
   b. in addition.   d. largely defined.

_____ 5. In paragraph 3, the word **curtail** means
   a. want.   c. promote.
   b. limit.   d. change.

Directions: _For items 6–10, write F next to each characteristic of folk culture and P next to each characteristic of popular culture._

_____ 6. Preserves traditions and resists change

_____ 7. Embraces innovation

_____ 8. Originates anywhere and spreads rapidly

_____ 9. Mostly rural

_____ 10. More closely related to social class

ANALYZING PATTERNS

Directions: *After reading the following passage, select the choice that best answers each of the questions that follow.*

1   Mormons lead healthy lifestyles and on average live longer than other Americans. In great part this is due to their adherence to the Word of Wisdom in the Mormon scriptures, which calls for abstinence from wine, strong drink, tobacco, and hot drinks; moderation in eating meat; and eating wholesome foods including fruits and grains.

2   The Mormons following the Word have had a head start on good health practices, and recent studies have shown just how beneficial this has been. A study of Mormons living in Utah found that they had one-third less cancer than non-Mormons also living in the state. Because they do not smoke, it is not surprising that the incidence of cancers associated with smoking—lung, oral, esophagus, stomach, and bladder—was about half that of non-Mormons.

3   There are some cancers for which Mormons have high incidence rates: skin cancer, lip cancer, and melanoma. But non-Mormons living in Utah also have high rates of these cancers, and research speculate they are due in part to genetic and environmental factors. A large percentage of Utah's population—both Mormons and non-Mormons—are of northern European ancestry and are considered more susceptible to cancers at sites of high sunlight exposure. Utah has a lot of sunlight.

4   The death rate from cardiovascular disease is also lower for Mormons. Another study found that Utah Mormons had a 35 percent lower death rate from coronary disease than the rest of the population. It is believed that this lower death rate is also associated with the fact that Mormons do not smoke. An additional contributing factor is their lower-fat diet, the result of eating only moderate amounts of meat.

—adapted from Pruitt and Stein, *HealthStyles,* p. 29

_____   1. The topic of the passage is
        a. religion in America.
        b. cardiovascular disease.
        c. health benefits of the Mormon lifestyle.
        d. the state of Utah.

_____ 2. Throughout this passage, the writers compare and contrast the health of
   a. Mormons and non-Mormons.
   b. residents of Utah and residents of other states.
   c. Americans and Northern Europeans.
   d. meat-eaters and vegetarians.

_____ 3. In addition to comparison/contrast, the writers use the organizational pattern known as
   a. chronological order.   c. spatial order.
   b. classification.   d. cause/effect.

_____ 4. The disease for which both Mormons and non-Mormons in Utah have high incidence rates is
   a. lung cancer.
   b. skin cancer.
   c. cardiovascular disease.
   d. coronary heart disease.

_____ 5. In paragraph 3, the word **susceptible** means
   a. resistant.   c. vulnerable.
   b. unwilling.   d. fearful.

Directions: *For items 6–10, write C next to each item from the passage that is a cause and E next to each item that is an effect.*

_____ 6. Lower-fat diet

_____ 7. Abstinence from smoking

_____ 8. Lower incidence of cancer

_____ 9. Lower death rate from cardiovascular disease

_____ 10. High sunlight exposure

THE MIND-BODY CONNECTION
Rebecca J. Donatelle

Have you ever wondered if laughter can heal or keep you healthy? Taken from a college health textbook, *Health: The Basics*, this reading explores the relationship between physical and mental health.

Vocabulary Preview

These are some of the difficult words in this essay. The definitions here will help you if you can't figure out the meanings from the sentence context or word parts.

empirical evidence (par. 3) evidence that can be proved by means of observation or experiment

cognitive ability (par. 7) related to one's mental process, including such aspects as perception, awareness, reasoning, and judgment

immune system (par. 8) a system that protects the body from disease

interferon (par. 8) a protein substance produced by the body that helps the immune system by protecting healthy cells

baseline (par. 9) standard of measurement to which other measurements are compared

adjuncts (par. 10) something extra or additional

1   Can negative emotions make a person physically sick? Can positive feelings help us stay well? Researchers are exploring the interaction between emotions and health, especially in conditions of uncontrolled, persistent stress. According to one theory, the brain of an emotionally overwrought person sends signals to the adrenal glands, which respond by secreting cortisol and epinephrine (adrenaline), the hormones that activate the body's stress response. These chemicals are also known to suppress immune functioning, so a persistently overwrought person may undergo subtle immune changes. What remains to be shown is how these changes affect overall health, if they do at all.

Happiness: A Key to Well-Being

2   Although we can list the actions that we should perform to become physically healthy, such as eating the right foods, getting enough rest, exercising, and so on, it is less clear how to achieve that "feeling-good state" that researchers call **subjective well-being**

(SWB). This refers to that uplifting feeling of inner peace and wonder that we call "happiness." Psychologists David Myers and Ed Deiner completed a major study of this thing called happiness and noted that people experience it in many different ways, based on age, culture, gender, and other factors. However, in spite of the differences in the way it is experienced, SWB is defined by three central components.

1. *Satisfaction with present life.* People who are high in SWB tend to like their work and are satisfied with their current personal relationships. They are sociable, outgoing, and willing to open up to others. They also like themselves and enjoy good health and self-esteem.

2. *Relative presence of positive emotions.* People with high SWB more frequently feel pleasant emotions, mainly because they evaluate the world around them in a generally positive way. They have an optimistic outlook, and they expect success in what they undertake.

3. *Relative absence of negative emotions.* Individuals with a strong sense of subjective well-being experience fewer and less severe episodes of negative emotions, such as anxiety, depression, and anger.

3   Do you have to be happy all of the time to achieve overall subjective well-being? Of course not. Everyone experiences disappointments, unhappiness, and times when life seems unfair. However people with SWB are typically resilient, are able to look on the positive side, get themselves back on track fairly quickly, and are less likely to fall into deep despair over setbacks. There are several myths about happiness: that it depends on age, gender, race, and socioeconomic status. Research and empirical evidence, however, have debunked these myths:

- *There is no "happiest age."* Age is not a predictor of SWB. Most age groups exhibit similar levels of life satisfaction, although the things that bring joy often change with age.

- *Happiness has no "gender gap."* Women are more likely than men to suffer from anxiety and depression, and men are more at risk for alcoholism and personality disorders. Equal numbers of men and women report being fairly satisfied with life.

- *There are minimal racial differences in happiness.* For example, African Americans and European Americans report nearly the same levels of happiness, and African Americans are slightly less vulnerable to depression. Despite racism and discrimination, members of disadvantaged minority groups generally seem to "think optimistically" by making realistic self-comparisons and attributing problems less to themselves than to unfair circumstances.

- *Money does not buy happiness.* Wealthier societies report greater well-being. However, once the basic necessities of food, shelter, and safety are provided, there is a very weak correlation between income and happiness.

Having no money is a cause of misery, but wealth itself does not guarantee happiness.

4   Fortunately, humans are remarkably resourceful creatures. We respond to great loss, such as the death of a loved one or a traumatic event, with an initial period of grief, mourning, and sometimes abject rage. Yet, with time and the support of loving family and friends, we can pick ourselves up, brush off the bad times, and manage to find satisfaction and peace. Typically, humans learn from suffering and emerge even stronger and more ready to deal with the next crisis. Most find some measure of happiness after the initial shock and pain of loss. Those who are otherwise healthy, in good physical condition, and part of a strong social support network can adapt and cope effectively.

Does Laughter Enhance Health?

5   Remember the last time you laughed so hard that you cried? Remember how relaxed you felt afterward? Scientists are just beginning to understand the role of humor in our lives and health. For example, laughter has been shown to have the following effects:

- Stressed-out people with a strong sense of humor become less depressed and anxious than those whose sense of humor is less well developed.
- Students who use humor as a coping mechanism report that it predisposes them to experiencing a positive mood.
- In a study of depressed and suicidal senior citizens, patients who recovered were the ones who demonstrated a sense of humor.
- Telling a joke, particularly one that involves a shared experience, increases our sense of belonging and social cohesion.

6   Laughter helps us in many ways. People like to be around people who are fun-loving and laugh easily. Learning to laugh puts more joy into everyday experiences and increases the likelihood that fun-loving people will keep company with us.

7   Psychologist Barbara Fredrickson argues that positive emotions such as joy, interest, and contentment serve valuable life functions. Joy is associated with playfulness and creativity. Interest encourages us to explore our world, enhancing knowledge and cognitive ability. Contentment allows us to savor and integrate experiences, an important step to achieving mindfulness and insight. By building our physical, social, and mental resources, these positive feelings empower us to cope more effectively with life's challenges. While the actual emotions may be transient, their effects can be permanent and provide lifelong enrichment.

8   Laughter also seems to have positive physiological effects. A number of researchers, such as Lee Berk, M.D., and Stanley Tan, M.D., have noted that laughter sharpens our immune systems by activating T-cells and natural killer cells and

increasing production of immunity-boosting interferon. It also reduces levels of the stress hormone cortisol.

9   In one experiment, Fredrickson monitored the cardiovascular responses of human subjects who suffered fear and anxiety induced by an unsettling film clip. Some of them then viewed a humorous film clip while others did not. Those who watched the humorous film returned more quickly to their baseline cardiovascular state, indicating that laughter may counteract some of the physical effects of negative emotions.

10   In another study, 50 women with advanced breast cancer who were randomly assigned to a weekly support group lived an average of 18 months longer than 36 cancer patients not in the support group. The implication of this finding is that the women in the support group cheered each other on and that this allowed them to sleep and eat better, which promoted their survival. Other researchers have found that a fighting spirit and the determination to survive are vital adjuncts to standard cancer therapy.

11   A large body of evidence points to an association between the emotions and physical health, although we still have much to learn about this relationship. Does an emotional state trigger negative behaviors that lead to decreased immune functioning? Or do emotions directly affect health by stimulating the production of hormones that tax the immune system? In the meantime, however, it appears that happiness and an optimistic mind-set don't just feel good—they are also good for you.

——— ▪ ———

Directions: Select the letter of the choice that best answers each of the following questions.

CHECKING YOUR COMPREHENSION

_____   1. The main point of the selection is that

   a. negative emotions can make people physically sick.

   b. most people are too stressed-out to be happy.

   c. a sense of humor is the most important factor in achieving good health.

   d. there is a connection between the emotions and physical health.

_____   2. The state that researchers call *subjective well-being* (SWB) refers to

   a. relaxation.   c. happiness.

   b. mental health.   d. physical health.

3. All of the following statements about SWB are true *except*
   a. People with SWB are able to look on the positive side of life.
   b. SWB depends on age, gender, race, and socioeconomic status.
   c. People experience SWB in many different ways, based on many factors.
   d. People with SWB are less likely to fall into deep despair over setbacks.

4. An experiment by psychologist Barbara Fredrickson showed that laughter may
   a. lead to a decrease in the production of Interferon.
   b. interfere with the functioning of the immune system.
   c. increase the levels of hormones that activate the body's stress response.
   d. counteract some of the physical effects of negative emotions.

5. A study of breast cancer patients indicated that, in comparison to patients who were not in a support group, those who *were* in a support group
   a. did not live as long.
   b. lived longer.
   c. lived the same length of time.
   d. needed extra cancer therapy.

USING WHAT YOU KNOW ABOUT PATTERNS

6. When the author discusses the connection between emotions and health, the overall pattern she is following is
   a. listing.
   b. chronological order.
   c. process.
   d. cause/effect.

7. The word or phrase that signals the author's pattern in paragraph 5 is
   a. "just beginning to understand."
   b. "the following effects."
   c. "the last time."
   d. "in a study."

8. In paragraph 8, the author explains the positive effects of laughter. She uses the transitional word *also* to suggest which of the following patterns?
   a. classification
   b. chronological order
   c. addition
   d. comparison/contrast

9. In paragraph 8, the *cause* that the author is discussing is
   a. laughter.
   b. activation of T-cells and natural killer cells.
   c. increased production of interferon.
   d. reduced levels of cortisol.

10. The pattern of organization that the author follows in paragraph 11 is
    a. definition.   c. process.
    b. example.   d. summary.

USING CONTEXT AND WORD PARTS

11. In paragraph 1, the word **suppress** means
    a. expand.   c. reduce or inhibit.
    b. strengthen.   d. endure.

12. In paragraph 3, the word **resilient** means
    a. active.   c. important.
    b. flexible.   d. resentful.

13. In paragraph 3, the word **debunked** means
    a. proved wrong.   c. lied about.
    b. supported.   d. disappointed.

14. In paragraph 5, the word **predisposes** means

           a. follows a path.

           b. prevents illness.

           c. differs in degree.

           d. creates favorable conditions.

         15. In paragraph 7, the word **transient** means

           a. permanent.

           b. significant.

           c. temporary or passing.

           d. unbelievable.

REVIEWING DIFFICULT VOCABULARY

Directions: *Complete each of the following sentences by inserting a word from the Vocabulary Preview on page 291 in the space provided.*

16. My mother recommended chicken noodle soup and a hot water bottle as _____ to my doctor's prescription.

17. The researchers relied upon _____ to support the findings of their study.

18. The patient's _____ X-rays from last year were compared with his new X-rays to determine any changes in his condition.

19. Vaccines are given to stimulate a person's _____ to produce antibodies against specific diseases.

20. Some intelligence tests are designed to measure the _____ of children under age 5.

QUESTIONS FOR DISCUSSION

1. How do you typically deal with disappointments or difficulties in your life? Do you ever use laughter as a coping mechanism?

2. What do you believe are the most important factors in achieving happiness? Discuss how this selection supports (or contradicts) these factors.

3. Discuss the influence of optimism and "subjective well-being" on the health of people close to you. With these people in mind, do you see a correlation between positive or negative emotions and physical health?

WRITING ACTIVITIES

1. Write a paragraph in which you describe how laughter or a sense of humor helped you cope with a difficult situation.

2. Brainstorm a list of ways that the information in the selection could be applied in a medical or therapeutic setting.

3. Explore the Web site for the organization Laughter Heals at http://laughterheals.org/. Create an outline of this group's history, purpose, and activities.

Chapter 8: Recognizing Comparison/Contrast and Cause/Effect Patterns

RECORDING YOUR PROGRESS

Test	Number Right		Score
Practice Test 8-1	_____	× 10 =	_____ %
Practice Test 8-2	_____	× 10 =	_____ %
Practice Test 8-3	_____	× 10 =	_____ %
Mastery Test 8-1	_____	× 10 =	_____ %
Mastery Test 8-2	_____	× 10 =	_____ %
Mastery Test 8-3	_____	× 5 =	_____ %

EVALUATING YOUR PROGRESS

Based on your test performance, rate how well you have mastered the skills taught in this chapter by checking one of the boxes below or by writing your own evaluation.

☐ **Need More Improvement**
Tip: Try completing the Patterns of Organization—New York Harbor module in the Reading Skills section on the MyReadingLab Web site at **http://www.ablongman.com/myreadinglab** to fine-tune the skills that you have learned in this chapter.

☐ **Need More Practice**
Tip: Try using the Patterns of Organization—New York Harbor module in the Reading Skills section on the MyReadingLab Web site at **http://www.ablongman.com/myreadinglab** to brush up on the skills taught in this chapter, or visit this textbook's Companion Web site at **http://www.ablongman.com/mcwhorter** for extra practice.

☐ **Good**
Tip: To maintain your skills, quickly review this chapter by using this textbook's Companion Web site at **http://www.ablongman.com/mcwhorter**.

☐ **Excellent**

YOUR EVALUATION: _____

_____

_____

_____

THINK ABOUT IT!

Look carefully at the photograph below. What is your overall impression of the photograph? What details in the photo give you that impression? Place a check mark next to each of the statements that are likely to be true based on the information shown in the photograph.

_____ 1. The person shown in the photograph is a deep sea diver.

_____ 2. The water shown is probably a canal.

_____ 3. The boat behind the man is a pleasure craft.

_____ 4. The man is near the shore.

When you analyze statements like these, you are using *inference*—you are going beyond the "facts" of the photograph and thinking about what the photographer meant to convey. This chapter will show you how to use inference as you read.

CHAPTER 9

Understanding Inference and the Author's Purpose

What Is Inference?

Just as you use inference when you study a photograph, you also use it when you try to figure out why a friend is sad or what an author's message is in a particular piece of writing. An **inference** is an educated guess or prediction about something unknown based on available facts and information. It is the logical connection that you draw between what you observe or know and what you do not know.

Here are a few everyday situations. Make an inference for each.

- A well-dressed man walks toward the front of your lecture hall on the first day of class.

- You see a young woman in a shopping mall wearing a wedding ring pushing a baby in a stroller with two young children following her.

In the first situation, a good inference might be that the man is the instructor because he is not dressed like the average student. However, it is possible that the man is a student who has an important appointment right after class. In the second situation, one inference is that the woman was married very young and had three children in a row; another possibility is that she is married but is just babysitting the children.

When you make inferences about what you read, you go beyond what a writer says and consider what he or she *means*. You have already done this, to some extent, in Chapters 2 and 5 as you inferred the meanings of words from context (see pp. 50–51) and figured out implied main ideas (see pp. 155–156). Thus you know that writers may directly state some ideas but hint at others. It is left to the reader, then, to pick up on the clues or suggestions and to figure out the writer's unstated message. This chapter will show you how to do so.

How to Make Inferences

Making an inference is a thinking process. As you read, you are following the writer's thoughts. You are also alert for ideas that are suggested but not directly stated. Because inference is a logical thought process, there is no simple, step-by-step procedure to follow. Each inference depends on the situation, the facts provided, and the reader's knowledge and experience.

However, here are a few guidelines to keep in mind as you read. These will help you get in the habit of looking beyond the factual level.

1. **Be sure you understand the literal meaning.** Before you can make inferences, you need a clear grasp of the facts, the writer's main ideas, and the supporting details.

2. **Notice details.** Often a particular detail provides a clue that will help you make an inference. When you spot a striking or unusual detail, ask yourself: Why did the writer include this piece of information? Remember that there are many kinds of details, such as descriptions, actions, and conversations.

3. **Add up the facts.** Consider all the facts taken together. Ask yourself: What is the writer trying to suggest with this set of facts? What do all these facts and ideas point toward?

4. **Look at the writer's choice of words.** A writer's word choice often suggests his or her attitude toward the subject. Notice, in particular, descriptive words, emotionally charged words, and words that are very positive or negative.

5. **Understand the writer's purpose.** An author's purpose, which is discussed in the next section, affects many aspects of a piece of writing. Ask yourself: Why did the author write this?

6. **Be sure your inference is supportable.** An inference must be based on fact. Make sure there is sufficient evidence to justify any inference you make.

Keep the preceding guidelines in mind as you read the following Hispanic folktale from New Mexico. Infer why the wife baked tortillas.

THE DAY IT SNOWED TORTILLAS

Here is a story about a poor woodcutter. He was very good at his work. He could swing his ax powerfully and cut down big trees. He would split them up into firewood to sell in the village. He made a good living.

But the poor man was not well educated. He couldn't read or write. He wasn't very bright either. He was always doing foolish things. But he was lucky. He had a very clever wife, and she would get him out of trouble.

One day he was working far off in the mountains, and when he started home at the end of the day, he saw three leather bags by the side of the trail.

He picked up the first bag and discovered that it was full of gold coins! He looked into the second. It was full of gold too. And so was the third.

He loaded the bags onto his donkey and took them home to show to his wife. She was aghast. "Don't tell anyone you found this gold!" she warned him. "It must belong to some robbers who have hidden it out in the mountains. If they find out we have it, they'll kill us to get it back!

But then she thought, "My husband! He can never keep a secret. What shall I do?"

She came up with a plan. She told her husband, "Before you do anything else, go into the village and get me a sack of flour. I need a big sack. Bring me a hundred pounds of flour."

The man went off to the village grumbling to himself, "All day I work in the mountains, and now I have to drag home a hundred pounds of flour. I'm tired of all this work." But he bought the flour and brought it home to his wife.

"Thank you," she told him. "Now, you've been working awfully hard. Why don't you go lie down for a while?" He liked that idea. He lay down on the bed and soon fell fast asleep.

As soon as her husband began to snore, the woman went to work. She began to make tortillas. She made batch after batch of tortillas. She made them until the stack reached clear up to the ceiling in the kitchen. She turned that whole hundred pounds of flour into tortillas. Then she took them outside and threw them all over the ground.

The woodcutter was so tired he slept all that evening and on through the night. He didn't wake up until morning. When he awoke, he stepped outside and saw that the ground was covered with tortillas. He called to his wife. "What's the meaning of this?" he asked.

His wife joined him at the door. "Oh, my goodness! It must have snowed tortillas last night!"

"Snowed tortillas? I've never heard of such a thing."

"What? You've never heard of it snowing tortillas? Well! You're not very well educated. You'd better go to school and learn something."

So she packed him a lunch and dressed him up and made him go off to school.

He didn't know how to read or write, so they put him in the first grade. He had to squeeze into one of the little chairs the children sat in. The teacher asked questions and the children raised their hands enthusiastically. He didn't know the answers to any of those questions. He grew more and more embarrassed.

Then he had to go to the blackboard and write. He didn't even know the alphabet. The little boy beside him began to write his name on the board, and the woodcutter tried to copy the boy's letters. When the other children saw the man writing the boy's name instead of his own, they began to laugh at him.

He couldn't stand it any longer. He stomped out of the school and hurried home. He seized his ax. "I've had enough education," he told his wife. "I'm going to go cut firewood."

"Fine," she called after him. "You go do your work."

About a week later, just as the woman had suspected, the robbers showed up at the house one day. "Where is that gold your husband found?" they demanded.

The wife acted innocent. "Gold?" She shook her head. "I don't know anything about any gold."

"Come on!" the robbers said. "Your husband's been telling everyone in the village he found three sacks of gold. They belong to us. You'd better give them back."

She looked disgusted. "Did my husband say that? Oh, that man! He says the strangest things! I don't know anything about your gold."

"That's a likely story. We'll find out. We'll wait here until he comes home." So the robbers waited around all day—sharpening their knives and cleaning their pistols.

Toward evening the woodcutter came up the trail with his donkey. The robbers ran out and grabbed him roughly. "Where's that gold you found?"

The woodcutter scratched his head. "Gold?" he mumbled. "Oh, yes. Now I remember. My wife hid it." He called out, "Wife, what did you do with that gold?"

His wife sounded puzzled. "What gold? I don't know what you're talking about."

"Sure you do. Don't you remember? It was just the day before it snowed tortillas. I came home with three bags of gold. And in the morning you sent me to school."

The robbers looked at one another. "Did he say, 'snowed tortillas'?" they whispered. "She sent him to school?" They shook their heads in dismay. "Why did we waste our time with this numbskull? He's out of his head!"

And they went away thinking the woodcutter was crazy and had just been talking a lot of nonsense.

From that day on, it didn't really matter whether he was well educated or clever. It didn't even matter if he was a good woodcutter. For he was a rich man. He and his wife had those three sacks of gold all to themselves. And the robbers never came back.

—Hayes, *The Day It Snowed Tortillas: Tales from Spanish New Mexico*, pp. 9–13

Of course, you realized that the wife baked tortillas to create an unbelievable situation that her husband would report to the robbers. Let us look at some of the clues the writer gives that lead to this inference.

- **Descriptive details:** The author describes the husband as not very bright and as a person who could "never keep a secret." The wife is described as clever and as someone who "would get him out of trouble."

- **Action details:** The wife's actions—baking hundreds of tortillas and sending her husband to school—suggest the wife was doing silly, implausible things.

- **Conversation details:** The wife's statement, "Snowed tortillas? I've never heard of such a thing," reveals the absurdity of the situation. The robbers' statement, "Why did we waste our time with this numbskull?" reveals that the wife's plan worked.

- **Word choice:** Although writing in simple language, the author chooses words that emphasize the wife's plot. She acted "innocent." The husband is a "numbskull." The robbers "shook their heads in dismay."

Exercise 9–1

Directions: *Read each of the following passages. Based on the information contained in the passage, use inference to determine whether the statements that follow it are likely to be true (T) or false (F). Indicate your answer in the space provided.*

A. While working for a wholesale firm, traveling to country stores by horse and buggy, Aaron Montgomery Ward conceived the idea of selling directly to country people by mail. He opened his business in 1872 with a one-page list of items that cost one dollar each. People could later order goods through a distributed catalog and the store would ship the merchandise cash on delivery (COD). The idea was slow to catch on because people were suspicious of a strange name. However, in 1875 Ward announced the startling policy of "satisfaction guaranteed or your money back." Contrasting with the former retailing principle of caveat emptor (Latin for "buyer beware"), this policy set off a boom in Ward's business.

—Frings, *Fashion: From Concepts to Consumer*, p. 11

_____ 1. Aaron Ward had experience in sales before he began his own business.

_____ 2. Ward's early experiences in wholesale with country people led him to develop a business aimed at them.

_____ 3. Customers had to pay for their merchandise before it could be delivered.

_____ 4. Ward's mistake was to give every item on the list the same price.

_____ 5. Other stores in operation at the time did not offer money back guarantees.

B.   **"Is Laughter the Best Medicine?"**

Lucy went to the hospital to visit Emma, a neighbor who had broken her hip. The first thing Lucy saw when the elevator door opened at the third floor was a clown, with an enormous orange nose, dancing down the hall, pushing a colorfully decorated cart. The clown stopped in front of Lucy, bowed, and then somersaulted to the nurses' station. A cluster of patients cheered. Most of them were in wheelchairs or on crutches. Upon asking for directions, Lucy learned that Emma was in the "humor room," where the film *Blazing Saddles* was about to start.

Since writer Norman Cousins's widely publicized recovery from a debilitating and usually incurable disease of the connective tissue, humor has gained new respectability in hospital wards around the country. Cousins, the long-time editor of the *Saturday Review,* with the cooperation of his physician, supplemented his regular medical therapy with a steady diet of Marx brothers movies and *Candid Camera* film clips. Although he never claimed that laughter alone effected his cure, Cousins is best remembered for his passionate support of the notion that, if negative emotions can cause distress, then humor and positive emotions can enhance the healing process (Cousins, 1979, 1989).

—Zimbardo and Gerrig, *Psychology and Life,* p. 501

_____ 6. The clown was at the hospital to celebrate a patient's birthday.

_____ 7. *Blazing Saddles* and Marx brothers movies would be found in the comedy section of a video store.

_____ 8. Cousins believed that humor should be only a part of a person's health-care plan.

_____ 9. Lucy watched the movie with Emma.

_____ 10. Emma probably used a wheelchair or crutches to reach the humor room.

Exercise
9–2

Directions: *After reading the following selection, select the choice that best answers each of the questions that follow.*

MARKETING IN ACTION

Dressing Up the Basics in Idaho

In almost any grocery store across the United States, consumers can purchase ten pounds of Idaho-grown potatoes for less than $5.00. Despite this fact, Rolland Jones Potatoes, Incorporated, has been extremely successful selling a "baker's dozen" of Idaho potatoes for $18.95. The potatoes are wrapped in a decorative box that uses Easter grass.

The Baker's Dozen of Idaho potatoes is only one example of a growing phenomenon. Laura Hobbs, marketing specialist for the Idaho Department of Agriculture, reports that more than 200 Idaho farms produce specialty or value-added products. These goods typically consist of basic farm commodities that have been "dressed-up" with packaging. Consumers can choose from these products: microwave popcorn that comes on the cob and pops right off the cob, a bag of complete chili ingredients that makers claim won't cause embarrassing side-effects, and chocolate-covered "Couch Potato Chips."

Idaho farmers are supported by two groups, the Idaho Specialty Foods Association and Buy Idaho, whose goals are to help producers market and promote unique items. With the help of the groups, Idaho farmers are getting quite savvy. The marketers have discovered, for example, that packaging certain items together can increase their attractiveness. Hagerman's Rose Creek Winery found that sales of its wines soared when they were packaged in gift baskets with jars of Sun Valley brand mustard.

According to Hobbs, consumers attracted to the unique packaging provide a market for an endless variety of products, all of which are standard commodities transformed into new products through packaging. The value added through the unique packaging also provides opportunities to charge prices in ranges far above the prices of standard products—like $18.95 for 12 potatoes!

—Kinnear et al., *Principles of Marketing*, p. 301

_____ 1. Which detail does the author want to immediately impress upon the reader?

    a. Rolland Jones is a potato company.

    b. People are buying 12 potatoes for $18.95.

    c. Most grocery stores in the U.S. sell potatoes grown in Idaho.

    d. The Baker's Dozen potatoes come in a decorative box.

_____ 2. What can you infer about the Idaho farmers' attitudes toward specialty and value-added products?

a. They think these products are frivolous and unmarketable.

b. They feel bad about exploiting customers, but they need the extra money.

c. They wanted to learn more about creating and marketing these products.

d. They want to go back to selling basic products.

_____ 3. What inference can you make about the consumers of these products?

a. They buy these products as gifts.

b. They do not like the taste of inexpensive potatoes.

c. They do not have high incomes.

d. They enjoy finding new and interesting items to buy.

_____ 4. Which fact contributes *least* to the author's overall message?

a. Laura Hobbs is a marketing specialist.

b. Idaho Specialty Foods Association and Buy Idaho are two entities helping farmers with marketing.

c. Many people can buy ten pounds of potatoes for less than five dollars.

d. Sun Valley is a brand of mustard.

_____ 5. What inferences can you make about Idaho Specialty Foods Association and Buy Idaho?

a. These groups are responsible for increased potato prices.

b. These groups are staffed by lawyers.

c. These groups are regarded positively by many potato farmers.

d. These groups have caused disagreements and competition among potato farmers.

Understanding a Writer's Purpose

Writers have many different reasons or purposes for writing. These purposes affect their style of writing, the language they use, and the details they include. Once you understand a writer's purpose, it becomes easier to make inferences about a particular piece of writing.

Read the following statements and try to decide why each was written:

1. Maria Montessori founded her first school for young children in Italy in 1906. Today there are thousands of Montessori schools throughout the world.

2. *New Baked Fat-Free Spicy Chips.* Finally a tasty snack without the fat. We bake them instead of frying and add your favorite spices. Try a bag today.

3. Children tell it like it is . . . sometimes to the embarrassment of their parents.

4. In case of an emergency, remain calm and proceed in an orderly manner to the nearest exit.

The statements above were written (1) to give information, (2) to persuade you to buy chips, (3) to amuse you and make a comment on human behavior, and (4) to give instructions.

In each of the examples, the writer's purpose was fairly clear, as it will be in most textbooks, newspaper articles, and reference books. However, in many other types of writing, authors have less obvious purposes. In these cases, an author's purpose must be inferred.

Suppose a writer says, "The recent actions of the president of the United States should be closely examined." You cannot tell whether the writer's purpose is to criticize presidential actions, or to suggest that the actions should be studied carefully and used in making future policy decisions.

Sometimes a writer wants to express an opinion indirectly or to encourage readers to think about a particular issue or problem. Writers achieve their purposes by controlling what they say and how they say it. This section focuses on the techniques writers use to achieve the results they want.

Style and Intended Audience

Are you able to recognize a friend just by his or her voice? Can you identify family members by their footsteps? You are able to do so because each person's voice and footsteps are unique. Have you noticed that a piece of writing has unique characteristics as well? One selection may include many examples; another may have few. One may have relatively short sentences, whereas another may use long, complicated ones. The characteristics that make a piece of writing unique are known as **style**. By changing style, writers can create different effects.

Writers may vary their styles to suit their intended audiences. For example, someone writing an article on the latest medical research for a newspaper or general magazine, such as *Time* or *Newsweek*, would use fairly straightforward language and would be careful to explain or define any uncommon medical or technical terms. The same person, writing for medical doctors in *JAMA: The Journal of the American Medical Association* could assume that readers would be familiar with the subject and thus would use more sophisticated language and details.

Depending on the group of people for whom an author is writing, he or she may change the level of language, choice of words, and method of presentation. One step toward identifying an author's purpose, then, is to ask yourself: Who is the intended audience? Your response will be your first clue to determining why the author wrote the article.

Exercise 9–3

Directions: *After reading each of the following statements, select the choice that best describes the audience for whom each was written.*

_____ 1. Don't worry. Many youngsters experience a case of hives sometime during childhood. Usually the hives last for three to four days and then disappear. You may never know what caused them.

a. medical students   c. parents

b. pediatricians   d. pharmacists

_____ 2. The abortion debate has taken away resources and attention from other important issues such as high Caesarian rates, poor child-care options, and employer discrimination against working mothers.

a. pregnant teenagers

b. high-school health instructors

c. scientists performing stem cell research

d. people interested in women's rights

_____   3. Now available—homeworkhelper.com—let our experts instantly provide you with "almost perfect" homework.

   a. parents looking for a tutor

   b. teachers who need lesson plan ideas

   c. students who have trouble completing their homework assignments on time and well

   d. guidance counselors looking for resources for students

_____   4. Theories of music origin come in two basic varieties: structural models and functional models. Structural models look to the acoustic properties of music as outgrowths of homologous precursor functions, whereas functional models look to the adaptive roles of music as determinants of its structural design features.

   a. students of music

   b. pop music stars

   c. piano tuners

   d. professors of music history

_____   5. As a computer user, you can save money on costly service visits and calls by learning to troubleshoot and fix simple problems yourself.

   a. network administrators

   b. computer store managers

   c. computer hackers

   d. computer owners who are unfamiliar with simple computer problems

Language: Denotation and Connotation

You already know that writers use different words to achieve different purposes. A reporter writing an objective newspaper account of a murder might use very different words than would a brother of the slain person. In this section you will learn more about the meanings of words and how they are clues to a writer's purpose.

Which of the following would you like to be: shrewd, brainy, tricky, smart, ingenious, sly, or resourceful? Each of these words has the same basic meaning: "clever and quick-witted." But each has a different *shade* of meaning. *Ingenious* suggests being skillful and original in idea formation. *Sly,* on the other hand, suggests secrecy, mischief, and deceit.

This example shows that words have two levels of meaning—a literal meaning and an additional shade of meaning. These two levels of meaning are called denotation and connotation. A word's **denotation** is the meaning stated in the dictionary—its literal meaning. A word's **connotation** is the additional implied meanings that a word may take on. A word's connotation often carries either a positive or negative, favorable or unfavorable, impression. The words *tricky* and *sly* have a negative connotation because they imply deception and dishonesty. *Smart* and *resourceful* have a positive connotation because they suggest intelligence and creativity.

Here are a few more examples. Would you prefer to be described as *old* or *mature?* As *centered* or *self-absorbed?* As *fun* or *amusing?* Notice that each pair of words has a similar denotation, but each word within the pair has a different connotation.

Depending on the words they choose, writers can suggest favorable or unfavorable impressions of the person, object, or event they are describing. For example, through the writer's choice of words, the two sentences below create two entirely different impressions. As you read them, underline the words that have a positive or negative connotation.

- The war protesters stormed through the streets, causing major traffic gridlock.
- The peace march spanned several blocks as motorists looked on.

It is important to pay attention to a writer's choice of words, especially when you are reading persuasive material. Often a writer may communicate subtle or hidden messages or encourage you to feel positive or negative toward the subject.

Read the following paragraph from Martin Luther King Jr.'s "Letter from Birmingham Jail" and, as you read, underline the words that have a strong positive or negative connotation.

> We have waited for more than 340 years for our constitutional and God-given rights. The nations of Asia and Africa are moving with jetlike speed toward gaining political independence, but we still creep at horse-and-buggy pace toward gaining a cup of coffee at a lunch counter. I guess it is easy for those who have never felt the stinging darts of segregation to say, "Wait." But when you have seen vicious mobs lynch your mothers and fathers at will and drown your sisters and brothers at whim; when you have seen hate-filled policemen curse, kick, and even kill your black brothers and sisters; when you see the vast majority of your 20 million Negro brothers smothering in an

airtight cage of poverty in the midst of an affluent society; when you suddenly find your tongue twisted and your speech stammering as you seek to explain to your six-year-old daughter why she can't go to the public amusement park that has just been advertised on television, and see tears welling up in her eyes when she is told that Funtown is closed to colored children, and see ominous clouds of inferiority beginning to form in her little mental sky, and see her beginning to distort her personality by developing an unconscious bitterness toward white people . . . then you will understand why we find it difficult to wait.

—King, "Letter from Birmingham Jail," *Why We Can't Wait*, p. 363

Exercise 9–4

Directions: *For each of the following pairs of words, underline the word with the more positive connotation.*

1.	fictitious	false
2.	persistent	stubborn
3.	absentminded	preoccupied
4.	decontaminate	cleanse
5.	nasty	disagreeable
6.	disturbance	riot
7.	whimsical	scatterbrained
8.	flimsy	fragile
9.	bother	harass
10.	old-fashioned	antiquated

Understanding More of What You Read

Now that you know about inference and about the various clues to look for in a piece of writing, you should gain a better understanding of everything you read—textbooks, newspapers, magazines, and other reading materials. A writer's purpose is one of the best clues to look for as you read. When you pay attention to style, audience, tone, and language, you come to understand the writer's motivation—the effect he or she is trying to have on you, the reader.

The Textbook Challenge

Part A: Current Issues Reader

Read the article "The High Cost of Being Poor" (p. 501), and write a few sentences describing the author's purpose.

Part A: A College Textbook

Using a textbook chapter or reading that you have read for one of your other courses, write a few sentences describing the author's purpose.

What Have You Learned?

Directions: *Match each term in column A with its meaning in column B.*

Column A	Column B
_____ 1. inference	a. specific words or phrases that describe what people or things are doing
_____ 2. action details	b. the characteristics that make a piece of writing unique
_____ 3. descriptive details	c. a word's literal meaning
_____ 4. audience	d. specific words or phrases that characterize people or things
_____ 5. denotation	e. a word's implied meaning
_____ 6. connotation	f. an educated guess or prediction based on the available information
_____ 7. style	g. the group of people for whom an author is writing

What Vocabulary Have You Learned?

Directions: *The words in column A appear in this chapter. Test your mastery of these words by matching each word in column A with its meaning in column B.*

Column A	Column B
_____ 1. commodities	a. change in an unfavorable way
_____ 2. transformed	b. suggesting something bad is going to happen
_____ 3. determinants	c. items that are bought or sold
_____ 4. ominous	d. factors that cause or influence
_____ 5. distort	e. changed dramatically

INFERENCE AND AUTHOR'S PURPOSE

A. Directions: *Match each word in column A with the word in column B that has the same denotation but a different connotation.*

	Column A		Column B
_____	1. modernize	a.	tranquilize
_____	2. pacify	b.	eccentric
_____	3. overlook	c.	renovate
_____	4. unconventional	d.	pandemonium
_____	5. commotion	e.	neglect

B. Directions: *After reading the following passage, select the choice that best answers each of the questions that follow. You will have to use inference in order to answer the questions.*

THE FOX AND THE WOODCUTTER

A Fox, running before the hounds, came across a Woodcutter felling an oak and begged him to show him a safe hiding-place. The Woodcutter advised him to take shelter in his own hut, so the Fox crept in and hid himself in a corner.

The huntsman soon came up with his hounds and inquired of the Woodcutter if he had seen the Fox. He declared that he had not seen him, and yet pointed, all the time he was speaking, to the hut where the Fox lay hidden. The huntsman took no notice of the signs, but believing his word, hastened forward in the chase.

As soon as they were well away, the Fox departed without taking any notice of the Woodcutter: whereon he called to him and reproached him, saying, "You ungrateful fellow, you owe your life to me, and yet you leave me without a word of thanks."

The Fox replied, "Indeed, I should have thanked you fervently if your deeds had been as good as your words, and if your hands had not been traitors to your speech."

—An Aesop's Fable from The Gutenburg Project Online E-texts
(http://www.ibiblio.org/gutenberg/etext91/aesop11.txt)

_____ 6. The fox started to leave without paying attention to the woodcutter because

    a. the fox was afraid of the woodcutter.

    b. the fox was angry with the woodcutter.

    c. the fox was in a hurry.

    d. the fox could not see the woodcutter.

_____ 7. When the fox begged for a hiding place, he assumed

    a. the woodcutter would not reveal the hiding place.

    b. the huntsman would not ask the woodcutter if he had seen the fox.

    c. the woodcutter would invite him to stay the night.

    d. the woodcutter did not know the huntsman.

_____ 8. The woodcutter gave signals to the huntsman about the fox's hiding place because

    a. he was afraid of the huntsman.

    b. he wanted to befriend the huntsman.

    c. he hated the fox.

    d. There is not enough information in the passage to make an inference about the woodcutter's motive.

_____ 9. The woodcutter was angry because

    a. the huntsman did not understand the signals.

    b. the fox did not show any gratitude.

    c. he risked his life for the fox.

    d. the huntsman went away so quickly.

_____ 10. What lesson can you learn from this story?

    a. Don't trust anyone.

    b. Be careful whom you trust.

    c. Don't forget to thank your host.

    d. Actions are as important, or more important, than words.

INFERENCE AND AUTHOR'S PURPOSE

Directions: *After reading the following passage, select the choice that best answers each of the questions that follow.*

SCAR

The mark on my face made me who I am

1   Growing up, I had a scar on my face—a perfect arrow in the center of my cheek, pointing at my left eye. I got it when I was 3, long before I knew that scars were a bad thing, especially for a girl. I knew only that my scar brought me attention and tenderness and candy.

2   As I got older I began to take pride in my scar, in part to stop bullies from taunting me, but mainly to counter the assumption that I should feel embarrassed. It's true, I was embarrassed the first couple of times someone pointed at my cheek and asked "What's that?" or called me Scarface. But the more I heard how unfortunate my scar was, the more I found myself liking it.

3   When I turned 15, my parents—on the advice of a plastic surgeon—decided it was time to operate on what was now a thick, shiny red scar.

4   "But I don't mind the scar, really," I told my father as he drove me home from the local mall, explaining that I would have the surgery during my summer vacation. "I don't need surgery." It had been years since I'd been teased. And my friends, along with my boyfriend at the time, felt as I did—that my scar was unique and almost pretty in its own way. After so many years, it was a part of me.

5   "You do need surgery," my father said, his eyes on the road, his lips tight.

6   "But I like it," I told him. "I don't want to get rid of it."

7   "You need surgery," he said again, and he lowered his voice. "It's a deformity."

8   I don't know what hurt more that day: hearing my father call my scar a deformity or realizing that it didn't matter to him how I felt about it.

9   I did have plastic surgery that summer. They cut out the left side of the arrow, leaving a thinner, zigzag scar that blended into the lines of my face when I smiled. The following summer they did the same to the right side of the arrow. Finally, when I was 18, the surgeon sanded my cheek smooth.

10   In my late 20s, I took a long look at my scar, something I hadn't done in years. It was still visible in the right light, but no one asked me about it anymore. I examined the small steplike pattern and the way it made my cheek dimple when I smiled. As I leaned in awkwardly toward the mirror, I felt a sudden sadness.

11   There was something powerful about my scar and the defiant, proud person I became because of it. I have never been quite so strong since they cut it out.

—Audet, "Scar," from *The Sun,* p. 96

1. The central thought of the reading is that
   a. the author's scar contributed to her self-identity and gave her power.
   b. parents should not make decisions for their children.
   c. people really do not notice deformities.
   d. beauty is in the eye of the beholder.

2. The writer's primary purpose is to
   a. provide autobiographical information.
   b. explain how she feels about her scar.
   c. give a general overview of plastic surgery.
   d. criticize her father.

3. What does the author mean when she says "scars were a bad thing, especially for a girl"?
   a. Faces reveal the inner person.
   b. Girls poke fun at other girls.
   c. Beauty is important for girls and a scar is thought to detract from beauty.
   d. Boys do not care about how they look.

4. The meaning of the word **taunting** in paragraph 2 is
   a. complimenting.   c. teasing.
   b. arguing with.   d. accompanying.

5. This article seems written primarily for which of the following audiences?
   a. plastic surgery patients
   b. audiences interested in personal stories
   c. children with serious physical disabilities
   d. parents who make decisions for their children

6. The connotation of the word **deformity** (paragraph 7) is
   a. strong and forceful act.
   b. frequently recurring problem.
   c. unsightly, unpleasant disability.
   d. unfortunate accident.

7. Which word best describes the author's attitude toward her scar?
   a. positive
   b. negative
   c. uncertain
   d. hateful

8. Based on the reading, the author is likely to agree that
   a. plastic surgeons should be more sensitive to their patients' needs.
   b. parents seldom have their children's best interest in mind.
   c. disabled people should be pitied.
   d. disabilities can be a source of strength.

9. The father probably wanted his daughter to have surgery because he
   a. thought she would look better without the scar.
   b. thought the scar disturbed her.
   c. blamed himself that she had a scar.
   d. knew she would be happier in the long run.

10. The author helps readers make inferences about the father's attitude toward the scar by
    a. examples.
    b. opinion of others.
    c. dialogue.
    d. comparisons.

INFERENCE AND AUTHOR'S PURPOSE

Directions: *After reading the following passage, select the choice that best answers each of the questions that follow.*

'DEADBEAT' DADS—OR JUST 'DEAD BROKE'?

1   Most divorced or never-married fathers with an outstanding child-support understand the high cost of falling behind. Those who don't pay up often face repercussions such as paycheck withholding, automobile-license suspension, even jail time.

2   Such aggressive pursuit of child-support dollars has not been without its problems—or critics. And perhaps surprisingly, the list of critics now includes more child-welfare advocates. Organizations including the Washington-based Children's Defense Fund (CDF) maintain that child-support policies need to recognize economic realities and be more flexible, particularly where low-income, noncustodial fathers are concerned.

3   "States are frequently not doing enough to help low-income fathers get employment so that they can pay child support," says Deborah Weinstein, director of CDF's Family Income Division.

4   "What we've found is that there's a fundamental tension here between what the fathers can actually financially contribute to their children and the children's needs," says Paula Roberts, senior staff attorney at the Center for Law and Social Policy (CLASP) in Washington.

Collection Rate Has Doubled

5   For decades, federal, state, and local governments have worked together to locate noncustodial parents, establish paternity, set child-support guidelines, and enforce court orders.

6   But efforts to collect really began to pick up steam in the 1990s, largely because of changes resulting from the 1996 welfare-reform package. The measure streamlined paternity establishment by threatening to cut benefits to welfare recipients who failed to help identify a child's father.

7   Once paternity was established, states were able to employ any number of tactics to ensure that fathers support their children, including liens on homes and the withholding of up to 65 percent of a parent's wages.

8   The enforcement has paid off: The U.S. child-support collection rate has doubled since 1995. In 2000, nearly $18 billion of the $23 billion owed by noncustodial parents was collected. Altogether, the support has been invaluable to many of the nation's 12 million single parents, nearly 10 million of whom are women, according to the U.S. Census Bureau.

9   But the collection efforts have also created almost insurmountable problems for some low-income parents who are trying to support their children. Most state child-support-enforcement programs could be doing a much better job of distinguishing between so-called "deadbeat" fathers and "dead broke" fathers, Ms. Roberts says.

—Talvi, *The Christian Science Monitor*

_____ 1. In paragraph 1, the word **repercussions** means
   a. noncustodial laws.
   b. results or reactions to an action.
   c. contributions.
   d. struggles and disagreements.

_____ 2. The central thought of the entire passage is that
   a. there is a distinction between deadbeat dads and dead broke dads.
   b. organizations such as CDF have acted irresponsibly.
   c. enforcement of existing laws has paid off.
   d. low-income fathers need help in finding employment.

_____ 3. In paragraph 2, the phrase "noncustodial fathers" refers to fathers who
   a. are behind in their child-support payments.
   b. do not have to pay child support.
   c. have their children living with them.
   d. do not have their children living with them.

_____ 4. The author's purpose is to
   a. defend deadbeat dads.
   b. explain why children must have more money.
   c. describe how collection techniques are unfair to some fathers.
   d. prove that children of divorced parents suffer economically.

_____ 5. For which audience is the article primarily intended?
   a. women who are considering divorce
   b. fathers who are looking to avoid their child-support responsibilities
   c. children of divorced parents
   d. people who are concerned about the fairness of child-support collection

6. The author quotes Deborah Weinstein and Paula Roberts in order to
   a. identify people who are trying to protect deadbeat dads.
   b. support his claims with information from experts.
   c. further the careers of these women.
   d. provide readers with people to contact for more information.

7. The connotation of the word **streamlined** in paragraph 6 is
   a. complicated.   c. popularized.
   b. made more efficient. d. allowed more leniency.

8. The statistics given in paragraph 8 suggest that
   a. about two million men are raising children on their own.
   b. more women than men are divorced.
   c. there are almost ten million deadbeat dads in the U.S.
   d. single women are becoming rich from child-support payments.

9. According to the article, some fathers are "dead broke" because
   a. they gamble away their earnings.
   b. they spend their money on their new wives and children.
   c. they are asked to pay more child support than they can afford.
   d. collection techniques are too successful.

10. This reading is an excerpt from a larger article. You might expect the remainder of the article to contain
   a. a historical perspective on deadbeat dads.
   b. proposals for how dead-broke dads can be helped.
   c. reasons why divorces occur and measures to pull families together.
   d. all of the above

INFERENCE AND AUTHOR'S PURPOSE

A. Directions: *Study the photograph below and then use inference to answer the questions that follow.*

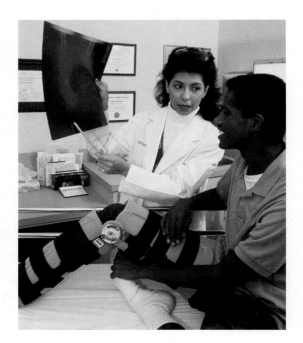

1. What is the relationship between the people in the photo?

    _____

2. What are the two people doing in the picture?

    _____

3. How might the man have come to be in this situation?

    _____

4. What details in the photo suggest that it was taken in a health-care setting?

    _____

    _____

B. Directions: *After reading the following passage, select the choice that best answers each of the questions that follow.*

EAT IT RAW

Raw food is not just for hippies anymore. It is being embraced by hip-hop stars and New York restaurateurs.

The raw-food diet, once the exclusive domain of '70s food faddists, is making a comeback for the same reasons it flourished 30 years ago: health and politics. Many find it helpful in relieving a variety of maladies—including allergies, fibromyalgia, obesity, gum disease, and mood swings—while others see raw food as a way to resist the unhealthy products of an industrialized food system. No matter how you slice it, excitement about a diet of uncooked food is running high.

"Anecdotally, there's been a definite rise in interest in raw-foods diets," says nutritionist Suzanne Havala Hobbs, adjunct assistant professor at the University of North Carolina–Chapel Hill's School of Public Health. "There's been a lot of information out about celebrities that are eating raw foods, and naturally many younger people are interested in trying it out. There's also been a wave of raw-foods cookbooks and restaurants." Hobbs, who also serves as nutrition advisor to the Baltimore-based Vegetarian Resource Group, is currently conducting a research survey on the topic, called the Raw Foods Project.

A raw-food diet consists of foods that have not been processed or heated above 118 degrees Fahrenheit. These might include fresh fruits, vegetables, cold-pressed oils, sprouted grains, nuts, seeds, and even organic wine—but not meat or fish. According to June Butlin in *Positive Health* (Aug. 2001), a proper raw-food diet provides high levels of natural, essential nutrients such as fiber, essential oils, antimicrobials, plant hormones, bioflavonoids, vitamins, minerals, chlorophyll, digestive enzymes, and antioxidants.

—Olson, *The Utne Reader*, pp. 20–22

_____ 5. The central thought of the passage is that

    a. a raw-food diet is the *most* healthy diet.

    b. interest in eating raw foods is growing in the U.S.

    c. raw foods improve mental health.

    d. the Raw Foods Project is studying the nutrition of raw foods.

_____ 6. Which of the following words or phrases has a somewhat negative connotative meaning?

    a. people

    b. restaurants

    c. food faddists

    d. degrees Fahrenheit

_____ 7. Which would *not* be part of a raw-food diet?

    a. cold-pressed olive oil

    b. fresh squeezed orange juice

    c. sunflower seeds

    d. bran muffin

_____ 8. Which describes the audience for whom this article was written?

    a. students studying nutrition

    b. businesspeople seeking new opportunities

    c. mothers looking for new dinner ideas

    d. people interested in alternative lifestyles and diets

_____ 9. The phrase "unhealthy products of an industrialized food system" refers to

    a. standard packaged grocery store food.

    b. raw food.

    c. all health foods.

    d. sugar-free and fat-free foods.

_____ 10. This reading is an excerpt from a larger article. You can expect the rest of the article to

    a. discuss other alternative diets.

    b. provide personal testimonies from people on a raw-food diet.

    c. explain why a raw-food diet is bad for you.

    d. teach you how to start a raw-food café.

INFERENCE AND AUTHOR'S PURPOSE

Directions: *After reading the following article, select the choice that best answers each of the questions that follow.*

WORKING MOMS: DON'T FEEL SO GUILTY

1   A study finds that children of career women do not lag behind their peers if their parents are attentive—and can afford quality child care.

2   As a working mother of two young boys, I found myself riveted by these recent headlines: "Study Links Working Mothers to Slower Learning" and "Study of Working Moms Finds Children Lag in Early Years." Oh, great, I thought. More ammunition for the ongoing guilt-slinging at working mothers.

3   The stories reported that three Columbia University researchers analyzed data from a three-year child-care study of 1,000 families in 10 cities. They found that 3-year-olds scored a significant six points less on the Bracken Test, which assesses children's knowledge of colors, letters, numbers, shapes, and comparisons, if their mothers worked more than 30 hours a week by the time the child was 9 months old. Considering that 75% of women are back on the job by a child's ninth month, myself included, I figured other working mothers were also assessing the damage they had inflicted on their children.

4   But first, consider the following: The women most likely to fret about this study are those who don't need to worry. They're likely to be highly educated, highly paid professionals, and their children tend to do well in school, notes Ellen Galinsky, president of the Families & Work Institute in New York.

5   These women also have the most flexible work and babysitting arrangements. Many have the option to work from home a couple of days a week or delay their return to the office. And they also are likely to have the resources to purchase high-quality child care. "For the woman who has the best child care possible and who is sensitive to her child when she is home," there is no difference between her children and those of mothers who stay home, says Jane Waldfogel, an associate professor of social work who is a co-author of the study.

6   One thing the study didn't account for was the father's contribution. In our family, my husband easily carries 50% of the home-life load, which definitely helps decrease my stress and increase my "maternal sensitivity"—my ability to be responsive to my children, which, along with quality of child care, number of hours in child care, and home environment, were the areas the researchers examined. While this study didn't include the impact of a father's efforts, Jeanne Brooks-Gunn, professor of child development and another co-author, is now researching the effects of shared caregiving on children under 3 who have two working parents. "The more shared caregiving there is among couples, the less likely there would be a negative effect on the children," she says.

7   Another thing to keep in mind is that studies are just that. They're helpful, but they don't account for many real-world situations. That means no working mother should second-guess the decisions she has made based on research findings.

8   What these study results can do is help with broader national policy decisions. The goal is to give women with lower incomes work flexibility and child-care arrangements similar to those enjoyed by higher-earning professionals. At this point, the debate returns to how best to increase quality child-care options, improve family-leave policies, and offer more part-time and flextime opportunities. Since the U.S. has among the worst work-family policies of all Western industrialized countries, those policies are certainly worth changing.

9   Yet while policy prescriptions may be useful for government planning, it's important for women to separate the public from the personal. If working moms don't focus on what is best for them and their families, they will only be adding stress to an already difficult job-vs.-home-life balance. And that does neither the mother, nor her children, any good.

—Gutner, *Business Week*

_____   1. The author of this article
   a. regrets she is forced to be a working mom.
   b. doesn't care if her children suffer because of her career.
   c. is concerned about the effect her career might have on her children.
   d. is confused about child-care studies.

_____   2. The primary intended audience of this article is
   a. working moms who can afford quality child care.
   b. fathers whose wives work full time.
   c. employers who hire women with young children.
   d. child-care center administrators.

_____   3. One purpose of the article is to
   a. examine the validity of child-care studies.
   b. offer child-care solutions for low-income working mothers.
   c. help high-earning mothers feel less guilty about sending their children to day care.
   d. expose the difficulties of a two-income household with children.

_____ 4. Which of the following statements best summarizes the writer's attitude toward research cited in this article?

  a. She mistrusts it.

  b. She feels it is flawed and poorly designed research.

  c. She feels it must be considered in light of family circumstances.

  d. She feels family studies have little practical value.

_____ 5. The author implies but does not directly state that

  a. women should not hold full-time jobs.

  b. fathers should be involved in day-care selection.

  c. children themselves determine the outcome of their day-care experiences.

  d. it is the children of low-income women who suffer from day care.

_____ 6. In paragraph 2, what is suggested by the phrase "ongoing guilt-slinging at working mothers"?

  a. Society doesn't approve of working moms so they try to make the moms feel guilty.

  b. Studies indicate that children of working moms suffer in some way.

  c. Working mothers make themselves feel guilty.

  d. Children make their mothers feel guilty.

_____ 7. The author of this selection is most likely a woman who is

  a. well educated and professionally employed.

  b. low paid and poorly educated.

  c. uncaring about her children.

  d. a strong advocate for better employee benefits.

_____ 8. The author mentions the contributions of the father because

  a. many working mothers are single.

  b. fathers can take a lot of stress off working mothers at home.

  c. most husbands do not contribute.

  d. the study did not mention their contribution.

_____ 9. The author feels that the research study should be used by
   a. mothers trying to decide if they should return to work.
   b. working mothers negotiating with their employers.
   c. policy makers, to create more options for low-income mothers.
   d. fathers trying to convince their wives to stay home.

_____ 10. The author concludes by suggesting that
   a. only mothers can know what is good for their children.
   b. research studies do not apply to daily life.
   c. government officials do not care about the struggles of working women.
   d. professional women should fight to help less fortunate working moms.

IF OUR SON IS HAPPY, WHAT ELSE MATTERS?
Scott Sherman

Originally published in *Newsweek*, this reading displays one family's struggle in the face of prejudice. Read it to discover why a child's adoption raised objections.

Vocabulary Preview

These are some of the difficult words in this essay. The definitions here will help you if you can't figure out the meanings from the sentence context or word parts.

spate (par. 1) large quantity

bias (par. 4) prejudice

autism (par. 7) a disorder characterized by self-absorption, little social interaction, and repetitive behavior

congenital (par. 10) present at birth

fundamental (par. 15) basic, essential

1   My son had a spate of bad falls. His black eye and leg cast made him look like he escaped a car crash, but just barely. People asked at every turn, "What happened to him?"

2   The honest answer would have been "What *didn't* happen to him?" He's had a rough life.

3   But since the truth is complicated, my answers tended to be flip. "You should see the other guy!" At one point, I said to my partner: "It's amazing no one's reported us for child abuse."

4   Then someone did. Unfortunately, it may not have been out of concern for our child's well-being, but because of bias toward his parents.

5   I had adopted Sasha seven months earlier from Eastern Europe. While we knew that not everyone approved of "gay adoption" as a concept, we couldn't believe that anyone would prefer that this specific child had been left in his orphanage. He wasn't exactly thriving there. At 17 months, Sasha was the size of an American 5-month-old. While most kids walk by 12 months, Sasha could barely crawl. He didn't babble or coo. His eyes were vacant and haunted.

6   Born 10 weeks premature and at less than four pounds, Sasha would have benefited from early intervention. But he spent his first 17 months lying alone in a crib. He was sickly and withdrawn. I asked one of the orphanage workers if Sasha ever smiled, and she replied "No, he's a serious child." Imagine a child who's never smiled.

7　　When children aren't loved, they drift away. Sasha lived in his own world. He cared for no one. It didn't matter who held him—we were all the same. Toys slipped unnoticed from his hands. Even when no longer confined to a crib, he just lay on his back sucking his thumb. At the orphanage, they told me he had "normal curiosity," but I think they meant normal for a stone. When I brought Sasha to an expert in the psychological assessment of orphaned children, he diagnosed Sasha as having institutional autism.

8　　Sasha's story would be unbearably sad if it weren't for how well he's done since coming home. By his 2nd birthday, he was grinning and laughing all the time. He went from being severely underweight to downright chubby. He's engaged and affectionate, and every day he wakes up happy.

9　　A speech therapist told us that, given Sasha's background, we shouldn't expect any words until 2. But when that birthday arrived, Sasha already had 60 words and phrases. He even says "please!"

10　　Sadly, Sasha's walking is still impeded by a congenital condition. But he's tenacious in his attempts to toddle around, and we encourage his trying. This leads to lots of bumps and bruises.

11　　Given his appearance, we weren't totally surprised that someone called the authorities. Done for the right reasons, that's the smart thing to do. But were the motivations here right?

12　　State investigators concealed the complainant's identity, but friends who knew her filled us in on what had happened. They said that the complainant had told them how terrible she thought it was that Sasha had two daddies. They believed her bias was what motivated her to call the authorities. My partner and I hope that's not true, but we may never know.

13　　To close the investigation, we had to take Sasha to a hospital for an assessment. We were there for six hours. He was kept up past his bedtime and endlessly poked and prodded. Worse, even after the attending physician was convinced that there was no mistreatment, hospital rules required that Sasha undergo a full-body skeletal exam. So, our hysterical, tired child was held down for half an hour, twisted this way and that on a cold metal table for 15 X-rays he never needed. At 2, my son learned how prejudice can—literally—hurt.

14　　But anti-gay prejudice hurts many children. Hundreds of thousands of them need homes. Yet some people would prefer that children be stuck in foster care or institutions rather than live with two loving parents of the same sex. I can't decide if that's more crazy or cruel.

15　　My partner and I don't feel like heroes for adopting Sasha. We're the lucky ones to have this wonderful child. But had we not taken a risk on a kid who wasn't looking too good at the time, Sasha might still be in that orphanage. His beautiful, inspiring light would have been lost. For the person who reported us for abuse and for the lawyers for the state of Florida (who recently defended that state's ban of gay adoption by claiming "there is not a fundamental right to adopt or to be adopted"), that loss would have been acceptable. If they really cared about kids, just one of Sasha's smiles would change their minds.

▬ ▪ ▬

Directions: *Select the letter of the choice that best answers each of the questions that follow.*

CHECKING YOUR COMPREHENSION

_____ 1. Sasha was bruised because he
  a. was in a car accident.
  b. had been abused at the orphanage.
  c. had difficulty walking and would fall.
  d. was hurt by his adoptive parents.

_____ 2. The workers at the orphanage attributed Sasha's withdrawn condition to his being
  a. born prematurely.   c. sick.
  b. "a serious child."   d. autistic.

_____ 3. In what way did Sasha improve after he was adopted?
  a. He gained weight and became happy and loving.
  b. He could speak at an early age.
  c. He moved out of a crib into a bed.
  d. He learned to play with new, more complex toys.

_____ 4. Who called the child-abuse authorities on Sherman and his partner?
  a. a concerned neighbor   c. a prejudiced acquaintance
  b. a worried babysitter   d. a hospital worker

_____ 5. Why did Sasha have to get so many X-rays?
  a. The attending physician saw signs of abuse.
  b. Sasha had broken bones.
  c. A court requested it.
  d. Hospital policy required it for the investigation.

USING WHAT YOU KNOW ABOUT INFERENCE AND THE WRITER'S PURPOSE

_____ 6. The audience that the author most likely intended this selection for is
  a. social workers.   c. gay couples.
  b. health-care professionals. d. the general public.

_____ 7. The author's main purpose for writing this selection is to
   a. expose the conditions in orphanages.
   b. show how painful anti-gay prejudice can be.
   c. show how loving same-sex couples can be toward children.
   d. evaluate the procedures of child protective agencies.

_____ 8. The author suggests that Sasha was in a bad way at the orphanage because
   a. he wasn't given proper nurturing and care from birth.
   b. the orphanage was crowded and dirty.
   c. Sasha had a serious personality.
   d. his congenital condition kept him from being happy and affectionate.

_____ 9. The author feels that people who want to report child abuse should
   a. mind their own business.
   b. do it for the right reasons.
   c. harass people they don't like.
   d. talk to the parents first.

_____ 10. The author believes that
   a. children are better off adopted by gay parents than no one at all.
   b. adoption is a fundamental right.
   c. Sasha might indeed be better off with parents of the same sex.
   d. orphanages should be better regulated in Eastern Europe.

CONTEXT AND WORD PARTS

_____ 11. In paragraph 5, the word **vacant** means
   a. unoccupied.   c. absent.
   b. clear.   d. expressionless.

_____ 12. In paragraph 7, **assessment** refers to
   a. evaluation.   c. record keeping.
   b. estimation.   d. approval.

_____ 13. In paragraph 8, the word **engaged** means
   a. getting married.   c. fastened.
   b. busy.   d. involved.

_____ 14. In paragraph 10, the word **impeded** means
   a. damaged.   c. hindered.
   b. endangered.   d. relieved.

_____ 15. In paragraph 10, the word **tenacious** means
   a. strong.   c. disconnected.
   b. reluctant.   d. persistent.

REVIEWING DIFFICULT VOCABULARY

Directions: _Complete each of the following sentences by inserting a word from the Vocabulary Preview on page 331 in the space provided._

16. Doctors agree that most _____ defects have no known cause.

17. Sahsa's parents wondered if he had a form of _____ since he didn't play with toys and didn't seem to notice those around him.

18. Many politicians believe that health care is a _____ right that the government should provide to all.

19. The glowing streak across the night sky caused a _____ of calls to the Channel Seven newsroom.

20. Unfortunately, after all the struggles of the Civil Rights movement, there still exists a great deal of _____ against minorities in our country.

QUESTIONS FOR DISCUSSION

1. What motivated the complainant to report child abuse? What did she hope to accomplish?
2. What issues or problems might children of a gay couple face in our society?
3. Hospital rules frustrated Sherman and his partner. Have you experienced similar frustration with institutional rules?

WRITING ACTIVITIES

1. Write a paragraph describing one form of prejudice you have observed or experienced.

2. Brainstorm a list of various prejudices and biases that are common in our society. Then choose one you feel strongly about and write a brief essay explaining what might be done to overcome or counteract it.

3. Visit the Web site http://www.pbs.org/independentlens/daddyandpapa/index.html for a documentary film called *Daddy & Papa* that was shown on PBS. Write a paragraph about the role of film in relation to sensitive issues such as gay adoption. For example, how does a film like this help or hinder a cause?

Chapter 9: Understanding Inference and the Author's Purpose

RECORDING YOUR PROGRESS

Test	Number Right			Score
Practice Test 9-1	_____	$\times\ 10$	$=$	_____ %
Practice Test 9-2	_____	$\times\ 10$	$=$	_____ %
Practice Test 9-3	_____	$\times\ 10$	$=$	_____ %
Mastery Test 9-1	_____	$\times\ 10$	$=$	_____ %
Mastery Test 9-2	_____	$\times\ 10$	$=$	_____ %
Mastery Test 9-3	_____	$\times\ 5$	$=$	_____ %

EVALUATING YOUR PROGRESS

Based on your test performance, rate how well you have mastered the skills taught in this chapter by checking one of the boxes below or by writing your own evaluation.

☐ **Need More Improvement**
Tip: Try completing the Purpose and Tone—The Getty Museum, California module in the Reading Skills section on the MyReadingLab Web site at **http://www.ablongman.com/myreadinglab** to fine-tune the skills that you have learned in this chapter.

☐ **Need More Practice**
Tip: Try using the Purpose and Tone—The Getty Museum, California module in the Reading Skills section on the MyReadingLab Web site at **http://www.ablongman.com/myreadinglab** to brush up on the skills taught in this chapter, or visit this textbook's Companion Web site at **http://www.ablongman.com/mcwhorter** for extra practice.

☐ **Good**
Tip: To maintain your skills, quickly review this chapter by using this textbook's Companion Web site at **http://www.ablongman.com/mcwhorter**.

☐ **Excellent**

YOUR EVALUATION: _____

_____

_____

_____

THINK ABOUT IT!

This cartoon's message is clear as soon as you realize that the scene shown is taking place in Juneau, Alaska. Do you agree that global warming is an important environmental problem? If you agree, you may say that the environment is rapidly changing due to harmful human activities, such as the burning fossil fuels and the destruction of tropical rainforests. You may offer the opinion that these changes are caused by humans and that humans must take responsibility for their actions.

What might someone say who has a different opinion on the issue of global warming? They might say that global warming is the result of natural causes, and that there have been similar periods in the past. They might offer the opinion that there is therefore no need to take action to decrease carbon dioxide levels in the atmosphere.

CHAPTER 10

Fact and Opinion

Is It Fact or Opinion?

The ability to distinguish between fact and opinion is an important part of reading critically. You must be able to evaluate ideas you encounter and determine whether they are objective information from a reliable source or whether they are one person's expression of a personal belief or attitude.

Facts

Facts are statements that can be verified. They can be proven true or false. Statements of fact are objective—they contain information but do not tell what the writer thinks or believes about the topic or issue. The statement "My car payments are $250 per month." is a fact. It can be proven by looking at your car loan statement. Here are a few more statements of fact:

EXAMPLES

1. The population of the United States in 2000 was 281,421,906. (You can check this by looking at Census figures found in various fact books and almanacs.)

2. In Washington State drivers must stop for pedestrians and bicyclists at crosswalks and intersections. (You can check this in the Washington State Drivers' Guide.)

3. Greenpeace is an organization dedicated to preserving the Earth's ability to support life in all its many forms. (You can check this by reading its mission statement or the "About Us" page on its Web site at http://www.greenpeace.org.)

Opinions

Opinions are statements that express a writer's feelings, attitudes, or beliefs. They are neither true nor false. They are one person's view about a topic or issue. The statement "My car payments are too expensive." is an opinion. It expresses your feelings about the cost of your auto payments. Others may disagree with you, especially the company that sold you the car or another person who pays twice as much as you are paying. As you evaluate what you read, think of opinions as one person's viewpoint that you are free to accept or reject. Here are a few more examples of opinions:

EXAMPLES

1. Bill Clinton was a better president than most people realize.
   (Those who dislike Clinton's policies or lifestyle would disagree.)

2. The slaughter of baby seals for their pelts should be outlawed.
   (Hunters who make their living selling pelts would disagree.)

3. Population growth should be regulated through mandatory birth control. (People who do not believe in birth control would disagree.)

Here is a list of the types of statements that are often opinions:

- Positions on controversial issues (gun control, abortion, animal experimentation)
- Predictions about things in the future (predicting that there will be ten major hurricanes next year; or speculating that the Federal Reserve Bank will reduce the interest rate by half a percent; or optimistically introducing a gubernatorial candidate as the "next governor")
- Evaluations of people, places, and things (a professor's teaching skills, a vacation spot, a movie)

Exercise 10-1

Directions: *Indicate whether each of the following statements is a fact (F) or an opinion (O).*

_____ 1. Alligators provide no physical care for their young.

_____ 2. Humans should be concerned about the use of pesticides that kill insects at the bottom of the food chain.

_____ 3. There are 28 more humans living on the earth now than there were ten seconds ago.

_____ 4. We must bear greater responsibility for the environment than our ancestors did.

_____ 5. Nuclear power is the only viable solution to our dwindling natural resources.

_____ 6. Between 1850 and 1900 the death rate in Europe decreased due to industrial growth and advances in medicine.

_____ 7. Dogs make the best pets because they can be trained to obey.

_____ 8. Solar energy is available wherever sunlight reaches the earth.

_____ 9. By the year 2010, many diseases, including cancer, will be preventable.

_____ 10. Hormones are produced in one part of the body and carried by the blood to another part of the body where they influence some process or activity.

Recognizing Judgment Words

When a writer or speaker expresses an opinion he or she often uses words or phrases that can tip you off that a judgment or opinion is being offered. Here are a couple of examples.

Professor Rodriguez is a _better_ teacher than Professor Harrigan.

The word _better_ suggests someone is deciding who is more skilled than someone else. Many students disagree about the qualities that make a good teacher.

My sister's behavior at the party was _disgusting_.

The word _disgusting_ reveals the author strongly disapproves and was sickened or horrified by the sister's behavior.

Here is a list of words that often suggest that the writer is interpreting, judging, evaluating, or expressing feelings.

Judgment Words				
bad	good	worthwhile	wonderful	frightening
worse	better	worthless	lovely	
worst	best	disgusting	amazing	

Exercise 10-2

Directions: *For each of the following statements, underline the judgment word or phrase that suggests the statement is an opinion.*

1. Purchasing a brand new car is a terrible waste of money.

2. Many wonderful vegetarian cookbooks are available in bookstores.

3. Of all the film versions of Victor Hugo's novel *Les Miserables*, the 1935 version starring Charles Laughton is the best.

4. The introductory biology textbook comes with an amazing CD-ROM.

5. Volunteers for Habitat for Humanity are engaged in a worthwhile activity.

Mixing Fact and Opinion

Writers often mix fact and opinion within a piece of writing. They may mix fact and opinion within a paragraph or even within a single sentence. Some writers deliberately include some factual information to make their writing appear substantive and thereby encourage readers to accept their opinions along with the facts.

Mixed Paragraphs

Here is an example of a paragraph that mixes fact and opinion. The statements of opinion are highlighted.

Cutting taxes was one of the best decisions President Bush has made during his presidency. Many Americans are pleased to find more money in their pockets after taxes. However, the legislation will expire in ten years unless laws are passed to make the cuts permanent. Unless made permanent, the tax rates will return to their Clinton-era levels in 2011. A return to the previous high levels will no doubt anger most Americans who have become accustomed to lower taxes.

In this paragraph, the writer presents some factual information about the tax cut timetable but also offers opinions about the value of the tax cuts.

To easily distinguish fact from opinion, ask yourself, "Is this information that can be verified, or is it what someone thinks about the topic?"

Exercise
10–3
Directions: *Each of the following paragraphs contains both fact and opinion. Read each paragraph and label each sentence as fact or opinion.*

A. [1] Flowering plants that are native to the South include purple coneflower and rose verbena. [2] In the view of many longtime gardeners, these two plants are an essential part of the Southern landscape. [3] Trees that are native to the South include a variety of oaks, as well as flowering dogwoods and redbuds. [4] Dogwoods are especially lovely, with their white, pink, or coral blossoms announcing the arrival of spring. [5] For fall color, the deep red of the Virginia willow makes a spectacular show in the native Southern garden.

Sentences: 1. _____   2. _____   3. _____
            4. _____   5. _____

B. [1] Today, many companies provide child-care assistance, either on- or off-site, for their employees. [2] This suggests that employers are becoming aware that their workers' family concerns can affect the company's bottom line. [3] The Eli Lilly pharmaceutical company, for example, has built two child-development centers with a total capacity of more than 400 children. [4] In addition to assistance with daily child care, Bank of America reimburses employees for child-care expenses related to business travel. [5] It seems clear that other, less progressive employers will have to follow these companies' leads in order to attract and retain the best employees.

Sentences: 1. _____   2. _____   3. _____
            4. _____   5. _____

C. [1] Preparing a will is an important task that people ignore because they prefer not to think about their own death. [2] However, if you die without a will, the courts will determine how your assets should be distributed, as directed by state law. [3] Even more important than establishing a will, in my opinion, is expressing your willingness to be an organ donor upon your death. [4] Each year, twenty-five thousand new patients are added to the waiting list for organ transplants. [5] The legacy of an organ donor is far more valuable than any material assets put in a will.

Sentences: 1. _____   2. _____   3. _____
            4. _____   5. _____

Mixed Sentences

Here is an example of a sentence that contains a mix of fact and opinion.

Chronic back pain affects millions of Americans, but there are many more important conditions that need immediate attention from our health-care professionals.

In this sentence, *Chronic back pain affects millions of Americans* is a fact, and *but there are many more important conditions that need immediate attention from our health-care professionals* expresses an opinion.

In the following sentence, you can see that the author blends fact and opinion to convince the reader that an article on soy products is reputable.

Dr. Athena Hunt, one of the best nutritionists, wrote an article titled, "Soy: The Amazing Miracle Bean."

Exercise 10–4

Directions: *Underline the portion of each sentence that contains an opinion.*

1. Earthquake preparedness is vital in Southern California where earthquakes are the worst imaginable disaster that could occur there.

2. Senior citizens can benefit from having a pet since cats and dogs are so friendly.

3. Children should be in mixed-aged classrooms since all children develop at different rates.

4. Most documentary films are dull because they deal with real-life events.

5. Food banks are always in need of donations to meet their costs because nobody realizes what valuable services they provide.

6. Healthy eating habits are important, but most exercise regimes are a waste of time.

7. Christmas has become too commercial; decorations go up right after Halloween in some stores.

8. Tree sitters get a great deal of media attention because they are so strange.

9. Many families with young children are now taking cruise vacations since these are the best travel deals.

10. No one goes to see community theater productions because the actors are not professionals.

Evaluating Fact and Opinion

Not every fact needs to be independently checked in another source. When using reliable sources such as textbooks, encyclopedias, and scholarly journals, it is usually safe to assume that the author is presenting accurate information. For example, if you are reading about the Cuban Missile Crisis in *The Cold War Encyclopedia,* it is safe to assume that facts about those thirteen days in October 1962 are accurate.

However, when using less reliable and less trustworthy sources such as personal Web sites, letters to the editor, and popular magazines, it may be necessary to verify the information by checking more reliable sources. For example, if you are researching voting patterns for a term paper, and find an editorial in your local newspaper with statistics about a recent county election, you should verify these numbers. You can find out the official counts by contacting the local board of elections by phone or on the Internet.

Here are some tips to use when cross-checking facts in a second source:

- **Use a reliable source.** If you need help identifying a second source, ask your instructor or a librarian.
- **Find current sources.** Some information can change quickly.
- **Look at primary sources when possible.** For example, most American demographic information originally comes from the U.S. Census.

Because opinions are an expression of someone's personal attitudes or feelings, they cannot be verified as either true or false. However, you can evaluate how well the writer supports or justifies his or her opinions. For example, a writer may offer the opinion that plastic shopping bags are harmful to the environment. She may substantiate that attitude by explaining that the bags do not biodegrade and offering statistics that reveal the number of such bags going into landfills each year.

Writers may substantiate a statement of opinion in the following ways:

1. **Giving reasons.** A writer may support the opinion that school uniforms should not be required by stating that they are expensive and some parents cannot afford them.
2. **Offering personal experience that supports the opinion.** An author may support public school attendance because he went through public schools and ended up "fine."
3. **Presenting statistics.** A writer may, for example, try to prove that expensive housing drives families out of cities by citing census figures that show how the percentage of children is lowest in expensive urban cores such as San Francisco and Seattle.

4. **Offering examples.** For instance, a writer may explain clichés by giving examples of several, such as: "A step in time saves nine" and "Don't bite the hand that feeds you."

Directions: *For each opinion, choose the type of information that the author could use to* best *support the opinion.*

_____ 1. Opinion: Parents should read to their children daily.

    a. an example of a mother who reads Mother Goose stories to her child

    b. an explanation that reading to children helps them see reading as fun

    c. statistics that report how many children's books are published each year

    d. the author's story of her children's reading preferences

_____ 2. Opinion: When teachers go on strike, the students suffer the most.

    a. quotes from a wide variety of students who express distress and hurt

    b. statistics that reflect the number of strikes that occur each year

    c. an explanation of why teachers choose to strike

    d. an interview with a teacher on strike

_____ 3. Opinion: The American prison system is doing a poor job of rehabilitating criminals.

    a. an interview with a prison guard

    b. statistics that show the numbers of inmates who are rearrested after release from prison

    c. examples of prisoners who go on to productive crime-free lives after their incarceration

    d. a list of the societal conditions that contribute to a person's tendency toward a life of crime

_____ 4. Opinion: Universities and colleges can do a great deal to stop underage drinking on campus.

    a. descriptions of the activities and successes of anti-drinking campaigns at various schools across the country

    b. interviews with students who have been punished for illegal drinking

       c. data from research studies that address the negative effects of alcohol on college students

       d. a list of Web sites that provide information for college students with alcoholism

_____ 5. Opinion: They'll never find a cure for the common cold.

       a. statistics that show the number of people who get sick with a cold every year

       b. examples of other diseases and conditions for which there are no cures

       c. an interview with a doctor who treats patients suffering from the common cold

       d. a description of the complex nature of the hundreds of cold viruses and the ease of transmission

Informed Opinions

The opinion of experts is known as informed opinion. For example, the surgeon general is regarded as an authority on the health of Americans, and his or her opinion on this subject is more trustworthy than that of casual observers or nonprofessionals.

Here are a few examples of expert opinions.

EXAMPLES

Alan Greenspan, chair of the Federal Reserve Board:

"The period of sub-par economic performance is not yet over."

Jane Goodall, primate expert and ethologist:

"Chimps are in massive danger of extinction from dwindling habitats—forest are being cut down at an alarming rate."

Arthur Sullivan, attorney specializing in divorce/child custody:

"Don't buy your child lavish gifts or take him or her to special places. Such activities may make the judge suspicious. Live normally."

Textbook authors, too, often offer informed opinion. As experts in their fields, they may make observations and offer comments that are not strictly factual. Instead, they are based on years of study and research. Here is an example from an American government textbook:

The United States is a place where the pursuit of private, particular, and narrow interests is honored. In our culture, following the teachings of Adam

Smith, the pursuit of self-interest is not only permitted but actually celebrated as the basis of the good and prosperous society.

—Greenberg and Page, *The Struggle for American Democracy*, p. 186

The author of this statement has reviewed the available evidence and is providing his expert opinion on what the evidence indicates about American political culture. The reader, then, is free to disagree and offer evidence to support an opposing view.

Some authors are careful to signal the reader when they are presenting an opinion. Watch for words and phrases such as:

Opinion Words and Phrases			
apparently	this suggests	in my view	one explanation is
presumably	possibly	it is likely that	according to
in my opinion	it is believed	seemingly	

In the following excerpt from a psychology textbook, notice how the author carefully distinguishes factual statements from opinion by using qualifying words and phrases (underlined) to express opinion.

Some research has suggested that day care can have problematic effects on children's development. For example, studies indicate that children who begin day care as infants are more aggressive, more easily distracted, less considerate of their peers, less popular, and less obedient to adults than children who have never attended day care or haven't attended for as long (Bates et al., 1994; Matlock & Green, 1990; Vandell & Corasaniti, 1990).

Other studies have found that day care is associated with adaptive behaviors. For example, researchers have reported that children who attend day care develop social and language skills more quickly than children who stay at home, although the children who don't attend day care catch up in their social development in a few years (Feagans et al., 1995; Mott, 1991). Poor children who go to day care are likely to develop better reading and math skills than poor children who stay at home (Caughy et al., 1994).

Further complicating this picture of day care's developmental effects are additional studies finding no differences between children who attended day care and those who didn't (e.g., Hegland & Rix, 1990; Reynolds, 1995; Roggman et al., 1994; Scarr et al., 1989). What can we conclude about the reasons for these different—and in some cases, contradictory—findings?

—Uba and Huang, *Psychology*, p. 323

| Exercise 10–6 | **Directions:** *Read each of the following statements. In each, underline the word or phrase that suggests that the author is offering an informed opinion.* |

1. It seems clear that parents who would bring a young child to an R-rated movie are putting their own interests ahead of what's best for the child.

2. Voters rejected the proposed rapid transit system connecting the southern and northern suburbs, possibly because of racial issues.

3. According to the city superintendent of schools, school uniforms lead to improved behavior and fewer disruptions in the classroom.

4. One explanation for low attendance at professional sporting events is the high price of tickets.

5. It is believed that most people practice some form of recycling in their daily lives.

The Textbook Challenge

Part A: Current Issues Reader

Using the article "His Name Is Michael" (p. 494), highlight three facts and underline three opinions.

Part B: A College Textbook

Using a textbook chapter or reading for one of your other courses, highlight three facts and underline three opinions.

What Have You Learned?

Directions: *To check your understanding of the chapter, select the word or phrase from the box below that best completes each of the following sentences. Not all of the words and phrases in the box will be used.*

personal Web sites	synthesize	objective
independently check	interpret	subjective
mix fact and opinion	quotes	informed opinion
personal experiences		

1. Statements of fact are _____, giving information, but not telling what the writer thinks or believes about the issue.

2. Writers express opinions when they evaluate, judge, predict, or _____.

3. Sometimes authors _____ in order to make their feelings appear to be the truth.

4. Writers try to substantiate their opinions with reasons, _____, statistics, or examples.

5. Experts can provide _____ based on research and professional observation.

6. Students do not need to _____ every fact they come across, especially when using textbooks and reference sources.

7. Facts from relatively unreliable sources such as _____, letters to the editor, and popular magazines should be checked.

What Vocabulary Have You Learned?

Directions: *The words in column A appear in this chapter. Test your mastery of these words by matching each word in column A with its meaning in column B. Please note that there are more meanings than words.*

Column A	Column B
_____ 1. regulated	a. favoring change or reform
_____ 2. reimburses	b. to keep employed, to hold secure
_____ 3. progressive	c. to prove guilty
_____ 4. retain	d. a gift given through a will
_____ 5. legacy	e. controlled by rules or laws
	f. collapsing, being destroyed
	g. pays back

NAME _____   SECTION _____
DATE _____   SCORE _____

PRACTICE TEST 10–1

IDENTIFYING FACT AND OPINION

A. Directions: *Indicate whether each of the following statements is a fact (F) or an opinion (O).*

KEEPING YOUR CHILDREN PHYSICALLY CLOSE TO YOU

[1] Advising parent/child proximity [physical closeness to protect them from abductions] accomplishes very little beyond making us feel guilty. [2] You can't always be less than 21 feet away from your preschooler. [3] It's impossible. [4] Many parents have multiple children under the age of 6. [5] Many family day cares [day care centers] require a maximum 6:1 child/adult ratio. [6] How do you take 6 kids to the playground and stay less than 21 feet away from all of them at the same time? [7] It's simple. [8] You don't. [9] You take reasonable precautions, of course. [10] You go to a playground that you know to be safe. [11] You instruct the kids to stay inside the fence. [12] You remind the kids to use the equipment appropriately.

[13] While we're being told to scrutinize the distance between ourselves and our charges, the Children's Defense Fund (May 6, 2002) reminds us that seven million children return to empty homes after school. [14] But, unlike the extremely rare cases of child abduction, the idea that many parents have to work two jobs to make ends meet is not exactly treated as a national emergency.

[15] The pictures in the paper of parents conscientiously trailing within a few feet of their children suggest that kids' safety is a minute-to-minute thing that is within your control if you are within arm's reach. [16] But let's get real. [17] Most tragedies that affect children unfold over a period of time and can only be averted by systematic changes in how wealth is distributed, how benefits are doled out, and how community is constructed.

—Peters, "On Being a Vigilant Parent," *Hyde Park Citizen*

_____ 1. Sentence 1

_____ 2. Sentence 5

_____ 3. Sentence 13

_____ 4. Sentence 14

_____ 5. Sentence 17

B. Directions: *After reading the following editorial that appeared in the* Buffalo News, *select the choice that best completes each of the statements that follow.*

LET STUDENT ATHLETES PAY THEIR OWN WAY

1   It seems like every day brings another newspaper, television or magazine story about Title IX [a federal law mandating equal public education sports programs for males and females] and how we should or should not fund high school and college athletics. Even though I am a proponent of sports participation on all levels by both males and females, I am sick of hearing this Title IX rhetoric. So, I have come up with the perfect solution to this problem: Eliminate all public funding for athletes and athletic teams.

2   In these current financial times, where our tax dollars are being spread thinner and thinner, I think money for amateur athletics should rank fairly low on our list of priorities. I am not advocating the elimination of high school and college sports. I am merely suggesting that we return to a time where student athletes paid their own way just as other extracurricular activity participants do.

3   If privately funded schools wish to give scholarships to people who run around tracks or kick soccer balls, more power to them. But I, as a taxpayer, don't feel that I should have to fund students for anything other than academics.

—Piechowicz, *Buffalo News*

_____   6. The central thought of the article is that
- a. athletics are a waste of time.
- b. taxpayers should be consulted on how their tax dollars are spent.
- c. Title IX has created a major problem within athletic programs.
- d. taxpayers should not have to pay for student athletic programs.

_____   7. Paragraph 2 contains
- a. mostly opinion.
- b. mostly fact.
- c. an even mix of fact and opinion.
- d. expert opinion.

_____ 8. Paragraph 3 contains
   a. mostly fact.
   b. all opinion.
   c. a mix of fact and opinion.
   d. unverifiable facts.

_____ 9. The first sentence of the editorial can be best verified by
   a. contacting the author.
   b. doing an Internet search for articles and stories about Title IX.
   c. contacting television stations.
   d. talking with a local news reporter.

_____ 10. The author could make a stronger case for his opinions by including
   a. stories of athletes who benefit from Title IX.
   b. facts about the added costs of operating athletic programs in high schools and colleges.
   c. examples of school districts that ignore Title IX rulings.
   d. facts about athletes who are graduates of colleges with strong athletic programs.

IDENTIFYING FACT AND OPINION

A. Directions: *This passage was taken from a book titled* Readings in Community-Based Nursing. *It is written for nurses and provides a viewpoint on the changes in the nursing profession. After reading the passage, select the choice that best completes each of the statements that follow.*

AN HOLISTIC APPROACH TO NURSING

Why are we justified as clinicians in speaking about soul and spirit in an age of science? Why not concentrate exclusively on the body, the sick organs, and the deranged biochemistry of our patients, as we've done for most of this century?

Our majestic predecessors in nursing, such as Florence Nightingale, spoke boldly about the need to honor the psychological and spiritual aspects of our patients. For her and many others, it was unthinkable to consider sick humans as mere bodies who could be treated in isolation from their minds and spirits. In Nightingale's holistic approach, the role of love and empathy was considered paramount. Early physicians agreed. As Paracelsus, the sixteenth-century Swiss physician and alchemist who discovered mercury as a treatment for syphilis, put it, "The main reason for healing is love." But with the rise of scientific, materialistic medicine in the nineteenth and twentieth centuries, these lessons in love, which had seemed so obvious throughout the history of healing, were set aside and virtually lost. Nurses and physicians set their sights almost exclusively on objective, physically based approaches. Emotional involvement, we learned, might get in the way and contaminate our clinical objectivity. We went to unbelievable lengths to sanitize health care, to rid it of the "subjective." For example, for most of this century, when one spoke of "the mind," what one really referred to was the chemistry and physiology of the brain. As a result, mental illness has increasingly been considered a biochemical or genetic derangement which can best be treated pharmacologically.

—Dossey and Dossey, *Readings in Community-Based Nursing*, p. 231

_____ 1. The authors begin their article with questions in order to

    a. focus the reader's thoughts.

    b. cast doubt upon their statements.

    c. summarize their ideas.

    d. quiz the reader.

        2. Florence Nightingale and Paracelsus are mentioned

    a. for dramatic effect.

    b. to provide expert evidence and informed opinion.

    c. to present opposing viewpoints.

    d. as authors of important research studies.

        3. The authors use such phrases as "virtually lost" and "almost exclusively" because

    a. these phrases leave room for exceptions.

    b. the authors are not sure of the facts.

    c. the authors are afraid to express opinions.

    d. these phrases signify that the statements are verifiable.

        4. The quotation by Paracelsus (Sentence 7)

    a. cannot be verified.   c. mixes fact and opinion.

    b. expresses an opinion.   d. is a fact.

        5. This passage is an excerpt from a longer article. You would expect the rest of the article to

    a. provide statistics on the religious affiliations of American nurses.

    b. enumerate the accomplishments of Florence Nightingale.

    c. describe ways in which nurses can address their patients' spiritual needs.

    d. make judgments about nurses who hold no religious beliefs.

B. Directions: *After reading the following excerpt, taken from an editorial titled "How the Media Distorts the News," select the choice that best completes each of the statements that follow.*

When I heard about veteran CBS reporter Bernard Goldberg's new book, *Bias: A CBS Insider Exposes How the Media Distort the News,* I knew I had to read it. It's not that I had to be convinced. I noticed the media's egregious bias years ago. This was just more proof coming from someone who was once actually a part of it all.

I have told people for years that if all they watched was the news on ABC, CBS, CNN or NBC, all they really "knew"—particularly about economic and social issues—was what they were told. Sadly, people formulate their political and social opinions on this "news," which is nothing more than left-wing indoctrination. This means their "thinking" can be controlled, directed and limited by a liberal media.

In his book, Goldberg discloses that network news steals just about everything from the major liberal (read socialistic and secular humanistic) newspapers. Therefore, if the *Washington Post* and the *New York Times* are against the flat tax, the networks can't and won't be far behind. This in itself is not surprising since polls show that 89 percent of people working in the media vote Democrat. They all share the same values.

—Davis, "How the Media Distorts the News," *Atlanta Inquirer,* July 13, 2002, p. 4

6. In the first paragraph, the word **egregious** means
   a. outstandingly bad.   c. friendly.
   b. unimportant.   d. emerging.

7. The author probably wanted to read Goldberg's book
   a. for new ideas about the media.
   b. as part of a research study on media bias.
   c. to gain more evidence to support the beliefs he already held.
   d. to review it for a scholarly journal on broadcasting.

8. In the second paragraph, the phrase "nothing more than left-wing indoctrination"
   a. mixes fact and opinion.   c. predicts behavior.
   b. expresses an opinion.   d. states a fact.

9. In the third paragraph, the author provides a statistic regarding the voting patterns of people working in the media. This statistic
   a. should be believed without question.
   b. cannot be verified.
   c. should be verified.
   d. must be true—it's in print.

10. The final sentence
   a. is a fact.
   b. is the result of research.
   c. is a logical conclusion drawn from a series of facts.
   d. is an opinion drawn from the statistic in the preceding sentence.

IDENTIFYING FACT AND OPINION

Directions: *After reading the following excerpt from a social work textbook, select the choice that best completes each of the statements that follow.*

SOCIAL WORK AS A PROFESSION

1   Social work is emerging as an important profession in the modern world. As we noted earlier, the National Association of Social Workers has 155,000 members. In December 1961, provision was made for professionally trained and experienced social workers to become members of the Academy of Certified Social Workers, which gave them additional professional status; more than 20,000 qualified. By 1998, some 59,000 were certified.

2   Social work today is utilized in a variety of settings and agencies. Some of the important ones are psychiatric, medical, marriage, and family counseling; the school; rehabilitation; corrections; public welfare; workplace; drug abuse; and child welfare. Schools of social work train a student to work in any agency, giving him or her the generic understandings, skills, and attitudes that make it possible to function adequately.

3   Social work is becoming more important because thousands of persons are benefiting from its services and are telling their friends and associates who have problems of its many values and services. People are not only being helped with personal and family problems but also with neighborhood, national and even international difficulties. A prominent American, upon returning from a trip abroad made the statement that what the United States needs most of all to improve its foreign policy and relations is to have trained social workers as State Department attachés where each of the official government representatives works and lives. Trained social workers in foreign countries would understand the people and work with them where they are, helping them to help themselves and interpreting the United States in a much more favorable light than in the past.

4   Current evidence indicates that social work is here to stay and that in the decades ahead it will likely grow and expand its services, helping even more people with personal, family and community problems, especially related to adequate social functioning.

—Farley, Smith, and Boyle, *Introduction to Social Work,* p. 13

_____   1. The first sentence

      a. states a fact.   c. cites a research study.

      b. expresses an opinion.   d. gives an example.

2. The statistics in the first paragraph
   a. cannot be verified.
   b. do not add useful information to the passage.
   c. create a historical backdrop for the rest of the passage.
   d. provide evidence in support of the first sentence.

3. The first sentence in paragraph 2
   a. states a fact.
   b. expresses an opinion.
   c. mixes fact and opinion.
   d. cannot be verified easily.

4. The author lists the social work environments in order to
   a. cite personal experiences with social work.
   b. express an opinion.
   c. give examples in support of the preceding sentence.
   d. cite the results of research.

5. Paragraph 3 expresses
   a. facts.
   b. informed opinion.
   c. unsupported opinion.
   d. a mix of fact and opinion.

6. Paragraph 3 begins with a sentence that
   a. states a fact.
   b. provides examples from personal experience.
   c. judges the people who need social workers.
   d. mixes fact and opinion.

7. The statement made by a "prominent American"
   a. expresses an informed expert opinion.
   b. states an opinion.
   c. states a verifiable fact.
   d. mixes fact and opinion.

8. According to the author, American social workers could help U.S. foreign policy by:

   a. teaching U.S. government officials about the problems facing citizens of other countries.

   b. helping the citizens of other countries.

   c. sending citizens of other countries to see the U.S. official in their area.

   d. convincing the citizens of other countries that the U.S. is a large nation with many problems.

9. Throughout the excerpt, the authors support their opinion that "social work is here to stay" by using

   a. mostly solid, verifiable facts.

   b. citations of research studies.

   c. analysis and interpretation.

   d. statistics, examples, and opinions.

10. Overall, the passage

    a. describes the state of social work as a field.

    b. gives an overview of a social worker's job description.

    c. explains the main philosophies of the discipline of social work.

    d. encourages students to become social workers.

IDENTIFYING FACT AND OPINION

Directions: *Indicate whether each of the following statements is either fact (F), opinion (O), or a mix of fact and opinion (M).*

RECONSIDERING THE BAN ON SCHOOL PRAYER

[1] Every morning, the first class, or homeroom, opened with "Our Father, who art in Heaven, hallowed be thy name; Thy Kingdom come, Thy will be done in Heaven as it is on earth, etc." [2] This was followed by the Pledge of Allegiance, with the phrase "one nation indivisible, with liberty and justice for all." [3] I don't remember when "one nation, under God, indivisible" was added, but it wasn't before 1941, when I graduated from high school in Clinton, Massachusetts.

[4] I can't recall any objections raised to the school by anyone in my hometown about the school prayer. [5] No mention was made in the school of any specific deity. [6] I'm certain that even if a specific name was mentioned, in the predominantly Christian environment, the Jewish community would probably not have raised a fuss. [7] We would probably have been instructed by our parents to remain silent if an offending name was mentioned. [8] Fortunately, we were never faced with that situation.

[9] At Christmas, we sang all of the carols—the words of which still remain in my failing memory; this was all fun and games without any converting influence. [10] I might add that several Jewish boys, who attended Holy Cross College in nearby Worcester, had to attend Mass every morning. [11] However, they matriculated there with this knowledge. [12] The important factor to our parents was that we had the opportunity to attend public school at no expense and minimal harassment, and have the opportunity to advance further.

[13] It is apparent that others were not so complacent about the school prayer, and started a movement to have it removed. [14] The leading advocate, a professed atheist named Madeline Murray O'Hare, probably encouraged by groups with a similar outlook, finally brought the matter to the Supreme Court, which in 1962, ruled that the prayer breached the concept of separation of church and state, and ruled school prayer unconstitutional. [15] President John F. Kennedy made the announcement, stating that we were still free to pray anywhere else, especially at home.

—Madoff, *The Jewish Chronicle,* July 25, 2002, p. 8

_____ 1. Sentence 1

_____ 2. Sentence 2

_____ 3. Sentence 3

_____ 4. Sentence 6

_____ 5. Sentence 7

_____ 6. Sentence 9

_____ 7. Sentence 10

_____ 8. Sentence 11

_____ 9. Sentence 14

_____ 10. Sentence 15

IDENTIFYING FACT AND OPINION

A. Directions: *After reading the following excerpt from a reference book, select the choice that best completes each of the statements that follow.*

THE RELATIONSHIP BETWEEN DRESS AND BEHAVIOR

An insightful example of the tension between conformity and individuality can be found in school uniforms. The present-day debate on school uniforms includes such questions as: Should students dress alike to emphasize learning and achievement? Do uniforms inhibit creativity and self-expression? President Clinton made school uniforms a national topic when he proposed uniforms in all public schools as a way to reduce violence (State of the Union Address, January 23, 1996).

Clothing researcher O'Neal (1997) has documented news reports about clothing related violence. However, there are still many unanswered questions about the proposed connection between reducing violence and wearing school uniforms. Several clothing researchers have tried to make connections between dress and behavior, but proving those connections is difficult and rare and heavily dependent on a specific situation. School uniforms serve as an excellent example of the difficulty in proving that dress affects behavior. Very often, schools implement several policies all at once, making it difficult to pinpoint a cause-effect relationship between dress and behavior.

—Miller, "Standing Out from the Crowd," in *The Meanings of Dress,* p. 212

_____ 1. The word "insightful" in the first sentence

    a. indicates how the author feels about the example she is presenting.

    b. means that the coming example is widely accepted.

    c. predicts the type of example.

    d. signals an informed opinion.

_____ 2. The best way to verify the information about President Clinton's statement would be to

    a. look on the Internet for Web sites about Clinton.

    b. look up Clinton in an encyclopedia.

    c. locate a transcript of the cited speech at the library.

    d. send an e-mail message to the White House.

_____ 3. The author uses the phrase "proposed connection" at the beginning of the second paragraph because she

    a. does not know for a fact that school uniforms and violence are related.

    b. is conducting research on school uniforms and violence.

    c. holds the opinion that uniforms and violence are not related.

    d. has read research that proves uniforms reduce violence.

_____ 4. In paragraph 2, the first sentence, which begins "Clothing researcher," is

    a. an opinion.   c. a mix of fact and opinion.

    b. a fact.   d. not verifiable.

_____ 5. This passage is an excerpt from a chapter in a reference book. You would expect the rest of the chapter to

    a. give instruction in creating your own uniform.

    b. provide the history of school uniforms.

    c. continue to explore the relationship between dress and behavior.

    d. give statistics showing the number of school shootings each year in America in schools where uniforms are not required.

B. Directions: _After reading the following passage, select the choice that best completes each of the statements that follow._

SCREENING FOOD SERVICE WORKERS

Impressions of the prospective employee gained in the interview and from the follow-up of references are admittedly incomplete. They may be checked or replaced by tests of various type, the most common being intelligence, trade, and aptitude. A number of companies, including food services, have improved the results of their selection decisions by the use of psychological tests. These companies have found that the benefits derived from psychological testing far exceed the costs. An applicant's probable tenure, customer relations, work values, and safety record may be predicted with such tests. To be considered legal, all psychological test questions must be job related and legal to ask. In addition, all applicants must be asked the same questions, and scoring methods must be the same for all applicants.

The physical fitness of an applicant for a food service appointment is highly important. A health examination should be required of all food service workers. Only physically fit persons can do their best work. Quite as important is the need for assurance that the individual presents no health hazard to the food service. Managers are well aware of the devastation that might result from the inadvertent employment of a person with a communicable disease.

Palaceo and Theis, eds., *West and Wood's Introduction to Food Service*

_____ 6. The first sentence of the excerpt
  a. gives examples of hiring techniques.
  b. judges the interviewer's style.
  c. states a fact.
  d. expresses an opinion.

_____ 7. The author believes that tests
  a. can provide useful information.
  b. do not take the place of an interview.
  c. should always be used in addition to an interview.
  d. provide no useful information.

_____ 8. In the first paragraph, sentence 3, which begins "A number of companies," expresses
  a. an expert opinion.　　c. a mix of fact and opinion.
  b. an opinion.　　d. a fact.

_____ 9. The writer of the passage
  a. expresses no doubts about using psychological tests in the hiring process.
  b. feels there is no merit to even the best formulated tests.
  c. holds no strong opinion about the tests.
  d. recommends a certain type of test.

_____ 10. In the second paragraph, the author
  a. offers expert opinion from food service managers.
  b. provides solid facts about food safety.
  c. expresses a strong opinion regarding health testing for food service workers.
  d. judges the quality of health monitoring programs in the food service industry.

CANINE CANDY STRIPERS
Margot Roosevelt

You've heard that a dog can be your best friend, but can a dog be a therapist, too? Preview and then read this article, which deals with a new technique in hospital care and physical therapy.

Vocabulary Preview

These are some of the difficult words in this essay. The definitions here will help you if you can't figure out the meanings from the sentence context or word parts.

succor (headnote) help, relief, or assistance in a time of need

barbershop quartet (par. 3) a group of four men singing songs in four-part harmony

evolved (par. 3) gradually developed

HMOs (par. 6) health maintenance organizations—groups that provide health care within a closed system of providers according to fixed rates and fees

physiology (par. 8) all the biological characteristics of a living creature

plummets (par. 8) falls or drops down suddenly

therapeutic (par. 9) related to medical treatment

peals (par. 9) loud sounds

Dogs in hospitals are treating human patients with succor, creature comfort, and unconditional love

1 The 65-year-old patient, hospitalized for quadruple-bypass surgery, had not moved or opened her eyes in days. Her relatives, grim-faced, stood around the bed. "They thought they had lost her," recalls Betty Walsh, a volunteer in the intensive-care unit at the UCLA Medical Center.

2 Then Walsh ushered in Kolya, a 145-lb. shaggy white Great Pyrenees, who climbed right up onto the woman's bed and snuggled against her body. Five minutes passed in silence. Then the woman's hand moved slowly toward the dog. She began to stroke his soft, thick coat. Another five minutes passed. The woman smiled and murmured, "So lovely . . ." "For half an hour she kept petting him and calling him 'my friend,'" says Walsh. "The whole time, I watched the blood-pressure monitor go down, down, down."

3 Kolya is not the only therapist making the rounds of the vast hospital complex at UCLA. There's also a poodle named Platinum, a pug named Egor and a greyhound named

Margot Roosevelt, "Canine Candy Stripers," *Time*, August 6, 2001. ©2001 Time Inc. Reprinted by permission.

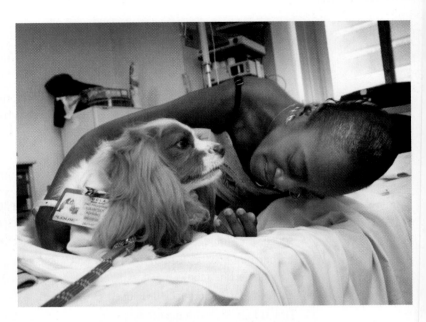

Aladdin—not to mention the eight golden retrievers, four black Labs, two German shepherds and several mutts. Canine candy-striping—which began in the 1980s as just another recreational activity for patients, like clown visits to children's hospitals or barbershop-quartet appearances at nursing homes—has evolved into an important and fast-growing component of modern patient care.

4   And not just at UCLA. At Mount Sinai Hospital in New York City, dogs have been incorporated into rehabilitation treatments for victims of brain and spinal-cord injuries. At the Medical College of Virginia in Richmond, Sandra Barker brings her own Lhasa apso to relax shock-therapy patients who are visibly trembling before treatment. In Texas, dogs are used to motivate children recovering in burn units and to calm residents in Alzheimer's wards.

5   "One patient was shaking the door handle and crying to get out," says Mara Baun, a University of Texas nursing professor who has co-authored 13 studies on the medical benefits of animal companions. "The staff could not get him away from the door. But the golden retriever—who had never been trained to do this—took him by the cuff of his sleeve, and he followed quietly."

6   Indeed, the animals are so good at what they do that it may be only a matter of time before they win over the real powers that be in the medical establishment—the HMOs. "Insurance companies will need to recognize the benefits of animal-assisted therapy and reimburse accordingly," predicts Richmond's Barker, whose study of 230 hospitalized patients treated with—and without—a dog in the room was published in the journal Psychiatric Services. The canine-assisted sessions measurably reduced anxiety in depressive and demented patients and cut the anxiety level of psychotic patients in half.

7   Most dogs practicing in hospitals today are certified either by Therapy Dogs International in New Jersey or by the Delta Society, a Seattle-based nonprofit organization that

screens dogs for personality, obedience and training in hospital protocols. Delta estimates that its 4,500 "pet partners" have provided services for 350,000 patients in 45 states.

8   UCLA's program began in 1994, when Kathie Cole, a cardiac-care nurse and dog lover, convinced the hospital that animals could lift the spirits of heart-transplant patients during the months they spend in the hospital waiting for an organ. "When depression sets in, the physiology plummets," she says. So successful were the cardiac dogs that the program expanded to 26 out of the hospital's 34 inpatient units, giving more than 17,000 patients the benefits of canine companionship. The 40 dogs now volunteering pass an hour-long evaluation in which they have to remain unflappable in the face of careening wheelchairs, screaming strangers and scary tangles of tubes. Handlers are coached in how to position the animals on beds, encourage dog-to-patient eye contact and wash patients' hands before and after visits. Every dog wears a laminated picture ID and a blue bandanna with a paw-print design.

9   Increasingly, researchers distinguish between animal-assisted activities, which are practiced in some 600 U.S. hospitals, and formal animal-assisted therapy, a newer discipline in which dogs are used by medical professionals to achieve a specific therapeutic goal. On a recent afternoon, peals of laughter echoed across the UCLA Medical Center's pediatric ward as Corky, a Yorkshire terrier, rolled over and danced for a two-year-old transplant patient. "I want him in my bed!" insisted the six-year-old next door.

10   Meanwhile, in a more focused intervention two floors away, a recreation therapist employed Ginger, an Australian shepherd, to help a brain-surgery patient recover his balance. Trailing an IV and secured with a harness, Chris Pereira, 26, bent down to groom the dog with his weak arm and then threw a ball for her to fetch. "I can't turn my neck, and my eyesight isn't good," Pereira says. "The dog gives me courage."

11   Although foundations and pet-food companies are financing studies, human-animal clinical research still struggles to attract the funding—and respect—its supporters feel it deserves. "Low-tech solutions in health care are often overlooked," complains Delta's Nancy Dapper, a former official with the federal Health Care Financing Administration. "But we are at a point where consumer demand will drive hospitals to offer animal-assisted services."

12   If so, the demand will come from consumers such as Daniel Uribe. Trapped in a UCLA hospital room bristling with IVs, monitors and other high-tech machinery, the 78-year-old heart patient is nuzzled lovingly in his bed by a big German shepherd named Si'sKa. "She is life," he says with a tender smile. "Like sun and air."

— ∎ —

Directions: *Select the letter of the choice that best completes each of the following statements.*

CHECKING YOUR COMPREHENSION

_____ 1. The central point of the article is that
   a. dogs make good companions.
   b. the use of dogs for therapy is not funded by most HMOs.
   c. the use of animal therapy is a growing field within the medical community.
   d. dogs can help children be more comfortable in hospitals.

_____ 2. What effect did Kolya have on the 65-year-old heart patient?
   a. He lowered her blood pressure.
   b. He brought her out of a coma.
   c. He had no effect.
   d. He caused the woman to wake up and address her family.

_____ 3. The dogs are good at
   a. delivering books and magazines to patients.
   b. keeping the people in waiting rooms occupied.
   c. cheering up depressed patients.
   d. performing medical procedures.

_____ 4. The dogs need to "win over" HMOs so that
   a. insurers will pay for the training of therapy dogs.
   b. the cost of animal-assisted therapy can be reimbursed.
   c. more research can be done on canine therapy.
   d. the value of using dogs in health care can be professionally accepted by physicians.

_____ 5. According to the article, human-animal research
   a. receives funding from the National Institutes of Health.
   b. proves that low-tech solutions do not work.
   c. does not receive enough funding.
   d. shows that only German shepherds perform well in hospitals.

USING WHAT YOU KNOW ABOUT FACT AND OPINION

_____ 6. The first sentence in paragraph 1
  a. mixes fact and opinion.   c. states a fact.
  b. expresses an opinion.   d. cannot be verified.

_____ 7. The experience described in paragraph 2 can be verified by
  a. searching on the Internet.
  b. asking a librarian.
  c. looking in a medical encyclopedia.
  d. speaking with the woman's doctor.

_____ 8. The author mentions the research of Baun and Barker in order to
  a. provide informed opinion.
  b. introduce founders of the animal-assisted therapy movement.
  c. present an opposing viewpoint.
  d. prove that HMOs treat animals unfairly.

_____ 9. In the article, it is predicted that
  a. the number of animals used in hospitals will not increase.
  b. consumer demand will cause hospitals to use animals more often.
  c. most patients will not want dogs in their hospital rooms.
  d. the government will begin to use animals in federally funded health-care programs for the poor.

_____ 10. The author provides evidence in favor of animal-assisted therapy using
  a. personal experiences.   c. examples.
  b. statistics.   d. all of the above.

CONTEXT AND WORD PARTS

_____ 11. In paragraph 3, the word **vast** means
- a. very big in size.
- b. with an obvious floor plan.
- c. hard to navigate.
- d. sterile and sanitized.

_____ 12. In paragraph 7, the word **protocols** means
- a. good manners.
- b. plans, procedures.
- c. ideas.
- d. viewpoints.

_____ 13. In paragraph 8, the word **unflappable** means
- a. not obvious.
- b. unrestrained.
- c. uncomplicated.
- d. not easily upset.

_____ 14. In paragraph 8, the word **careening** means
- a. airborne.
- b. swerving while in motion.
- c. coming downhill.
- d. circling around.

_____ 15. In paragraph 12, the word **bristling** means
- a. frightening.
- b. lacking.
- c. covered with, full of.
- d. deafening, very loud.

REVIEWING DIFFICULT VOCABULARY

Directions: *Complete each of the following sentences by inserting a word from the Vocabulary Preview on page 365 in the space provided. A word should be used only once.*

16. Her favorite song from "The Music Man" is the

    _____ piece sung by four of the River City men.

17. Federally funded universal health care for Americans is not favored by

    the heads of most _____.

18. The residents of Rochester, New York, were overwhelmed by the number of people from other cities who provided great

    _____ after the devastating ice storm.

19. A student's grade in a course _____ when he

    or she works too many hours or is distracted by personal problems.

20. Cindy was much more interested in her _____

    class than her biology class.

QUESTIONS FOR DISCUSSION

1. Think about a time when you were sick. What made you feel better? With your classmates, organize the responses of each student into categories.

2. As a class, brainstorm other ideas for lifting the spirits of patients in hospitals and nursing homes. Consider carrying out some of these ideas.

3. Discuss the ethical issues surrounding the use of animals by humans. What limits should there be and who should impose and enforce them?

WRITING ACTIVITIES

1. Write a paragraph about a memorable experience with an animal, either positive or negative. What happened and how did you respond?

2. Write a letter to a patient in a nursing home. Include news, personal information, and some cheerful comments.

3. Study the Web site for Therapy Dogs International at http://www.tdi-dog.org/. Write a short speech that describes the purpose, goals, and activities of this organization.

Chapter 10: Fact and Opinion

RECORDING YOUR PROGRESS

Test	Number Right			Score	
Practice Test 10-1	_____	× 10	=	_____	%
Practice Test 10-2	_____	× 10	=	_____	%
Practice Test 10-3	_____	× 10	=	_____	%
Mastery Test 10-1	_____	× 10	=	_____	%
Mastery Test 10-2	_____	× 10	=	_____	%
Mastery Test 10-3	_____	× 5	=	_____	%

EVALUATING YOUR PROGRESS

Based on your test performance, rate how well you have mastered the skills taught in this chapter by checking one of the boxes below or by writing your own evaluation.

☐ **Need More Improvement**
Tip: Try completing the Critical Thinking—American Southwest module in the Reading Skills section on the MyReadingLab Web site at **http://www.ablongman.com/myreadinglab** to fine-tune the skills that you have learned in this chapter.

☐ **Need More Practice**
Tip: Try using the Critical Thinking—American Southwest module in the Reading Skills section on the MyReadingLab Web site at **http://www.ablongman.com/myreadinglab** to brush up on the skills taught in this chapter, or visit this textbook's Companion Web site at **http://www.ablongman.com/mcwhorter** for extra practice.

☐ **Good**
Tip: To maintain your skills, quickly review this chapter by using this textbook's Companion Web site at **http://www.ablongman.com/mcwhorter**.

☐ **Excellent**

YOUR EVALUATION: _____

_____

_____

_____

_____

THINK ABOUT IT!

The two photographs below show two demonstrations. Notice that the first creates a negative feeling. It depicts confrontation, stress, and conflict. In contrast, the second photograph presents a positive image. It represents national pride, and the participants seem happy and spirited. The two photographs reveal the photographer's attitude toward their subjects through the details they show. Writers also express their attitudes, but they do so through the words they choose and the facts they choose to present about a topic. In this chapter you will evaluate a writer's tone—his or her attitude toward the subject. You will also learn to uncover bias—the expression of an unfair preference for or dislike toward a subject.

CHAPTER 11

Tone and Bias

Tone

The tone of a speaker's voice helps you interpret what he or she is saying. If a friend says to you, "Would you mind closing the door?" you can tell by her tone of voice whether she is being polite, insistent, or angry. Or if your brother asks, "Where did you get that coat?" he may mean that he wants to know where you bought it, or maybe he is being sarcastic and really dislikes it. You can tell by his tone of voice. The speaker's tone of voice, then, reveals the intended meaning. Writers also convey a tone, or feeling, through writing. **Tone** refers to the attitude or feeling a writer expresses about his or her subject. Think of tone as the feelings, mood, or emotions that a writer expresses through a piece of writing.

Recognizing Tone

A writer can express a variety of different tones. In the following example, notice how each writer reveals a different attitude toward the same subject:

- We cannot trust our police chief; he is corrupt and completely ignorant of our community's problems.
- Our feelings of disappointment over the police chief's actions are overwhelming; we truly believed he would be the one to turn our community around, but he has betrayed us just like his predecessor.

TABLE 11-1	Words Frequently Used to Describe Tone			
abstract	condemning	flippant	irreverent	playful
absurd	condescending	forgiving	joyful	reverent
amused	convincing	formal	loving	righteous
angry	cynical	frustrated	malicious	sarcastic
apathetic	depressing	gentle	melancholic	satiric
arrogant	detached	grim	mocking	sensational
assertive	disapproving	hateful	nostalgic	serious
awestruck	disrespectful	humorous	objective	solemn
bitter	distressed	impassioned	obsequious	sympathetic
caustic	docile	incredulous	optimistic	tragic
celebratory	earnest	indignant	outraged	uncomfortable
cheerful	excited	indirect	pathetic	vindictive
comic	fanciful	intimate	persuasive	worried
compassionate	farcical	ironic	pessimistic	

- Is anyone really surprised by the scandal surrounding our police chief? Trusting a city official is like trusting a fox in a hen house.

In the first example, the writer is angry, in the second the writer is sad and disappointed, and in the third the writer is cynical.

As you can see, writers can express a wide range of tones. Table 11-1 lists words that are often used to describe tone. Here are six that are commonly used:

- **An instructive tone.** The writer values his or her subject and thinks it is important for the reader. Information about the subject is presented in a straightforward, helpful manner.

EXAMPLE

When purchasing a piece of clothing, one must be concerned with quality as well as with price. Be certain to check for the following: double-stitched seams, matched patterns, and ample linings.

- **A sympathetic tone.** The writer reveals sympathy or sorrow toward the subject.

EXAMPLE

The forlorn, frightened-looking child wandered through the streets alone, searching for someone who would show an interest in helping her find her parents.

- **A convincing tone.** The writer feels his or her ideas are correct and is urging the readers to accept them.

EXAMPLE

Child abuse is a tragic occurrence in our society. Strong legislation is needed to control the abuse of innocent victims and to punish those who are insensitive to the rights and feeling of others. Write to your congressional representative today.

- **An entertaining tone.** The writer finds the subject light and amusing and wishes to share this with his or her readers.

EXAMPLE

Gas prices are climbing again, which means some super-hard driving decisions in our family. Driving to the gym is definitely out—besides, walking builds character as well as muscle. And when Cousin Stanley comes to town, I hope he does not expect to be chauffeured around; walking may help him lose a couple of pounds that need to go. Of course, the 50-mile trek to Edgar's Easter Egg Extravaganza is a no-go this spring. Tough times = tough choices!

- **A nostalgic tone.** The writer is thinking about past times or events. The writer is often sentimental, recalling the past with happiness, sadness, or longing.

EXAMPLE

Television is not what it used to be. There was a time when TV shows were truly entertaining and worthwhile. Wouldn't it be wonderful to see shows like *I Love Lucy* or *Batman* again?

- **An outraged tone.** The writer expresses anger and indignation toward something he or she finds offensive.

EXAMPLE

It is appalling that people sit on bus seats talking loudly on their cell phones and expecting me to listen to their ignorant conversations. I'd like to grab their cell phones and throw them out the window.

A writer's tone is intended to rub off on you, so to speak. Tone is also directly tied to the author's purpose (see Chapter 9). A writer whose tone is humorous hopes you will be amused. A writer whose tone is convincing hopes you will accept his or her viewpoint.

Exercise 11–1

Directions: *Indicate whether the tone in each of the following statements is instructive (I), sympathetic (S), convincing (C) entertaining (E), outraged (O), or nostalgic (N).*

_____ 1. Try yoga for your back pain. Students of yoga agree that your discomfort will disappear while you gain strength and flexibility. Just five minutes a day to better back health.

_____   2. I am sick of seeing billboards and signs plastered all over our beautiful countryside. These are visual pollution, and I never want to see another.

_____   3. Most newcomers to our country are hoping for a better life. Unfortunately, before they can achieve that, they must face a myriad of problems. Seemingly endless bureaucracy and prejudice are just two of the major hurdles tragically placed in the way of these hardworking immigrants.

_____   4. Yesterday, I saw a true sign of spring: a cute squirrel playing in the backyard. He was trying to get a piece of string that held up last summer's climbing peas. The squirrel tugged and tugged, spinning around and flipping, until he finally rolled the string into a ball. With this ball in his mouth, he gave one last tremendous pull that snapped the string from the post to which it had been tacked! With his mission accomplished, he scurried up the nearest tree with his treasure.

_____   5. Parents need help raising their children. Since many families now have two income earners, mothers and fathers are increasingly turning to outside institutions and individuals for child care. Our government should assist these families with subsidies, health insurance, and parental leave in order to ensure stable futures for our country's youth.

_____   6. Today's cameras come in many formats with a wide range of features. First, you must decide if you want to go digital. Then, you must consider your budget. Finally, you should try out a variety of models to find the best fit for you.

_____   7. Public high school teachers work very hard at one of the most difficult jobs in our country. How do we reward them? We give them long hours and low salaries. No wonder so many teachers burn out quickly and turn to more lucrative jobs in the business world.

_____   8. After four years of surpluses, the federal budget is now returning to deficit spending. Write your senators and repre-sentatives and let them know that this is unacceptable. We do not need surpluses to be spent on tax cuts that benefit the wealthiest Americans. What we do need is a government that sets a good fiscal example for its citizens.

_____   9. Every living creature has different nutritional needs. For example, humans need water, oxygen, and a complicated combination of minerals, vitamins, and other substances. Other mammals have different needs. Even plants and microorganisms have their own set of nutritional requirements.

_____ 10. Public libraries have become much more than the quiet, relaxing places they used to be. Nowadays there is so much activity—there's free Internet access, games, and software. Some libraries even have espresso stands. I vote for a return to the good old days when a library meant books and only books.

Tone and Connotative Meanings

Look again at the examples of tone on pages 376–377. Notice that each writer uses particular words to convey tone. Often writers choose words that have a strong connotative or emotional meaning. (See Chapter 9 for a review of connotative meanings.) In the first example, the writer offers advice in a straightforward way, using the words *must* and *be certain*. In the second example, the writer wants you to feel sorry for the child and uses words such as *forlorn* and *frightened-looking*. In the third example, the writer tries to convince the reader that action must be taken to prevent child abuse. The use of such words as *tragic, innocent victims,* and *insensitive* establish this tone. In the fourth example, the writer uses exaggeration *(super-hard)* and silly expressions *(Edgar's Easter Egg Extravaganza)* to create humor.

Exercise 11-2

Directions: *Select a word from the box below that best describes the tone of each of the following statements. Not all of the words will be used.*

optimistic—hopeful, positive
angry—extremely annoyed, mad
admiring—approving, holding a high opinion
cynical—distrustful, doubting
excited—feeling enjoyment and pleasure
humorous—amusing, making people laugh
disapproving—disliking, condemning
formal—serious, official
informative—factual
sarcastic—saying the opposite of what is meant
apathetic—lacking enthusiasm, energy, or interest

1. Taking a young child to a PG-13 movie is inappropriate and shows poor judgment on the part of the parents. _____

2. The brown recluse spider has a dark, violin-shaped marking on the upper section of its body. _____

3. The dedication and determination of the young men and women participating in the Special Olympics were an inspiration to everyone there. _____

4. It does not matter to me which mayoral candidate wins the election, so I won't bother to vote. _____

5. Nobody is ever a complete failure; he or she can always serve as a bad example. _____

6. The councilman once again demonstrated his sensitivity toward the environment when he voted to allow commercial development in an area set aside as a nature preserve. _____

7. The success of the company's youth mentoring program will inspire other business groups to establish similar programs.

_____

8. Professional athletes have no loyalty toward their teams or their fans anymore, just their own wallets. _____

9. We were thrilled to learn that next year's convention will be held in San Antonio—we've always wanted to see the Alamo!

_____

10. To be considered for president's student-of-the year award, an individual must demonstrate academic excellence as well as outstanding community service, and the individual must furnish no fewer than four letters of reference from faculty members. _____

Identifying Tone

It is sometimes difficult to find the right word to describe a writer's tone. To identify a writer's tone ask yourself the following questions:

- What feelings does the author reveal toward his or her subject?
- How is the writer trying to make me feel about the subject?
- What words reveal the writer's feelings toward the subject?

Exercise 11–3

Directions: *Select a word from the box below that best describes the tone of each of the following statements. Not all of the words will be used.*

flippant	outraged	excited
awestruck	earnest	compassionate
sarcastic	worried	ironic

1. Our senator should be ousted from Congress. He no longer listens to the concerns of the people. He makes a mockery of the entire legislative process. _____

2. I still remember the first time I laid my eyes upon the New York City skyline. Having grown up in a rural town, I was amazed and a little frightened by the huge stretch of enormous buildings.

   _____

3. My niece is an aspiring actress, and I can't wait to see her star in the next production at the Children's Theatre.

   _____

4. It is scary that on some college campuses free thinking and critical debate are discouraged these days. What will happen if our students are not allowed to explore all sides of important issues?

   _____

5. As your best friend, I will do anything in my power to help you, so please let me know if there's anything I can do for you.

   _____

Tone: The Relationship Between the Writer and the Reader

Tone can also be used to help establish a relationship between reader and writer. Through tone a writer can establish a sense of a shared communication with the reader, drawing them closer together. Or a writer may establish a distance from the reader. In the excerpts that follow, notice how in the first passage a formality, or distance, is evident, and in the second, how a familiarity and friendliness are created.

Passage 1

Meditation, which focuses awareness on a single stimulus, generally brings a subjective sense of well-being and relaxation, along with such physiological changes as decreased heart and respiratory rates and shifting EEG patterns of brain activity. There are three main types of meditation: concentrative, in which the meditator focuses on one chosen image or word; opening-up, in which the meditator's surroundings become part of the meditation; and mindfulness, in which the meditator focuses on whatever is most prominent at the moment.

—Kosslyn and Rosenberg, *Psychology: The Brain, the Person, the World*, p. 162

Passage 2

To begin evaluating a poem, first try to understand your own subjective response—don't pretend it doesn't exist. Admit, at least to yourself, whether the poem delights, moves, bores, or annoys you. Then try to determine what the poem seems designed to make you think and feel. Does it belong to some identifiable form or genre? (Is it, for instance, a love sonnet, narrative ballad, satire, or elegy?) How does its performance stack up against the expectations it creates? Considering those questions will give you some larger sense of perspective from which to evaluate the poem.

—Kennedy and Gioia, *Literature*, p. 789

Understanding how tone affects communication is particularly important for your writing classes, where you will be asked to choose a tone that is appropriate for your audience.

Exercise 11-4

Directions: *Indicate whether each of the following statements is formal or friendly.*

1. Virus protection software helps to create a secure computing environment. The B-Safe program runs at all times and is constantly updated for maximum benefit. _____

2. Children who experience violence in the home are more likely to be the perpetrators of violence in school. Educators should be trained to recognize the signs of physical abuse in their students. _____

3. It takes stamina to keep up with technological advances. Just when you have mastered your VCR, it is time to get a DVD player. Right after you have finally gotten your scanner's software to run properly, you buy a digital camera. Perhaps we need a device to help us keep track of all the changes and skills required to function in the modern world!

_____

4. Becoming a professional magician takes a great deal of work. First, one must master the basic skills necessary for the core tricks. Then, there must be the development of complex, original illusions. Finally, the magician must begin the long process of working at clubs and parties until an agent who can foster a career notices him.

_____

5. The aurora borealis, or northern lights, are a spectacular sight. If you ever hear that they are visible in your area, be sure to find a spot to look for this beautiful show in the sky. Do not miss the opportunity to see the effects of solar wind and geomagnetic activity in our atmosphere. _____

Exercise 11–5

Directions: *After reading each of the following passages, select the choice that best describes the tone that the writer is expressing.*

_____ 1. Before you begin any knitting project, always check your gauge. Using the yarn and needles called for in the instructions, knit a two-inch swatch and then compare it with the scale given in the pattern. By making adjustments before beginning the project, you can avoid problems later on.

   a. excited   c. sentimental

   b. instructive   d. casual

_____ 2. After the helpless whales had beached themselves for a third time, the exhausted volunteers abandoned their rescue efforts and looked on grimly while the dying whales were euthanized.

a. persuasive   c. sympathetic

b. instructive   d. humorous

_____ 3. Use your frequent flyer programs to donate to charity. Your frequent flyer points may be used to help people with life-threatening medical conditions travel by plane to obtain the treatment they need, or to transport emergency relief personnel to the site of natural disasters, or simply to enable seriously ill children and their families to enjoy a trip to Disney World. You will be glad you helped others.

a. persuasive   c. sympathetic

b. angry   d. impersonal

_____ 4. "A boy can run like a deer, swim like a fish, climb like a squirrel, balk like a mule, bellow like a bull, eat like a pig, or act like a jackass, according to climate conditions. A boy is a piece of skin stretched over an appetite. However, he eats only when he is awake. Boys imitate their Dads in spite of all efforts to teach them good manners."

—former President Herbert Hoover; **www.hooverassoc.org**

a. persuasive   c. logical

b. grim   d. humorous

_____ 5. The handwritten letter is a vanishing art. Although the convenience of e-mail can't be beat, when someone sits down with pen and paper to write a good, old-fashioned letter, it reminds us of a simpler, more thoughtful time.

a. instructive   c. persuasive

b. nostalgic   d. angry

Understanding Irony and Sarcasm

If while walking in a blinding snowstorm, a friend comments, "I really love this weather," you know that he means just the opposite. When someone says the opposite of what they mean, it is called **irony**. Here are a few examples:

- You want me to buy Girl Scout cookies? Sure, those will help me stay on my diet.
- Of course we should tear down this historic building for a parking lot. The city needs more pavement and less beautiful architecture.
- Oh, there's nothing better than waiting in line at the financial aid office!

Writers also use irony to humorously or lightly criticize, poke fun at, or indirectly comment on an issue or situation. Here is an example:

Americans respond well to reality TV. We should hold our presidential elections this way—voters could just call in their votes after each debate.

In this example, the writer is suggesting that voter turnout would be better if our elections were held in the style of a reality TV show.

Sarcasm is a harsher, more bitter form of irony. Sarcasm is usually intended to ridicule, mock, or injure someone. Here is an example:

When a woman at a dinner party told Winston Churchill he was drunk, he replied, "And you madam are ugly. But tomorrow I will be sober."

Here the humor is implied, but the meaning is clear. Here is another example:

If you say to someone who has just come back from getting a haircut, "The barber shop was closed, huh?" you are making a sarcastic remark about the person's new hairdo.

Exercise 11-6

Directions: *Place a check mark in front of each statement that expresses irony or sarcasm.*

_____   1. Violent crime is dropping due to the decrease in cocaine use.

_____   2. Flight attendants have the most glamorous jobs—waitresses in the sky.

_____   3. If you know your neighbor has an illegal immigrant working around the house, you should report it.

_____   4. It is cruel and unusual punishment to force inmates at the Buffalo jail to shovel the snow. It is wrong to expect criminals to work or support themselves.

_____   5. Gregory never says anything at our meetings; it's like working with a mummy.

Bias

Suppose a classmate who is failing her psychology class tells you that the textbook for the course is difficult, that there are frequent unannounced quizzes, and that class participation is required. However, she fails to tell you that the instructor provides study guides for each textbook chapter, that students are allowed to retake quizzes to improve their grades, and that class participation often involves fun activities such as role-playing or simulated experiments. Obviously, the failing student is deliberately attempting to make her psychology class sound difficult and unappealing by presenting some facts and deliberately omitting others.

What Is Bias?

When a writer or speaker deliberately presents a one-sided picture of a situation, it is known as bias. **Bias,** then, refers to an author's partiality, inclination toward a particular viewpoint, or prejudice. Now, think of a television commercial you have seen recently. Let's say it is for a particular model of car. The ad tells you its advantages—why you want to buy the car—but does it tell you its disadvantages? Does it describe ways in which the model compares unfavorably with competitors? Certainly not. Do you feel the ad writer is being unfair? Now let's say you know nothing about Ebook readers and want to learn about them. You find an article titled "What you need to know about Ebook readers." If the author of this article told you all the advantages of Ebook readers, but none of their disadvantages, would you consider the article unfair? We expect advertisers to present a one-sided view of their products. In most other forms of writing, however, we expect writers to be honest and forthright. If a writer is explaining instant messaging he or she should explain it fully, revealing both strengths and weaknesses. To do otherwise is to present a biased point of view. You can think of bias as a writer's prejudice.

How to Detect Bias

To detect bias, ask the following questions:

- Is the author acting as a reporter—presenting facts—or as salesperson—providing only favorable information?

- Does the author feel strongly about or favor one side of the issue?

- Does the author seem to be deliberately creating a positive or negative image?

- Does the author seem emotional about the issue?

- Are there other views toward the subject that the writer does not recognize or discuss?

The author's language and selection of facts also provide clues about his or her bias. Specifically, words with strong connotative (emotional) meanings or words that elicit an emotional response on the part of the reader suggest bias. In the following excerpt from a biology textbook, the author's choice of words (see underlining) and sarcastic comment in parentheses reveal his attitudes toward Greenpeace and those it opposes.

> Greenpeace is an organization dedicated to the preservation of the sea and its great mammals, notably whales, dolphins, and seals. Its ethic is <u>nonviolent</u> but its <u>aggressiveness</u> in protecting our oceans and the life in them is becoming legendary.
>
> Greenpeace volunteers routinely place their lives in <u>danger</u> in many ways, such as by riding along the backs of whales in inflatable zodiacs, keeping themselves between the animal and the harpoons of ships giving <u>chase</u>. They have pulled alongside Dutch ships to stop the <u>dumping</u> of <u>dangerous toxins</u> into the sea. They have placed their zodiacs directly in the paths of ships <u>disrupting delicate</u> breeding grounds of the sea with soundings and have forced some to turn away or even abandon their efforts. They have confronted hostile sealers on northern ice floes to try to stop them from <u>bludgeoning</u> the baby seals in the birthing grounds, skinning them on the spot, and leaving the mother sniffing at the <u>glistening red corpse</u> of her baby as its skin is <u>stacked</u> aboard the ship on the way to warm the <u>backs of very fashionable people</u> who gather where the bartender knows their favorite drink. (The mother seal would be <u>proud</u> to know that her dead baby had nearly impressed some bartender.) They have petitioned the International Whaling Commission to establish rules and enact bans.
>
> —Wallace, *Biology: The World of Life*, p. 754

Exercise 11-7

Directions: *Place a check mark in front of each statement that reveals bias.*

_____ 1. Cities should be designed for the pedestrian, not the automobile.

_____ 2. There are more channels than ever before on cable television.

_____ 3. The current system of voter registration is a sham.

_____ 4. Professional sports has become elitist.

_____ 5. Space exploration costs millions of dollars each year.

Exercise 11-8

Directions: *After reading each passage, select the choice that best answers each of the questions that follow.*

A. The greatest immediate danger to the future of our firearm rights is the media hype typified in a *Washington Times* headline, "Gun Control Drops Off the Screen." Don't for one second buy into it. The goal of the anti-gun-rights crowd this election year is power—total control of the national legislature—and they will try to get it by lulling gun owners into thinking the threat has passed. They want gun owners to stay home on election day.

—LaPierre, "Standing Guard," *American Rifleman,* August 2002, p. 12

_____ 1. The author seems biased against

a. anti-gun-rights advocates.

b. voting.

c. elections.

d. the media.

_____ 2. Which of the following phrases best reveals the author's bias?

a. "*Washington Times* headline"

b. "Gun Control Drops Off the Screen"

c. "total control"

d. "on election day"

B. Those clamoring to shut down the farmers, however, should look hard at the prospect of a prairie full of subdivisions and suburban pollution: car exhaust, lawn and garden fertilizers, wood stoves, sewage. Certainly, the smoke from field burning is an annoyance, particularly to the hard-hit Sandpoint area, and to some it's a health hazard. But the benefits the sturdy farmers produce 50 weeks of the year shouldn't be dismissed casually.

—"Burning Will Go; That's Not All Good," *Spokesman Review,* July 24, 2002

_____ 3. The author seems to be biased against

    a. farmers.   c. rural development.

    b. wood smoke.   d. Sandpoint.

_____ 4. Which of the following phrases best suggests the author's bias?

    a. "smoke from field burning is an annoyance"

    b. "prairie full of subdivisions"

    c. "hard-hit Sandpoint area"

    d. "50 weeks of the year"

C. Money doesn't grow on trees, but some trees might as well be pure gold. The world's voracious (and growing) appetite for wood, paper, and other forest products is driving a stampede to mow down forests. Much of this logging is illegal.

—Haugen, "Logging, Illogic," *World Watch,* September/October 2002

_____ 5. The author seems to be biased against

    a. paper product users.   c. recycling.

    b. economic growth.   d. reckless logging.

_____ 6. Which phrase best suggests the author's bias?

    a. "a stampede to mow down forests"

    b. "Money doesn't grow on trees"

    c. "trees might as well be"

    d. "wood, paper, and other forest products"

The Textbook Challenge

Part A: Current Issues Reader

Using the article "His Name Is Michael" (p. 494), describe the author's tone. Then compare this tone with that of the textbook excerpt "Hold It Right There, and Drop That Camera" (p. 507). How do they differ?

Part B: A College Textbook

Using a textbook chapter or reading that you have read for one of your other courses, describe the author's tone. Compare it with the tone of a chapter in a different textbook or reading in that course or another course.

What Have You Learned?

Directions: *To check your understanding of the chapter, select the word or phrase from the box below that best completes each of the following statements. Not all of the words in the box will be used.*

denotative	sarcasm	relationship
connotative	bias	tone
irony	wit	

1. _____ refers to the author's attitude or feelings toward the subject.

2. The _____ meanings of words often convey tone.

3. Tone helps establish a _____ between the reader and the writer.

4. When writers use _____ they say the opposite of what they mean.

5. _____ is a harsh, bitter form of irony used to ridicule, mock, or injure someone.

6. _____ refers to an author's partiality toward a particular viewpoint.

What Vocabulary Have You Learned?

Directions: *The words in column A appear in this chapter. Test your mastery of these words by matching each word in column A with its meaning in column B.*

	Column A		Column B
_____	1. subsidies	a.	not impartial, based on opinion
_____	2. subjective	b.	producing profit or wealth
_____	3. lucrative	c.	financial help with expenses
_____	4. myriad	d.	large number, wide range of
_____	5. stamina	e.	strength and endurance

NAME _____   SECTION _____

DATE _____   SCORE _____

IDENTIFYING TONE

Directions: *Indicate whether the tone in each of the following statements is instructive (I), sympathetic (S), convincing (C), entertaining (E), outraged (O), or nostalgic (N).*

_____   1. When you see an automobile accident, call 911 immediately for assistance. If it is safe for you to do so, check the occupants of the vehicles for injuries. Stay until police arrive and identify yourself as a witness. The police will ask you to describe what you saw happen and will take your name and phone number in case your testimony is needed in a future investigation or in court.

_____   2. Oil spills are devastating to the environment. These accidents cause massive damage to birds and marine mammals. Their sensitive bodies are simply not equipped to deal with the destructive effects of oil in their habitat.

_____   3. Camping is a fun and educational experience for young children. They will delight in all the new sights and sounds of the forest and learn a great deal about our natural areas. Parents should not miss this important opportunity to enrich the lives of their children.

_____   4. Regrettably, there are very few movies made these days that tell a good story. Most filmmakers simply rely on violence and special effects to attract viewers, disregarding character and plot development. Movies used to be so interesting, involved, and intellectual; now they are just visual candy.

_____   5. Our government should make more of an investment in passenger trains. Many people do not like to fly and would rather have a leisurely railroad excursion. Also, trains use less fuel than airplanes and create less pollution. Finally, taking a train is much safer than flying. I am sure that most Americans would welcome a revival of train travel.

_____   6. Who would ever think of taking a baby to a movie theater? Everyone there wants to hear the movie—not some burping, crying, sniveling baby. Do parents stupidly believe these babies will sleep through the whole movie? Send them to drive-in movies, or point them to the nearest video store!

_____ 7. If you want to do your taxes online, be just as prepared as if you were completing the paper form. You will need all your records at your computer with you. However, most programs give you the option to stop and save your work while you go hunt for important documents. If you use the same program year after year, you will be able to transfer some information. This feature saves you time. Finally, you will have to pay some sort of fee for the service so have your credit card handy, too.

_____ 8. The holidays are fast approaching, which other years has meant huge amounts of stress. This year I have scaled back. Gone are the personalized gingerbread houses for all my neighbors. They know what their houses look like—I don't have to create models with dough and frosting. Gone, too, is the 500,000-light outdoor display. Why should I light up the neighborhood? I did not set up a tree in every room of the house this year, either. The family was complaining that the house looked like a Christmas Wonderland store; I hope they're happy! Now I'm so stress free that I am looking in every corner for something to worry about or do.

_____ 9. Our peace organization is holding a demonstration tomorrow. We need protesters who are willing to practice civil disobedience and risk being arrested. If you are really committed to this cause, then you will take this chance. Please join us and act on your true beliefs and principles.

_____ 10. In learning about archaeologists, you will discover that these professionals do not just find and date objects; they also place these objects into a cultural context. Therefore, the job of archaeologist can be described as the science of bringing the past to life.

ANALYZING TONE

Directions: *Select the word from the box that best describes the tone of each of the following statements. Not all of the words in the box will be used.*

amused	nostalgic	fanciful
forgiving	docile	indignant
indirect	apathetic	condemning
intimate	optimistic	pessimistic
sensational	loving	frustrated

1. You better watch out for the big storm today! It's going to be life threatening. Record rainfall, flooding, and high winds are expected; everyone should just stay home and stay safe. _____

2. We know deep in our hearts that our teachers' union and the school board will reach an understanding soon. Certainly, these educators do not want to miss any more school days. _____

3. I am having a difficult time finding employment. Every job I want requires experience, but I just got out of school and have no experience in my field yet. _____

4. It is harvest time in the life of the urban gardener; time to begin the great zucchini hand-off. I take them to work and church; perhaps my kids can give them away at their lemonade stand, or do you think that would drive away their customers? _____

5. In the old days, young men and women respected their parents. No one got into trouble because we had no drugs and no violence. Those were different, more innocent times. _____

6. The city will never fix up this neighborhood. The mayor has it in for us and will not give our ward any money. This area will just keep deteriorating until there is nothing left except rubble. _____

7. The prescription drug companies should be prosecuted for charging poor people extravagant prices for medicine. These manufacturers are immoral and murderous. _____

8. How dare that police officer give me a speeding ticket! I was only going one mile an hour over the limit. _____

9. Many abusive parents were abused themselves as children. They do not know how to discipline or show anger in a healthy way. We must help *all* the members of a violent household. _____

10. So many voters like myself just do not care enough to get out to the polls every November. There are simply no issues or candidates that are worth voting for. _____

NAME _____ SECTION _____

DATE _____ SCORE _____

EVALUATING TONE AND BIAS

Directions: *After reading each of the following passages, select the choice that best answers each of the questions that follow.*

A. When I was just a school boy, cigarettes were referred to as "coffin nails." Every puff was another nail in the coffin. We were aware even then of the dangerous effects of tobacco upon health, but at that time, in the early 1940s, there was not much factual evidence. Today, there is. Yet surprisingly, cigarette smoking has actually increased. Billions of dollars are being spent trying to find a cure for cancer without any regard for its cause. We want our bad habits and good health, too. It can never happen, for we are defying nature's laws. If we remove the causes of disease, we can have natural good health. Some of these causes are difficult to remove because they are created by impure air, pollution from industry and motor vehicles. But we can always stop smoking.

—Gitananda, "Smoking Yogis, Beware!" *Hinduism Today,* September 30, 2002, p. 66

_____ 1. The author reveals his bias against

    a. 1940s doctors.   c. industry.

    b. modern medicine.   d. smoking cigarettes.

_____ 2. The tone of the passage is

    a. malicious.   c. sincere.

    b. irreverent.   d. mocking.

_____ 3. Which one of the following phrases reveals the author's bias against cigarette smoking?

    a. school boy   c. defying nature's laws

    b. difficult to remove   d. cure for cancer

B. Cell phone use has not just increased in recent years, but has become commonplace, normal, and expected. Even children as young as 11 are toting their own phones under the pretense of keeping in touch with their parents. Our new method of communication has led us down a frightening path of familiarity, and as we all know, familiarity breeds contempt. Sitting in a library, a final bastion of civility and quietude, you can hear one-sided cell phone conversations about pet ailments, baby diaper contents, and last night's alcohol-fueled escapades. People have no qualms about discussing the details of their plane reservations, résumés, and potential purchases. All this unintentional openness at such high volumes pushes us further from loving our neighbors and closer to abandoning them. After all, they have someone on the other end of the "line" that cares about them, right?

_____ 4. The author's tone is
   a. worried.   c. alarmist.
   b. condescending.   d. irritated.

_____ 5. The passage reveals the author's bias against
   a. parents.   c. libraries.
   b. cell phone users.   d. children.

_____ 6. Which of the following groups of words best reveals the author's bias?
   a. "commonplace, normal, and expected."
   b. "toting their own cell phones."
   c. "new method of communication."
   d. "frightening path of familiarity."

C. There have been two serious accidents at the intersection of 155th Avenue and Broad Street within the past six days—ten in the past year. Angry residents have been demanding that our city council make traffic safety improvements at this very dangerous corner. However, our leaders are obviously waiting for a couple hundred people to be killed before they act. More important matters are at hand, such as a skateboard park and pay raises for the mayor and his staff. In this year's election, five council members (half of the total) are up for re-election. My guess is that the intersection will be made safer just before Election Day . . . after about six more accidents.

_____ 7. The author reveals a bias against
   a. the city council.   c. drivers.
   b. city residents.   d. traffic engineers.

_____ 8. The author's overall tone is
   a. grim.   c. irreverent.
   b. outraged.   d. mocking.

_____ 9. When the author writes that the council is "waiting for a couple hundred people to be killed," she is being
   a. pessimistic.   c. disapproving.
   b. sarcastic.   d. flippant.

_____ 10. What important fact might the author be purposely leaving out?

    a. The mayor's raise goes into effect next year.

    b. Last year's election brought two incumbents back.

    c. Three pedestrians were injured over the past year.

    d. The city council has met with the residents and several plans of action were discussed.

EVALUATING TONE AND BIAS

A. Directions: *Select the word from the box below that best describes the tone of each of the following statements.*

instructive	indignant	persuasive
impassioned	insulting	

1. Even though our country has made great advances in race equality over the past fifty years, we still have a long, hard road ahead of us. Shamefully, all people are still not presented with the same level of respect and opportunity in the United States. _____

2. In order to master a musical instrument, students must practice, practice, practice. Visit the college library's music collection, and just start selecting pieces to learn. Also, try to find a practice space away from the distractions of your dorm. _____

3. With mortgage rates so low right now, buying a house has become a better deal than renting. You will have your very own home and be building equity for your future. You cannot afford to miss out. Call your realtor today and start house shopping! _____

4. I cannot believe how many parents allow their children to misbehave in restaurants! I am still shocked each time I see children throwing food, crawling under tables, and shouting and screaming.

   _____

5. Our totally incompetent and cowardly town council voted secretly last night to put a sewage treatment plant right near a public beach. These idiots have ruined the only waterfront access our children have without consulting their constituents. _____

B. Directions: *Briefly identify the bias in each of the following statements.*

6. Modern farmers are harming our children with their new, stronger pesticides. Young kids all over the country are developing health problems from the chemicals in their foods. I am only going to buy certified organically grown products from now on. They may cost more, but their purity is worth it.

_____

7. So many of my neighbors have peace symbols and slogans in their windows and on their lawns. Do they really think that these signs make a difference? Some people are so naïve.

_____

8. Health insurance companies have no right to dictate treatment plans. They should stay out of the personal lives of their patients and go back to the old ways of doing business. Leave the treatment to the doctors—doctors that we choose!

_____

9. Millions of unwanted animals are euthanized each year. If it weren't for all the uncaring pet owners out there who don't have their animals spayed or neutered, animal shelters wouldn't even have to exist. When is everyone going to get on board with pet birth control?

_____

10. People who drive gas-guzzling vehicles should be ashamed of themselves. Our country needs to limit its dependence on foreign oil, not create a hot new demand for it.

_____

ANALYZING TONE AND BIAS

Directions: *After reading each passage, select the choice that best completes each of the statements that follow.*

A. My daughter stared at her reflection as she brushed her teeth. Our eyes met in the mirror as she said, "Mama, I'm sad that you're different from us." My heart sank. "We all have brown eyes and yours are blue. Don't you wish you had brown eyes too?" My heart lightened. I had thought Claire was going to ask me about my being the only Catholic in our interfaith household.

Before my wedding, Mother worried about how I would feel if I married a Jewish man and raised Jewish children, and asked if I'd considered converting. I assured my mother that having a different religion or a different last name (I was keeping my maiden name, another source of concern for her) did not mean I had to feel like an outsider in my own family. At 31 I had a strong sense of who I was and what I wanted. My fiancé and I had attended an interfaith couples group and discussed likely scenarios for birth rituals, raising children, and celebrating holidays, and we agreed that the interfaith aspects of our household would be open to reinterpretation as our lives changed. I had tried to think through all the challenges.

It was my idea to raise any future children Jewish. Even though I was no longer attending Mass regularly, I knew I wanted to raise a family that participated together in a religious community. In addition, I was comfortable in synagogues, while Barry was decidedly uncomfortable in churches. So, if I wanted Barry to participate in our children's religious upbringing, the only thing that made sense was to raise them Jewish. If I felt like an outsider at services, I could handle that. I would experience what it feels like to be the minority. Wasn't that what Jews experience all too often?

—McMahon, "The Outsider: Being a Catholic in Temple,"
Lilith, January 31, 2003, p. 48

_____ 1. The author's tone is
a. earnest.   c. gentle.
b. joyful.   d. worried.

_____ 2. At first the author thought her daughter
a. was angry at her.
b. had a condemning tone.
c. might reveal bias against her mother's being Catholic.
d. did not understand why her mother had a different religion.

3. The author's mother's tone was probably

   a. disapproving.

   b. sarcastic.

   c. pessimistic.

   d. concerned.

4. The author suggests her husband may have had a bias against Catholicism by writing that he

   a. was uncomfortable in churches.

   b. attended an interfaith couples group.

   c. has a different last name.

   d. had a strong attachment to the Jewish faith.

5. The author felt that she might

   a. develop bias against Jewish people.

   b. experience bias at temple for not being Jewish.

   c. miss the Catholic Church.

   d. pass on her biases to her children.

B. It's a great day for minority kids, for children in the inner cities, and for parents who desperately want to give their children a better education in a safer environment. It's a great day for parents who want the same benefits for their children enjoyed by the offspring of Jesse Jackson, Bill Clinton, our representatives and senators, the wealthy and many public school principals and teachers. It's the opportunity to choose the school where they want their children to go.

   Sometime in June this year, in the case involving Cleveland Schools, the U.S. Supreme Court ruled that it is legal for Americans to choose vouchers as an alternative to traditional government-sponsored public education. Essentially, the High Court ruled that government programs permitting vouchers are constitutional, even if the vouchers are used toward tuition at religious schools. "Closing its 2001–2002 term, the Court endorsed a six-year-old pilot program in inner-city Cleveland that provides parents a tax-supported education stipend. Parents may use the money to opt out of one of the worst-rated public school systems in the nation," wrote Anne Gearan of the Associated Press.

   When it comes to educating our children, choice is good. This ruling is good. For too long now, liberal politicians and their supporters in the education establishment have created a climate that tells parents who can't afford private schools—most of us—that choice in education is a bad ideal. "Let's save our public schools. Let's improve them. Don't throw the baby out with the bathwater," are common responses. Well, now we can take the baby out of the bath water and put him in a different tub. Now parents have choice.

An inner city single mom can send her kid to a private school, a school that might indeed teach the values that she wants her children to learn, in a safe environment, away from the gangs, the drugs and discipline problems. Isn't this good for all of us?

But the liberal education establishment says choice in education is bad. Want to know a dirty little secret? Check out the percentage of public school principals and teachers who send their own children to private schools. They fight feverishly to keep that very same options they enjoy from others—especially from parents in the inner city who need that choice most of all.

—Gibbs, "It's a Great Day for Choice," *New York Voice Inc.*

_____ 6. The author's overall tone is
    a. critical of the Court's decision.
    b. solemn.
    c. indirect and evasive.
    d. approving of the Court decision.

_____ 7. The "different tub" referred to in paragraph 3 is
    a. a new building with modern conveniences.
    b. an improved public school.
    c. a school of the parent's choice.
    d. a school where racial problems do not exist.

_____ 8. The author reveals bias against
    a. private schools.   c. public schools.
    b. politicians.   d. parents.

_____ 9. The author thinks that
    a. the Supreme Court is biased against liberals.
    b. inner city parents should not give up on their neighborhood schools.
    c. private schools will welcome students from the inner city.
    d. liberal politicians are biased against lower- and middle-class families.

_____ 10. The tone of Anne Gearan's quote is
  a. critical of the Court decision.
  b. factual and supportive of parents.
  c. intended to be entertaining.
  d. grim and angry.

EXPLAINING AWAY THE HATE
Terry Hong

Why do people hate other people? In this reading, which first appeared in *Asian Week*, the author considers this difficult question. Read it to find out how seeing protesters on the street led the author to explore the meaning of hate.

Vocabulary Preview

These are some of the difficult words in this essay. The definitions here will help you if you can't figure out the meanings from the sentence context or word parts.

rhetorical (par. 1) not expecting an answer; just for effect

vehemence (par. 1) intensity, power, passion

arbitrary (par. 1) randomly chosen based on personal whim

permutations (par. 3) arrangements, sets

unconditional (par. 5) absolute, limitless

dogma (par. 6) doctrine, code of beliefs

diverged (par. 8) moved in different directions from a common starting point

mulling over (par. 11) thinking over, considering

dismay (par. 11) disturbance, shock

---

1   I want to understand hate. This is not a rhetorical statement. I want someone to explain to me, patiently and logically, how people learn to hate with such blindness, vehemence and violence. I want to know how a child can be taught to hate based on such arbitrary factors as what a person looks like, what a person might believe in or who a person might love. I want to know how that child grows up to be a hateful adult. And I want to know how it becomes possible that it is God who supposedly teaches this hate.

2   Last weekend, as I was driving my two young children to a birthday party in the pouring rain, I saw a group of approximately a dozen men carrying large, fluorescent placards. They were posted at the entrance of the very church where I had spent most Sunday mornings growing up. So determined were the demonstrators to make sure their message was loud and clear that these hideous signs were untouched by the downpour—the demonstrators had the foresight to seemingly waterproof them.

3   "God Hates Fags!" the signs screamed in various permutations.

4 "Oh my God!" I shouted in response. My shocked 5-year-old, who is discouraged from using that phrase, asked with great concern, "What's wrong, Mommy?" And somehow I had to explain that the people with the signs had written "not nice" and "mean" messages on their posters, that they thought that God didn't like a certain group of people. Ironically, back at home visiting for the weekend was one of our closest friends, who just happened to be homosexual. I cringed, thinking our friend might drive this way.

5 "But Mommy," my daughter said, "God loves everybody. That's why he's God." And I thought to myself how grateful I am for the innocence of my children. And I silently prayed that my children would never lose that sense of God's unconditional love.

6 I'm not a religious person. Disappointed with dogma, I left the Catholic Church years ago. My husband and children attend a non-denominational Christian church on a fairly regular basis. When our children get older, we plan to expose them to other religious choices, as my husband was so exposed. The son of a United Church of Christ/Congregational minister who marched with Martin Luther King Jr. and Gloria Steinem, my husband and his siblings were taken to synagogues, Muslim temples, Buddhist services, as well as various Christian houses of worship. My father-in-law wanted his children to have a choice about other religions. In so doing, he taught them so much about tolerance.

7 How do we teach tolerance today in a world so filled with hate—hate that happens in the name of God?

8 The Palestine/Israel conflict is on the front page of every newspaper nearly every day. Two groups of people, who share a common ancestry that once included a common God, diverged in their beliefs some 5,000 years ago and continue to this day to kill each other in the name of their different gods.

9 In Gujarat, India, a report with information gathered in late March by a group of women activists is surfacing, documenting the hideous violence, especially the sexual torture and mass burning of Muslim girls and women by uncontrollable Hindu mobs. All in the name of God.

10 Take a worldwide poll, and the hate and violence seem endless. Look back just a decade—there's the continuing violence in Northern Ireland, the Hutus and the Tutsis in Africa and ethnic cleansing in Bosnia and Serbia. And think back to the Matthew Shepard tragedy in Wyoming, with the same placards outside the Laramie courthouse eerily duplicating the "God hates fags" signs.

11 Which brings me back to last week. My daughter had the final word. After mulling over my dismay, she said with such amazing clarity, "But Mommy, God loves those hating people too."

— ▪ —

Directions: *Select the letter of the choice that best completes each of the following statements.*

CHECKING YOUR COMPREHENSION

_____ 1. The central thought of the reading is that the author is struggling to understand

    a. why people believe in God.

    b. how children learn to hate adults.

    c. how God has become associated with hate.

    d. why God hates some people.

_____ 2. The author is disturbed about the demonstrators' message because it

    a. used God to justify their hate.

    b. was written on fluorescent placards.

    c. seemed insensitive and rude.

    d. was being delivered at her childhood church.

_____ 3. From the information presented in the reading, it is apparent that the author believes in the freedom to

    a. carry weapons.

    b. choose a religion.

    c. select marriage partners.

    d. hold unpopular political views.

_____ 4. How did the author's husband learn about tolerance?

    a. by marching with Martin Luther King Jr.

    b. by being exposed to a variety of religious experiences

    c. from having a minister for a father

    d. from the Catholic Church

_____ 5. The author mentions the worldwide incidents of hate and violence in order to

    a. educate the reader on international affairs.

    b. illustrate that widespread conflict in the name of God exists.

    c. show that homosexuals are discriminated against in many countries.

    d. comment on the problem of intolerance inherent in organized religions across the globe.

USING WHAT YOU KNOW ABOUT TONE AND BIAS

_____ 6. The author's overall tone is
   a. angry.   c. flippant.
   b. distressed.   d. pessimistic.

_____ 7. The demonstrators are biased against
   a. people of different faiths.
   b. atheists.
   c. homosexuals.
   d. anyone not like themselves.

_____ 8. The daughter's comments reveal
   a. bias against the demonstrators.
   b. a trusting, innocent tone.
   c. an uncaring tone.
   d. bias against mean people.

_____ 9. What word best describes the tone expressed on the demonstrators' placards?
   a. hateful   c. fearful
   b. reluctant   d. hurtful

_____ 10. What is at the root of the hatred described by the author?
   a. disputes from ancient times
   b. bias taught in churches
   c. the tone of the Bible
   d. the perceived biases of God

USING CONTEXT AND WORD PARTS

_____ 11. In paragraph 1, the word **blindness** means
   a. lack of rational thought.
   b. lack of sight.
   c. hiding.
   d. darkness.

_____ 12. In paragraph 2, the word **hideous** means
       a. laughable.
       b. impolite.
       c. indifferent.
       d. horrible and disgusting.

_____ 13. In paragraph 9, the word **surfacing** means
       a. rising from under the water.
       b. coming to the forefront of your mind.
       c. coming into public view.
       d. arriving at a new interpretation.

_____ 14. In paragraph 10, the word **eerily** means
       a. with a ghostly appearance.
       b. oddly, differently from the norm.
       c. unnervingly or mysteriously.
       d. coldly and unresponsively.

_____ 15. In paragraph 11, the word **clarity** means
       a. clear and exact thought.
       b. wrongful and inappropriate thought.
       c. rambling and wordy thought.
       d. correct and logical thought.

REVIEWING DIFFICULT VOCABULARY

Directions: _Complete each of the following sentences by inserting a word from the Vocabulary Preview on page 405 in the space provided. A word should be used only once._

16. With so many difficult relationships in my life, I need the
_____ affection of my dog.

17. To the professor's _____, no one turned in his or her homework today.

18. The CEO and the board have recently _____ in their ideas of how the company should operate.

19. The professor's choice of student assistants from among those who applied seemed _____.

20. My daughter protested with such _____ against going to visit my sister that I just couldn't take her along.

QUESTIONS FOR DISCUSSION

1. Bring a newspaper to class. Find reports of events that reveal bias. Then categorize them according to the type of bias they demonstrate, for example, religious, racial, ethnic, or gender bias. What do these news reports reveal about our world?

2. Brainstorm ideas for reducing hate and violence in your community. Consider acting on at least some of these as a group.

3. Discuss how the tone of our political leaders affects our attitudes toward government. What types of speeches motivate us?

WRITING ACTIVITIES

1. Describe your day in three different tones. What does this exercise reveal about your daily life?

2. Create a collage that contrasts love and hate or peace and war.

3. Explore the FBI's site on hate crime at http://www.fbi.gov/hq/cid/civilrights/hate.htm. Write a paragraph that explains how the FBI defines hate crimes and what is done about them.

Chapter 11: Tone and Bias

RECORDING YOUR PROGRESS

Test	Number Right			Score	
Practice Test 11-1	_____	× 10	=	_____	%
Practice Test 11-2	_____	× 10	=	_____	%
Practice Test 11-3	_____	× 10	=	_____	%
Mastery Test 11-1	_____	× 10	=	_____	%
Mastery Test 11-2	_____	× 10	=	_____	%
Mastery Test 11-3	_____	× 5	=	_____	%

EVALUATING YOUR PROGRESS

Based on your test performance, rate how well you have mastered the skills taught in this chapter by checking one of the boxes below or by writing your own evaluation.

☐ **Need More Improvement**
Tip: Try completing the Critical Thinking—American Southwest module in the Reading Skills section on the MyReadingLab Web site at **http://www.ablongman.com/myreadinglab** to fine-tune the skills that you have learned in this chapter.

☐ **Need More Practice**
Tip: Try using the Critical Thinking—American Southwest module in the Reading Skills section on the MyReadingLab Web site at **http://www.ablongman.com/myreadinglab** to brush up on the skills taught in this chapter, or visit this textbook's Companion Web site at **http://www.ablongman.com/mcwhorter** for extra practice.

☐ **Good**
Tip: To maintain your skills, quickly review this chapter by using this textbook's Companion Web site at **http://www.ablongman.com/mcwhorter**.

☐ **Excellent**

YOUR EVALUATION: _____

_____

_____

_____

THINK ABOUT IT!

Study the photograph below showing an employee participating in a picket line. The sign the demonstrator holds and the labels on his shirt take a position on an issue: The company is guilty of unfair labor practice. All that is lacking is evidence or reasons to convince us that the company is using unfair labor practices. In this chapter you will learn to read and evaluate arguments and discover errors or common flaws in reasoning.

CHAPTER 12

Reading Arguments

What Is an Argument?

An argument between people can be an angry onslaught of ideas and feelings. Family members might argue over household chores or use of the family car. Workers may argue over work assignments or days off from the job. To be effective, however, an argument should be logical and should present well-thought-out ideas. It may involve emotion, but a sound argument is never simply a sudden, unplanned release of emotions and feelings.

An argument, then, always presents logical reasons and evidence to support a viewpoint. In a government course, you might read arguments for or against free speech; in a literature class, you may read a piece of literary criticism that argues for or against the value of a particular poem, debates its significance, or rejects a particular interpretation.

Parts of an Argument

An argument has three essential parts—issue, claim, and support. It may also include a fourth part, refutation.

The Issue

An argument must address an **issue**—a problem or controversy about which people disagree. Abortion, gun control, animal rights, capital punishment, and drug legalization are all examples of issues.

The Claim

An argument must take a position on an issue. This position is called a **claim.** An argument may claim that capital punishment should be outlawed or that medical use of marijuana should be legalized. Here are a few more claims:

- Animals should have the same rights that humans do.
- Within ten years, destruction of the rain forest should be halted because it will make hundreds of plant and animal species extinct.
- Requiring community service is a good idea because it will create more community-minded graduates.

**Exercise
12–1**

Directions: *For each of the following issues, choose the statement that takes a position on the issue and place a check mark in front of it.*

1. Issue: Community service

   _____ a. Twenty hours of community service is required at Dodgeville High School.

   _____ b. Community service should be required of all high school students.

   _____ c. Some students voluntarily perform many hours of community service yearly.

2. Issue: Health insurance

   _____ a. Millions of Americans do not have health insurance.

   _____ b. Many insurance companies are finding it difficult to control costs.

   _____ c. Health insurance is a basic right that the federal government should provide to all people.

3. Issue: Public libraries and the Internet

   _____ a. People should be able to view whatever sites they choose at the public library.

   _____ b. Filtering software cannot block all offensive Web sites.

   _____ c. Many public libraries filter their Internet access.

4. Issue: The Equal Rights Amendment (ERA)

_____ a. All citizens should be in favor of the principles outlined in the ERA.

_____ b. Women made gains in the struggle for equality in the first half of the twentieth century.

_____ c. Feminists did not agree about the value of pushing for the ERA.

5. Issue: Sports fan behavior

_____ a. Many football stadiums now have alcohol-free seating areas.

_____ b. Tickets to athletic events are expensive, so fans should be free to act however they choose.

_____ c. Sports arena security forces eject unruly fans.

Exercise 12–2

Directions: *For each of the following issues, write a statement that takes a position on the issue. Write your claim in the space provided.*

1. Issue: Minimum wage

Claim: _____

_____

2. Issue: Global climate changes

Claim: _____

_____

3. Issue: Air travel safety

Claim: _____

_____

4. Issue: Alternative medicine

Claim: _____

_____

5. Issue: Pop music

Claim: _____

Support

A writer supports a claim by offering reasons and evidence that the claim should be accepted. A **reason** is a general statement that backs up a claim. Here are a few reasons that support an argument in favor of parental Internet controls:

1. The Internet contains millions of sites that are not appropriate for children, so parents must accept responsibility for controlling what their children see.

2. Parental controls are needed because the Internet can be a place for sexual predators to find victims.

3. Parental controls are needed because the Internet is not controlled by any other entity.

However, for any of these reasons to be believable and convincing, they need to be supported with evidence. **Evidence** consists of facts, personal experience, examples, statistics, and comparisons that demonstrate why the claim is valid.

- **Facts.** Facts are true statements. Writers may use facts to lead readers to a conclusion. However, the conclusion does not always follow from the facts presented. For example, a writer may state that you will not get a cold if you eat a lot of oranges because oranges have vitamin C. It is true that oranges have vitamin C, but that does not necessarily mean that eating them will keep you cold free.

- **Personal experience.** A writer may use his or her own personal account or observation of a situation. For example, in supporting the claim that Internet controls are useful, a writer may report that she has put a filter on her child's computer and her child has never come across a pornographic Web site. Although a writer's personal experience may provide an interesting perspective on an issue, personal experience should not be accepted as proof.

- **Examples.** Examples are descriptions of particular situations that are used to illustrate or explain a principle, concept, or idea. In supporting the statement that people would rather drive their own cars than use public transportation, a writer may give the example that almost no one in his office takes the bus to work. Examples should not be used by themselves to prove the concept or idea they illustrate. The writer's experience may be atypical, or not representative, of what is common.

- **Statistics.** Statistics—the reporting of figures, percentages, averages, and so forth—is a common method of support. For example, in an argument about the overuse of elective surgery in hospitals, a writer may present statistics showing the increase in Caesarean sections over the past few years. However, this increase could be due to other factors such as physicians' assessment of risk during childbirth or patients' physical conditions. Statistics can be misused, misinterpreted, or used selectively to give other than the most objective, accurate picture of a situation.

- **Comparisons and analogies.** Comparisons or analogies (extended comparisons) serve as illustrations. Their reliability depends on how closely the comparison corresponds or how similar it is to the situation to which it is being compared. For example, Martin Luther King Jr., in his famous letter from the Birmingham jail, compared nonviolent protesters to a robbed man. To evaluate this comparison, you would need to consider how the two are similar and how they are different.

Exercise 12–3

Directions: *Read each of the following sets of statements. Identify the statement that is a claim and label it C. Label the one statement that supports the claim as S.*

1. _____ Year-round school is advantageous for both parents and children.

   _____ Continuous, year-round application of skills will prevent forgetting and strengthen students' academic preparation.

   _____ Year-round school may be costly to school districts.

2. _____ Many celebrities have been in trouble with the law lately because of their involvement with theft, drunk driving, violence, and even murder.

   _____ Celebrities do not act as positive role models for the people who admire them.

   _____ Acquiring fame and fortune does not automatically relieve a person of stress and suffering.

3. _____   Millions of students cannot afford to attend college because tuition costs and fees are so high.

_____   States should find ways to control tuition costs at public colleges and universities.

_____   Officials at private institutions of higher learning do not have to worry about budget issues since they have huge endowments.

4. _____   Drug companies should not be allowed to advertise on television.

_____   My grandparents are easily persuaded to buy expensive medications they do not need.

_____   Physicians do not provide all the necessary information patients need.

5. _____   Today's artists receive more media attention than in previous decades.

_____   Modern art is confusing.

_____   I am never sure what an abstract painting represents.

Exercise 12–4

Directions: *Each item below begins with a claim, followed by supporting statements. Identify the type(s) of evidence used to support each claim. Choose from among the following types: personal experience (PE), examples (E), statistics (S), and comparisons (C).*

_____   1. Library hours should be extended to weekends to make the library more accessible. My sisters have part-time jobs that require them to work late afternoons and evenings during the week. They are unable to use the library during the week.

_____   2. Because parents have the right to determine their children's sexual attitudes, sex education should take place in the home, not at school. Teaching children about sex in school is like teaching them to sit in assigned seats and walk around quietly in single file at home.

_____   3. It is more expensive to own a dog than a cat. According to the American Veterinary Medical Association, a dog visits the vet twice as many times as a cat.

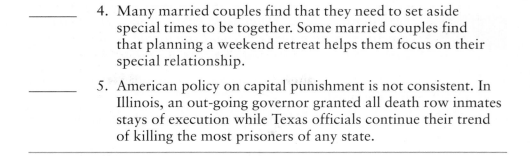

_____ 4. Many married couples find that they need to set aside special times to be together. Some married couples find that planning a weekend retreat helps them focus on their special relationship.

_____ 5. American policy on capital punishment is not consistent. In Illinois, an out-going governor granted all death row inmates stays of execution while Texas officials continue their trend of killing the most prisoners of any state.

Questions for Evaluating Arguments

Not all arguments are reasonable and not all arguments are sound and logical. Use the following questions to help you evaluate arguments.

Is the Evidence Relevant?

Evidence that is offered in support of a claim must directly relate to that claim. That is, to be relevant, evidence must apply specifically to the issue at hand. For example, a friend may offer as a reason for his tardiness that he had a flat tire, but this fact is not relevant because he would have had to walk only one block to see you. Writers may intentionally or unintentionally include information that may seem convincing but when analyzed more closely does not directly apply to the issue. Here is an example. Can you identify the irrelevant information the paragraph contains?

> Business students, especially those in MBA programs, need to take more classes in ethics. Stricter requirements in this area will ensure that tomorrow's corporate executives will be more responsible and honest than they have been in the past. More women should be admitted to the top business schools. The trust and confidence that employees and investors have lost can be built back if today's professors commit to teaching right and wrong. Future businesspeople will then move the economy forward without the setbacks created by corporate scandal and bankruptcy.

In this paragraph, the sentence about women being admitted to business school is not relevant because the argument is not about whether women are more honest than men or whether higher numbers of women would make a difference in the ethical business climate.

To decide whether a statement is relevant, reread the claim and then immediately afterward reread the statement in question. Ask yourself, "Are the two logically connected?"

Directions: *For each claim listed below, place a check mark in front of those statements that provide relevant supporting evidence. The number of relevant statements varies, but there are always at least two.*

1. Claim: Alcohol abuse is common among teenagers and needs to be curtailed.

    _____ a. Thousands of young people die each year in alcohol-related crashes.

    _____ b. According to the National Institute on Alcohol Abuse and Alcoholism, young people who drink have an increased chance of developing problems with alcohol later in life.

    _____ c. People who take medication need to limit or cease their alcohol intake.

    _____ d. Many teens who drink have a parent who is an alcoholic.

2. Claim: Fish populations are decreasing because of overfishing.

    _____ a. The UN Food and Agriculture Organization reports that because of overharvesting, four of the fifteen main fishing areas in the world are depleted and another nine are declining.

    _____ b. Regulations to save fish populations will hurt fishermen.

    _____ c. The fish cannot reproduce fast enough to keep up with the rate they are harvested.

    _____ d. These days people are eating less red meat for health reasons.

3. Claim: Recycling helps the environment.

    _____ a. Products made from recycled materials are expensive.

    _____ b. Buying items in bulk reduces the need for extra packaging.

    _____ c. Recycling keeps reusable materials out of landfills.

    _____ d. It takes less energy to make a new product from recycled material.

4. Claim: Controversial art should not be exhibited in public places.

    _____ a. Children might see disturbing images, causing them behavioral problems.

    _____ b. Taxpayers do not want their money going to fund obscene art.

_____ c. Public funds have to be used for security if there are protesters.

_____ d. Art is covered under the "Freedom of Speech" amendment.

5. Claim: Any stock or bond investment is risky and must be researched before money exchanges hands.

_____ a. The Securities and Exchange Commission collects financial data on public companies.

_____ b. Day traders sometimes use borrowed money for their activities.

_____ c. Stocks and bonds may lose their value.

_____ d. Not all brokers are responsible with their clients' money.

Exercise 12–6

Directions: *Each of the following paragraphs contains one sentence that does not support the claim. Identify the sentence and write its number in the space provided.*

_____ 1. [1] Modern architecture makes our cities look and feel sterile and unfriendly. [2] Today's building materials—glass and steel—reflect the world they face instead of inviting the world inside. [3] The lack of ornamental details has rendered our downtowns void of beauty and emotion. [4] Commuters flood the city centers with cars and pollution. [5] Architecture should welcome workers with the same warm and comfortable styles, colors, and materials of our homes to reduce stress in the workplace.

_____ 2. [1] Being an environmentalist does not mean being against economic growth. [2] There are many ways to keep jobs and even create new ones while making responsible choices with regard to the environment. [3] For example, when states such as California require the use of low-emissions vehicles, they are opening up new markets to car manufacturers. [4] Some celebrities even own these special vehicles. [5] Also, oil companies can create new businesses by developing alternative fuels. [6] Meanwhile, employees can be retrained to work with the new technologies.

_____   3. [1] Despite years of education, antismoking advertising, and skyrocketing prices, cigarettes remain popular among Americans. [2] According to the National Institute on Drug Abuse, 60 million Americans aged 12 and over are smokers. [3] Most people who smoke start smoking when they are teenagers. [4] Since nicotine is extremely addictive, once people start smoking, they find it very difficult to stop even if they have learned about the health hazards. [5] Also, smoking is still perceived as cool and glamorous by millions of young people who see movie and rock stars take part in this proven unhealthy behavior.

_____   4. [1] Digital photography has brought families and friends closer together. [2] These days, most of us have relatives and friends living more than a day's drive or even a day's flight away, and we cannot see them as often as we would like. [3] New York City to Hong Kong is over 20 hours in the air. [4] By using digital cameras and the Internet, we can provide regular updates with pictures on everything from our garden to Junior's soccer season. [5] Using technology for highly enjoyable purposes like this not only keeps us in touch, but also balances out all the more routine computer work we do in our work and school environments.

Is the Evidence Sufficient?

There must be a sufficient number of reasons or pieces of evidence to support a claim. The amount and degree of detail of supporting evidence will vary with the issue, its complexity, and its importance. For any serious issue, it is not usually sufficient to offer a single reason or piece of evidence. For example, to say that our oceans are dying due to coastal development is not convincing because only a portion of the world's oceans are affected by coastal development. Other evidence to support this claim could include industrial waste dumping, oil drilling, ecosystem imbalance, and rising water temperatures.

The evidence a writer offers must also be sufficiently detailed to be convincing and believable. For instance, the statement, "A parrot is an ideal pet because it can be taught to mimic language" does not provide sufficient information to persuade anyone to choose a parrot as a pet. To be convincing, more details would be needed about the habits, personality, longevity, and beauty of parrots.

Exercise 12-7

Directions: *For each of the claims listed below, find three pieces of evidence in the box below that support it. Write the letters of the evidence in the space provided. Not all pieces of evidence will be used.*

Claims

_____   1. People are becoming ruder in our country.

_____   2. Many children who receive special education services do not really need them.

_____   3. Parents and teachers should fight to keep art and music in the schools.

_____   4. Standardized tests do not accurately represent what American students know.

Evidence

A. Research shows that children need a variety of ways to express themselves.
B. The media bombard our children with images of violence.
C. Telemarketers just will not take no for an answer.
D. Celebrities live public lives of immorality, making promiscuity, drugs, reckless behavior, and divorce seem normal and even glamorous.
E. Incidents of road rage are increasing every year.
F. Not all teachers realize that every child has a different learning style.
G. Teachers are quick to label any child who needs extra help with a learning disorder.
H. Our society puts pressure on children to be consumers at a young age.
I. Learning to play an instrument helps with math skills.
J. Many students experience test anxiety, which can have a negative impact on their scores.
K. Many people have been storming out of stores because of insulting customer service.
L. In some schools there is tremendous pressure on teachers to boost test scores, forcing teachers to "teach to the test."
M. Studies have shown that learning to read music helps students with their regular reading skills.
N. Special education teachers are too aggressive in identifying students who need their services just so they can keep their jobs.
O. Test writers understand education only in theory and do not write questions that are relevant to today's students.

Does the Author Recognize and Refute Opposing Viewpoints?

Many arguments recognize opposing viewpoints. For example, an author may argue that gays should be allowed to serve in the military. However, the author may recognize or admit that opponents believe that the presence of gays in a military unit may compromise its cohesiveness.

Many arguments also attempt to refute the opposing viewpoint (explain why it is wrong, flawed, or unacceptable). For example, a writer may refute the notion that gays will compromise cohesiveness by stating that soldiers are unified against the enemy, not each other. Basically, then, refutation is a process of finding weaknesses in the opponent's argument.

When reading arguments that address opposing viewpoints, ask yourself the following questions.

- Does the author address opposing viewpoints clearly and fairly?
- Does the author refute the opposing viewpoint with logic and relevant evidence?

Does the Author Use Emotional Appeals and Are They Used Unfairly?

Emotional appeals are ideas that are targeted toward needs or values that readers are likely to care about. Needs include physiological needs (food, drink, shelter) and psychological needs (sense of belonging, sense of accomplishment, sense of self-worth). An argument on gun control, for example, may appeal to a reader's need for safety, while an argument favoring restrictions on banks sharing personal or financial information may appeal to a reader's need for privacy and financial security.

Unfair emotional appeals attempt to involve or excite readers by appealing to their emotions, thereby controlling the reader's attitude toward the subject. Several types of emotional appeals are described below.

1. **Emotionally Charged or Biased Language.** By using words that create an emotional response, writers establish positive or negative feelings. For example, an advertisement for a new line of fragrances promises to "indulge," "refresh," "nourish," and "pamper" the user. An ad for an automobile uses phrases such as "limousine comfort," "European styling," and "animal sleekness" to interest and excite readers.

2. **False Authority.** False authority involves using the opinion or action of a well-known or famous person. We have all seen athletes endorsing underwear or movie stars selling shampoo. This type of appeal works on the notion that people admire celebrities and strive to be like them, respect their opinion, and are willing to accept their viewpoint.

3. **Association.** An emotional appeal also is made by associating a product, idea, or position with others that are already accepted or highly regarded. Patriotism is already valued, so to call a product All-American in an advertisement is an appeal to the emotions. A car being named a Cougar to remind you of a fast, sleek animal, a cigarette ad picturing a scenic waterfall, or a speaker standing in front of an American flag are other examples.

4. **Appeal to "common folk."** Some people distrust those who are well educated, wealthy, highly artistic, or in other ways distinctly different from the average person. An emotional appeal to this group is made by indicating that a product or idea originated from, is held by, or is bought by ordinary citizens. A commercial may advertise a product by showing its use in an average household. A politician may describe her background and education to suggest that she is like everyone else; a salesperson may dress in styles similar to his clients.

5. *Ad hominem.* An argument that attacks the holder of an opposing viewpoint rather than his or her viewpoint is known as *ad hominem,* or an attack on the man. For example, the statement, "How could a woman who does not even hold a college degree criticize a judicial decision?" attacks the woman's level of education, not her viewpoint.

6. **"Join the crowd" appeal.** The appeal to do, believe, or buy what everyone else is doing, believing, or buying is known as crowd appeal or the bandwagon appeal. Commercials that proclaim their product the "#1 best-selling car in America" are appealing to this motive. Essays in support of a position that cite opinion polls on a controversial issue—"68 percent of Americans favor capital punishment"—are also using this appeal.

Exercise 12-8

Directions: *For each of the following statements, indicate the type of emotional appeal it represents.*

a. emotionally charged or biased language

b. false authority

c. association

d. appeal to common folk

e. *ad hominem*

f. join the crowd

_____ 1. Laura Bush, wife of President George Bush, recommends the book *Beloved,* by Toni Morrison; it must be very good.

_____ 2. We must preserve our historic neighborhoods in order to save the memories of the hardworking men and women who built our cities with their sweat and blood.

_____ 3. Don't go to that restaurant; the owner can't even keep her garden growing.

_____ 4. Everyone who cares about education is voting for Proposition E.

_____ 5. The mayor eats Mrs. Baker's pecan sandies; they must be the best.

_____ 6. Mandatory DNA collection of criminals will stop all brutal sexual assaults on our helpless women and innocent children.

_____ 7. We provide quality service just like in the good old days.

_____ 8. Join together with your brothers and sisters in the union; don't let rich managers and executives oppress you any longer.

_____ 9. No one dresses like that anymore.

_____ 10. My dentist is awful; he drives an old car.

Errors in Logical Reasoning

Errors in reasoning, often called logical fallacies, are common in arguments. These errors invalidate the argument or render it flawed. Several common errors in logic are described next.

Circular Reasoning

Also known as begging the question, this error involves using part of the conclusion as evidence to support it. Here are two examples.

Cruel medical experimentation on defenseless animals is inhumane.

Female police officers should not be sent to crime scenes because apprehending criminals is a man's job.

In circular reasoning, because no evidence is given to support the claim, there is no reason to accept the conclusion.

Hasty Generalization

This fallacy means that the conclusion has been derived from insufficient evidence. Here is one example: You taste three tangerines and each is sour, so you conclude that all tangerines are sour. Here is another: By observing one performance of a musical group, you conclude the group is unfit to perform.

Non Sequitur ("It Does Not Follow")

The false establishment of cause/effect is known as a *non sequitur*. To say, for example, that "Because my doctor is young, I'm sure she'll be a good doctor" is a non sequitur because youth does not cause good medical practice. Here is another example: "Arturio Alvarez is the best choice for state senator because he is an ordinary citizen." Being an ordinary citizen will not necessarily make someone an effective state senator.

False Cause

The false cause fallacy is the incorrect assumption that two events that follow each other in time are causally related. Suppose you walked under a ladder and then lost your wallet. If you said you lost your wallet because you walked under a ladder, you would be assuming false cause.

Either-Or Fallacy

This fallacy assumes that an issue is only two sided, or that there are only two choices or alternatives for a particular situation. In other words, there is no middle ground. Consider the issue of censorship of violence on television. An either-or fallacy is to assume that violence on TV must be either allowed or banned. This fallacy does not recognize other alternatives such as limiting access through viewing hours, restricting certain types of violence, and so forth.

Exercise 12–9

Directions: *Identify the logical fallacy in each of the following statements and write its letter in the space provided.*

a. circular reasoning

b. hasty generalization

c. *non sequitur*

d. false cause

e. either-or fallacy

_____   1. All African-American students in my biology class earned A grades, so African-Americans must excel in life sciences.

_____   2. If you are not for nuclear arms control, then you're against protecting our future.

_____   3. My sister gets nervous when asked to do mathematical computations or balance her checkbook because she has math anxiety.

_____   4. A well-known mayor, noting a decline in the crime rate in the four largest cities in his state, quickly announced that his new "get-tough on criminals" publicity campaign was successful and took credit for the decline.

_____   5. I always order a fruit pastry for dessert because I am allergic to chocolate.

Arguments in Academic Writing

While textbooks do not usually address popular controversial issues, you will still encounter arguments in your assigned textbook readings. Textbook authors often take a position on pertinent topics within their discipline. A health and fitness textbook author may make a claim that cardiovascular exercise is essential to long-term health. Or a psychology textbook author may argue that compulsive shopping should be officially declared a mental illness.

As when reading any other source of argument, pay attention to the reasons and evidence offered to support the claim. Textbook authors are careful to provide relevant and sufficient evidence. Close attention to evidence is important, though, since it is the evidence that you will need to understand and recall the material for upcoming quizzes and exams.

Exercise 12-10

Directions: *After reading each of the following paragraphs from college textbooks, select the choice that best answers each of the questions that follow.*

A. As technology continues to develop and change, so must businesses change and adapt to keep pace. The Internet, telecommunications, computers, robotics—all have an impact on business. For example, growing numbers of businesses have Web sites; increasing numbers of employees are telecommuting (working at home); and small robots are used increasingly in manufacturing. Awareness of technology will keep you on the cutting edge of business growth and change.

—McWhorter, *Academic Reading*, p. 385

_____ 1. What issue is being considered?

    a. the role of robots in business

    b. the role of technology in business

    c. the speed of change in business due to technology

    d. the use of the Internet in business

_____ 2. What claim is the author making?

    a. Businesses must keep up with technology.

    b. Technology is too complicated for small businesses.

    c. Robots should replace humans in factories.

    d. Business owners should have Web sites and allow workers to telecommute.

_____ 3. What evidence is used to support the claim?

    a. circular reasoning that technology drives business so businesses must adopt technology

    b. comparison of old and new business technologies

    c. emotional language meant to frighten those who are behind in technology

    d. examples of ways in which businesses have adapted technology

B. Literature describes human experience. It is a creative record of the thoughts, feelings, emotions, or experiences of other people. By reading literature, you can learn about yourself and understand both painful and joyful experiences without actually going though them yourself. For example, you can read a poem about the birth of a child and come to understand the range of feelings parents share, even though you may not be a parent. In other words, literature allows you to live vicariously, sharing the lives of others without physical participation.

_____ 4. What issue is being considered?

    a. the role of literature in the lives of children

    b. the value of literature

    c. literature as therapy

    d. why people write books

_____ 5. What claim is the author making?

    a. Novels teach you just as much as nonfiction books.

    b. Reading literature expands your range of emotional experiences.

    c. People who read a lot are in better touch with their emotions.

    d. Books can help you solve problems.

_____ 6. Which of the following is used as evidence to support the claim?

    a. an example of a way in which literature can affect your feelings

    b. an explanation of how to read with emotion

    c. hasty generalization about the value of literature

    d. a comparison between the experience of reading and the pain of childbirth

The Textbook Challenge

Part A: Current Issues Reader

For the article "Hold It Right There and Drop That Camera" (p. 507), choose one claim made in the selection and list the evidence given to support it.

Part B: A College Textbook

Using a textbook chapter or reading that you have read for one of your other courses, choose one claim made in the selection and list the evidence given to support it.

What Have You Learned?

Directions: *To check your understanding of the chapter, select the word or phrase from the box below that best completes each of the following statements. Not all of the items in the box will be used.*

argument	*non sequitur*	*ad hominem*	emotional appeal	relevant
evidence	refute	issue	circular reasoning	sufficient
claim	statistics	examples	either-or fallacy	facts

1. An author may introduce counterarguments and then
   _____ them in order to support a claim.

2. Evidence must directly pertain to the claim; it must be
   _____.

3. The general topic an argument addresses is the _____.

4. An _____ targets a reader's values and feelings.

5. Supporting _____ could be facts, statistics, or personal experiences.

6. _____ uses the conclusion of an argument to prove that same argument.

7. An argument that presents an issue as having only two distinct sides contains an _____.

8. An _____ presents logical evidence and reasons to support a viewpoint.

9. In order for evidence to be _____, it must be complete and detailed.

10. The position an argument takes on a subject is the
    _____.

What Vocabulary Have You Learned?

Directions: *The words in column A appear in this chapter. Test your mastery of these words by matching each word in column A with its meaning in column B.*

	Column A		Column B
_____	1. endowments	a.	cut short, made less
_____	2. rendered	b.	donated funds for continual support
_____	3. vicariously	c.	very careful, responsible, and attentive
_____	4. conscientious	d.	caused; made to happen
_____	5. curtailed	e.	through another's experience

ANALYZING SUPPORTING EVIDENCE AND ERRORS
IN REASONING

A. Directions: *Read each claim and determine which three statements provide relevant support for it. Write their letters in the space provided.*

_____   1. Claim: DNA technology is critical to our criminal justice system and law enforcement agencies.

   a. Innocent prisoners can be released when new DNA evidence is presented.

   b. Suspects are linked to victims by the presence of their DNA at the crime scene.

   c. Most Americans have a basic understanding of the properties of DNA.

   d. Researchers are using DNA to find cures for diseases.

   e. DNA evidence is more reliable than fingerprints and eyewitness testimony.

_____   2. Claim: Watching motion pictures lifts our spirits during hard economic times.

   a. Some movie theaters now have espresso stands.

   b. Movies help us imagine, remember, or hope for better times.

   c. Many video rental stores guarantee the availability of all the latest releases.

   d. By renting or borrowing video tapes, families can enjoy happy times together without spending a great deal of money.

   e. Theater attendance increased dramatically during the Great Depression.

_____   3. Claim: The United States fills a large humanitarian and peacekeeping role in the world.

   a. According to White House statistics, America gave away over $3 billion in 2000 to help other countries.

   b. The United States stayed out of WWII until 1941.

   c. U.S. troops take part in peacekeeping missions in several countries in Africa.

    d. Protestors marched in Washington against the war in Vietnam in the sixties.

    e. Millions of refugees have found asylum on American shores.

_____ 4. Claim: The government should subsidize the high cost of quality child care so that single mothers can work.

    a. Some single moms have relatives who take care of their children.

    b. Many of the children in Head Start live with only one parent.

    c. Many single mothers prefer to work than to receive welfare, but are unable to do so.

    d. Quality child care is expensive; the workers are well educated and command higher rates of pay.

    e. Millions of single mothers go without financial support from their ex-husbands or the fathers of their children.

_____ 5. Claim: Children should not be raised in an urban environment.

    a. Families that live in the suburbs spend more time in the car than families who live in the city.

    b. Asthma rates for children living in cities are rising.

    c. Crime rates are rising in urban centers.

    d. Cities generally offer many cultural opportunities.

    e. Children need lots of wide open spaces for running and playing.

B. Directions: *Choose the type of emotional appeal or logical fallacy used in each set of statements.*

_____ 6. Today's young people are out of control. The only alternative is to impose strict discipline. Otherwise, there will be total chaos in our society.

    a. biased language

    b. join the crowd

    c. either-or fallacy

    d. circular reasoning

_____ 7. Tall people have an advantage in the workplace. My boss and supervisor are taller than average and no one in a managerial position is short. You must be tall to get a promotion where I work.

   a. appeal to common folk

   b. hasty generalizations

   c. false authority

   d. _non sequitur_

_____ 8. Your tax dollars are being wasted on overly expensive campaigns. Don't let your hard-earned money pay for extravagant parties and leisure travel for candidates you don't support.

   a. _ad hominem_

   b. association

   c. either-or fallacy

   d. emotionally charged language

_____ 9. Every city has at least one charter school. We must encourage our city to keep up with other communities across the country by funding at least one charter school.

   a. join the crowd

   b. circular reasoning

   c. _non sequitur_

   d. false authority

_____ 10. Try the musical theater instead of opera. The stories reflect the problems of daily life; the songs are familiar; the lyrics are in a language we understand.

   a. false authority

   b. join the crowd

   c. appeal to common folk

   d. circular reasoning

ANALYZING CLAIMS AND EVIDENCE

Directions: *Read the following paragraphs. Answer the questions about their claims and evidence.*

A. [1] Many young people find themselves in some sort of trouble at school during their teen years. [2] Usually a talk and simple punishment from teachers or school administrators are enough to keep children from repeating their offenses. [3] However, some youths are not affected by lectures or detention, and unfortunately they go on to more serious crimes such as vandalism or theft. [4] In these cases, schools should hold parents responsible for their child's behavior. [5] If a father has to pay for the window his son smashed, he will take a more active role in controlling that son's behavior. [6] Discipline and control begin at home where parents are responsible for instilling values in their children.

_____   1. The author of the paragraph makes the claim that

   a. teachers and parents should communicate more.

   b. students do not respond to school-imposed punishments.

   c. parents should be held accountable for how their kids act.

   d. schools have no control over students.

_____   2. The type of evidence used in sentence 5 is a(n)

   a. comparison.

   b. example.

   c. fact.

   d. reason.

B. People who live in the suburbs do not experience the tight-knit community of a city neighborhood. Big houses with large backyard decks and streets with no sidewalks keep suburban dwellers focused on themselves. When I lived in the city, I sat on the front porch with my family in the evening and talked with neighbors who were on their nearby front porches or taking a leisurely stroll. We all knew and cared about each other. Whenever someone had a problem, we all helped. In the suburbs, you cannot walk around safely or linger in front of your house comfortably. People tend to stay inside or in the backyard and never get to know who lives around and among them.

_____ 3. The author of the paragraph makes the claim that
    a. city dwellers know their neighbors better than suburban-ites know theirs.
    b. suburban houses are too big.
    c. there are no backyards in city neighborhoods.
    d. people who live in the city are more interested in knowing their neighbors.

_____ 4. The author uses which type of evidence?
    a. analogy   c. statistics
    b. fact   d. personal experience

C. [1] Building more roads in and around our cities will not alleviate traffic. [2] Commuters will just fill up those new roads too, creating even bigger backups. [3] Simply stated, people must leave their cars at home. [4] In the first half of the twentieth century, most U.S. cities had extensive streetcar lines. [5] Buses and trains, rapid transit, and monorail systems should be funded by the federal and state governments in order to remove automobiles from the pavement. [6] At the very least, strict carpooling requirements should be established and enforced.

_____ 5. The author of the paragraph makes the claim that
    a. our traffic will never end.
    b. carpooling does very little to alleviate traffic.
    c. new road construction will not decrease traffic congestion.
    d. existing roads should be improved before new roads are constructed.

6. Circle the number of the sentence that is irrelevant.

    1   2   3   4   5   6

D. Western doctors should use more of the so-called alternative medical remedies. *The New England Journal of Medicine* reports that 33 percent of Americans do! However, most of these patients do so without telling their physicians. If traditional doctors were to learn more about these treatments and incorporate them into their recommended therapies, patients would have a wider variety of health care options. In addition, medical costs would go down because alternative medicine takes more of a preventive stance, so people would be sick less often.

_____ 7. The author of the paragraph makes the claim that
   a. alternative medicine is better than traditional medicine.
   b. alternative medicine should be embraced by Western doctors.
   c. patients are not honest with their health care providers.
   d. patients want more health care choices.

_____ 8. The author uses which type of evidence?
   a. statistics   c. comparison
   b. personal experience   d. emotional appeal

E.   [1] Our society values youth at the expense of the elderly. [2] These days no one respects older people anymore. [3] Instead of being looked upon as wise and experienced, senior citizens are seen as foolish and burdensome. [4] Instead of asking their advice, we shush them and take away their freedom. [5] Younger people shy away from these unglamorous yet valuable members of our society just because wrinkles and arthritis have slowed them down a bit. [6] Putting elderly parents in a nursing home can be very difficult. [7] Families should teach respect for older relatives.

_____ 9. The author of the paragraph makes the claim that
   a. young people hate old people.
   b. our society must change its attitude toward the elderly.
   c. senior citizens are not valued as useful members of society.
   d. older people have a lot to offer.

10. Circle the number of the sentence that is irrelevant.

        1   2   3   4   5   6   7

ANALYZING ARGUMENTS

Directions: *After reading each of the paragraphs below, select the choice that best answers each of the questions that follow.*

A. [1] A majority of Americans follow at least one professional sport. [2] Unfortunately, rising costs are making it impossible for the average fan to watch his or her favorite athlete or team in person. [3] According to *Team Marketing Report,* the average ticket price in the NFL is $50.02, and in the NBA it's $43.65. For professional baseball, the average ticket price is $18.30, while in hockey, it's $41.56. [4] Soccer is the most popular professional sport in the world. [5] Some argue that the high prices are justified. [6] After all, they say, in order to please fans, teams must win more games than they lose. [7] The best way to win is to have the top players, but teams must spend large amounts of money to get these players. [8] These costs are passed on to the fans through ticket prices and merchandising. [9] However, instead of raising ticket prices, team owners should raise the fees paid by corporations who sponsor stadiums and put their logo on the TV next to the score or advertise in the arena, making use of the real money in the hands of big business. [10] The love of sports cuts across socioeconomic lines; the ability to enjoy a game in person should too.

_____ 1. The issue being addressed is
  a. corporate greed.
  b. the cost of professional sports tickets.
  c. economic disparity.
  d. the entertainment value of professional sports.

_____ 2. The author makes the claim that
  a. athletes and team owners are greedy.
  b. teams should give away tickets for free.
  c. only extremely wealthy people can afford to attend sports events.
  d. ticket prices are too high for most fans of professional sports.

_____ 3. The author uses which type of evidence in this argument?
  a. analogy   c. statistics
  b. direct quote   d. personal experience

_____ 4. The author includes

    a. an opposing viewpoint.

    b. a "join the crowd" emotional appeal.

    c. figurative language.

    d. circular reasoning.

_____ 5. Which sentence provides irrelevant evidence?

    a. 2   c. 6

    b. 4   d. 8

B. [1] For the past eleven years, United Nations members have voted against the United States' embargo [trade restrictions] against Cuba. [2] Perhaps it is time for our country to listen to the rest of the world and allow trade and tourism with this island nation. [3] The embargo only hurts the regular people—citizens of Cuba and their American relatives—not Fidel Castro. [4] In fact, he feels the embargo strengthens his cause since it requires him and his country to survive without aid from the wealthiest nation on the planet. [5] Furthermore, this tropical country no longer poses any kind of threat to our national security. [6] Americans regularly and freely travel to countries that our current administration sees as more dangerous and menacing, such as North Korea. [7] Clearly there is no reason to put Cuba into the "axis of evil." [8] In fact, the resumption of American tourism in Cuba could help its residents demand freedom as they are exposed to American values of democracy and liberty. [9] Cuba has an old world charm because of its long isolation. [10] Most important, however, to restore trade and tourism with Cuba is to cooperate with the rest of the world instead of continuing to disregard the wishes of the majority.

_____ 6. The issue being addressed is

    a. the lack of freedom in Cuba.

    b. the U.S. embargo against Cuba.

    c. the effect capitalism would have on Cuba.

    d. American economic policy.

_____ 7. The author makes the claim that

    a. Fidel Castro does not want to resume trade with the U.S.

    b. Cuba should be part of the "axis of evil."

    c. The U.S. should change its policy on Cuba.

    d. More Cubans should seek asylum in America.

_____ 8. The mention of U.S. policy toward North Korea
   a. serves as a comparison.
   b. is an important statistic.
   c. demonstrates circular reasoning.
   d. is a hasty generalization.

_____ 9. The author includes
   a. a "join the crowd" emotional appeal.
   b. an *ad hominem* statement.
   c. a refutation.
   d. a false cause error.

_____ 10. Which sentence provides irrelevant evidence?
   a. 3   c. 7
   b. 5   d. 9

ANALYZING ARGUMENTS

Directions: *After reading the following paragraphs, select the choice that best answers each of the questions that follow.*

A. [1] As the Internet becomes more and more central to the search for information, students and scholars are demanding that more items in library collections be digitized and made available on the Web. [2] Library directors also see this method of preservation as a perfect way to provide more service for less money. [3] Many library directors are out of touch with the librarians who work for them. [4] However, librarians caution that digital preservation is not without its faults. [5] Many small libraries do not have the budgets to provide equipment and personnel needed to undertake such a project. [6] More important, however, technologies are changing so quickly that files preserved today in one format will not be usable with future formats. [7] If paper documents are scanned and discarded, our heritage will be lost forever somewhere down the road on the digital bandwagon.

_____ 1. The issue the argument focuses on is
   a. meeting the needs of scholars and researchers.
   b. treating small libraries unfairly.
   c. reducing library costs.
   d. converting library collections from paper to digital format.

_____ 2. To best strengthen this argument, the author could add the following evidence:
   a. actual dollar amounts for the cost of digital preservation to small libraries.
   b. interviews with professors who use digital collections in their research.
   c. comparisons of currently available scanning software.
   d. examples of online collections at small libraries.

_____ 3. Which sentence contains information irrelevant to the article?
   a. 2   c. 5
   b. 3   d. 7

B. Mandatory retirement rules hurt businesses and families. When my grandfather was required to give up his job of thirty years at age 65, he was forced into economic hardship. His boss was a cold-hearted bachelor with no family. He received a pension and other benefits, but they were not enough to sustain him and his ill wife in their comfortable existence for the rest of their earthly days. Had his employer kept him on for ten or fifteen more years, my grandparents' elderly years would have been much happier. Furthermore, his company would have continued to benefit from his many years of accumulated knowledge and experience in the industry. Employers should treat all employees on a case-by-case basis instead of laying down policies that hurt some and help others.

_____ 4. The author uses which type of evidence in the argument?

    a. statistics   c. comparison

    b. analogy   d. personal experience

_____ 5. Which statement best expresses the author's claim?

    a. Pension benefits should be increased for retirees.

    b. The author's grandfather was treated unfairly.

    c. Mandatory retirement is unfair and detrimental.

    d. Employers need to be more considerate of the needs of their employees.

_____ 6. To best strengthen the argument, the author could add

    a. quotations from the boss and grandfather.

    b. a sample retirement plan.

    c. statistics about the average pension income retirees receive.

    d. the opinion of a member of Congress.

_____ 7. In describing the father's boss, the author uses which of the following emotional appeals?

    a. *ad hominem*

    b. "join the crowd" emotional appeal

    c. association

    d. false authority

C. Costly medical research requires foundations and universities to spend a great deal of money. In addition American taxpayers contribute to federal research grants that sometimes go to fund controversial projects. Meanwhile, many practicing physicians and their patients feel removed from the entire research process and think the studies being conducted do not directly apply to them. All in all, the entire medical research structure needs a complete overhaul to reduce expenses, educate the public, and demonstrate real progress for real people.

_____ 8. The author's claim is that
   a. doctors must become more aware of late-breaking research.
   b. the medical community spends too much money on research.
   c. the medical research system needs to be changed.
   d. medical research should be controlled by the government.

_____ 9. To best strengthen this argument, the author could add the following evidence:
   a. personal statements from researchers about their studies.
   b. a breakdown of medical research funding costs and sources.
   c. the names of the major research foundations.
   d. a comparison of funding practices in several states.

_____ 10. The first sentence is an example of
   a. the false cause fallacy.
   b. a _non sequitur_.
   c. circular reasoning.
   d. the either-or fallacy.

ANALYZING ARGUMENTS

Directions: *After reading the following argument, select the choice that best answers each of the questions that follow.*

MISSTEP ON VIDEO VIOLENCE

1   In the booming world of video games, there are more than a few dark corners: Murder and mayhem. Blood and gore. Explicit sex and abuse of women. In one of the best-selling series, Grand Theft Auto, car stealing is accompanied by drug use, shootouts that kill police and bystanders, and simulated sex with comely prostitutes who are beaten with baseball bats afterward.

2   Small wonder some parents are concerned over what game-crazed teens may be up to. And small wonder, too, that legislators in several states are playing to these concerns by trying to outlaw the sale of violent and sexually explicit games to minors. A bill banning the sale of such games to anyone younger than 18 is awaiting the governor's signature in Illinois. A similar proposal is moving in the Michigan Legislature. The issue has been raised this year in at least nine other states and the District of Columbia. But to what useful end?

3   This is the latest chapter in a very old story. When teenage entertainment offends adult sensibilities—think Elvis Presley's pulsating hips or the arrival on newsstands of Hugh Hefner's Playboy—the first response is to see the new phenomenon as a threat to social order. The second is to attempt to ban it. Parents—former teenagers all—seem to forget history's lesson: The bans never work. And they're probably not constitutional, anyway. Courts have ruled that today's sophisticated video games are protected as creative expression. If communities want to limit access, they must show overriding evidence that the games pose a public threat. That evidence does not exist.

4   Lawmakers and activist groups assert that the thrill of engaging in virtual criminal activity will spur teens to try the real thing. But the violent crime rate has gone down nearly 30% since the first bloody shoot-'em-up games debuted in the early 1990s. Youth crime rates have dropped even more. And a Federal Trade Commission survey found parents already involved in 83% of video-game purchases and rentals for minors.

5   Judges have repeatedly rejected as flawed the studies that advocates say show a link between fantasy violence and anti-social behavior. To the extent there is a threat, it is mainly to the individual, vulnerable teenager, and it can be addressed only by parents.

6   Unknown to many parents, they're getting some help. The game industry's rating system classifies games in six categories from "early childhood" to "adults only" and requires detailed content descriptions. Also, newer models of popular games include

parental controls that can block their use for age-inappropriate games. Manufacturers have announced an expanded ratings-education program, and major retailers are tightening their restrictions on sales to minors.

7   There will always be a market for the dark, tasteless, even the outrageous, and parents ought to keep kids away from it. But even with the best intentions of legislators, the problem is beyond their reach. New laws are likely to give parents only the false impression that someone else is solving that problem for them.

—*USA Today*, June 6, 2005

_____   1. The author addresses which of the following issues?

   a. the proven effectiveness of legislation in controlling behavior

   b. parents' inability to monitor their children's video game usage

   c. the reluctance of game companies to rate their games

   d. the impact of violent video games on teen behavior

_____   2. The author's claim is that

   a. violent video games do not result in violent behavior.

   b. Grand Theft Auto is appropriate for teens.

   c. more laws need to be passed regulating video games.

   d. parents are already too involved in video game choices.

_____   3. Which type of evidence does the author use to support the argument?

   a. personal experience   c. comparison

   b. statistics   d. analogy

_____   4. This argument could best be strengthened by adding

   a. information about studies that show no link between violent video games and violent behavior.

   b. evidence that laws banning violent video games reduce violent behavior.

   c. examples of teens who play video games and have no history of violence.

   d. details about the type of violence portrayed in other violent video games.

_____ 5. The purpose of this argument is to
   a. urge readers to support legislation banning violent video games.
   b. convince readers that violent video games have actually contributed to a reduction in violent crime.
   c. cast doubt upon the belief that violent video games lead to violent behavior.
   d. describe ways parents can limit video game usage.

_____ 6. The use of "false authority" can be found where the author argues
   a. that judges have found no link between fantasy violence and behavior.
   b. that new legislation in Illinois is unnecessary.
   c. manufacturers are taking steps to limit access to violent games.
   d. parents need to have more control over their children's game activities.

_____ 7. Legislators who think that all violent video games must either be banned for anyone under 18 or be available to all teens have made what error in reasoning?
   a. circular reasoning
   b. _non sequitur_
   c. either-or fallacy
   d. _ad hominem_ attack

_____ 8. The author's mention of Elvis and _Playboy_ is a type of supporting evidence known as
   a. personal experience.
   b. example.
   c. statistics.
   d. appeal to the common folk.

_____ 9. Which of the following would further support the author's argument?

    a. statistics about the growth of the market for violent games

    b. the author's describing a personal experience of how easy it is to buy violent games

    c. statistics demonstrating the relationship between gender and level of violent behavior

    d. the results of a study that tracks teenage behavior after playing violent video games

_____ 10. The author fails to offer sufficient supporting evidence when he or she writes

    a. "But the violent crime rate has gone down nearly 30% since the first bloody shoot-'em up games debuted" (par. 4).

    b. "Unknown to many parents, they're getting some help." (par. 6).

    c. "A bill banning the sale of such games to anyone younger than 18 is awaiting the governor's signature in Illinois" (par. 2).

    d. "The bans never work" (par. 3).

NAME _____ SECTION _____
DATE _____ SCORE _____

MASTERY TEST 12-3

ANWR OIL: AN ALTERNATIVE TO WAR OVER OIL
Walter J. Hickel

Originally published in the magazine *The American Enterprise*, this reading takes a position on drilling for oil in the Arctic National Wildlife Refuge. Read it to discover why the author supports oil exploration.

Vocabulary Preview

These are some of the difficult words in this essay. The definitions here will help you if you can't figure out the meanings from the sentence context or word parts.

precarious (par. 1) lacking stability; potentially dangerous

devoid (par. 4) without the usual accompaniment

lichen (par. 4) an arctic moss eaten by caribou

tundra (par. 4) a treeless arctic plain with frozen subsoil

supplant (par. 11) to substitute, take the place of

seismic (par. 12) related to earthquakes

pristine (par. 14) pure, clean, unspoiled

desecration (par. 14) a violation of respect

1   The Senate Democrats have stubbornly refused to allow any oil exploration along the rim of the Arctic National Wildlife Refuge (ANWR) in Alaska. Despite this latest vote, however, the issue is not going to go away. Given our continuing precarious dependence on overseas oil suppliers ranging from Saddam Hussein to the Saudis to Venezuela's Castro-clone Hugo Chavez, sensible Americans will continue to press Congress in the months and years ahead to unlock America's great Arctic energy storehouse.

2   I'm an Alaskan who believes the coastal plain of ANWR should be opened for intelligent exploration of its energy potential. ANWR is owned by all Americans. The very small portion of the refuge with oil potential can be explored and drilled without damaging the environment. At a time when America is dependent for vital energy supplies on overseas oil-producing countries, some of which are allied with terrorist groups, it makes no sense for us to ignore a region within our own borders that could supply up to a third of a trillion dollars worth of domestic energy—enough to replace completely all imports from Saudi Arabia or Iraq for a generation. There are already 171 million acres of land in Alaska fenced off for conservation and wilderness preservation. That's an area larger than the state of Texas.

3   ANWR's coastal plain, the only part of the refuge where oil is suspected to exist, is a flat and featureless wasteland that experiences some of the harshest weather conditions in the world. Temperatures drop to nearly −70°F. There are no forests or trees. At all.

4   For ten months a year, the plain is covered with snow and ice and is devoid of most living things. Then, for a few weeks, a carpet of lichen and tundra emerges from beneath the snow. During that brief period, the migratory Porcupine caribou herd (named for the Porcupine River), one of Alaska's 20 caribou herds, may graze and calve on the plain. The animals seek breezes from the Beaufort Sea to help them cope with the blizzard of mosquitoes that hatch with the spring.

5   In 2001, the Porcupine herd didn't calve on the coastal plain. It gave birth to its young many miles to the east, across the Canadian border. It calved in Canada the previous year as well. There is nothing magical about the area.

6   It's unlikely that exploration and drilling on the coastal plain will harm the caribou. Most biologists expect the animals will react to the presence of human activity the same way the Central Arctic herd adjusted to oil development at Prudhoe Bay (the region to the immediate west of ANWR's coastal plain). That herd has not only survived, but flourished. In 1977, as the Prudhoe region started delivering oil to America's southern 48 states, the Central Arctic caribou herd numbered 6,000; it has since grown to 27,128.

7   It is important to note that in the Arctic, oil drilling is restricted to the wintertime. And from early fall to early May, the Porcupine herd is not on the coastal plain at all. It roams south to the Porcupine Mountains and east into Canada.

8   ANWR covers an enormous area nearly as much as New Hampshire, Vermont, Massachusetts, and Connecticut combined. The most beautiful sections of ANWR—8 million acres—are federally mandated wilderness areas where the only tolerated human activity is hiking, backpacking, camping, and rafting. No motorized vehicles are permitted, and no development of any kind is allowed. This wilderness heart of ANWR includes the mountains of the Brooks Range. Journalists often use images of these mountains when describing the coastal plain region and its rich energy supplies, but the Brooks Range will not be touched by development.

9   When it set up ANWR, Congress recognized that the 1.5 million-acre coastal plain possesses unique potential for large oil and gas reserves. It was stipulated that these resources could be developed at any time if Congress so voted. As a result, scientists have studied this area for more than 20 years, and their work has produced estimates of recoverable oil ranging up to 16 billion barrels. Most of these scientists recommend that exploration be allowed.

10   To compare how much petroleum may lie beneath ANWR, consider that the entire rest of the U.S. contains 21 billion barrels of recoverable oil. The monetary value of ANWR's pumpable oil is projected by the U.S. Energy Information Agency to be between $125 billion and $350 billion. This doesn't even count the region's vast natural gas potential.

11   How much would an oil reservoir that size, just a few miles from the already-built-and-paid-for trans-Alaska pipeline, mean to America and our energy future? The

government estimates the coastal plain could produce 600,000 to 1,900,000 barrels of oil per day. This new source of Alaskan oil could more than supplant all of our annual oil imports from Saudi Arabia or Iraq and ensure that the trans-Alaska oil pipeline would continue to deliver domestically produced energy to American consumers for decades to come.

12   I have visited many oil-producing regions throughout the world. The production techniques are often primitive and risky, both for the workers and the environment. The technology used in Alaska's Arctic to find and develop oil is the best in the world. When and if development takes place on the ANWR coastal plain, there will be little traceable disturbance. Seismic tests to locate the oil, and the actual drilling after that, will take place in the winter, using ice roads that will melt later. Small gravel drilling pads, only six acres in size, will be used to tap vast fields and will be removed when drilling is complete. Alaska's "North Slope" oil workers take pride in challenging visitors to find any trace of winter work activities after the snow melts.

13   If oil is discovered in ANWR, the size of the surface area disturbed will be dramatically less than when Prudhoe Bay was developed 30 years ago. Experts estimate that less than 2,000 acres will be touched—out of the 1.5 million acres on the coastal plain, and the 19 million acres in ANWR as a whole.

14   The opposition to opening ANWR "isn't really economic, humanitarian, or even environmental. It is spiritual," wrote a *New York Daily News* columnist. "If all the oil in the refuge could be neatly sucked up with a single straw, the naturalists would still oppose it because [to them] human activity in a pristine wilderness is, in itself, an act of desecration."

15   That is an extreme philosophical position. America's access to energy is a serious national security issue. Overdependence on foreign oil exposes us to energy blackmail and compromises our ability to protect our citizens and assist our friends in times of crisis. Our goal as Americans must be to produce as much energy as we can for ourselves. This need not undermine efforts to conserve energy nor undercut the push to discover alternate energy sources. We must extend the energy sources that are practical today, even as we pursue possible alternatives for the future.

16   Rather than shutting down the Alaska pipeline and our other Arctic oil infrastructure we should be linking them to the vast untapped resources that await us on ANWR's coastal plain. That will not only make America safer and stronger economically; it will provide the rest of the world with an environmentally responsible model of how to produce energy the right way.

17   It makes no sense to ignore a region within our own borders that could supply up to a third of a trillion dollars worth of domestic energy—enough to replace completely all annual imports from Saudi Arabia. Oil development would touch less than 2,000 acres in ANWR. Meanwhile, 171 million acres of land in Alaska are already fenced off for conservation and wilderness preservation.

—   ▪   —

Directions: *Select the letter of the choice that best completes each of the following statements.*

CHECKING YOUR COMPREHENSION

1. The central thought of the article is that
   a. the ANWR coastal plain is uninhabitable.
   b. oil drilling is unnecessary, since reserves exceed demand.
   c. the ANWR coastal plain should be used for oil drilling.
   d. conservation is more important that oil drilling.

2. The author states that scientists believe caribou will react to humans drilling in the ANWR by
   a. grazing and calving on the coastal plain.
   b. dying out.
   c. going to Canada.
   d. flourishing—just like a herd near Prudhoe Bay.

3. Which mountains are found within the "wilderness heart" of the ANWR?
   a. the Brooks Range
   b. the Porcupine Range
   c. the Beaufort Mountains
   d. the Cascade Range

4. The author feels that access to ANWR oil
   a. should be Congress' top priority.
   b. will solve our energy problems.
   c. is a national security issue.
   d. will do more harm than good.

5. According to the author, drilling in the Coastal Plain will benefit the world by
   a. replacing our imports from the Middle East.
   b. giving an example of the right way to produce energy.
   c. showing how to respect wildlife.
   d. discovering new drilling technologies.

USING WHAT YOU KNOW ABOUT ARGUMENT

_____ 6. The author discusses which of the following issues?

    a. congressional energy policies

    b. oil drilling techniques

    c. preserving the wildlife on the Coastal Plain

    d. drilling for oil in the ANWR

_____ 7. The author is making the claim that

    a. the Coastal Plain should be opened to drilling.

    b. oil is more important than animals.

    c. American drilling technology is the best in the world.

    d. Congress will vote to open the ANWR to drilling.

_____ 8. By linking oil drilling with national security (paragraph 15) and terrorism (paragraph 2), the author is using which type of emotional appeal?

    a. false authority   c. _ad hominem_

    b. association   d. join the crowd

_____ 9. When the author associates the flourishing Prudhoe Bay caribou herd with oil development, he is using which type of logical fallacy?

    a. either-or fallacy   c. circular reasoning

    b. _non sequitur_   d. false cause

_____ 10. The quote from the _New York Daily News_ columnist

    a. includes a refutation.

    b. uses a false authority emotional appeal.

    c. proposes a solution.

    d. is an either-or fallacy.

USING CONTEXT AND WORD PARTS

_____ 11. In paragraph 2, the word **allied** means

    a. indefinite about.   c. opposite of.

    b. unclear toward.   d. associated with.

_____ 12. In paragraph 4, the word **blizzard** means
     a. a long, severe snowstorm.   c. a strong gale with fine snow.
     b. a frozen treat.   d. an overwhelming number.

_____ 13. In paragraph 9, the word **stipulated** means
     a. separated.   c. specified.
     b. substituted.   d. preferred.

_____ 14. In paragraph 15, a **philosophical position** concerns
     a. serious questions of life.   c. unpopular ideas.
     b. practical matters.   d. unrealistic problems.

_____ 15. In paragraph 15, the word **overdependence** means
     a. spending money.   c. undue importance.
     b. redistributing.   d. excessive reliance.

REVIEWING DIFFICULT VOCABULARY

Directions: _Complete each of the following sentences by inserting a word from the Vocabulary Preview on page 449 in the space provided. A word should be used only once._

16. Nuclear energy is not _____ of harmful waste products.

17. Burning the American flag is a _____ of our country itself.

18. My professor's new theory is bound to _____ those held by his predecessors.

19. The stock market seems like a _____ investment in these tight economic times.

20. I can't wait to see the beautiful _____ wilderness of the Australian outback.

QUESTIONS FOR DISCUSSION

1. As a class, brainstorm some ideas for new fuels or fuel-saving technologies.
2. Consider the opposing viewpoint: oil drilling should not be allowed in the ANWR. Identify reasons to support this position.

WRITING ACTIVITIES

1. Write a letter to your congressperson about your feelings on the issue of oil drilling in the ANWR.
2. Make a list of ways you could conserve energy and other resources. Keep track of your efforts.
3. Evaluate the ANWR Web site at http://www.anwr.org/. Write a paragraph that summarizes your evaluation of the site.

Chapter 12: Reading Arguments

RECORDING YOUR PROGRESS

Test	Number Right		Score
Practice Test 12-1	_____	× 10 =	_____ %
Practice Test 12-2	_____	× 10 =	_____ %
Practice Test 12-3	_____	× 10 =	_____ %
Mastery Test 12-1	_____	× 10 =	_____ %
Mastery Test 12-2	_____	× 10 =	_____ %
Mastery Test 12-3	_____	× 5 =	_____ %

EVALUATING YOUR PROGRESS

Based on your test performance, rate how well you have mastered the skills taught in this chapter by checking one of the boxes below or by writing your own evaluation.

☐ **Need More Improvement**
Tip: Try completing the Critical Thinking—American Southwest module in the Reading Skills section on the MyReadingLab Web site at **http://www.ablongman.com/myreadinglab** to fine-tune the skills that you have learned in this chapter.

☐ **Need More Practice**
Tip: Try using the Critical Thinking—American Southwest module in the Reading Skills section on the MyReadingLab Web site at **http://www.ablongman.com/myreadinglab** to brush up on the skills taught in this chapter, or visit this textbook's Companion Web site at **http://www.ablongman.com/mcwhorter** for extra practice.

☐ **Good**
Tip: To maintain your skills, quickly review this chapter by using this textbook's Companion Web site at **http://www.ablongman.com/mcwhorter**.

☐ **Excellent**

YOUR EVALUATION: _____

_____

_____

_____

Part II

Student Resource Guide

Online Guide

Real-World Learning Strategies

http://www.ablongman.com/mcwhorter

Learning from Textbooks

Use Effective Recall Strategies

Using Review to Increase Recall

Review refers to the process of going back over something you have already read. There are two types of review: immediate and periodic. Both types can greatly increase the amount you can remember from a printed page.

Immediate Review   When you finish reading an assignment, your first inclination may be to breathe a sigh of relief, close the book, and go on to another task. Before you do this, however, take a few minutes to go back over the material. Briefly review the overall organization and important ideas presented. Think of review as a postreading activity similar to previewing (see Chapter 1, p. 6). In reviewing you should reread the parts of the article or chapter that contain the most important ideas. Concentrate on titles, introductions, summaries, headings, graphic material, and depending on the length of the material, topic sentences. Also review any notes you made and any portions of the text that you highlighted.

Considerable research has been conducted on how individuals learn and remember. These experiments have shown that review immediately following reading greatly improves the amount remembered. However, the review must be *immediate;* it will not produce the same effects if you do it after a ten-minute break or later in the evening. To get the full benefit, you must review while the content of the article or chapter is still fresh in your mind.

Review before you have had a chance to forget and before other thoughts and ideas interfere or compete with what you have read.

Periodic Review   Although immediate review is very effective and will increase your ability to recall information, it is not sufficient for remembering material for long periods. To remember facts and ideas permanently, you need to review them periodically, going back and refreshing your recall on a regular basis. For example, suppose you are reading a chapter on criminal behavior in your sociology text, and a midterm exam is scheduled in four weeks. If you read the chapter, reviewed it immediately, and then did nothing with it until the exam a month later, you would not remember enough to score well on the exam. To achieve a good grade, you need to review the chapter periodically. You might review the chapter once several days after reading it, again a week later, and once again a week before the exam.

Other Aids to Recall

Review and repetition are primary methods of increasing retention. Other aids or methods for increasing your recall include the following:

Building an Intent to Remember   Very few people remember things that they do not intend to remember. Do you remember what color of clothing a friend wore last week? Can you name all the songs you heard on the radio this morning? Can you remember exactly what time you got home last Saturday night? If not, why not? Most likely you cannot remember these facts because at the time you did not see the importance of remembering them. Of course, if you had known that you would be asked these questions, you would most likely have remembered the items. You can see, then, that you must intend to remember things to be able to do so effectively. The same principle holds true for reading and retention. To remember what you read, you must have a clear and strong intent to do so. Unless you have defined what you intend to remember before you begin reading, you will find that it is difficult to recall specific content.

In Chapter 1 you saw how guide questions can help you keep your mind on what you are reading. Now you can see that they also establish an intent to remember.

Before you begin to read an assignment, define as clearly as possible what you intend to remember. Your definition will depend on the type of material, why you are reading it, and how familiar you are with the topic. For instance, if you are reading an essay assigned in preparation for a class discussion, plan to remember not only key ideas but also points of controversy, applications, and opinions with which you disagree. Your intent might be quite different in reviewing a chapter for an essay exam. Here you would be looking for important ideas, trends, guiding or controlling principles, and significance of events.

As you read a text assignment, sort important information from that which is less important. Ask and continually answer questions such as:

1. **How important is this information?**
2. **Will I need to know this for the exam?**
3. **Is this a key idea or is it an explanation of a key idea?**
4. **Why did the writer include this?**

Organizing and Categorizing   Information that is organized, or that has a pattern or structure, is easier to remember than material that is randomly arranged. One effective way to organize information is to *categorize* it, to arrange it in groups according to similar characteristics. Suppose, for example, that you had to remember the following list of items to buy for a picnic: cooler, candy, 7-Up, Pepsi, napkins, potato chips, lemonade, peanuts, paper plates. The easiest way to remember this list would be to divide it in groups. You might arrange it as follows:

Drinks	Snacks	Picnic Supplies
7-Up	peanuts	cooler
Pepsi	candy	paper plates
lemonade	potato chips	napkins

By grouping the items into categories, you are putting similar items together. Then, rather than learning one long list of unorganized items, you are learning three shorter, organized lists.

Now imagine you are reading an essay on discipline in public high schools. Instead of learning one long list of reasons for disruptive student behavior you might divide the reasons into groups such as peer conflicts, teacher-student conflicts, and so forth.

Associating Ideas   Association is a useful way to remember new facts and ideas. It involves connecting new information with previously acquired knowledge. For instance, if you are reading about divorce in a sociology class and are trying to remember a list of common causes, you might try to associate each cause with a person you know who exhibits that problem. Suppose one cause of divorce is lack of communication between the partners. You might remember this by thinking of a couple you know whose lack of communication has caused relationship difficulties.

Suppose you are taking an introductory physics course and are studying Newton's Laws of Motion. The Third Law states: To every action there is always opposed an equal reaction. To remember this law you could associate it with a familiar everyday situation such as swimming that illustrates the law. When you swim you push water backward with your feet, arms, and legs, and the water pushes you forward.

Association involves making connections between new information and what you already know. When you find a connection between the known and the unknown, you can retrieve the new information from your memory along with the old.

Using a Variety of Sensory Modes   Your senses of sight, hearing, and touch can all help you remember what you read. Most of the time, most of us use just one sense—sight—as we read. However, if you are able to use more than one sense, you will find that recall is easier. Activities such as underlining, highlighting, note-taking, and outlining involve your sense of touch and reinforce your learning. Or, if you are having particular difficulty remembering something, try to use your auditory sense as well. You might try repeating the information out loud or listening to someone else repeat it. Most of us tend to rely only on our strengths. Visual learners tend to rely on visual skills; and auditory learners tend to depend on their auditory skills, for example. To become a more efficient learner, try to engage additional sensory modes, even if they are not your strengths.

Visualizing   Visualizing, or creating a mental picture of what you have read, often aids recall. In reading descriptive writing that creates a mental picture, visualization is an easy task. In reading about events, people, processes, or procedures, visualization is again relatively simple. However, visualization of abstract ideas, theories, philosophies, and concepts may not be possible. Instead, you may be able to create a visual picture of the relationship of ideas in your mind or on paper. For example, suppose you are reading about the invasion of privacy and learn that there are arguments for and against the storage of personal data about each citizen in large computer banks. You might create a visual image of two lists of information—advantages and disadvantages.

Using *Mnemonic* Devices   Memory tricks and devices, often called mnemonics, are useful in helping you recall lists of factual information. You might use a rhyme, such as the one used for remembering the number of days in each month: "Thirty days hath September, April, June, and November. . . ." Another device involves making up a word or phrase in which each letter represents an item you are trying to remember. If you remember the name Roy G. Biv, for example, you will be able to recall the colors in the light spectrum: red, orange, yellow, green, blue, indigo, violet.

Exercise A-1

Directions: *Five study-learning situations follow. Indicate which of the retention aids described in this section—organization/categorization, association, sensory modes, visualization, and mnemonic devices—might be most useful in each situation.*

1. In a sociology course, you are assigned to read about and remember the causes of child abuse. How might you remember them easily?

   _____

2. You are studying astronomy and you have to remember the names of the eight planets: Mercury, Venus, Earth, Mars, Jupiter, Saturn, Uranus, and Neptune. What retention aid(s) could help you remember them?

   _____

3. You are taking a course in anatomy and physiology and must learn the name and location of each bone in the human skull. How could you learn them easily?

   _____

4. You have an entire chapter to review for a history course, and your instructor has told you that your exam will contain 30 true/false questions on Civil War battles. What could you do as you review to help yourself remember the details of various battles?

   _____

5. You are taking a course in twentieth-century history and are studying the causes of the Vietnam War in preparation for an essay exam. You find that there are many causes, some immediate, others long-term. Some have to do with international politics; others, with internal problems in North and South Vietnam. How could you organize your study for this exam?

   _____

The SQ3R Reading/Study System

The SQ3R system has been used successfully for more than 50 years. Considerable experimentation has been done, and the system has proven effective in increasing students' retention. It is especially useful for studying textbooks and other highly factual, well-organized materials. Basically, SQ3R is a way of learning as you read.

How to Use SQ3R

Each of the steps in the SQ3R system will be briefly summarized, and you will then see how it can be applied to a sample selection.

1. **Survey.** Become familiar with the overall content and organization of the material. You have already learned this technique and know it as prereading.

2. **Question.** Formulate questions about the material that you expect to be able to answer as you read. As you read each successive heading, turn it into a question. This step is similar to establishing guide questions discussed in Chapter 1.

3. **Read.** As you read each section, actively search for the answer to your guide questions. When you find the answers, highlight or mark portions of the text that concisely state the information.

4. **Recite.** Probably the most important part of the system, "recite" means that you should stop after each section or after each major heading, look away from the page, and try to remember the answer to your question. If you are unable to remember, look back at the page and reread the material. Then test yourself again by looking away from the page and "reciting" the answer to your question.

5. **Review.** Immediately after you have finished reading, go back through the material again and read titles, introductions, summaries, headings, and graphic material. As you read each heading, recall your question and test yourself to see if you can still remember the answer. If you cannot, reread that section again.

Now, to give you a clear picture of how the steps in the SQ3R method work together to produce an efficient approach to reading-study, the method will be applied to a textbook chapter. Suppose you have been assigned to read the following excerpt, "Meanings and Messages," taken from *Human Communication* by Joseph DeVito for a class that is studying verbal and nonverbal communication. Follow each of the SQ3R steps in reading the selection.

1. **Survey.** Preread the article, noticing introductions, headings, first sentences, and the last paragraph. From this prereading you should have an overall picture of what this article is about and what conclusions the author draws about the listening process.

2. **Question.** Using the headings as a starting point, develop several questions that you might expect the article to answer. You might ask questions such as these:

   How are meanings and messages related?

   How can meanings be "in people"?

   What besides words and gestures makes up meanings?

   What makes meanings unique?

   What is the difference between denotative and connotative meanings?

   How does context affect meaning?

3. **Read.** Now read the entire selection, keeping your questions in mind as you read. Stop at the end of each major section and proceed to step 4.

4. **Recite.** After each section, stop reading and check to see if you can recall the answers to your questions.

5. **Review.** When you have finished reading the entire article, take a few minutes to reread the headings and recall your questions. Check to see that you can still recall the answers.

MEANINGS AND MESSAGES

Meaning is an active process created by cooperation between source and receiver—speaker and listener, writer and reader. Here are a few important corollaries concerning meaning.

Meanings Are in People

Meaning depends not only on messages (whether verbal, nonverbal, or both) but on the interaction of those messages and the receiver's own thoughts and feelings. You do not receive meaning; you create meaning. You construct meaning out of the messages you receive combined with your own social and cultural perspectives (beliefs, attitudes, and values, for example). Words do not mean; people mean. Consequently, to discover meaning, you need to look into people and not merely into words.

An example of the confusion that can result when this relatively simple fact is overlooked is provided by Ronald D. Laing, H. Phillipson, and A. Russell Lee in

Interpersonal Perception and analyzed with insight by Paul Watzlawick in *How Real Is Real?* A couple on the second night of their honeymoon are sitting at a hotel bar. The woman strikes up a conversation with the couple next to her. The husband refuses to communicate with the couple and becomes antagonistic toward his wife as well as the couple. The wife then grows angry because he has created such an awkward and unpleasant situation. Each becomes increasingly disturbed, and the evening ends in a bitter conflict in which each is convinced of the other's lack of consideration. Eight years later, they analyze this argument. Apparently the idea of honeymoon had meant very different things to each of them. To the husband it had meant a "golden opportunity to ignore the rest of the world and simply explore each other." He felt his wife's interaction with the other couple implied there was something lacking in him. To the wife, honeymoon had meant an opportunity to try out her new role as wife. "I had never had a conversation with another couple as a wife before," she said. "Previous to this I had always been a 'girlfriend' or 'fiancée' or 'daughter' or 'sister.'"

One very clear implication of this principle is that meaning is always ambiguous to some extent. Each person's meaning is somewhat different from each other person's, therefore you can never know precisely what any given word or gesture means. Nonverbal gestures—with the obvious exception of emblems—are usually more ambiguous than verbal messages.

Meanings Are More Than Words and Gestures

When you want to communicate a thought or feeling to another person, you do so with relatively few symbols. These represent just a small part of what you are thinking or feeling, much of which remains unspoken. If you were to try to describe every feeling in detail, you would never get on with the job of living. The meanings you seek to communicate are much more than the sum of the words and nonverbal behaviors you use to represent them.

Because of this, you can never fully know what another person is thinking or feeling. You can only approximate it on the basis of the meanings you receive, which, as already noted, are greatly influenced by who you are and what you are feeling. Conversely, others can never fully know you; they too can only approximate what you are feeling. Failure to understand another person or to be understood are not abnormal situations. They are inevitable, although you should realize that with effort you can always understand another person a little better.

Meanings Are Unique

Because meanings are derived from both the messages communicated and the receiver's own thoughts and feelings, no two people ever derive the same meanings. Similarly, because people change constantly, no one person can derive the same meanings on two separate occasions. Who you are can never be separated from the meanings you create. As a result, you need to check your perceptions of another's meanings by asking questions, echoing what you perceive to be the other person's feelings or thoughts, and seeking elaboration and clarification—in general, practicing all the skills identified in the discussion on effective interpersonal perception and listening.

Also recognize that as you change, you also change the meanings you created out of past messages. Thus, although the message sent may not have changed, the meanings you created from it yesterday and the meanings you create today may be quite different. Yesterday, when a special someone said, "I love you," you created certain meanings. But today, when you learn that the same "I love you" was said to three other people or when you fall in love with someone else, you drastically change the meanings you perceive from those three words.

Meanings Are Both Denotative and Connotative

To understand the nature of denotative and connotative meaning, consider a word such as *death*. To a doctor this word might mean, or denote, (the point at which the heart stops beating. To a doctor, *death* is a word signifying an objective description of an event; the word is basically denotative. To a mother whose son has just died, the words mean much more. It recalls the son's youth, his ambitions, his family, his illness, and so on. To her the word is emotional, subjective, and highly personal. These emotional, subjective, and personal reactions are the word's connotative meanings.

Nonverbal behaviors may also be viewed in terms of their denotation and connotation. Some nonverbal behaviors are largely denotative (for example, a nod signifying yes) while others are primarily connotative (for example, a smile, raised eyebrows, or a wink).

Another distinction between the two types of meaning has already been implied: the denotative meaning of a message is more general or universal; most people would agree with the denotative meanings and would give similar definitions. Connotative meanings, however, are extremely personal, and few people would agree on the precise connotative meaning of a word or nonverbal behavior. Test this idea by trying to get a group of people to agree on the connotative meanings of such words as *religion, racism, democracy, wealth,* and *freedom* or of such nonverbal behaviors as raised eyebrows, arms folded in front of one's chest, or sitting with one's legs crossed. Chances are very good that it will be impossible to reach an agreement.

Meanings Are Context-Based

Verbal and nonverbal communications exist in a context, and that context to a large extent determines the meaning of any verbal or nonverbal behavior. The same words or behaviors may have totally different meanings when they occur in different contexts. For example, the greeting, "How are you?" means "Hello" to someone you pass regularly on the street but means "Is your health improving?" when said to a friend in the hospital. A wink to an attractive person on a bus means something completely different from a wink that signifies a put-on or a lie. Similarly, the meaning of a given signal depends on the behaviors it accompanies or is close to in time. Pounding a fist on the table during a speech in support of a politician means something quite different from that same gesture in response to news of a friend's death. Divorced from the context, it is impossible to tell what meaning was intended just from examining signals. Of course, even if you know the context in detail, you still may not be able to decipher the meaning of the verbal or nonverbal message.

—DeVito, *Human Communication,* pp. 108–110

How SQ3R Helps You Learn

The SQ3R system improves your reading efficiency in three ways: It increases your comprehension, increases your recall, and saves you valuable time by encouraging you to learn as you read.

Your comprehension is most directly improved by the S and Q steps. By surveying or prereading you acquire an overview of the material that serves as an outline to follow as you read. In the "Question" step, you are focusing your attention and identifying what is important to look for as you read.

Your recall of the material is improved through the "Recite" and "Review" steps. By testing yourself while reading and immediately after you have finished, you are building a systematic review pattern that will provide the necessary repetitions to ensure learning and recall.

Finally, because you are learning as you are reading, you will save time later when you are ready to study the material for an exam. Because you have already learned the material through recitation and review, you will find that you need much less time to prepare for an exam. Instead of learning the material for the first time, all you need to do is refresh your memory and review difficult portions.

Adapting SQ3R to Different Textbooks

Your texts and other required readings vary greatly from course to course. For example, a mathematics text is structured and written quite differently from a sociology text. A chemistry text contains numerous principles, laws, formulas, and problems, whereas a philosophy text contains mostly reading selections and discussions. To accommodate this wide variation in your textbooks and other assigned readings, use the SQ3R system as a base or model. Add, vary, or rearrange the steps to fit the material. For example, when working with a mathematics text, you might add a "Study the

Sample Problems" step in which you analyze the problem-solving process. When reading an essay, short story, or poem for a literature class, add a "React" step in which you analyze various features of writing, including the writer's style, tone, purpose, and point of view. For textbooks with a great deal of factual information to learn, you might add "Highlight," "Take Notes," or "Outline" steps.

Exercise A-2

Directions: *Read one of the selections in Part Three of this book using the SQ3R system and follow each of the steps listed here. Add to or revise the system as necessary. After you complete the "Review" step, answer the multiple-choice questions that follow the selection.*

1. **Survey.** Preview the article to get an overview of its organization and content.

2. **Question.** Write the questions you expect to be able to answer when you read the article.

   _____

   _____

3. **Read.** Read the selection, looking for the answers to your questions. As you find them, write them in this space.

   _____

   _____

4. **Recite.** After each boldface heading, stop and recall your questions and their answers.

5. **Review.** After finishing the article, quickly go back through the article reviewing the major points.

Use Self-Testing to Prepare for Exams

Have you ever taken an exam for which you studied hard and felt prepared, only to find out you earned just an average grade? Although you spent time reviewing, you did not review in the right ways; you probably focused on recalling factual information, and you probably did not use self-testing.

What Is Self-Testing?

Self-testing is a study strategy that uses writing to discover and relate ideas. It involves writing possible exam questions and drafting answers to them. This activity combines the use of factual recall with interpretation and evaluation. Self-testing is an active strategy that gets you involved with the material and forces you to think about, organize, and express (in your own words) ideas. Self-testing is also a sensible and effective way to prepare for an exam. How would you prepare for a math exam? By solving problems. How would you prepare to run a marathon? By running. Similarly, you should prepare for an exam by testing yourself.

Constructing potential test questions is fun and challenging and can be done with a classmate or in groups. It is usually best to write answers yourself, however, to get maximum benefit from the technique. After writing, compare and discuss your answers with classmates. If you prefer to work alone, be sure to verify your answers by referring to your text and/or lecture notes.

What kinds of questions you ask depends on the type of material you are learning as well as on the type or level of analysis your instructor expects. Sample questions for various types of material that you may be required to study are listed in Table A-1 (p. 470).

How to Ask Good Questions

To construct and answer possible test questions, use the following hints.

1. Do not waste time writing multiple-choice or true/false questions. They are time-consuming to write, and you know the answer before you start.

2. Matching tests are useful, but they are limited to information that requires only factual recall.

3. Open-ended questions that require sentence answers are best, because they tend to require more levels of thought.

4. Consult Table A-1 for ideas on how to word your questions.

5. You are interested in long-term retention of information, so it is best to write the questions one day and answer them a day or two later.

6. As you answer your questions, respond in complete sentences. Writing complete sentences usually involves careful and deliberate thought and therefore leads to more effective learning.

7. Take time to review and critique your answers. This process will also contribute to learning.

TABLE A-1	Questions to Provoke Thought

Type of Material	Questions
Report of research studies and experiments	What was the purpose of the study? What are the important facts and conclusions? What are its implications? How can these results be used?
Case studies	What is it intended to illustrate? What problems or limitations does it demonstrate'? To what other situations might this case apply?
Models	How was the model derived? What are its applications? What are its limitations? Do other models of the same process exist?
Current events	What is the significance of the event? What impact will this have in the future? Is there historical precedent?
Supplementary readings	Why did your instructor assign the reading? How is it related to course content? What key points or concepts does the reading contain? Does the reading present a particular viewpoint?
Sample problems	What processes or concepts does the problem illustrate? What is its unique feature? How is it similar to and different from other problems?
Historical data (historical reviews)	Why were the data presented? What trends or patterns are evident? How is this information related to key concepts in the chapter or article?
Arguments	Is the argument convincing? How is the conclusion supported? What persuasive devices does the author use? Do logical flaws exist? Is the author's appeal emotional?
Poetry	What kinds of feelings does the poem evoke? What message or statement is the poet making? How does the poet use language to create feelings?
Essays	What is the author's purpose? What thought patterns are evident? How does the author support his or her key point (thesis)?
Short stories	What does the title mean? Beyond the plot, what does the story really mean? (What is the theme?) What kinds of comments does it make about life? How do the plot, setting, and tone contribute to the overall meaning?

8. Rewrite any answers that you found to be poorly written or incomplete. This repetition will facilitate learning.

9. Save your answers, and review them once again the evening before the exam.

Many students who use self-testing as a review strategy are pleasantly surprised when they take their first exam: They discover that some (or many!) of their questions actually appear on the exam. This discovery boosts their confidence during the exam and saves them time as well. As you will see later in this chapter, self-testing is an important part of the SQ3R system—a systematic approach to learning and study.

Exercise A-3

Directions: *Write a list of questions that might be asked on an exam covering one of the textbook excerpts in Part Three of this book. Answer them and then verify the correctness of your answers by consulting the excerpt.*

Exercise A-4

Directions: *Write a list of questions for an upcoming exam in one of your courses. Answer each. Save your questions, and after you have taken the exam, mark those that appeared on the exam. (Do not expect the actual questions to use the same wording or format as those you constructed.)*

Test-Taking Strategies: A Review

Taking exams demands sharp thinking and reasoning skills. This appendix is intended to show you how to approach all types of exams with an advantage and how to apply thinking and reasoning skills to objective exams.

Starting with an Advantage

One key to success on any type of examination is to approach it in a confident, organized, and systematic manner.

Bring the Necessary Materials

When going to any examination, take along any materials you might be asked or allowed to use. Be sure you have a watch and an extra pen, and take several number 2 pencils in case you must make a drawing or diagram or fill in an electronically scored answer sheet. Take paper—you may need it for computing figures or writing essay answers. Take along anything you have been allowed to use throughout the semester, such as a pocket calculator, conversion chart, or dictionary. If you are not sure whether you may use them, ask the instructor.

Time Your Arrival Carefully

Arrive at the examination room a few minutes early, in time to get a seat and get organized before the instructor arrives. If you are late, you may miss instructions and feel rushed as you begin the exam. If you arrive too early (more than 15 minutes ahead of time), you risk anxiety induced by panic-stricken students who are questioning each other, trading last-minute memory tricks, and worrying about how difficult the exam will be.

Sit in the Front of the Room

The most practical place to sit in an exam is in the front. There, you often receive the test first and get a head start. Also, it is easier to concentrate and avoid distractions.

Listen Carefully to Your Instructor's Directions

Your instructor may give specific instructions that are not included in the exam's written directions. If these are detailed instructions jot them down on your exam paper or on scrap paper.

Preview the Exam

Before you start to answer any of the questions, quickly page through the exam, noticing the directions, the length, the type of questions, the general topics covered, the number of points the questions are worth, and where to put your answers. Previewing provides an overview of the whole exam and helps to reduce anxiety.

Plan Your Time

After previewing, you will know the number and types of questions included. The next step is to estimate how much time you should spend on each part of the exam, using the point distribution as your guide.

Avoid Reading Too Much into Questions

Most instructors word their questions so that what is expected is clear. Do not anticipate hidden meanings or trick questions.

General Suggestions for Objective Exams

Before we examine particular types of objective exams, here are a few general suggestions to follow in approaching all types of objective exams.

- **Read the directions.** Before answering any questions, read the directions. Often, an instructor will want the correct answer marked in a particular way (for example, underlined rather than circled). The directions may contain crucial information that you must be aware of in order to answer the questions correctly. In the items below, if you did not read the directions and assumed the test questions were of the usual type, you could lose a considerable number of points.

True/False Directions: Read each statement. If the statement is true, mark a T in the blank to the left of the item. If the statement is false, add and/or subtract words in order to make the statement correct.

Multiple-Choice Directions: Circle all the choices that correctly complete the statement.

- **Leave nothing blank.** Before turning in your exam, check through it to be sure you have answered every question. If you have no idea about the correct answer to a question, guess. You might be right!

  Students frequently turn in tests with some items unanswered because they leave difficult questions blank, planning to return to them later. Then, in the rush to finish, they forget them. To avoid this problem, when you are uncertain, choose what looks like the best answer, and then mark the question number with an X or check mark so you can return to it; then, if you have time at the end of the exam, give it further thought. If you run out of time, you will have an answer marked.

- **Look for clues.** If you encounter a difficult question, choose what seems to be the best answer, mark the question with an X or check mark so that you can return to it, and keep the item in mind as you go through the rest of the exam. Sometimes you will see some piece of information later in the exam that reminds you of a fact or idea.

- **Write your answers clearly.** If your instructor cannot be sure of the answer you wrote, he or she will mark it wrong. Answer with block letters on multiple-choice and matching tests to avoid confusion. Write or print responses to fill-in-the-blank tests legibly. Be sure that your answers to short-answer questions not only are written neatly but are to the point and express complete thoughts.

- **Check over your answers before you turn in the exam.** As mentioned earlier, reserve some time at the end of the exam for reviewing your answers. Check to be sure you didn't use the same matching-test answer twice. Be sure your multiple-choice answers are written in the correct blanks or marked in the correct place on the answer grid. One answer marked out of sequence could lead to a series of answers being in error. If there is a separate answer sheet, verify that your fill-in-the-blanks and short answers correspond to the correct question numbers.

- **Don't change answers without a good reason.** When reviewing your answers during an exam, don't make a change unless you have a reason for doing so. Very often your first impressions are correct. If clues from a later test item prompt your recall of information for a previous item, change your answer.

Techniques for Taking Multiple-Choice Tests

Multiple choice is the most frequently used type of exam and is often the most difficult to answer. The following suggestions should improve your success in taking this type of exam.

- **Begin by reading each question as if it were a fill-in-the-blank or short-answer question.** Cover up the choices and try to answer the question from your knowledge of the subject. In this way, you will avoid confusion that might arise from complicated choices. After you have formed your answer, compare it with each of the choices, and select the one that comes closest to your answer.

- **Read all choices first, considering each.** Do not stop reading after the second or third choice, even if you are certain that you have found the correct answer. Remember, on most multiple-choice tests your job is to pick the *best* answer, and the last choice may be a better answer than any of the first three.

- **Read combination choices.** Some multiple-choice tests include choices that are combinations of previously listed choices, as in the following item:

   The mesodermal tissue layer contains cells that will become
   a. skin, sensory organs, and nervous systems.
   b. skin, sensory organs, and blood vessels.
   c. bones and muscle.
   d. stomach, liver, and pancreas.
   e. a and c
   f. b, c, and d
   g. a, c, and d

The addition of choices that are combinations of the preceding choices tends to make items even more confusing. Treat each choice, when combined with the stem, as a true or false statement. As you consider each choice, mark it true or false. If you find more than one true statement, then select the choice that contains the letters of all the true statements you identified.

- **Use logic and common sense.** Even if you are unfamiliar with the subject matter, you can sometimes reason out the correct answer. The following test item is taken from a history exam on Japanese-American relations after World War II:

> Prejudice and discrimination are
> a. harmful to our society because they waste our economic, political, and social resources.
> b. helpful because they ensure us against attack from within.
> c. harmful because they create negative images of the United States in foreign countries.
> d. helpful because they keep the majority pure and united against minorities.

Through logic and common sense, it is possible to eliminate choices *b* and *d*. Prejudice and discrimination are seldom, if ever, regarded as positive, desirable, or helpful since they are inconsistent with democratic ideals. Having narrowed your answer to two choices, *a* or *c*, you can see that choice *a* offers a stronger, more substantial reason why prejudice and discrimination are harmful. The attitude of other countries toward the United States is not as serious as a waste of economic, political, and social resources.

- **Examine closely items that are very similar.** Often, when two similar choices are presented, one is likely to be correct. Carefully compare the two choices. First, try to express each in your own words, and then analyze how they differ. Often, this process will enable you to recognize the right answer.

- **Pay special attention to the level of qualifying words.** Qualifying words are important. Since many statements, ideas, principles, and rules have exceptions, be careful in selecting items that contain such extreme qualifying words as *best, always, all, no, never, none, entirely,* and *completely,* all of which suggest that a condition exists without exception. Items containing words that provide for some level of exception, or qualification, are more likely to be correct. Here are a few examples of such words: *often, usually, less, seldom, few, more,* and *most.* Likewise, numerical answers that are about in the middle of a range of choices are probably correct. In the following example, notice the use of the italicized qualifying words:

In most societies

a. values are *highly* consistent.

b. people *often* believe and act on values that are contradictory.

c. *all* legitimate organizations support values of the majority.

d. values of equality *never* exist alongside prejudice and discrimination.

In this question, items *c* and *d* contain the words *all* and *never,* suggesting that those statements are true without exception. Thus, if you did not know the answer to this question based on content, you could eliminate items *c* and *d* on the basis of the level of qualifiers.

- **Some multiple-choice questions require application of knowledge or information.** You may be asked to analyze a hypothetical situation or to use what you have learned to solve a problem. Here is an example taken from a psychology test:

  Carrie is uncomfortable in her new home in New Orleans. When she gets dressed and leaves her home and goes to the supermarket to buy the week's groceries, she gets nervous and upset and thinks that something is going to happen to her. She feels the same way when walking her four-year-old son Jason to the park or playground.
  Carrie is suffering from

  a. shyness.

  b. a phobia.

  c. a personality disorder.

  d. hypertension.

  In answering questions of this type, start by crossing out unnecessary information that can distract you. In the preceding example, distracting information includes the woman's name, her son's name, where she lives, why she goes to the store, and so forth.

- **Jot down the essence.** If a question concerns steps in a process or order of events or any other information that is easily confused, ignore the choices and use the margin or scrap paper to jot down the information as you can recall it. Then select the choice that matches what you wrote.

- **Avoid the unfamiliar.** Avoid choosing answers that are unfamiliar or that you do not understand. A choice that looks complicated or uses difficult words is not necessarily correct. If you have studied carefully, a choice that is unfamiliar to you or contains unfamiliar terminology is probably incorrect.

- **Eliminate choices that are obviously false.** Treat each choice in a troublesome question like you would a statement on a true/false test.

- **Choose the longest or most inclusive answers.** As a last resort, when you do not know the answer and are unable to eliminate any of the choices as wrong, guess by picking the one that seems most complete and contains the most information. This is a good choice because instructors are usually careful to make the correct answer complete. Thus, the answer often becomes long or detailed.

- **Be careful of "all of the above" and "none of the above" questions.** This type of question can be particularly difficult, since it usually involves five choices and can lead to confusion. To make it easier, first try to eliminate "all of the above." If even *one* choice is incorrect "all of the above" will be incorrect. If you think that at least *one* of the choices is correct, you can eliminate "none of the above." If you think two choices are correct but you are unsure of the third one, you should choose "all of the above." When questions such as these occur only a few times in a test, "all" or "none" is probably the correct choice.

- **Make educated guesses.** In most instances, you can eliminate one or more of the choices as obviously wrong. Even if you can eliminate only one choice, you have increased your odds on a four-choice item from one in four to one in three. If you can eliminate two choices, you have increased your odds to one in two, or 50 percent. Don't hesitate to play the odds and make a guess—you may gain points.

Exercise B–1

Directions: *The following multiple-choice items appeared on a psychology exam. Study each item and use your reasoning skills to eliminate items that seem incorrect. Then, making an educated guess, choose the letter of the choice that best completes the statement.*

_____   1. Modern psychological researchers maintain that the mind as well as behavior can be scientifically examined primarily by

   a. observing behavior and making inferences about mental functioning.

   b. observing mental activity and making inferences about behavior.

   c. making inferences about behavior.

   d. direct observation of behavior.

_____ 2. Jane Goodall has studied the behavior of chimpanzees in their own habitat. She exemplifies a school of psychology that is concerned with

   a. theories.

   b. mental processes.

   c. the individual's potential for growth.

   d. naturalistic behavior.

_____ 3. If a psychologist were personally to witness the effects of a tornado upon the residents of a small town, what technique would he or she be using?

   a. experimentation   c. observation

   b. correlational research   d. none of the above

_____ 4. A case study is a(n)

   a. observation of an event.

   b. comparison of similar events.

   c. study of changes and their effects.

   d. intense investigation of a particular occurrence.

_____ 5. Events that we are aware of at a given time make up the

   a. unconscious.   c. consciousness.

   b. subconscious.   d. triconscious.

_____ 6. Unlocking a combination padlock

   a. always involves language skills.

   b. always involves motor skills.

   c. seldom involves concentration skills.

   d. seldom involves memory skills.

Achieving Success with Standardized Tests

At various times in college, you may be required to take standardized tests. These are commercially prepared; they are usually lengthy, timed tests that are used nationally or statewide to measure specific skills and abilities. Your score on these tests compares your performance with that of large numbers of other students throughout the country or state.

Preparing for the Test

Use the following suggestions for preparing for standardized tests:

- **Find out as much as possible about the test.** Meet with your advisor or check the career center to obtain brochures and application forms. Find out about its general content, length, and timing. Determine its format and the scoring procedures used. Know when and where the test is given.

- **Take a review course.** Find out if your college offers a preparatory workshop to help you prepare for the test.

- **Obtain a review book.** Review books are available to help you prepare for many standardized tests. Purchase a review book at your college bookstore, at a large off-campus bookstore, or through the Internet. If you cannot purchase a review book, you may be able to borrow one from your college library or public library.

- **Begin your review early.** Start to study well ahead of the exam so that you can fit the necessary review time into your already hectic schedule.

- **Start with a quick overview of the test.** Most review books contain a section that explains the type of questions on the test and offers test-taking strategies. If a brief review of the subject matter is offered, read through it.

- **Take practice tests.** To become as comfortable as possible with the test, take numerous timed practice tests and score them. Make your practice tests as much like the actual test as possible. Work at a well-lighted desk or table in a quiet setting and time yourself carefully.

- **Review your answers.** Thoroughly review the questions you answered incorrectly. Read through the explanations given in your review book and try to see why the keyed answer is best.

- **Keep track of your scores.** Keep a record of both your total score and subtest scores on practice tests. This will help you judge your progress and can give you insights into areas of weakness that require extra review.

Taking the Test

Use the following suggestions to get as many points as possible on a standardized test:

- **Arrive in the exam room prepared.** Get to the testing site early so you can choose a good seat and become comfortable with the surroundings.

Wear a watch, and bring two sharpened pencils with erasers (in case one breaks) and two pens (in case one runs out).

- **Get organized before the timing begins.** Line up your answer sheet and test booklet so you can move between them rapidly without losing your place. Carefully fill out your answer sheet.

- **Skim the instructions.** This can save you valuable time. If you have prepared yourself properly, you should be very familiar with the format of the test and the instructions. A quick reading of the directions will be all that is necessary to assure yourself that they have not changed.

- **Work quickly and steadily.** Most standardized tests are timed, so the pace you work at is a critical factor. You need to work at a fairly rapid rate, but not so fast as to make careless errors.

- **Don't plan on finishing the test.** Many of these tests are designed so that most people do not finish. So work on the easier questions first, and make a mark next to the harder ones so you can return to them if time permits.

- **Don't expect to get everything right.** Unlike classroom tests or exams, you are not expected to get most of the answers correct.

- **Find out if there is a penalty for guessing.** If there is none, then use the last 20 or 30 seconds to randomly fill in an answer for each item that you have not had time to complete. The odds are that you will get one out of every five correct. If there is a penalty for guessing, guess only if you can narrow the answer down to two choices. Otherwise, leave the item blank.

- **Check your answer sheet periodically.** If you have skipped a question, make sure that later answers match their questions. If the test has several parts, check to see that you are marking answers in the correct answer grid.

- **Don't just stop if you finish early.** If you have time left over, use it. Redo marked questions you skipped. Review as many answers as you can. Check over your answer sheet for stray marks and darken your answer marks.

Reading and Evaluating Internet Sources

Reading Electronic Text

Reading electronic sources demands a different type of thinking from reading print sources. A print source is linear—it goes in a straight line from idea to idea. Electronic sources, due to the presence of links, tend to be multidirectional; you can follow numerous paths.

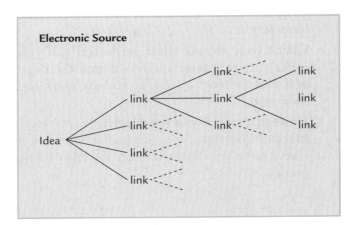

Reading electronic text also requires new strategies. The first steps to reading electronic text easily and effectively are to understand how it is different and to realize that you must change and adapt how you read. Here are some specific suggestions.

Focus on Your Purpose

Focus clearly on your purposes for visiting the site. What information do you need? Because you must create your own path through the site, you must fix in mind what you are looking for to avoid wandering aimlessly, wasting valuable time, or even becoming lost, following numerous links that lead you farther and farther away from the site at which you began.

Get Used to the Site's Design and Layout

Each Web site has unique features and arranges information differently.

1. **When you reach a new site, spend a few minutes getting used to it and discovering how it is organized.** Scroll through it quickly to determine how it is organized and what information is available. Ask yourself the following questions.

   - What information is available?
   - How is it arranged on the screen?
   - Can you search the site using a search box or other search option?
   - Is there a site map?

   On large and complex sites, especially, you have a number of different choices for locating the information you need. Be sure to spend time exploring your choices before choosing a particular path for your search.

2. **Expect the first screen to grab your attention and make a main point.** (Web site authors know that many people who read a Web page do not scroll down to see the next screenful.)

3. **Get used to the Web site's design before you attempt to obtain information from the site.** Your eye may have a tendency to focus on color or movement, rather than on print. Because some Web sites are highly visual, they require visual as well as verbal thinking. The author intends for you to respond to photos, graphics, and animation.

4. **Consider both the focus of and limitations of your learning style.** Are you a spatial learner? If so, you may have a tendency to focus too heavily on the graphic elements of the screen. If, on the other hand, you tend to focus on words, you may ignore important visual elements or signals. If you focus *only* on the words and ignore color and graphics on a particular screen, you probably will miss information or may not move through the site in the most efficient way.

Pay Attention to How Information Is Organized

Because you can navigate through a Web site in many different ways, it is important to have the right expectations and to make several decisions before you begin. Some Web sites are much better organized than others. Some have clear headings and labels that make it easy to discover how to proceed; others do not and will require more thought. For example, if you are reading an article with as many as ten or 15 underlined words (links), there is no prescribed order to follow and these links are not categorized in any way. Below are some suggestions on how to stay organized when using a Web site.

1. **Use the site map, if provided, to discover what information is available and how it is organized.** A site map can help you navigate the site.

2. **Consider the order in which you want to take in information.** Choose an order in which to explore links; avoid randomly clicking on link buttons. Doing so is somewhat like randomly choosing pages to read out of a reference book. Do you need definitions first? Do you want historical background first? Your decision will be partly influenced by your learning style.

3. **Consider writing brief notes to yourself as you explore a complicated Web site.** Alternatively, you could print the home page and jot notes on it. You can also save Web pages onto a disk or on your computer, as a text file.

4. **Expect shorter, less detailed sentences and paragraphs.** Much online communication tends to be briefer and more concise than in traditional sources. As a result, you may have to mentally fill in transitions and make inferences about relationships among ideas. For example, you may have to infer similarities and differences or recognize cause and effect connections.

Directions: *Visit two Web sites on the same topic. On a separate sheet of paper write a few sentences comparing and contrasting their organization and design.*

Use Links to Find the Information You Need

Links are unique to electronic text. Here's how to use them.

1. **Plan on exploring links to find complete and detailed information.** Links, both remote links (those that take you to another site) and related links within a site, are intended to provide more detailed information on topics introduced on the home page.

2. **As you follow links, be sure to bookmark your original site and other useful sites you come across so you can find them again.** Bookmarking is a feature of your Internet browser that allows you to record Web site addresses and access them later simply by clicking on the site name. Different search engines use different terms for this function. Microsoft's Internet Explorer refers to bookmarks as *Favorites*.

3. **If you use a site or a link that provides many pages of continuous paragraphs, print the material and read it offline.**

4. **If you find you are lacking background on a topic, use links to help fill in the gap or search for a different Web site on the same topic that is less technical.**

5. **If you get lost, most Internet browsers have a history feature.** It allows you to backtrack or retrace the links you followed in a search. For example, clicking on "Back," will take you back one link at a time; "History" keeps track of all searches over a given period and allows you to go directly to a chosen site rather than backtracking step-by-step.

Directions: *For one of the Web sites you visited earlier or for a new site of your choice, follow at least three links and then, on a separate sheet of paper, answer the following questions.*

1. What type of information did each link contain?

2. Which was the easiest to read and follow? Why?

Evaluating Internet Sources

Although the Internet contains a great deal of valuable information and resources, it also contains rumor, gossip, hoaxes, and misinformation. In other words, not all Internet sources are trustworthy. You must evaluate a source before accepting it. Here are some guidelines to follow when evaluating Internet sources.

Discover the Purpose of Web Sites

There are many thousands of Web sites and they vary widely in purpose. Five primary types of Web sites are summarized in Table C-1.

TABLE C-1	Types of Web Sites		
Type	**Purpose and Description**	**Domain**	**Sample Sites**
Informational	To present facts, information, and research data. May contain reports, statistical data, results of research studies, and reference materials.	.edu or .gov	**http://www.haskins.vale.edu/** **http://www.census.gov/**
News	To provide current information on local, national, and international news. Often supplements print newspapers, periodicals, and television news programs.	.com or .org	**http://news.yahoo.com/** **http://www.theheart.org/index.cfm**
Advocacy	To promote a particular cause or point of view. Usually concerned with a controversial issue; often sponsored by nonprofit groups.	.com or .org	**http://www.goveg.com/** **http://www.bradycampaign.org/**
Personal	To provide information about an individual and his or her interests and accomplishments. May list publications or include the individual's résumé.	Varies . . . may contain .com, .org, .biz, .edu, .info. May contain a tilde (~).	**http://www.jessamyn.com/** **http://www.srmi.biz/resumeJohn.html** **http://www.maryrusell.info/**
Commercial	To promote goods or services. May provide news and information related to their products.	.com, .biz, .info	**http://www.nmgroup.biz/** **http://www.alhemer.com/** **http://vintageradio.info/**

Exercise C–3

Directions: *Determine the purpose of each of the following Web sites using the information in Table C-1. Some sites may have more than one purpose. Be sure to investigate the whole site carefully and explain your choices on a separate piece of paper.*

1. Tibetan Children's Educational and Welfare Fund: http://www.tcewf.org/index.html

2. Realty Times: http://realtytimes.com/

3. Israel—A Country Study: http://lcweb2.loc.gov/frd/cs/iltoc.html

4. Center for Science in the Public Interest: http://www.cspinet.org/

5. Professor Hunt's Dog Page: http://www.cofc.edu/~huntc/dogpage.html

Evaluate the Content of a Web Site

When evaluating the content of a Web site, evaluate its appropriateness, its source, its level of technical detail, its presentation, its completeness, and its links.

Evaluate Appropriateness   To be worthwhile a Web site should contain the information you need. It should answer one or more of your search questions. If the site only touches upon answers to your questions and does not address them in detail, check the links on the site to see if they will lead you to more detailed information. If they do not, search for another more useful site.

Evaluate Source   Another important step in evaluating a Web site is to determine its source. Ask yourself "Who is the sponsor?" and "Why was this site put up on the Web?" The sponsor of a Web site is the person or organization who paid for it to be created and placed on the Web. The sponsor will often suggest the purpose of a Web site. For example, a Web site sponsored by Nike is designed to promote its products, while a site sponsored by a university library is designed to help students learn to use its resources more effectively.

If you are uncertain of who sponsors a Web site, check its URL, its copyright, and the links it offers. The ending of the URL often suggests the type of sponsorship, as you saw in Table C-1. The copyright indicates the owner of the site. Links may also reveal the sponsor. Some links may lead to commercial advertising; others may lead to sites sponsored by nonprofit groups, for example. Another way to check the ownership of a Web site is to try to locate the site's home page. You can do this by using only the first part of its URL—up to the first slash (/) mark. For example, suppose you found some information on Medicare on the Internet and you wanted to track its source. Its URL is http://www.pha.org.au/friends_of_medicare/frame_friends_of_medicare.html. This page deals with Medicare, but it begins by talking about Australia. If you go back in the URL to http://www.pha.org.au you will discover that the sponsoring organization is the Public Health Association of Australia.

Evaluate Level of Technical Detail   A Web site should contain the level of detail that is suited to your purpose. Some sites may provide information that is too sketchy for your search purposes; others assume a level of background knowledge or technical sophistication that you lack. For example, if you are writing a short, introductory-level paper on global warming, information on the University of New Hampshire's NASA Earth Observing System site (http://www.cos-ids.sr.unh.edu/) may be too technical and contain more information than you need unless you have some previous knowledge in that field.

Evaluate Presentation   Information on a Web site should be presented clearly; it should be well written. If you find a site that is not clear and well written, you should be suspicious of it. If the author did not take time to present ideas clearly and correctly, he or she may not have taken time to collect accurate information, either.

Evaluate Completeness   Determine whether the site provides complete information on its topic. Does it address all aspects of the topic that you feel it should? For example, if a Web site on important twentieth-century American poets does not mention Robert Frost, then the site is incomplete. If you discover that a site is incomplete, search for sites that provide a more thorough treatment of the topic.

Evaluate Links   Many reputable sites supply links to other related sites. Make sure that the links work and are current. Also check to see if the sites to which you were sent are reliable sources of information. If the links do not work or the sources appear unreliable, you should question the reliability of the site itself. Also determine whether the links provided are comprehensive or present only a representative sample. Either is acceptable, but the site should make clear the nature of the links it is providing.

Exercise C–4

Directions: *Evaluate the content of two of the following sites. On a separate sheet of paper explain why you would either trust or distrust the site's content.*

1. http://www.freedombox.info/

2. http://www.earlham.edu/~peters/knotlink.htm

3. http://www.age-of-the-sage.org/psychology/

Evaluate the Accuracy of the Web Site

When using information on a Web site for an academic paper, it is important to be sure that you have found accurate information. One way to determine the accuracy of a Web site is to compare it with print sources (periodicals and books) on the same topic. If you find a wide discrepancy between the Web site and the print sources, do not trust the Web site. Another way to determine accuracy of information on a site is to compare it with other Web sites that address the same topic. If discrepancies exist, further research is needed to determine which site is more accurate.

The site itself will also provide clues about the accuracy of its information. Ask yourself the following questions:

- **Are the author's name and credentials provided?** A well-known writer with established credentials is likely to author only reliable, accurate information. If no author is given, you should question whether the information is accurate.

- **Is contact information for the author included on the site?** Often, sites provide an e-mail address where the author can be contacted.

- **Is the information complete or in summary form?** If it is a summary, use the site to find the original source. Original information has less chance of error and is usually preferred in academic papers.

- **If opinions are offered, are they presented clearly as opinions?** Authors who disguise their opinions as facts are not trustworthy. (See Chapter 10, "Fact and Opinion," p. 339.)

- **Does the writer make unsubstantiated assumptions or base his or her ideas on misconceptions?** If so, the information presented may not be accurate.

- **Does the site provide a list of works cited?** As with any form of research, sources used to put information up on a Web site must be documented. If sources are not credited, you should question the accuracy of the Web site.

It may be helpful to determine if the information is available in print form. If it is, try to obtain the print version. Errors may occur when the article or essay is put up on the Web. Web sites move, change, and delete information, so it may be difficult for a reader of an academic paper to locate the Web site that you used in writing it. Also, page numbers are easier to cite in print sources than in electronic ones.

Exercise C–5

Directions: *Evaluate the accuracy of two of the following Web sites and write your comments on a separate piece of paper.*

1. http://www.amguard.net/
2. http://www.krysstal.com/democracy.html
3. http://www.idausa.org/facts/pg.html

Evaluate the Timeliness of the Web Site

Although the Web is well known for providing up-to-the-minute information, not all Web sites are current. Evaluate a site's timeliness by checking

- the date on which the Web site was mounted (put on the Web).
- the date when the document you are using was added.
- the date when the site was last revised.
- the date when the links were last checked.

This information is usually provided at the end of the site's home page or at the end of the document you are using.

Exercise C–6

Directions: *Evaluate the timeliness of two of the following Web sites, using the directions given for each site. Write your comments on a separate piece of paper.*

1. http://www.hwg.org/resources/?cid=30

   See when these links were last checked. Find out what the consequences of this are by checking the links yourself.

2. http://www.chebucto.ns.ca/Urbancap/

   Evaluate whether this site contains up-to-date information and links on the Community Access Program in Nova Scotia.

3. http://www.mediasurface.com//news/pressreleases/?view=standard

   Examine this Web page carefully. How does its timeliness relate to the service being offered?

**Exercise
C–7**

Directions: *Evaluate each of the sites listed below. Assign each a rating of 1–5 (1 = low reliability; 5 = high reliability). Be prepared to discuss your ratings.*

1. A Virtual Visit to Expo '74

   http://pw2.netcom.com/~mffuller/index.html

2. Ten Commandments of How to Work Effectively with Lawyers

   http://web.mit.edu/entforum/res_hadzima/commandments.html

3. Meteorology

   http://www.schooltv.com/meteorology.htm

4. U.S. Economy at a Glance

   http://www.bls.gov/eag/eag.us.htm

5. How to Communicate with Journalists

   http://www.fair.org/activism/communicate.html

Part III

Current Issues Reader

ISSUE #1

ISSUE #1: EQUITY IN EDUCATION

His Name Is Michael: A Lesson on the Voices We Unknowingly Silence
Donna M. Marriott

This reading from *Education Week* magazine describes how a teacher learned an important lesson from a child who did not assert his identity in her classroom. The author is an early-literacy program manager in the San Diego, California, city schools.

Vocabulary Preview

These are some of the difficult words in this passage. The definitions here will help you if you can't figure out the meanings from the sentence context or word parts.

full-inclusion (par. 2) the practice of including children with disabilities in a regular classroom full time

progressive teacher (par. 2) one who believes in informal classroom procedures, encouragement of self-expression, and an emphasis on the individual child

curriculum (par. 2) a set of courses

assessment (par. 2) the evaluation of a student's performance

la maestra (par. 10) in Spanish, "the teacher"

complicity (par. 11) involvement as an accomplice in a questionable act

polarized (par. 12) at opposite extremes

pedagogy (par. 13) the principles and methods of teaching

1   This is a true story—one that both haunts and inspires me. I wish I could say that the names have been changed to protect the innocent. The names were changed, but, sadly, no one was protected.

2   I was teaching that year in a full-inclusion, multiage class. My teaching partner and I had 43 children ranging in age from 5 to 9, ranging in ability from average to labeled, ranging in experience from indulged to adequate. I boasted about being a progressive teacher—a teacher bent on changing the system. As I looked around my classroom, I could see evidence of all the latest and greatest in education: child-directed learning, meaning-driven curriculum, responsive teaching, authentic assessment. It took a little boy to show me what I couldn't see: Beneath this veneer of "best practice," there was a layer of fundamental ignorance.

3   He appeared at my classroom door in the middle of a busy morning gripping the hand of a harried school secretary. He was a tiny child with carefully combed hair, wearing a crisply pressed shirt, tightly clutching his lunch money. The secretary handed this child to me and rattled off the institutional essentials: "His name is Michael. He is a bus rider. He doesn't speak English." Not much of an introduction, but that's how it happens in schools. New students appear in the office at times that make sense in their lives—not in our lives. These children are unceremoniously placed in whatever classroom has an extra chair. It's not very welcoming—but that's the drill. We did all the usual new-kid things that day. We played the name game. The kid of the day gave him the grand tour of our room. He got to sit on the couch even though it wasn't really his turn. The children insisted that Michael have a buddy for absolutely everything—learning buddy, recess buddy, bathroom buddy, lunch buddy, cubby buddy, line buddy, water buddy, rug buddy, bus buddy. They thought it would be great if he had a sleepover buddy, too, but I was able to convince them otherwise. We were genuinely glad to have this youngster in our learning family. But Michael didn't become part of our family.

4   Michael existed marginally on the outside of the group. Sometimes he was on the outside looking in; sometimes he was on the outside looking out. I often saw him with his eyes closed—looking somewhere hidden. He was well-mannered, punctual, respectful, cute-as-a-button—but completely detached from me, from the children, and from the learning.

5   I met with the bilingual resource teacher to chat about concerns and possibilities. She told me she could come do an informal observation "a week from tomorrow." It was a long wait, but that's how it is in schools. She came. She watched. She listened. On her way out she said, "You might have better results, dear, if you call him Miguel."

6   I could not have been more embarrassed or confused. How could I have been calling this child the wrong name? I was a progressive teacher: How could I have made such a mistake? How could the school secretary have made such a mistake? Why hadn't the parents corrected her? Why hadn't the child corrected me?

7   Miguel didn't stay with us for long. His family moved on to follow their own calendar of opportunities. We didn't get to say goodbye, but that's how it happens in schools.

8   Miguel's paperwork arrived about three weeks after he had moved away. I was going through the folder, updating it for his next teacher, when I noticed something that made me catch my breath. His name wasn't Michael. It wasn't Miguel. His name was David.

9   I wondered how it was that this child could have been part of my classroom for more than a month, and in that entire time he never had enough personal power to tell me that his name was David. What was it about me, about the other children, about the school that made David feel he had to give up his name? No child should have to forfeit his identity to walk through our classroom doors. No child. Ever. It is much too high a price to pay.

10   I have to do a bit of guessing about what was going on in David's head. I am guessing that he was told to respect la maestra—to "be good" in school. I am guessing that he thought if the teacher decided to change his name, well then . . . that was that. I am guessing that he didn't connect school to any known reality. He could be David at home, but at school he was expected to become someone else.

11   I don't have to do much guessing at my own complicity. It never occurred to me that his name would be anything other than Michael. In the entire breadth of my experience, people had called me by my given name. In those few instances when someone mispronounced my name, I would offer a polite but prompt correction. I was taught to speak up for myself. I was given the power to be me—in my school, in my neighborhood, in my life. I never considered checking in with David about his name. It was beyond the scope of my experience. It was beyond the lens of my culture.

12   Our power distance was huge. I had all the power. I was white; I was the teacher; I spoke English. David had no power. He was brown; he was a child; he spoke Spanish. Our sense of individualism clashed. I expected him to have a sense of himself—to stand up for himself, to speak up. He denied himself. David expected and accepted that he was "less than" in the culture of school. Our perception of reality was polarized. I trusted in the precision of the system. The name on the registration card just had to be correct. That's how it works in schools. David accepted the imprecision of the system. Having his name changed was just part of the whole befuddling experience.

13   I have learned many difficult lessons in the years since David sat submissively on the edge of my classroom. I have learned lessons about passive racism—the kind that we cannot see in ourselves, don't want to see in ourselves, and vehemently deny. I have learned lessons about implicit power and explicit powerlessness—about those voices we choose to hear and those voices we unknowingly silence. I have learned that being a good teacher is as much about rapport and relationships as it is about progressive curriculum, pedagogy, and assessment.

14   If I could go back to that day when the secretary brought in a little boy with carefully combed hair wearing a crisply pressed shirt, I would shake his hand and say, "Hello. My name is Mrs. Marriott. What's your name?" I believe that if I had simply asked him, he would have told me.

━━ · ━━

Directions: Select the letter of the choice that best completes each of the following statements.

CHECKING YOUR COMPREHENSION

_____   1. The statement that best expresses the central thesis of the selection is

a. The procedures for enrolling children in schools should be revised so that new students are made to feel welcome.

b. Cultural differences and false assumptions can prevent children from having a voice in their own lives.

c. Students who do not speak English are at a major disadvantage in American schools.

     d. The overcrowding of classrooms results in many students getting overlooked by their teachers.

_____ 2. The author's primary purpose is to

     a. compare her own experience as a child with that of her students.

     b. criticize parents who move their children during the school year.

     c. describe what she learned from her experience with a particular student.

     d. discuss what it means to be a progressive teacher in an inclusive classroom.

_____ 3. The topic of paragraph 3 is

     a. the classroom.   b. the secretary.

     c. Michael.   d. the teacher.

_____ 4. The question that the author is attempting to answer in paragraph 10 is

     a. Why did David let people call him by the wrong name at school?

     b. Why did David's family remove him from school?

     c. What did David's parents call him at home?

     d. How did the school secretary get the wrong name for David?

_____ 5. The main idea of paragraph 11 is that the teacher

     a. should have known she was calling her student by the wrong name.

     b. made incorrect assumptions about a student based on her own experience.

     c. was taught to speak up for herself in every aspect of her life.

     d. did not even consider asking her student about his name.

_____ 6. In paragraph 12, the author uses the comparison and contrast organizational pattern to discuss the differences between

     a. teachers and students.

     b. adults and children.

     c. herself and David.

     d. school culture and home life.

_____ 7. Of the following statements from the selection, which one is an opinion?

a. "My teaching partner and I had 43 children ranging in age from 5 to 9." (par. 2)

b. "I met with the bilingual resource teacher to chat about concerns and possibilities." (par. 5)

c. "His name was David." (par. 8)

d. "No child should have to forfeit his identity to walk through our classroom doors." (par. 9)

_____ 8. The bilingual resource teacher's comment in paragraph 5 indicates that she

a. understood exactly why the student did not participate in class.

b. thought the classroom teacher was doing a poor job.

c. also made an incorrect assumption about the student's name.

d. did not think the student was having any problems.

_____ 9. The phrase "power distance" in paragraph 12 refers to the

a. difference between the physical strength of adults compared to children.

b. distance each student and teacher must travel to come to school.

c. total amount of power people have when they work together for a common goal.

d. difference between the amount of power or status that two people possess.

_____ 10. The tone of the selection can best be described as

a. angry and bitter.

b. cheerful and optimistic.

c. honest and heartfelt.

d. indifferent and resigned.

USING CONTEXT AND WORD PARTS

_____ 11. In paragraph 2, the word **veneer** refers to

a. speech.   b. difficulty.

c. decoration.   d. surface appearance.

_____ 12. In paragraph 3, the word **harried** means
     a. distressed.   b. carefree.
     c. stubborn.   d. confident.

_____ 13. In paragraph 4, the word **marginally** means
     a. importantly.   b. strongly.
     c. just barely.   d. carefully.

_____ 14. In paragraph 9, the word **forfeit** means
     a. allow.   b. insist on.
     c. leave.   d. give up.

_____ 15. In paragraph 13, the word **vehemently** means
     a. strangely.   b. forcefully.
     c. poorly.   d. gaily.

REVIEWING DIFFICULT VOCABULARY

Directions: _Complete each of the following sentences by inserting a word from the Vocabulary Preview on page 494 in the space provided._

16. The two politicians were so strongly _____ about the issues that it seemed they could agree on nothing.

17. Although the woman did not actually burglarize the store, her _____ was clear when she drove the getaway car.

18. When Ted entered medical school, he found the _____ to be overwhelming.

19. The education major learned quite a lot about _____ from her professors and textbooks, which she hoped to be able to put into use in a classroom setting someday.

20. The practice exam offered a good _____ of Emma's performance in class and preparation for the final exam.

QUESTIONS FOR DISCUSSION

1. Discuss the subtitle, "A Lesson on the Voices We Unknowingly Silence." What other voices do you think might be silenced in the culture of school? Where else might voices be silenced?

2. Define "passive racism" (par. 13). Have you ever experienced or witnessed passive racism? Discuss how and where it can appear.

3. The author writes, "that's how it is in schools" (par. 5), "that's how it happens in schools" (par. 7), and "that's how it works in schools" (par. 12). Discuss why the author repeats this assertion throughout the selection. How are things in your school? Are there procedures that are followed without thought and assumptions that are made?

ACTIVITES FOR WRITING

1. Brainstorm a list of various prejudices and biases that are common in our society. Then choose one that is important to you and write a brief essay explaining what might be done to overcome or counteract it.

2. Write a paragraph that explains how important names are and what it means when someone gets a name wrong.

3. Listen to this story from NPR about tracking the children of migrant workers through the education system: http://www.npr.org/templates/story/story.php?storyId=4751388& sourceCode=RSS. Write a paragraph that summarizes the program and indicates whether you think it will help or hurt migrant workers.

ISSUE # 2: POVERTY IN AMERICA

THE HIGH COST OF BEING POOR

Barbara Ehrenreich

     This article first appeared on the author's blog. In it the author refers to an experience in which she held several low-paying jobs in order to understand the problems and lifestyle of the poor. She published her findings in the book titled *Nickel and Dimed*. Read this selection to find out why it is so difficult to overcome poverty.

Vocabulary Preview

These are some of the difficult words in this passage. The definitions here will help you if you can't figure out the meanings from the sentence context or word parts.

the simple life (par. 1) a free and unhindered existence

altercations (par. 1) arguments, quarrels

Brookings Institute (par. 2) an organization devoted to examining public policies and issues

hypothetical (par. 5) not real, for the purposes of discussion

socialized medicine (par. 6) medical care that is paid for and run by the government

hypertension (par. 6) high blood pressure

siphoned (par. 7) drained or taken away

1   There are people, concentrated in the Hamptons and Beverly Hills, who still confuse poverty with the simple life. No cable TV, no altercations with the maid, no summer home maintenance issues—just the basics like family, sunsets and walks in the park. What they don't know is that it's expensive to be poor.

2   In fact, you, the reader of middling income, could probably not afford it. A new study from the Brookings Institute documents the "ghetto tax," or higher cost of living in low-income urban neighborhoods. It comes at you from every direction, from food prices to auto insurance. A few examples from this study, by Matt Fellowes, that covered 12 American cities:

- Poor people are less likely to have bank accounts, which can be expensive for those with low balances, and so they tend to cash their pay checks at check-cashing businesses, which in the cities surveyed, charged $5 to $50 for a $500 check.

- Nationwide, low-income car buyers, defined as people earning less than $30,000 a year, pay two percentage points more for a car loan than more affluent buyers.

- Low-income drivers pay more for car insurance. In New York, Baltimore and Hartford, they pay an average $400 more a year to insure the exact same car and driver risk than wealthier drivers.
- Poorer people pay an average of one percentage point more in mortgage interest.
- They are more likely to buy their furniture and appliances through pricey rent-to-own businesses. In Wisconsin, the study reports, a $200 rent-to-own TV set can cost $700 with the interest included.
- They are less likely to have access to large supermarkets and hence rely on the far more expensive, and lower quality offerings of small grocery and convenience stores.

3   I didn't live in any ghettoes when I worked on *Nickel and Dimed*—a trailer park, yes, but no ghetto—and on my average wage of $7 an hour, or about $14,400 a year, I wasn't in the market for furniture, a house or a car. But the high cost of poverty was brought home to me within a few days of my entry into the low-wage life, when, slipping into social-worker mode, I chastised a co-worker for living in a motel room when it would be so much cheaper to rent an apartment. Her response: Where would she get the first month's rent and security deposit it takes to pin down an apartment? The lack of that amount of capital—probably well over $1,000—condemned her to paying $40 a night at the Day's Inn.

4   Then there was the problem of sustenance. I had gone into the project imagining myself preparing vast quantities of cheap, nutritious soups and stews, which I would freeze and heat for dinner each day. But surprise: I didn't have the proverbial pot to pee in, not to mention spices or Tupperware. A scouting trip to K-Mart established that it would take about a $40 capital investment to get my kitchenette up to speed for the low-wage way of life.

5   The food situation got only more challenging when I, too, found myself living in a motel. Lacking a fridge and microwave, all my food had to come from the nearest convenience store (hardboiled eggs and banana for breakfast) or, for the big meal of the day, Wendy's or KFC. I have no nutritional complaints; after all, there is a veggie, or flecks of one, in Wendy's broccoli and cheese baked potato. The problem was financial. A double cheeseburger and fries is a lot more expensive than that hypothetical homemade lentil stew.

6   There are other tolls along the road well-traveled by the working poor. If your credit is lousy, which it is likely to be, you'll pay a higher deposit for a phone. If you don't have health insurance, you may end up taking that feverish child to an emergency room, and please don't think of ER's as socialized medicine for the poor. The average cost of a visit is over $1,000, which is over ten times more than what a clinic pediatrician would charge. Or you neglect that hypertension, diabetes or mystery lump until you end up with a $100,000 problem on your hands.

7   So lets have a little less talk about how the poor should learn to manage their money, and a little more attention to all the ways that money is being systematically

siphoned off. Yes, certain kinds of advice would be helpful: skip the pay-day loans and rent-to-pay furniture, for example. But we need laws in more states to stop predatory practices like $50 charges for check cashing. Also, think what some micro-credit could do to move families from motels and shelters to apartments. And did I mention a living wage?

8   If you're rich, you might want to stay that way. It's a whole lot cheaper than being poor.

━━ ∎ ━━

Directions: *Select the letter of the choice that best completes each of the following statements.*

CHECKING YOUR COMPREHENSION

_____ 1. The author's purpose in writing this selection is to
   a. blame the government for not supporting low-income citizens.
   b. suggest ways in which we can eliminate poverty.
   c. demonstrate why low-income people cannot get ahead financially.
   d. offer statistics on the number of low-income families in the United States.

_____ 2. Poor people tend to pay to cash their checks because
   a. it is the least expensive way to get paid.
   b. they cannot afford the costs of low-balance bank accounts.
   c. they are unfamiliar with banks.
   d. most employers will not pay in cash.

_____ 3. Purchasing furnishings through a rent-to-own business is
   a. more convenient than other methods.
   b. a wise investment.
   c. not available to low-income people.
   d. more expensive than outright purchases.

_____ 4. Because there are few large supermarkets in their areas, low-income people
   a. are forced to shop at more expensive convenience stores.
   b. bring their own carts when they shop.
   c. can save money by buying fewer items.
   d. lobby frequently for development by large stores.

_____ 5. Apartments are out of reach for many low-income people because
   a. they cannot come up with first and last months' rent and a security deposit.
   b. motels are more convenient.
   c. many landlords turn away low-income applicants.
   d. there are no available units due to high demand.

_____ 6. The main idea of paragraph 4 is that
   a. healthy cooking is an expensive proposition.
   b. trailer home kitchens are not intended for serious cooking.
   c. it is possible to eat well no matter where you live.
   d. fast-food restaurants should offer better choices.

_____ 7. Low-income people often use emergency rooms for medical care because
   a. medical care for children is free there.
   b. they do not have insurance.
   c. there are few doctors' offices in their neighborhoods.
   d. it is possible to give incorrect contact information and never have to pay the bills.

_____ 8. The author's tone is one of
   a. pity.   b. outrage.
   c. fear.   d. snobbishness.

_____ 9. The author believes that
   a. poor people can help themselves.
   b. most solutions have already been tried and failed.
   c. many solutions are too expensive to be possible.
   d. states should propose legislation that helps.

_____ 10. Which of the following is an opinion expressed by the author?

    a. low-income people pay higher interest rates when buying a car.

    b. low-income drivers pay more for car insurance.

    c. low-income people should not use pay-day loans.

    d. low-income people pay higher interest rates on mortgages.

USING CONTEXT AND WORD PARTS

_____ 11. In paragraph 2, the word **middling** means

    a. professional.   b. undefined.

    c. average.   d. unreported.

_____ 12. In paragraph 2, the word **hence** means

    a. later.   b. therefore.

    c. however.   d. unhappily.

_____ 13. In paragraph 3, the word **chastised** means

    a. scolded.   b. interrupted.

    c. blocked.   d. rewarded.

_____ 14. In paragraph 4, the word **sustenance** means

    a. food.   b. taxes.

    c. affordability.   d. boredom.

_____ 15. In paragraph 7, the word **predatory** means

    a. exploitative.   b. unruly.

    c. irrational.   d. conservative.

REVIEWING DIFFICULT VOCABULARY

Directions: _Complete each of the following sentences by inserting a word from the Vocabulary Preview on page 501 in the space provided._

16. Doctors agree that _____ is a serious medical condition.

17. The hockey players had several _____ during the game, which resulted in one of them being benched.

18. The accountant sneakily _____ off money from his client's account once a month.

19. Yolanda considered the _____ case of inheriting a large sum of money.

20. Because Sweden has _____, its citizens have fewer medical problems, and the country spends much less than the United States on health care.

QUESTIONS FOR DISCUSSION

1. How do you think the author felt as she lived the life of a low-income person?
2. What solutions are available for the ghetto taxes the author lists in the article?
3. How are low-income people thought of by others? Do they blame them, understand them, resent them, or something else?

ACTIVITIES FOR WRITING

1. Brainstorm a list of strategies a low-income person could use to begin to climb out of poverty.
2. Should the government take steps to eliminate the ghetto tax? Write a paragraph defending your position.
3. Explore the Web site of the Center for Responsible Lending at http://www.responsiblelending.org/. Write a fact sheet on predatory lending. Your audience is new college graduates.

ISSUE #3: THE RIGHT TO PRIVACY

HOLD IT RIGHT THERE AND DROP THAT CAMERA
Jo Napolitano

This article first appeared in the *New York Times*. Read the article to find out about the issues surrounding the use of cell phone cameras in public spaces.

Vocabulary Preview

These are some of the difficult words in this passage. The definitions here will help you if you can't figure out the meanings from the sentence context or word parts.

alderman (par. 1) a member of Chicago's city council

consensus (par. 3) agreement

American Civil Liberties Union (par. 3) a nonprofit organization that works to preserve the constitutionally guaranteed rights of Americans, especially those of free speech and privacy

transgressions (par. 5) actions that go beyond what is allowable

proactively (par. 7) taking steps in advance to deal with an anticipated problem

indiscretions (par. 12) moral errors

Nokia (par. 12) major wireless company that manufactures cell phones, multimedia systems, and business networks

---

1   "What grabbed my attention," said Alderman Edward M. Burke, "was that TV commercial when the guy is eating the pasta like a slob, and the girl sends a photo of him acting like a slob to the fiancee." The commercial, for Sprint PCS, was meant to convey the spontaneity and reach afforded by the wireless world's latest craze, the camera phone. But what Mr. Burke saw was the peril. "If I'm in a locker room changing clothes," he said, "there shouldn't be some pervert taking photos of me that could wind up on the Internet." Accordingly, as early as Dec. 17, the Chicago City Council is to vote on a proposal by Mr. Burke to ban the use of camera phones in public bathrooms, locker rooms and showers. There will be no provision to protect messy restaurant patrons. But Mr. Burke wanted to ban the use of camera phones in places where "the average Chicagoan would expect a reasonable right to privacy."

2   Not that tiny cameras couldn't be spirited into intimate settings before. But now it is a matter of numbers: only a year after camera phones began to appear in the United

States, there were six million of them, according to the market-research firm IDC. And when you marry a camera to a phone that can transmit the pictures instantly, legislation increasingly results. The Chicago proposal, setting a fine of $5 to $500 for offenders, echoes restrictions adopted in several smaller jurisdictions. What remains to be seen is how and when such laws will be enforced.

3   While privacy experts, municipalities and the American Civil Liberties Union agree that photos should not be taken without consent in public bathrooms and showers, there is no consensus on the best method of balancing the camera owner's rights with those of the unsuspecting citizen. The town of Seven Hills, Ohio, backed down less than two weeks after proposing a ban to avoid possibly costly court challenges. The mayor, David A. Bentkowski, said he would leave the matter to state and federal legislation.

4   Trying to distinguish between a camera phone and any other cell phone has also complicated matters. The Elk Grove Park District in suburban Chicago enacted a ban in November that covered the possession of any cell phone—not just camera phones—in park-owned restrooms, locker rooms and showers. "There is no reason to have a cell phone while you're changing and showering," said Ron Nunes, one of the park district's commissioners. "I'd rather protect the children and the public more than someone who wants to call home and see what's for dinner." Fresh in the town's memory was a 2001 incident in which a man used a fiber-optic camera to secretly take pictures of children in a park shower.

5   So far, there have been no complaints in Elk Grove about cell phone transgressions. But Mr. Nunes concedes, "It's darn near impossible to enforce." There will be no searches of bags, he said, and park officials will not summon the police if a cell phone is found in a restricted area. "We're not going to arrest someone for making a phone call in a locker room," he said. "We're counting on people to just say, 'Shut it off.' " Though they are permitted in gym areas, patrons say they often leave their phones in the car when they work out there because they usually have to use the changing room first, where the phones are not permitted. Nancy Funteas, a business owner, said she was worried about missing calls while at the park district gym. "You feel protected in the locker room, but out here if you need it for business it's not a good idea," she said after finishing an upper-body workout. Desi Leyba, a 30-year-old gym member, admitted: "Sometimes I forget and I bring it in. I wonder if they're going to make a case of it."

6   L. Richard Fischer, a Washington lawyer who deals with privacy issues, said the park district's ban goes too far. "People have to pass laws very carefully and recognize there is a broad but flexible standard of reasonable expectation of privacy," he said. "You have to do it very selectively or you really are treading on people's rights." Banning cell phones from some locations could invite lawsuits from people who might have to use a phone in an emergency and be unable to summon help, he said. "What they've done is go to the extreme," he said. "They've threatened the rights of the majority of people to try to control the conduct of a few, and that's just beyond the balance." He added that the only way to deter people from taking photos of others was to punish them for taking surreptitious pictures rather than banning the phones.

7   Des Peres, Mo., a St. Louis suburb, passed a more limited and specific law in September that bans taking photos of a person who is partly unclothed without consent in an area where they should expect privacy. "The ordinance would provide the city with some teeth for the ability to prosecute someone," said Jason McConachie, the assistant city administrator, adding, "I don't believe there is any way to proactively enforce it, like putting police officers in locker rooms." He said the city would help an aggrieved citizen pursue legal action against someone for taking pictures in a restricted area without consent—an occurrence as yet unreported.

8   Some courthouses have extended existing bans on picture taking to include camera phones. Representative Michael G. Oxley of Ohio felt that the federal government should draft its own provision, so he and a fellow Ohio Republican, Senator Mike DeWine, broadened the language in a law proposed by Mr. Oxley, the Video Voyeurism Prevention Act of 2003, to include camera phones. "I think if we can nip it in the bud, we can avoid a lot of embarrassing situations or gross invasions of privacy," Mr. Oxley said. "Our bill would only apply to federal property, but it would spur the states to pass similar legislation." The law would prohibit the use of camera phones in restrooms in federal park districts and federal buildings. Breaking the law would result in a fine, up to a year in prison, or both.

9   Chris J. Hoofnagle, legislative counsel for the Electronic Privacy Information Center, a nonprofit group in Washington, acknowledged that the proliferation of camera phones had helped give new life to "up skirt" or "down blouse" photography. "Clearly, this is going to get worse," Mr. Hoofnagle said. "There is a remarkable lack of sensitivity to the subjects of the photographs." But he said changing the norms of society, rather than its laws, was likely to be a more effective response.

10   Barry Steinhardt, director of the year-old technology and liberty program for the A.C.L.U., suggested that the camera-phone quandary reflected a larger problem: that technology has developed at the speed of light and American law is "stuck in the Stone Ages." "The rest of the developed world have fairly advanced laws that incorporate privacy and fair information that we invented in the 1960's but didn't implement," he said. While he would not comment on specific measures in Chicago and elsewhere, he said that privacy laws were justifiable but had to be very specific. What the United States needs, he added, is to establish a privacy commissioner to enforce existing rules and investigate the need for new ones. Technology for surveillance and data gathering is "becoming more powerful every day," he said. "In the U.S., our response to this has been to bury our heads in the sand and say, 'It'll all work out.' "

11   Meanwhile, cameras are becoming not only more numerous among the nation's 160 million cell phones, but also more capable. Alex Slawsby, an analyst with IDC, said that by next year the typical camera phone sold in the United States would have a resolution of at least one megapixel, about three times the current average—doing wonders, no doubt, for the rendering of sloppy restaurant patrons.

12   Whatever indiscretions arise in a camera phone's use, the makers plead, don't blame the equipment. "There are people who would use things they shouldn't," said Keith

Nowak, a spokesman for Nokia. "There is not a product made that somebody somewhere with a good enough imagination couldn't figure out how to misuse."

━━ ▪ ━━

Directions: *Select the letter of the choice that best completes each of the following statements.*

CHECKING YOUR COMPREHENSION

_____ 1. The main point of the entire selection is

    a. there is growing concern about the use of cell phone cameras in public spaces and the violation of privacy.

    b. legislation against cell phone cameras should be enforced.

    c. cell phone cameras should be banned from public places.

    d. not enough has been done to protect Americans from cell phone camera users.

_____ 2. Which of the following is *not* true about the Elk Grove situation?

    a. People cannot have any kind of cell phone in a park-owned locker room.

    b. Children were the victims of a man using a camera in park-owned showers.

    c. Locker room users are leaving their cell phones in their cars.

    d. The new law is being enforced frequently and strictly.

_____ 3. According to the article, the Video Voyeurism Prevention Act of 2003 would

    a. prohibit the use of video cameras in federal courtrooms.

    b. ban camera phones from restrooms in federal buildings.

    c. penalize violators with fines from $5 to $500.

    d. require states to enact similar legislation.

_____ 4. One concern not mentioned in the article is
   a. the lack of sensitivity to the subjects of photographs.
   b. a person's right to expect a reasonable amount of privacy in a public setting.
   c. whether private establishments should make rules about camera phone use.
   d. the rights of camera phone owners.

_____ 5. The Nokia spokesperson feels that
   a. cameras will have such high resolution in the future that offensive pictures will be even more common.
   b. cell phone manufacturers should take more responsibility for how their products are used.
   c. federal legislators are not doing enough to protect the privacy of Americans.
   d. people will come up with ways to misuse a product no matter what laws are in place.

_____ 6. The overall tone of this article is
   a. alarmist.   b. informative.
   c. indifferent.   d. angry.

_____ 7. The author's primary purpose is to
   a. offer a personal opinion on a current topic of interest.
   b. argue in favor of a particular position.
   c. make a comparison.
   d. explore a problem.

_____ 8. The main idea of paragraph 6 is that
   a. one lawyer thinks that some laws go too far in their restrictions.
   b. people will not be able to call 911 for help if they cannot use a cell phone in a park.
   c. the majority is being punished.
   d. cell phones should not be banned; taking pictures with cell phones should be banned.

9. The author began the article with Alderman Burke's experience in order to
   a. present an opposing viewpoint.
   b. establish a time frame for the article.
   c. grab the reader's attention with an interesting example.
   d. make a comparison.

10. Fischer and Hoofnagle would agree that
   a. nothing can be done to stop people from taking inappropriate photos.
   b. camera phones don't take inappropriate photos; people take inappropriate photos.
   c. only federal legislation will solve the camera phone problem.
   d. not enough has been done to stop privacy violations.

USING CONTEXT AND WORD PARTS

11. In paragraph 1, the word **provision** means
   a. change.   b. notice.
   c. legal clause.   d. idea.

12. In paragraph 2, the word **spirited** means
   a. carried away.   b. openly brought.
   c. banned.   d. animated.

13. In paragraph 2, the word **echoes** means
   a. sounds.   b. imitates.
   c. authorizes.   d. distinguishes.

14. In paragraph 6, the word **surreptitious** means
   a. silly.   b. inappropriate.
   c. large amounts.   d. secret.

15. In paragraph 7, the word **aggrieved** means
   a. sad.   b. wronged.
   c. angry.   d. frustrated.

REVIEWING DIFFICULT VOCABULARY

Directions: *Complete each of the following sentences by inserting a word from the Vocabulary Preview on page 507 in the space provided.*

16. The firefighters acted _____ to prevent the collapse of the burning building.

17. The state representatives reached a _____ about the state budget and finally passed it.

18. The school board reviewed the high school seniors' _____ and decided upon appropriate punishment.

19. The man's wife accused him of a variety of _____ during their marriage and was going to file for divorce.

20. The immigrant who was being held against his will with no charges filed against him contacted the _____.

QUESTIONS FOR DISCUSSION

1. Discuss the use of cell phones in public places. Where on campus should they be used or not used? What about camera phones?

2. Consider the taking of photographs in public places. How would you feel if your photo were taken without your permission? How do you think celebrities feel? Should the rules be different for celebrities?

3. Discuss with your classmates how you could find out more information about some of the bans and legislation mentioned in the article. Do some follow-up work to find out what happened in these communities since the article was written. Ask your librarian for help, if necessary.

ACTIVITIES FOR WRITING

1. Write a policy for camera phone use for various places on your campus.

2. Brainstorm a list of ways camera phone use could be controlled and limited.

3. Read an article about a different use for camera phones at http://yaleglobal.yale.edu/display.article?id=6075 and then write a paragraph describing your reaction to it.

ISSUE #4

ISSUE #4: VOTING RIGHTS AND RESPONSIBILITIES

WHETHER TO VOTE: A CITIZEN'S FIRST CHOICE

George C. Edwards III, Martin P. Wattenberg, and Robert L. Lineberry

This reading is taken from the "Elections and Voting Behavior" chapter of the book *Government in America*. Read this textbook excerpt to discover why voting is important, how voting in the United States compares to other countries, and how technology may change the voting process.

Vocabulary Preview

These are some of the difficult words in this passage. The definitions here will help you if you can't figure out the meanings from the sentence context or word parts.

virtually (par. 1) almost but not quite

proportionately (par. 2) comparatively

electoral (par. 2) having to do with voting

incentive (par. 5) reason to act

impelled (par. 6) urged on, forced to act

stimulus (par. 9) something that spurs on action

referendum (par. 12) a public vote on a specific question or issue

Suffrage: The legal right to vote, extended to African Americans by the Fifteenth Amendment, to women by the Nineteenth Amendment, and to people over the age of 18 by the Twenty-sixth Amendment

1   Over two centuries of American electoral history include greatly expanded **suffrage** — the right to vote. In the election of 1800, only property-owning White males over the age of 21 were typically allowed to vote. Now virtually everyone over the age of 18—male or female, White or non-White, rich or poor—has the right to vote. The two major exceptions concern noncitizens and convicted criminals. No state currently permits residents who are not citizens to vote. Some immigrant groups feel that this ought to at least be changed at the local level. State law varies widely when it comes to crime and voting: 46 states deny prisoners the right to vote, 32 states extend the ban to people on parole, and 10 states impose a lifetime ban on convicted felons.

2   Interestingly, as the right to vote has been extended, proportionately fewer of those eligible have chosen to exercise that right. In the past 100 years, the 80 percent turnout in the 1896 election was the high point of electoral participation. In 2004, only 55 percent of the adult population voted in the presidential election (see Figure A).

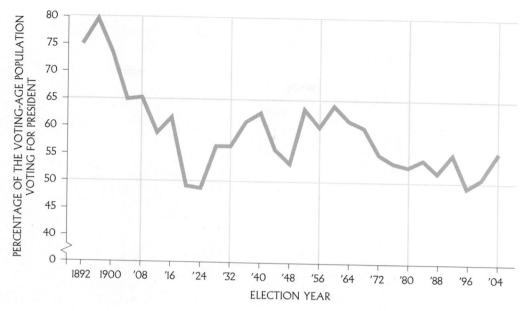

FIGURE A   The Decline of Turnout: 1892–2004

Sources: For data up to 1968, *Historical Statistics of the United States* (Washington, D.C.: Government Printing Office, 1975), part 2, 1071. For 1972–1988, *Statistical Abstract of the United States*, 1990 (Washington, D.C.: Government Printing Office, 1990), 264. Subsequent years from census reports and authors' calculations.

Deciding Whether to Vote

3   Realistically, when over 100 million people vote in a presidential election, as they did in 2004, the chance of one vote affecting the outcome is very, very slight. Once in a while, of course, an election is decided by a small number of votes, as occurred in Florida in 2000. It is more likely, however, that you will be struck by lightning during your lifetime than participate in an election decided by a single vote.

4   Not only does your vote probably not make much difference to the outcome, but voting is somewhat costly. You have to spend some of your valuable time becoming informed, making up your mind, and getting to the polls. If you carefully calculate your time and energy, you might rationally decide that the costs of voting outweigh the benefits. Indeed, the most frequent response given by nonvoters in the 2000 Census Bureau survey on turnout was that they could not take time off from work or school that day. Some scholars have therefore proposed that one of the easiest ways to increase American turnout levels would be to move election day to Saturday or make it a holiday.

5   Economist Anthony Downs, in his model of democracy, tries to explain why a rational person would ever bother to vote. He argues that rational people vote if they believe that the policies of one party will bring more benefits than the policies of the other party. Thus people who see policy differences between the parties are more likely to join the ranks of voters. If you are an environmentalist and you expect the Democrats to pass

■ *Young people have one of the lowest rates of election turnout. Music stars like P. Diddy have tried to change this by actively participating in events that encourage young people to vote.*

more environmental legislation than the Republicans, then you have an additional incentive to go to the polls. On the other hand, if you are truly indifferent—that is, if you see no difference whatsoever between the two parties—you may rationally decide to abstain.

political efficacy: 6
The belief that one's political participation really matters—that one's vote can actually make a difference.

Another reason why many people vote is that they have a high sense of **political efficacy**—the belief that ordinary people can influence the government. Efficacy is measured by asking people to agree or disagree with statements, such as "I don't think public officials care much what people like me think." Those who lack strong feelings of efficacy are being quite rational in staying home on Election Day because they don't think they can make a difference. Yet even some of these people will vote anyway, simply to support democratic government. In this case, people are impelled to vote by a sense of civic duty. The benefit from doing one's **civic duty** is the long-term contribution made toward preserving democracy.

civic duty: The belief that in order to support democratic government, a citizen should always vote.

Why Turnout in the United States Is So Low Compared to Other Countries

7   Despite living in a culture that encourages participation, Americans have a woefully low turnout rate compared to other democracies. There are several reasons given for Americans' abysmally low turnout rate. Probably the reason most often cited is

the American requirement of voter registration. The governments of many, but not all, other democracies take the responsibility of seeing to it that all their eligible citizens are on the voting lists. In America, the responsibility for registration lies solely with the individual. If we were to be like the Scandinavian countries and have the government take care of registering every eligible citizen, no doubt our turnout rate would be higher.

8   A second difference between the United States and other countries is that the American government asks citizens to vote far more often. Whereas the typical European voter may be called upon to cast two or three ballots in a four-year period, many Americans are faced with a dozen or more separate elections in the space of four years. Furthermore, Americans are expected to vote for a much wider range of political offices. With 1 elected official for every 442 citizens and elections held somewhere virtually every week, it is no wonder that it is so difficult to get Americans to the polls. It is probably no coincidence that the one European country that has a lower turnout rate—Switzerland—has also overwhelmed its citizens with voting opportunities, typically asking people to vote three times every year.

9   Finally, the stimulus to vote is low in the United States because the choices offered Americans are not as stark as in other countries. This is because the United States is quite unusual in that it has always lacked a major left-wing, socialist party. When European voters go to the polls, they are deciding on whether their country will be run by parties with socialist goals or by conservative (and in some cases religious) parties. The consequences of their vote for redistribution of income and the scope of government are far greater than the ordinary American voter can imagine.

Registering and Voting by E-Mail?

10   Future reform designed to increase turnout may well focus on conducting elections through e-mail. Although modern technology is widely available, Americans have not harnessed much of it to improve democracy. Though many precincts now use computer touch screens to record votes, the high-tech age has not yet made much of an impact on the voting process. There is good reason to expect that this will change in the twenty-first century.

11   The development of the personal computer and the World Wide Web are likely to facilitate the process of voter registration. Already, one can go to the website of the Federal Election Commission (http:www.fec.gov/votregis/vr.htm) and download the "National Mail Voter Registration Form." Twenty-two states currently accept copies of this application printed from the computer image, signed by the applicant, and mailed in the old-fashioned way. As e-mail becomes ever more popular and "snail mail" fades into a method reserved for packages, the entire voter registration process may someday be conducted mostly through electronic means. In an age where personal computers in the

home are nearly as common as television sets are today, this technology would clearly make registering to vote more user-friendly.

12   If people can register by computer, the next step is voting by e-mail. A growing trend in the Pacific Coast states has been voting by mail. In 1998, Oregon voters approved a referendum to eliminate traditional polling places and conduct all future elections by mail. In California, approximately 25 percent of the votes cast currently come in via the post office. Again, as e-mail takes the place of regular mail, why not have people cast their votes through cyberspace?

13   Voting through the Internet would be less costly for the state, as well as easier for the average citizen—assuming that computer literacy reaches near-universal proportions sometime in the future. The major concerns, of course, would be ensuring that no one votes more than once and preserving the confidentiality of the vote. These security concerns are currently being addressed by some of the world's top computer programmers, as commercial enterprises look toward using the Internet to conduct business. If the technology can be perfected to allow trillions of dollars of business to be conducted via the Internet, then it seems reasonable that similar problems can be overcome with regard to the voting process.

14   Whether these possible developments will improve democracy in America is debatable. Making voting more user-friendly should encourage turnout, but people will still have to be interested enough in the elections of the future to send in their e-mail ballots. If old-style polling places are relegated to the history books and everyone votes electronically in the convenience of their own homes, the sense of community on Election Day may be lost. This loss could lead to even lower turnout. You be the policymaker: Do the benefits of voting by e-mail outweigh the potential costs?

Directions: *Select the letter of the choice that best completes each of the following statements.*

CHECKING YOUR COMPREHENSION

_____ 1. The central thesis of this selection is that
    a. voting is a right that not everyone chooses to exercise.
    b. computer voting will increase turnout.
    c. voter turnout in the United States is low.
    d. people in other countries are more inclined to vote.

_____ 2. Which group cannot vote in any state?
    a. convicted felons   b. prisoners
    c. people on parole   d. noncitizens

3. As more types of people have been given the right to vote, the voter turnout has
   a. decreased.
   b. increased.
   c. stayed the same.
   d. It is impossible to know how the voter turnout has been affected.

4. The Florida 2000 election (paragraph 3) refers to a
   a. gubernatorial election.   b. senatorial election.
   c. presidential election.   d. judicial election.

5. According to economist Anthony Downs,
   a. the voter registration process is too complicated for the average citizen.
   b. people vote if they perceive a difference between parties.
   c. environmentalists vote more than other groups.
   d. voters only consider issues that are important to them.

6. The author's primary purpose is to
   a. present information on voting history, statistics, and innovations.
   b. persuade readers to exercise their right to vote.
   c. explain why voter turnout is lower in the United States than in Europe.
   d. argue that today's citizens do not deserve the right to vote.

7. Of the following statements from the reading, which is an opinion?
   a. "Interestingly, as the right to vote has been extended, proportionally fewer of those eligible have chosen to exercise that right." (paragraph 2)
   b. "If we were to be like the Scandinavian countries and have the government take care of registering every eligible citizen, no doubt our turnout rate would be higher." (paragraph 7)
   c. "State law varies widely when it comes to crime and voting." (paragraph 1)
   d. "Some scholars have therefore proposed that one of the easiest ways to increase American turnout levels would be

to move election day to Saturday or make it a holiday."
(paragraph 4)

8. The authors compare the United States with other countries
   a. to embarrass American voters.
   b. to explain why American voter turnout may be low.
   c. to describe places to which civic-minded Americans might want to move.
   d. to prove that no country is perfect when it comes to voter turnout.

9. The main idea of paragraph 4 is that
   a. Election Day should be a national holiday.
   b. people might not vote because it takes too much time and energy.
   c. not everyone can take time off from work to vote.
   d. elections decided by one vote are very rare.

10. Overall, the authors' attitude toward voter turnout in the United States seems to be
   a. indifferent.   b. hopeful.
   c. concerned.   d. amused.

USING CONTEXT AND WORD PARTS

11. In paragraph 1, the word **suffrage** means
   a. suffering.   b. the right to vote.
   c. politics.   d. opportunities.

12. In paragraph 4, the word **calculate** means
   a. subtract.   b. estimate.
   c. consider.   d. test.

13. In paragraph 7, the word **woefully** means
   a. encouragingly.   b. remarkably.
   c. surprisingly.   d. distressingly.

14. In paragraph 10, the word **harnessed** means
   a. ridden.   b. displayed.
   c. directed.   d. withdrawn.

_____ 15. In paragraph 12, the word **cast** means
     a. delivered.   b. submitted.
     c. withheld.   d. removed.

REVIEWING DIFFICULT VOCABULARY

Directions: *Complete each of the following sentences by inserting a word from the Vocabulary Preview on page 514 in the space provided.*

16. The promise of extra credit provided a great _____ for the students to attend the guest lecturer's speech.

17. After the thunderstorm, _____ all the lights in the city went out.

18. Being laid off from work was the _____ Rick needed to go back to school.

19. The city council held a _____ about how many terms of office the mayor may hold.

20. After learning that the crime victim had died, Rosa was _____ to come forward and report a disturbance she had witnessed the previous day.

QUESTIONS FOR DISCUSSION

1. Discuss the situation of low voter turnout. Why do you think more eligible Americans do not vote? What do you think would boost voter turnout?

2. Discuss whether or not you have voted in an election and what reasons were behind your decision to vote or not.

3. Interview someone from another country about voting behavior. Report your findings to the class.

ACTIVITES FOR WRITING

1. Pick a target group. Discuss strategies aimed at that group encouraging them to vote.

2. Write a paragraph that defends your position on whether convicted criminals should be permitted to vote.

3. Read this short article on the findings of one study on voter behavior at http://www.princeton.edu/main/news/archive/S11/83/38S10/index.xml?section=topstoris. Write a paragraph on the extent to which you think physical appearance matters in a political race.

ISSUE #5: THE ENVIRONMENT AT RISK

AIR POLLUTION AND GLOBAL WARMING
James M. Henslin

Taken from a textbook on social problems, this selection discusses how air pollution is affecting global warming, and considers the debate among scientists about how humans really are affecting the planet.

ISSUE #5

Vocabulary Preview

These are some of the difficult words in this passage. The definitions here will help you if you can't figure out the meanings from the sentence context or word parts.

accumulates (par. 1) collects or gathers

derived (par. 2) obtained from

refineries (par. 3) facilities where oil is used to produce gasoline

incineration (par. 4) burning to ashes

stratosphere (par. 5) region of the earth's atmosphere, six to ten miles above the earth's surface

industrial revolution (par. 7) period of history in the late 1700s when machinery began to replace human labor

hieroglyphics (par. 9) a writing system that uses pictures

Three Main Sources of Air Pollution:

1   In 1952, a "killer smog" settled on London. In just 5 days, 4,000 people were dead. People became fearful. Slowly, facts about air pollution emerged. Air pollution is essentially a poison that accumulates in the human body. Besides causing eye, nose, and throat irritations, it causes bronchitis, emphysema, and lung cancer, which lead to a slow, agonizing death.

1. Burning of Fossil Fuels

2   What causes air pollution? The main cause is the burning of fossil fuels, that is, substances derived from living things—wood, coal, petroleum, and natural gas. To produce our electricity and the goods we consume, power plants and factories pour pollutants into the air. The worst polluter, however, is the internal combustion engine. The exhausts of cars, trucks, and buses emit poisons—sulphur dioxide, nitrogen, oxide, hydrocarbons, and carbon monoxide. The vehicles also leave behind a **carcinogenic** (cancer-causing) trail from the asbestos particles in their brake linings.

3   On occasion, pollution is the result of deliberate, spiteful acts. The most dramatic example occurred in 1991, when Iraqi troops ignited 600 oil wells, storage tanks, and refineries in Kuwait. The soot from the fires circled the globe.

Waste incineration is a second major source of air pollution. Burning plastics is especially damaging to our health because it creates PCBs (polychlorinated biphenyls), a potent toxin. Plastics are not **biodegradable;** that is, they do not disintegrate after being exposed to normal bacteria. Even steel rusts, but plastics endure almost indefinitely. Consequently, we burn them.

A third source of air pollution is fluorocarbon gases. These gases are suspected of damaging the **ozone shield,** the layer in the earth's upper stratosphere that screens out much of the sun's ultraviolet rays. High-intensity ultraviolet radiation harms most life forms. In humans, it causes skin cancer and cataracts; in plants, it reduces growth and causes genetic mutations. When the danger of fluorocarbon gases was realized, their use in aerosol cans, refrigerators, and air conditioners was reduced or eliminated. The damage to the ozone is expected to be repaired.

Air pollution may lead to what is known as the **greenhouse effect**. Carbon dioxide and water vapor form an invisible blanket around the globe that allows the sun's light to enter, but traps the heat. Without this blanket, temperatures would plummet, and the earth would be unable to support life. If the blanket is too thick, however, it traps too much heat and has devastating consequences for our environment.

The blanket seems to be growing thicker. Because of the industrial revolution, we burn more fossil fuels than humans did in the past, releasing more carbon dioxide into the air. In effect, the carbon dioxide blocks the atmospheric window through which our earth's daily heat escapes to outer space. The increased temperature of the earth is known as **global warming.**

Peru's 7.5. mile long mountain glacier, the Quelcayya, is the world's largest tropical glacier. Sitting at 18,600 feet above sea level, it often gets snow but never rain. The Quelcayya is shrinking by about 100 feet a year. As the ice receded, researchers discovered a moss-like plant that had been frozen in the glacier. Carbon dating showed the plant to be over 5,000 years old.

To get an idea of how extensive today's global warming is, consider this: The last time this plant wasn't covered with snow and ice, the Egyptians were busy inventing *hieroglyphics.*

If global warming continues, some scientists say that it will disrupt the earth's climate and biological system. If so, we can expect these consequences:

1. Climate boundaries will move about 400 miles north, resulting in a longer growing season in the United States, Canada, and Russia.

2. The oceans will rise about two feet as the polar ice caps melt.

3. The world's shorelines will erode (Most of the beaches on the U.S. east coast will be gone in a generation.)

4. Some small island nations will be destroyed, and the United States will lose an area of land the size of Massachusetts.

5. Coastal fisheries will be damaged.

6. Summers will be hotter, increasing the demand for electricity.
7. There will be more forest fires, droughts, floods, and outbreaks of pests.
8. There will be outbreaks of diseases—malaria, dengue fever, cholera.
9. Many species of plants and animals will become extinct.
10. Problems in the Least Industrialized Nations will be worse, as they have fewer resources to meet the crisis.

11   The Maldives are a little island nation of just 270,000 people. Their maximum altitude is about five feet above sea level. With the threat of the polar ice caps melting and the oceans rising, the ministry of tourism considered making their national slogan, "Come see us while we're still here."

Differences of Opinion

12   Because the earth goes through periods of warming and cooling (it was an ice age that formed the glaciers that once covered huge parts of North America), scientists disagree on whether global warming is due to natural or human causes. They point out that during the past 3,000 years the earth has had five extended periods that were warmer than today. Atmospheric temperatures are rising, but they have been rising for 300 years (from a cold period called "the Little Ice Age"), and current temperatures remain below the 3,000 year average. Some even conclude that if carbon dioxide increases, it may *lower* sea levels. A warmer earth would increase evaporation from the warmer oceans, and more rain would fall over Greenland and the Antarctic. This would thicken the polar ice caps, removing vast amounts of water from the oceans.

13   In 1998, 15,000 scientists signed a petition asking that the United States revoke the Kyoto agreements to cut emissions of carbon dioxide. The petition was accompanied by a letter from a former president of the National Academy of Sciences. He said that higher carbon dioxide did not pose a threat to the climate, and that it might actually benefit the world. More carbon dioxide would increase plant growth and be "a wonderful and unexpected gift from the industrial revolution." Confused, members of Congress called the National Academy of Sciences; its current president assured them that the greenhouse effect poses a threat to the world.

14   This argument has heated up science: One side claims that the case for global warming is overblown, whereas those convinced about global warming call the other side silly. Because scientists who examine the same data disagree, we will have to await more data.

Changes in U.S. Air Pollution

15   With today's pollution control devices and the agitation of environmentalists, is our air getting cleaner? There have been some striking improvements. The change in the amount of lead in our air is stunning; it is now only 2 percent of what it was in 1970. The primary reason for this welcome change is lead-free gasoline. But results are mixed. We now have slightly more nitrogen dioxide in our air than in 1970. Certainly the picture is far from rosy. Our air still contains 188 chemicals that have been linked to cancer, birth defects, and other serious health problems.

━━ ▪ ━━

Directions: *Select the letter of the choice that best completes each of the following statements.*

CHECKING YOUR COMPREHENSION

_____ 1. The author's main purpose for writing this selection is to
   a. expose the dangers of burning plastics.
   b. argue that we need stricter air pollution regulations.
   c. demonstrate how to reduce internal combustion engine emissions.
   d. show how air pollution affects the biosphere.

_____ 2. Air pollution can be deadly because it
   a. decreases visibility, causing automobile accidents.
   b. is a poison that accumulates in the body.
   c. is linked to asthma.
   d. is difficult to detect.

_____ 3. The primary cause of air pollution is
   a. burning fossil fuels.   b. the greenhouse effect.
   c. waste incineration.   d. landfills.

_____ 4. Internal combustion engines can be found in all of the following except
   a. cars.   b. buses.
   c. computers.   d. trucks.

_____ 5. Plastics are burned because
   a. they are biodegradable.
   b. they take up so much space in landfills.
   c. that is the safest way to dispose of them.
   d. they do not disintegrate on their own.

_____ 6. The ozone shield is important because it
   a. creates a blanket that holds oxygen in the atmosphere.
   b. screens out ultraviolet rays from the sun.
   c. contains gases needed to prevent evaporation of the oceans.
   d. is an important component of the greenhouse effect.

_____ 7. An increase in carbon dioxide in the atmosphere is believed to cause temperatures to
   a. rise.
   b. fall.
   c. rise during the day and fall at night.
   d. remain the same.

_____ 8. The main idea of paragraph 5 is that
   a. the stratosphere is rapidly deteriorating.
   b. ultraviolet radiation is damaging the ozone shield.
   c. fluorocarbon gases may damage the ozone shield.
   d. the ozone shield is permanently damaged.

_____ 9. The sentence, "Come see us while we're still here" (paragraph 11), means
   a. because of rising oceans, the country of the Maldives may not be there for much longer.
   b. global warming has reduced tourism costs in the Maldives.
   c. air pollution makes the Maldives difficult to see from the air.
   d. due to air pollution, the entire population of the Maldives may soon move elsewhere.

_____ 10. The author believes that
   a. carbon dioxide emissions are damaging the earth.
   b. carbon dioxide emissions are beneficial to the earth.
   c. more data are needed to determine whether carbon dioxide emissions are harmful or beneficial.
   d. carbon dioxide emissions are harmful to some parts of the earth and beneficial to others.

USING CONTEXT AND WORD PARTS

_____ 11. In paragraph 4, the word **biodegradable** means
   a. environmentally friendly.
   b. decaying through natural processes.
   c. fluorocarbon based.
   d. not radioactive.

_____ 12. In paragraph 6, the word **plummet** means
   a. adjust slowly.   b. normalize.
   c. increase rapidly.   d. fall quickly.

_____ 13. In paragraph 10, the word **erode** means
   a. wear away   b. increase.
   c. rebuild.   d. change chemically.

_____ 14. In paragraph 14, the word **overblown** means
   a. underestimated.   b. too detailed.
   c. exaggerated.   d. reduced.

_____ 15. In paragraph 15, the word **striking** means
   a. impressive.   b. relentless.
   c. dangerous.   d. questionable.

REVIEWING DIFFICULT VOCABULARY

Directions: _Complete each of the following sentences by inserting a word from the Vocabulary Preview on page 523 in the space provided._

16. The mummy's marble coffin was covered with colorful

   _____.

17. The trophy _____ dust as it sits untouched on the shelf.

18. The oil-producing nation of Kuwait has many _____ within it.

19. The cotton gin is considered to be the first important invention in the period known as the _____.

20. Although the movie was _____ from the book of the same title, they have different endings.

QUESTIONS FOR DISCUSSION

1. Why do you think there is no clear consensus among scientists about the effects of carbon dioxide emissions? What kind of information is needed to come to a conclusion?

2. How could humans adapt if global warming does continue and changes the earth?

3. How can more people become informed about the dangers of global warming? What would you do to increase awareness?

ACTIVITIES FOR WRITING

1. Write a paragraph describing ways you can personally help reduce air pollution.

2. Explain in a paragraph why you think people are or are not reluctant to take steps to reduce air pollution.

3. Explore the Web site for the film *An Inconvenient Truth*: http://www.cli-matecrisis.net/. Write a paragraph that explains your beliefs and opinions on the topic of global warming.

ISSUE #6: SPECIES LOSS

THE BIODIVERSITY CRISIS

Neil A. Campbell, Jane B. Reece, and Eric J. Simon

Taken from a college biology textbook, *Essential Biology*, this excerpt discusses extinction and its implications for humans and for the planet.

Vocabulary Preview

These are some of the difficult words in this passage. The definitions here will help you if you can't figure out the meanings from the sentence context or word parts.

Cretaceous (par. 1) a geologic time period in which the dinosaurs became extinct

dexterous (par. 1) physically skillful in the use of hands

biodiversity (par. 2) variety of animal and plant life within a system

biosphere (par. 3) the section of the earth that supports life

habitats (par. 4) natural conditions and environments in which plants and animals live

degradation (par. 8) wearing away of land

1   The seventh mass extinction in the history of life is well under way. Previous episodes, including the Cretaceous crunch that claimed the dinosaurs and many other groups, pale by comparison. The current mass extinction is both broader and faster, extinguishing species at a rate at least 50 times faster than just a few centuries ago. And unlike past poundings of biodiversity, which were triggered mainly by physical processes, such as climate change caused by volcanism or asteroid crashes, this latest mass extinction is due to the evolution of a single species—a big-brained, manually dexterous, environment-manipulating toolmaker that has named itself *Homo sapiens*.

2   We do not know the full scale of the biodiversity crisis in terms of a species "body count," for we are undoubtedly losing species that we didn't even know existed; the 1.7 million species that have been identified probably represent less than 10% of the true number of species. However, there are already enough signs to know that the biosphere is in deep trouble:

- About 11% of the 9,040 known bird species in the world are endangered. In the past 40 years, population densities of migratory songbirds in the mid-Atlantic United States dropped 50%.

- Of the approximately 20,000 known plant species in the United States, over 600 are very close to extinction.

FIGURE A   A hundred heartbeats from extinction.
The Philippine eagle is one of the many members of what E. O. Wilson calls the Hundred Heartbeat Club, species with fewer than 100 individuals remaining on Earth.

- Throughout the world, 970 tree species have been classified as critically endangered. At least 5 of those species are down to fewer than a half dozen surviving individuals.
- About 20% of the known freshwater fishes in the world have either become extinct during historical times or are seriously threatened. The toil on amphibians and reptiles has been almost as great.
- Harvard biologist Edward O. Wilson, a renowned scholar of biodiversity, has compiled what he grimly calls the Hundred Heartbeat Club. The species that belong are those animals that number fewer than 100 individuals and so are only that many heartbeats away from extinction (Figure A).
- Several researchers estimate that at the current rate of destruction, over half of all plant and animal species will be gone by the end of this new century.

3   Unless we can reverse the current trend of increasing loss of biodiversity, we will leave our children and grandchildren a biosphere that is much less interesting and much more biologically impoverished.

The Three Main Causes of the Biodiversity Crisis

4   **Habitat Destruction** Human alteration of habitats poses the single greatest threat to biodiversity throughout the biosphere (Figure B, p. 532). Assaults on diversity at the

FIGURE B   Habitat destruction: clearing a rain forest

ecosystem level result from the expansion of agriculture to feed the burgeoning human population, urban development, forestry, mining, and environmental pollution. The amount of human-altered land surface is approaching 50%, and we use over half of all accessible surface fresh water. Some of the most productive aquatic habitats in estuaries and intertidal wetlands are also prime locations for commercial and residential developments. The loss of marine habitats is also severe, especially in coastal areas and coral reefs.

5   **Introduced Species** Ranking second behind habitat loss as a cause of the biodiversity crisis is human introduction of exotic (non-native) species that eliminate native species through predation or competition. For example, if your campus is in an urban setting, there is a good chance that the birds you see most often as you walk between classes are starlings, rock doves (often called "pigeons"), and house sparrows—all introduced species that have replaced native birds in many areas of North America. One of the largest rapid-extinction events yet recorded is the loss of freshwater fishes in Lake Victoria in East Africa. About 200 of the 300 species of native fishes, found nowhere else but in this lake, have become extinct since Europeans introduced a non-native predator, the Nile perch, in the 1960s (Figure C).

6   **Overexploitation** As a third major threat to biodiversity, overexploitation of wildlife often compounds problems of shrinking habitat and introduced species. Animal species whose numbers have been drastically reduced by excessive commercial harvest or sport hunting include whales, the American bison, Galápagos tortoises, and numerous fishes.

FIGURE C Introduced species: Nile perch

Many fish stocks in the ocean have been overfished to levels that cannot sustain further human exploitation (Figure D, p. 534). In addition to the commercially important species, members of many other species are often killed by harvesting methods; for example, dolphins, marine turtles, and seabirds are caught in fishing nets, and countless numbers of invertebrates are killed by marine trawls (big nets). An expanding, often illegal world trade in wildlife products, including rhinocerous horns, elephant tusks, and grizzly bear gallbladders, also threatens many species.

Why Biodiversity Matters

7   Why should we care about the loss of biodiversity? First of all, we depend on many other species for food, clothing, shelter, oxygen, soil fertility—the list goes on and on. In the United States, 25% of all prescriptions dispensed from pharmacies contain substances derived from plants. For instance, two drugs effective against Hodgkin disease and certain other forms of cancer come from the rosy periwinkle, a flowering plant native to the island of Madagascar. Unfortunately most of Madagascar's species are in serious trouble. People have lived on the island for only about 2,000 years, but in that time, Madagascar has lost 80% of its forests and about 50% of its native species. Madagascar's dilemma represents that of much of the developing world. The island is home to over 10 million

FIGURE D Overexploitation: North Atlantic bluefin tuna being auctioned in a Japanese fish market

people, most of whom are desperately poor and hardly in a position to be concerned with environmental conservation. Yet the people of Madagascar as well as others around the globe could derive vital benefits from the biodiversity that is being destroyed.

8   Another reason to be concerned about the changes that underlie the biodiversity crisis is that the human population itself is threatened by large-scale alterations in the biosphere. Like all other species, we evolved in Earth's ecosystems, and we are dependent on the living and nonliving components of these systems. By allowing the extinction of species and the degradation of habitats to continue, we are taking a risk with our own species' survival.

━ ∙ ━

Directions: *Select the letter of the choice that best completes each of the following statements.*

CHECKING YOUR COMPREHENSION

_____   1. The author's main purpose for writing this selection is to

a. explain how we can increase biodiversity.

b. argue that there is a need for greater protection of endangered animals.

c. explain the importance of biodiversity and show how human behavior is affecting it.

d. compare and contrast various environmental policies.

_____ 2. Mass extinction

a. is currently happening for the seventh time in the history of life.

b. has never happened on earth before.

c. is a process for which there is no explanation.

d. is currently under way for humans.

_____ 3. The current extinction is unique because it is caused by

a. volcanoes.

b. global warming.

c. the evolution of one species.

d. the cooling down of the sun.

_____ 4. The Hundred Heartbeat Club is made up of

a. animals whose hearts beat faster than 100 beats per minute.

b. animals with less than 100 left per species.

c. humans who are environmentally conscious.

d. extinct animals.

_____ 5. The three ways humans are causing extinction are

a. genetic engineering, overexploitation, and habitat destruction.

b. financial mismanagement, pollution, and sport hunting.

c. genetic engineering, introduced species, and pollution.

d. habitat destruction, introduced species, and overexploitation.

_____ 6. Introducing a non-native species into a habitat

a. eliminates native species through competition or predation.

b. increases biodiversity.

c. is illegal.

d. demonstrates the adaptive powers of a species.

7. The main idea of paragraph 6 is that
   a. rhinoceroses are a protected species and killing them is illegal.
   b. humans think only of themselves.
   c. animals least able to defend themselves from hunting are most likely to become extinct.
   d. killing animals for sport or products or by mistake is among the ways in which humans decrease biodiversity.

8. The authors included the bullet points in paragraph 2 in order to
   a. offer a definition of what biodiversity is.
   b. provide evidence of the damage that has been done to the biosphere and biodiversity.
   c. defend the actions humans have taken and demonstrate that there is no permanent harm to the biosphere.
   d. illustrate how small changes can create important positive results.

9. The authors believe that
   a. humans are themselves at risk because of changes to the biosphere.
   b. humans cannot control the damage they do to the biosphere.
   c. animal and plant species are resilient and can survive much of the damage done by humans.
   d. humans rely too heavily on animals and plants for food, medicine, clothing, and shelters.

10. The authors' tone is
    a. determined.   b. concerned.
    c. argumentative.   d. annoyed.

USING CONTEXT AND WORD PARTS

11. In paragraph 1, the word **extinguishing** means
    a. eliminating.   b. restraining.
    c. enhancing.   d. reproducing.

_____ 12. In paragraph 1, the word **volcanism** refers to
  a. water shortages.   b. seismic activity.
  c. volcanic activity.   d. aliens.

_____ 13. In paragraph 4, the word **intertidal** means
  a. endangered water.
  b. the area between the low and high tide.
  c. aquatic species.
  d. an area that is always submerged.

_____ 14. In paragraph 5, the word **exotic** means
  a. useful.   b. endangered.
  c. high-demand.   d. non-native.

_____ 15. In paragraph 5, the word **predation** means
  a. prayer.   b. capturing prey.
  c. fearfulness.   d. coming earlier.

REVIEWING DIFFICULT VOCABULARY

Directions: _Complete each of the following sentences by inserting a word from the Vocabulary Preview on page 530 in the space provided._

16. The jeweler used his _____ fingers to insert the diamond in its setting.

17. The zoo displays many animals in their natural _____.

18. Because of the extensive _____ on this planet, we have barely begun to catalog the many species that exist.

19. Due to the many mudslides in that area, the _____ of the land was so complete, no homes could be rebuilt.

20. Damage to the earth's _____ affects all the animal and plant life on the planet.

QUESTIONS FOR DISCUSSION

1. How can we balance human needs with the needs of the biosphere?
2. Do you think people today are more sensitive to the fragility of earth's biodiversity? Why or why not?
3. How can you personally have an impact in helping prevent the loss of biodiversity?

ACTIVITIES FOR WRITING

1. Research one species that has become extinct in the last 100 years. Write a paragraph explaining what brought about the extinction.
2. Consider where your college is located. Describe what kinds of habitats might have been destroyed when it was built.
3. Figure out your ecological footprint by visiting http://www.myfootprint.org/. Write a list of things you could do to lessen your impact on the environment.

Current Issues Reader

RECORDING YOUR PROGRESS

Reading	Test	Number Right	Score
1 His Name Is Michael	Checking Your Comprehension	_____ × 10 =	_____ %
2 The High Cost of Being Poor	Checking Your Comprehension	_____ × 10 =	_____ %
3 Hold It Right There and Drop That Camera	Checking Your Comprehension	_____ × 10 =	_____ %
4 Whether to Vote	Checking Your Comprehension	_____ × 10 =	_____ %
5 Air Pollution and Global Warming	Checking Your Comprehension	_____ × 10 =	_____ %
6 The Biodiversity Crisis	Checking Your Comprehension	_____ × 10 =	_____ %

Credits

Photo Credits

Page 2 (top): Purestock/Jupiter Images; 2 (bottom): Mitch Ranger/Workbook Stock/Jupiter Images; 33: Ronnie Kaufman/Corbis; 40: Elmer Martinez/AFP/Getty Images; 80: Robyn Beck/AFP/Getty Images; 118: Gary Conner/PhotoEdit Inc. 148: Warren Miller/Cartoon Bank; 152: Billy E. Barnes/ PhotoEdit Inc.; 154: Spencer Grant/PhotoEdit Inc.; 175 (left): Dr. John Brackenbury/Photo Researchers; 175 (right): Chris Pizzello/AP Wide World Photos; 220 (top): J Group Photo; 220 (bottom): Shangara Singh/Alamy; 253: Gallo Images/Corbis; 260, left: Gary Conner/PhotoEdit Inc.; 260, right: image100/Jupiter Images; 300: Andrew Milligan/PA Photos; 324: Robert E. Daemmrich/Getty Images; 338: Horsey. Copyright © 2003, Tribune Media Services. Reprinted with permisson.; 366: Cheryl Himmelstein Photography; 374 (top): Ron Haviv/VII; 374 (bottom): Spencer Platt/Getty Images; 412: Todd Soqui/Corbis; 530: Mary Altaffer/AP Wide World Photos; 545: Bullit Marquez/AP Wide World Photos; 546: Wayne Lawler/Corbis; 547: Gary Kramer; 548: Koichi Kamoshida/Getty Images.

Text Credits

CHAPTER 1

Ronald J. Ebert and Ricky W. Griffin, from *Business Essentials*, Fourth Edition. Copyright © 2003 Pearson Education, Inc. Reprinted by permission of Pearson Education, Inc., Upper Saddle River, NJ.

Rebecca J. Donatelle, from *Health: The Basics*, Fifth Edition, pp. 58-61. Copyright © 2003 Pearson Education, Inc., publishing as Benjamin Cummings. Reprinted by permission.

James Henslin, from *Sociology: A Down to Earth Approach*, Sixth Edition, pp. 623-624. Published by Allyn and Bacon, Boston, MA. Copyright © 2003 James Henslin. Reprinted/adapted by permission of the publisher.

James Henslin, from *Social Problems*, Seventh Edition, pp. 293, 295, 296. Copyright © 2006. Reprinted by permission of Pearson Education, Inc.

James Henslin, "Diversity in U.S. Families," from *Sociology: A Down-To-Earth Approach*, Eighth Edition, pp. 462-465. Published by Allyn and Bacon, Boston, MA. Copyright © 2007 by James Henslin. Reprinted by permission of the publisher.

CHAPTER 2

William J. Germann and Cindy Stanfield, from *Principles of Physiology*, First Edition, p. 9. Copyright © 2002 Pearson Education, Inc., publishing as Benjamin Cummings. Reprinted by permission.

Palmira Brummett, et al., *Civilization: Past & Present, Concise Version*, pp. 239-240. New York: Longman, 2001.

Mark Carnes and John Garraty, *The American Nation: A History of the United States*, Eleventh Edition, pp. 175-176. New York: Longman, 2003.

Audesirk, Audesirk, and Byers, from *Life on Earth*, Third Edition, pp. 95, 104. © 2003 Pearson Education, Inc. Reprinted by permission of Pearson Education, Inc, Upper Saddle River, NJ.

CHAPTER 3

Rebecca J. Donatelle, *Health: The Basics*, Seventh Edition, p. 283. San Francisco: Pearson/Benjamin Cummings, 2007.

Joseph A. DeVito, *Human Communication: The Basic Course*, Ninth Edition, p. 178. Boston: Allyn and Bacon, 2003.

Warren K. Agee et al., *Introduction to Mass Communications*, Twelfth Edition, p. 153. New York: Longman, 1997.

Robert C, Nickerson, *Business and Information Systems*, p. 30. Reading, MA: Addison-Wesley, 1998.

Laura Uba and Karen Huang, *Psychology*, p. 148. New York: Longman, 1999.

Donald C. Mosley, et al., *Management: Leadership in Action*, Fifth Edition, p. 317. New York: HarperCollins College Publishers, 1996.

Warren K. Agee, et al., *Introduction to Mass Communications*, Twelfth Edition, p. 225. New York: Longman, 1997.

Joseph A. DeVito, from *Human Communication: The Basic Course*, Seventh Edition, p. 182. Published by Allyn and Bacon, Boston MA. Copyright © 1997 by Pearson Education. Reprinted by permission of the publisher.

Josh R. Gerow, *Psychology: An Introduction*, Third Edition, p. 700. New York: HarperCollins College Publishers, 1992.

Robert A. Wallace, *Biology: The World of Life*, Sixth Edition, p. 283. New York: HarperCollins College Publishers, 1992.

James Coleman and Donald Cressey, *Social Problems*, Sixth Edition, p. 130. New York: HarperCollins College Publishers, 1996.

Michael Mix, et al., *Biology: The Network of Life*, Second Edition, p. 532. New York: HarperCollins College Publishers, 1996.

Duane Preble, et al., *Artforms: An Introduction to the Visual Arts*, Sixth Edition, p. 64. New York: Longman, 1999.

Roger LeRoy Miller, *Economics Today*, Eighth Edition, p. 213. New York: HarperCollins College Publishers, 1994.

Joyce Brothers, "What Dirty Words Really Mean," *Good Housekeeping*, May 1973.

Elaine N. Marieb, *Essentials of Human Anatomy and Physiology*, Fifth Edition, p. 119. Menlo Park, CA: The Benjamin Cummings Publishing Co., 1997.

Alex Thio, *Sociology*, Fourth Edition, p. 180. New York: HarperCollins College Publishers, 1996.

Robert C. Nickerson, *Business and Information Systems*, p. 249.

Karen Timberlake, *Chemistry: An Introduction to General, Organic, and Biological Chemistry*, Sixth Edition, p. 30. New York: HarperCollins College Publishers, 1996.

Richard Weaver II, *Understanding Interpersonal Communication*, Seventh Edition, p. 220. New York: HarperCollins College Publishers, 1996.

S.A. Beebe, et al., *Interpersonal Communication: Relating to Others*, Third Edition, pp. 243, 248. Boston: Allyn & Bacon, 2002.

Audesirk, Audesirk, and Byers, from *Life on Earth*, Third Edition, p. 201. © 2003 Pearson Education, Inc. Reprinted by permission of Pearson Education, Inc, Upper Saddle River, NJ.

James Henslin, from *Sociology: A Down to Earth Approach*, Sixth Edition, p. 246. Published by Allyn and Bacon, Boston, MA. Copyright © 2003 James Henslin. Reprinted/adapted by permission of the publisher.

Ronald J. Ebert and Ricky W. Griffin, from *Business Essentials*, Fourth Edition, p. 208. Copyright © 2003 Pearson Education, Inc. Reprinted by permission of Pearson Education, Inc., Upper Saddle River, NJ.

Daniel M. Dunn and Lisa J. Goodnight, from *Communication: Embracing Difference*, First Edition, p. 92. Published by Allyn and Bacon, Boston, MA. Copyright © 2003 by Pearson Education. Reprinted/adapted by permission of the publisher.

Alex Thio, *Sociology: A Brief Introduction*, Fifth Edition, p. 187. Boston: Allyn and Bacon, 2003.

Alex Thio, *Sociology: A Brief Introduction*, Fifth Edition, p. 187. Boston: Allyn and Bacton, 2003.

Mark A. Bishop, from *Introduction to Chemistry*, p. 750. Copyright © 2002 Pearson Education, Inc., publishing as Benjamin Cummings. Reprinted by permission of Pearson Education, Inc.

Dunn and Goodnight, from *Communication: Embracing Difference*, First Edition, p. 103. Copyright © 2003 by Pearson Education. Reprinted/adapted by permission of the publisher.

Rebecca J. Donatelle, from *Health: The Basics*, Fifth Edition, p. 105. Copyright © 2003 Pearson Education, Inc., publishing as Benjamin Cummings. Reprinted by permission.

Rebecca J. Donatelle, from *Health: The Basics*, Fifth Edition, p. 418. Copyright © 2003 Pearson Education, Inc., publishing as Benjamin Cummings. Reprinted by permission.

CHAPTER 4

James Henslin, from *Sociology: A Down to Earth Approach*, Sixth Edition, pp. 380-381. Published by Allyn and Bacon, Boston, MA. Copyright © 2003 James Henslin. Reprinted/adapted by permission of the publisher.

Stephen M. Kosslyn and Robin S. Rosenberg, from *Fundamentals of Psychology: The Brain, The Person, The World*, First Edition, pp. 368-369. Published by Allyn and Bacon, Boston, MA. Copyright © 2003 by Pearson Education. Reprinted/adapted by permission of the publisher.

Joseph A. DeVito, from *Messages: Building Interpersonal Communication Skills*, Fifth Edition, p. 121. Published by Allyn and –Bacon, Boston, MA. Copyright © 2002 by Pearson Education. Reprinted by permission of the publisher.

Joseph A. DeVito, from *Messages: Building Interpersonal Communication Skills*, Fifth Edition, p. 197, 199. Published by Allyn and Bacon, Boston, MA. Copyright © 2002 by Pearson Education. Reprinted by permission of the publisher.

Daniel M. Dunn and Lisa J. Goodnight, from *Communication: Embracing Difference*, First Edition, pp. 100-101. Published by Allyn and Bacon, Boston, MA. Copyright © 2003 by Pearson Education. Reprinted/adapted by permission of the publisher.

Ronald J. Ebert and Ricky W. Griffin, from *Business Essentials*, Fourth Edition. © 2003 Pearson Education, Inc. Reprinted by permission of Pearson Education, Inc., Upper Saddle River, NJ.

Sherry Amatenstein, "Talking a Stranger Through the Night," from *Newsweek*, November 18, 2002. All rights reserved. Reprinted by permission.

CHAPTER 5

Joseph A. DeVito, from *Messages: Building Interpersonal Communication Skills*, Fifth Edition, p. 290. Published by Allyn and Bacon, Boston, MA. Copyright © 2002 by Pearson Education. Reprinted by permission of the publisher.

Michael R. Solomon, from *Consumer Behavior: Buying, Having, and Being*, Fourth Edition. © 1999. Reprinted by permission of Pearson Education, Upper Saddle River, NJ.

Laura Uba and Karen Huang, *Psychology*, p. 148. New York: Longman, 1999.

Josh Gerow, *Psychology: An Introduction*, Third Edition, p. 700. New York: HarperCollins College Publishers, Inc., 1992.

Nora Newcombe, *Child Development: Change Over Time*, Eighth Edition, p. 354. New York: HarperCollins College Publishers, Inc., 1996.

Joseph A. DeVito, *Elements of Public Speaking*, Seventh Edition, pp. 132-133. New York: Longman, 2000.

Jeffrey Bennett, et al., *The Solar System*, Second Edition, p. 40. San Francisco: Addison-Wesley, 2002.

Nanda Bandyo-padhyay, *Computing for Non-Specialists*, p. 4. New York: Addison-Wesley, 2000.

George C. Edwards III, Martin P. Wattenberg, and Robert Lineberry, from *Government in America: People, Politics, and Policy*, Tenth Edition, p. 422. © 2002 Addison-Wesley Educational Publishers. Reprinted by permission of Pearson Education, Inc.

Roy A. Cook, et al., *Tourism: The Business of Travel*, Second Edition, p. 370. Upper Saddle River, NJ: Prentice-Hall, 2002.

Elaine N. Marieb, from *Human Anatomy & Physiology*, Fifth Edition, p. 9. © 2001 by Benjamin Cummings. Reprinted by permission of Pearson Education, Inc.

Joseph A. DeVito, from *Messages: Building Interpersonal Communication Skills*, Fifth Edition, p. 161. Published by Allyn and Bacon, Boston, MA. Copyright © 2002 by Pearson Education. Reprinted by permission of the publisher.

Edward Bergman and William Renwick, from *Introduction to Geography: People, Places, and Environment*, Updated Second Edition, p. 265. © 2003 Pearson Education, Inc. Reprinted by permission of Pearson Education, Inc., Upper Saddle River, NJ.

Michael R. Solomon, *Consumer Behavior*, Fifth Edition, p. 19. Upper Saddle River, NJ: Prentice-Hall, 2002.

David Mas Masumoto, 6 paragraphs from *Epitaph for a Peach: Four Seasons on My Family Farm* by David Mas Masumoto. Copyright © 1995 by David Mas Masumoto. Reprinted by permission of HarperCollins Publishers.

Audesirk, Audesirk, and Byers, from *Life on Earth*, Third Edition, pp. 515, 535. © 2003 by Pearson Education, Inc. Reprinted by permission of Pearson Education, Inc., Upper Saddle River, NJ.

CHAPTER 6

Rebecca J. Donatelle, from *Health: The Basics*, Fifth Edition, p. 286. Copyright © 2003 Pearson Education, Inc., publishing as Benjamin Cummings. Reprinted by permission.

Steve Russo and Mike Silver, *Introductory Chemistry: Essentials*, Second Edition, pp. 3-4. San Francisco: Benjamin Cummings, 2002.

Michael R. Solomon, from *Consumer Behavior: Buying, Having, Being*, Fourth Edition, p. © 1999. Reprinted by permission of Pearson Education, Inc., Upper Saddle River, NJ.

Michael R. Solomon, from *Consumer Behavior: Buying, Having, –Being*, Fourth Edition, p. 316. © 1999. Reprinted by permission of Pearson Education, Inc., Upper Saddle River, NJ.

Alex Thio, *Sociology*, Fifth Edition, pp. 70-71. New York: Longman, 1998.

George C. Edwards III, Martin P. Wattenberg, and Robert Lineberry, from *Government in America: People, Politics, and Policy*, Tenth Edition, pp. 196-197. © 2002 Addison-Wesley Educational Publishers. Reprinted by permission of Pearson Education, Inc.

Joseph A. DeVito, from *Messages: Building Interpersonal Communication Skills*, Fifth Edition, p. 317. Published by Allyn and Bacon, Boston, MA. Copyright © 2002 by Pearson Education. Reprinted by permission of the publisher.

Audesirk, Audesirk, and Byers, from *Life on Earth*, Third Edition, pp. 584-585. © 2003 by Pearson Education, Inc. Reprinted by permission of Pearson Education, Inc., Upper Saddle River, NJ.

Edward Bergman and William Renwick, from *Introduction to Geography: People, Places, and Environment*, Updated Second Edition, pp. 504-505. © 2003 Pearson Education, Inc. Reprinted by permission of Pearson Education, Inc., Upper Saddle River, NJ.

Rebecca J. Donatelle, Health: The Basics, Fifth Edition, p. 350. Copyright © 2003 Pearson Education, Inc., publishing as Benjamin Cummings. Reprinted by permission.

Duane Preble and Sarah Preble, *Artforms: An Introduction to the Visual Arts*, Seventh Edition, p. 110. Upper Saddle River, NJ: Prentice-Hall, 2002.

Stephen M. Kosslyn and Robin S. Rosenberg, from *Fundamentals of Psychology: The Brain, The Person, The World*, First Edition, pp. 259-260. Published by Allyn and Bacon, Boston, MA. Copyright © 2003 by Pearson Education. Reprinted/adapted by permission of the publisher.

William E. Thompson and Joseph V. Hickey, *Society in Focus: An Introduction to Sociology*, Fourth Edition, p. 147. Boston: Allyn and Bacon, 2002.

Michael R. Solomon and Elnora Stuart, from *Marketing: Real People Real Choices*, Second Edition. © 2000 Prentice-Hall, Inc. Reprinted by permission of Pearson Education, Inc., Upper Saddle River, NJ.

Ronald J. Ebert and Ricky W. Griffin, from *Business Essentials*, Fourth Edition, pp. 266-267. © 2003 Pearson Education.

Reprinted by permission of Pearson Education, Inc., Upper Saddle River, NJ.

Wendy Lehnert, from *Light on the Web: Essentials to Make the Net Work*, pp. 29-31. © 2002 Pearson Education, Inc. Reproduced by permission of Pearson Education, Inc. All rights reserved.

CHAPTER 7

Bergman and Renwick, *Introduction to Geography*, Second Edition, p. 356. Upper Saddle River, NJ: Prentice-Hall, 2002, and Carnes and Garraty, *The American Nation*, Tenth Edition, p. 916. New York: Longman, 2000.

B.E. Pruitt and Jane Stein, from *HealthStyles: Decisions for Living Well*, Second Edition, p. 100. Copyright © 1999. by Allyn and Bacon. Reprinted by permission of Pearson Education, Inc.

B.E. Pruitt and Jane Stein, from *HealthStyles: Decisions for Living Well*, Second Edition, p. 100.

B.E. Pruitt and Jane Stein, from *HealthStyles: Decisions for Living Well*, Second Edition, p. 100.

Edward Bergman and William Renwick, from *Introduction to Geography: People, Places, and Environment*, Updated Second Edition, p. 80. © 2003 Pearson Education, Inc. Reprinted by permission of Pearson Education, Inc., Upper Saddle River, NJ.

Rebecca J. Donatelle, from *Access to Health*, Seventh Edition, p. 65. © 2002 Pearson Education, Inc., publishing as Benjamin Cummings. Reprinted by permission.

Elaine N. Marieb, *Essentials of Human Anatomy and Physiology*, Sixth Edition, p. 3. San Francisco: Benjamin Cummings, 2000.

Jeffrey Bennett, et al., *The Cosmic Perspective*, Brief Edition, p. 28. San Francisco: Addison Wesley Longman, 2000.

X.J. Kennedy and Dana Gioia, *Literature: An Introduction to Fiction, Poetry, and Drama*, Third Compact Edition, p. 7. New York: Longman, 2003.

Elaine N. Marieb, from *Human Anatomy & Physiology*, Fifth Edition, p. 387. Copyright © 2001 by Benjamin Cummings. Reprinted by permission of Pearson Education, Inc.

Mark Carnes and John Garraty, *The American Nation: A History of the United States*, Eleventh Edition, p. 518. New York: Longman, 2003.

Roy A. Cook, et al., *Tourism: The Business of Travel*, Second Edition, p. 102. Upper Saddle River, NJ: Prentice-Hall, 2002.

Elaine N. Marieb, from *Human Anatomy & Physiology*, Fifth Edition, p. 13. Copyright © 2001 by Benjamin Cummings. Reprinted by permission of Pearson Education, Inc.

Carnes and Garraty, *The American Nation: A History of the United States*, Eleventh Edition, p. 455.

Kathleen German, et al., *Principles of Public Speaking*, Fourteenth Edition, p. 24. New York: Longman, 2001.

Rebecca J. Donatelle, from *Access to Health*, Seventh Edition, p. 17. Copyright © 2002 Pearson Education, Inc., publishing as Benjamin Cummings. Reprinted by permission.

William J. Germann and Cindy Stanfield, from *Principles of Physiology*, First Edition, pp. 606-607. Copyright © 2002 Pearson Education, Inc., publishing as Benjamin Cummings. Reprinted by permission.

Jeffrey Bennett, et al., *The Solar System*, Second Edition, pp. 58-59. San Francisco: Addison-Wesley, 2002.

Stephen M. Kosslyn and Robin S. Rosenberg, from *Fundamentals of Psychology: The Brain, The Person, The World*, First Edition, p. 331. Published by Allyn and Bacon, Boston, MA. Copyright © 2003 by Pearson Education. Reprinted by permission of the publisher.

Wendy Lehnert, from *Light on the Web: Essentials to Make the Net Work*, pp. 32-33. © 2002 Pearson Education, Inc. Reproduced by permission of Pearson Education, Inc. All rights reserved.

Audesirk, Audesirk, and Byers, from *Life on Earth*, Third Edition, pp. 533-534. © 2003 Pearson Education, Inc. Reprinted by permission of Pearson Education, Inc., Upper Saddle River, NJ.

CHAPTER 8

Jeffrey Bennett, et al., *The Cosmic Perspective*, Second Edition, p. 249. San Francisco: Addison-Wesley, 2002.

Rebecca J. Donatelle, from *Health: The Basics*, Fifth Edition, p. 324. Copyright © 2003 Pearson Education, Inc., publishing as Benjamin Cummings. Reprinted by permission.

William J. Germann and Cindy Stanfield, from *Principles of Physiology*, First Edition, p. 622. Copyright © 2002 Pearson Education, Inc., publishing as Benjamin Cummings. Reprinted by permission.

Ronald J. Ebert and Ricky W. Griffin, from *Business Essentials*, Fourth Edition, p. 117. © 2003 Pearson Education, Inc. Reprinted by permission of Pearson Education, Inc., Upper Saddle River, NJ.

Nanda Bandyo-padhyay, *Computing for Non-Specialists*, p. 260. New York: Addison-Wesley, 2000.

James Henslin, from *Sociology: A Down to Earth Approach*, Sixth Edition, p. 637. Published by Allyn and Bacon, Boston, MA. Copyright © 2003 James Henslin. Reprinted/adapted by permission of the publisher.

Edward Bergman and William Renwick, from *Introduction to Geography: People, Places, Environment*, Updated Second Edition, p. 404. © 2003 Pearson Education, Inc. Reprinted by permission of Pearson Education, Inc., Upper Saddle River, NJ.

Germann and Stanfield, *Principles of Human Physiology*, First Edition, pp. 303-304. Copyright © 2002 Pearson Education, Inc., publishing as Benjamin Cummings. Reprinted by permission.

Stephen M. Kosslyn and Robin S. Rosenberg, from *Fundamentals of Psychology: The Brain, the Person, the World*, First Edition, p. 197. Published by Allyn and Bacon, Boston, MA. Copyright © 2003 by Pearson Education. Reprinted by permission of the publisher.

Elaine N. Marieb, *Anatomy and Physiology*, pp. 402-403. San Francisco: Benjamin Cummings, 2002.

Joseph A. DeVito, *The Essential Elements of Public Speaking*, p. 46. Boston: Allyn and Bacon, 2003.

Ronald J. Ebert and Ricky W. Griffin, from Business Essentials, Fourth Edition, p. 254. Copyright © 2003 Pearson Education, Inc. Reprinted by permission of Pearson Education, Inc., Upper Saddle River, NJ.

Michael R. Solomon, *Consumer Behavior*, 5/e, p. 89. Upper Saddle River, NJ: Prentice-Hall, 2002.

X.J. Kennedy and Dana Gioia, *Literature: An Introduction to Fiction, Poetry, and Drama*, Third Compact Edition, pp. 885-886. New York: Longman, 2003.

Tim Curry et al., *Sociology for the Twenty-First Century*, Second Edition, p. 148. Upper Saddle River, NJ: Prentice-Hall, 1999.

Ronald J. Ebert and Ricky W. Griffin, from *Business Essentials*, Fourth Edition, pp. 212-213. Copyright © 2003 Pearson Education, Inc. Reprinted by permission of Pearson Inc., Upper saddle River, NJ.

Jeffrey Bennett, et al., The Cosmic Perspective, Second Edition, p. 326

Edward Bergman and William Renwick, Introduction to Geography: People, Places, Environment, Updated Second Edition, pp. 215-217. © 2003 Pearson Education, Inc. Reprinted by permission of Pearson Education, Inc, Upper Saddle River, NJ.

B.E. Pruitt and Jane Stein, *HealthStyles: Decisions for Living Well*, Second Edition, p. 29. Copyright © 1999 by Allyn and Bacon. Reprinted by permission of Pearson Education, Inc.

Rebecca J. Donatelle, Health: The Basics, Fifth Edition pp. 39-40. Copyright © 2003 Pearson Education Inc. publishing as Benjamin Cummings. Reprinted by permission.

CHAPTER 9

"The Day It Snowed Tortillas" is from *The Day It Snowed Tortillas / El día que nevaron tortillas*, Folktales as told by Joe Hayes. Copyright © 2003 by Joe Hayes. Published by Cinco Puntos Press, El Paso, Texas, (www.cincopuntos.com). Reprinted by permission.

Gini Stephens Frings, *Fashion: From Concepts to Consumer*, Sixth Edition, p. 11. Upper Saddle River, NJ: Prentice-Hall, 1999.

Philip Zimbardo and Richard Gerrig, *Psychology and Life*, Fourteenth Edition, p. 501. New York: HarperCollins College Publishers, 1996.

Thomas Kinnear et al., *Principles of Marketing*, Fourth Edition, p. 301. New York: HarperCollins College Publishers, 1995.

Steven Brown, "The Musilanguage Model of Music Evolution," *The Origins of Music*, Wallin, Merker, Brown, eds., p. 271. Cambridge, MA: Massachusetts Institute of Technology, 2000.

Martin Luther King, Jr., from "Letter from Birmingham Jail," *Why We Can't Wait*, New York: Harper & Row, 1964.

Aesop, "The Fox and the Woodcutter," *Aesop's Fables*, translated by George Fyler Townsend.

Cynthia Audet, "Scar" from *The Sun*, Issue 325, January 2003. Reprinted by permission of the author.

Silja Talvi, from "'Deadbeat' Dads-Or Just 'Dead Broke'?" from *The Christian Science Monitor*, February 4, 2002. Reprinted by permission of the author.

Karen Olson, from "Eat it Raw." Reprinted with permission from *Utne Reader*, March/April 2002.

Toddi Gutner, "Working Moms," *Business Week*, 9/23/02. Reprinted by permission.

Scott Sherman, "If Our Son Is Happy, What Else Matters?" from *Newsweek*, September 16, 2002. All rights reserved. Reprinted by permission.

CHAPTER 10

Edward Greenberg and Benjamin Page, *The Struggle for Democracy*, Second Edition, p. 186. New York: HarperCollins College Publishers, 1995.

Laura Uba and Karen Huang, *Psychology*, p. 323. New York: Longman, 1999.

Cynthia Peters, from "On Being a Vigilant Parent," *The Hyde Park Citizen*, September 19, 2002. Reprinted by permission of The Chicago Citizen Newspaper Group.

Dick Piechowicz, "Let Student Athletes Pay Their Own Way" as appeared in *The Buffalo News*, February 8, 2003. Reprinted by permission of the author.

Barbara M. Dossey and Larry Dossey, from "Attending to Holistic Care," *American Journal of Nursing*, 1998; 98(8), 35-38. Reprinted by permission of Lippincott Williams & Wilkins.

R.D. Davis, from "How the Media Distorts the News," *The Atlanta Inquirer*, July 13, 2002. Reprinted by permission of The Atlanta Inquirer, Atlanta, GA.

Farley, Smith, and Boyle, from *Introduction to Social Work*, Ninth Edition, p. 13. Published by Allyn and Bacon, Boston, MA. Copyright © 2003 by Pearson Education. Reprinted by permission of the publisher.

Henry Madoff, from "Reconsidering the Ban on School Prayer," *The Jewish Chronicle of Pittsburgh*, July 25, 2002. Reprinted by permission of the publisher and author.

Kimberly Miller, *The Meanings of Dress*, Damhorst, Miller, and Michelman, eds., p. 212. New York: Fairchild Publications, 1999.

June Payne Palaceo and Monica Theis, eds., *West and Wood's Introduction to Foodservice*, Upper Saddle River, NJ: Prentice-Hall, 2001.

Margot Roosevelt, "Canine Candy Stripers," *Time*, August 6, 2001. © 2001 Time Inc. Reprinted by permission.

CHAPTER 11

Stephen M. Kosslyn and Robin S. Rosenberg, *Psychology: The Brain, the Person, the World*, First Edition, p. 162. Boston: Allyn and Bacon, 2001.

X.J. Kennedy and Dana Gioia, *Literature: An Introduction to Fiction, Poetry, and Drama*, Second Compact Edition, p. 789. New York: Longman, 2000.

Robert A. Wallace, *Biology: The World of Life*, Sixth Edition, p. 754. New York: HarperCollins College Publishers, 1992.

Wayne LaPierre, from "Standing Guard," *American Rifleman*, August 2002. Reprinted by permission of The National Rifle Association.

D.F. Oliveria, "Burning Will Go, That's Not All Good," *Spokesman Review*, July 24, 2002.

Christine Haugen, "Logging Illogic," *World Watch*, September/October 2002.

Dr. Swami Gitananda, from "Smoking Yogis, Beware!" in *Hinduism Today*, September 30, 2002. Reprinted by permission of *Hinduism Today*.

Teresa McMahon, "The Outsider: Being a Catholic in Temple," *Lilith*, January 31, 2003. Reprinted by permission.

Murdock Gibbs, from "It's a Great Day for Choice," *New York Voice Inc./Harlem USA*, October 2, 2002. Reprinted by permission of the author.

Terry Hong, "Voices from the Community: Explaining Away the Hate" from *Asian Week*, July 31, 2002. Reprinted by permission of the author.

CHAPTER 12

Kathleen McWhorter, *Academic Reading*, Sixth Edition, p. 385. New York: Longman, 2007.

"Misstep on Video Violence," *USA Today*, June 6, 2005. Reprinted with permission of USA Today.

Walter J. Hickel, "ANWR Oil: An Alternative to War Over Oil," *The American Enterprise*, June 2002, Vol. 13, Issue 4. Reprinted with permission from *The American Enterprise*, a magazine of Politics, Business, and Culture. On the web at www.TAEmag.com.

PART 2

Joseph A. DeVito, from *Human Communication: The Basic Course*, Seventh Edition, pp. 108-110. Published by Allyn and Bacon, Boston, MA. Copyright © 1997 by Pearson Education. Reprinted by permission of the publisher.

"Adult Participation in Selected Leisure Activities by Frequency," *Statistical Abstract of the United States: 2006*, Table 1230, p. 792. Washington DC: U.S. Census Bureau, 2006.

Susan Gilbert, "Noise Pollution," *Science Digest*, March 1985. Reprinted by permission of the author.

Stephanie Rice, "Pilot Project to Give Jurors a Raise," *The Columbian*, October 10, 2006. Reprinted by permission of The Columbian, Vancouver, WA.

Richard Folkers, "Why Do Dogs Bark?" from *U.S. News & World Report*, August 18/25, Copyright 1997 U.S. News & World Report, L.P. Reprinted with permission.

CURRENT ISSUES READER

Donna M. Marriott, "His Name Is Michael," *Education Week*, October 9, 2002. Reprinted by permission of the author.

Barbara Ehrenreich, "The High Cost of Being Poor," *Alternet*, posted July 21, 2006. First appeared in the author's blog. Reprinted by permission of International Creative Management, Inc. Copyright © 2006 by Barbara Ehrenreich.

Jo Napolitano, "Hold It Right There, and Drop That Camera," *The New York Times*, December 11, 2003. Copyright © 2003 by The New York Times Co. Reprinted by permission.

George C. Edwards III, Martin P. Wattenberg, and Robert Lineberry, from "Whether to Vote: A Citizen's First Choice," *Government in America: People, Politics, and Policy*, Twelfth Edition, pp. 304, 305, 308, 309. Copyright © 2006 by Pearson Education, Inc. Reprinted by permission.

Martin P. Wattenberg. Reprinted by permission of the publisher from *Where Have All the Voters Gone?* by Martin P. Wattenberg, p. 15. Cambridge, Mass: Harvard University Press, Copyright © 2002 by the President and Fellows of Harvard College.

James Henslin, from *Social Problems*, Seventh Edition, pp. 464-466. Copyright © 2006. Reprinted by permission of Pearson Education, Inc.

Neil A. Campbell, Jane B. Reece, and Eric J. Simon, from "The Biodiversity Crisis," *Essential Biology with Physiology*, pp. 452-455. Copyright © 2004 Pearson Education, Inc., publishing as Benjamin Cummings. Reprinted by permission.

Index